*A*dventure Guide to the ™ *to the*
Yucatán
including
Cancún & Cozumel

Bruce & June Conord

HUNTER

HUNTER PUBLISHING, INC.
130 Campus Drive
Edison NJ 08818-7816, USA
Tel (732) 225 1900; Fax (732) 417 1744
E-mail: hunterpub@emi.net
Web site: www.hunterpublishing.com

1220 Nicholson Road
Newmarket, Ontario L3Y 7V1, CANADA
Tel (800) 399 6858; Fax (800) 363 2665

ISBN 1-55650-792-5

© 1998 Hunter Publishing

Visit Our Web Site!

For complete information about the hundreds of other travel guides and language courses offered by Hunter Publishing, see us online at:

www.hunterpublishing.com

Every effort has been made to ensure that the information in this book is correct, but the publisher and authors do not assume, and hereby disclaim, any liability to any party for any loss or damage caused by errors, omissions, misleading information or any potential problem caused by information in this guide, even if these are a result of negligence, accident or any other cause. All opinions expressed in this book stem from the authors' personal experience only or from those of their contributors; consequently, neither they nor the contributors can be held accountable for a reader's personal experience while traveling.

All photos by the authors
Cover: Maya women in Izamal
Maps by Kim André

Dedication

This book is dedicated to the ones we love. We hope that life offers them many adventures full of wonder and delight.

Acknowledgements

The authors wish to thank the Mexico Ministry of Tourism and the individual State Offices of Tourism for their invaluable help in preparing this guide. Thank you Kim André, our editor at Hunter, for your confidence and talented editing. We also need to acknowledge the generous assistance of the following people: Maité Hernández, Alejandro Serrano López, Gabriel Escalante, Gerardo Magaña, Steve Cochrane of Aeromexico, Amigos de Sian Ka'an, Marisa López, Erik Medicuti Polanco, Giada Bresaola, Monserrat Alfaro, Judith Fernandez, Joyce Kelly, and Matthew Hill – who takes care of our house and geriatric dog when we are away. Gracias tambien to the countless others who aided us in Mexico and really meant it when they said "Mi casa es su casa." Finally, we must thank Ofelia Casa Madrid, who rescued Bruce one night when he became locked in with the ghosts at Fort Bacalar.

About The Authors

Bruce and June Conord have been travel hounds for years, but Mexico kept luring them back with its charm and beauty. They drew on their knowledge and experience of the area for this book and its companion Hunter travel guide, *Cancún & Cozumel Alive*.

Both Conords collaborate on a monthly travel column and Bruce has written numerous magazine articles as well as three biographies for children and young adults. He graduated Rutgers University and studied Spanish at Forester Instituto in Costa Rica.

June was born in Plymouth, England and spent part of her childhood in a picturesque fishing village in Cornwall. She attended Plymouth Art College before emigrating to the United States.

Together their travels have taken them to 15 different countries around the world, but they always come home to New Jersey.

GOING METRIC!

To make your adventures in and around the Yucatán a little easier, we have provided the following charts that show metric equivalents for the measurements you are familiar with.

1 kilometer	=	.6124 miles
1 mile	=	1.6093 kilometers
1 foot	=	.304 meters
1 inch	=	2.54 centimeters
1 square mile	=	2.59 square kilometers
1 pound	=	.4536 kilograms
1 ounce	=	28.35 grams
1 imperial gallon	=	4.5459 liters
1 US gallon	=	3.7854 liters
1 quart	=	.94635 liters

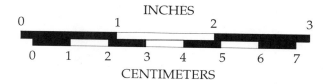

For Fahrenheit: Multiply Centigrade by 1.8 and add 32.

For Centigrade: Subtract 32 from Fahrenheit and divide by 1.8.

CENTIGRADE		FAHRENHEIT
40°	=	104°
35°	=	95°
30°	=	86°
25°	=	77°
20°	=	64°
15°	=	59°
10°	=	50°

Contents

Maps

Introduction

Don't be a tourist.

– Travel Channel slogan, 1997

 This guide book is about adventure, excitement and fun in a vibrant land alive with both natural wonders and contemporary culture amid the fragments of departed grandeur. You don't have to speak Spanish to enjoy the superb attractions of Mexico's Yucatán Peninsula – English is welcome everywhere – and we know of few destinations that offer more all-around pleasure.

Whether your definition of adventure is lying on the beach and sipping margaritas, or hiking into the jungle to explore the spectacular ruins of the lost Maya civilization, this book has you covered. Plus, we give first-hand evaluations of hundreds of hotels and restaurants, so you can get more for your money. We give you the absolute best values in lodging, meals and shopping.

We'll show you where to enjoy the best of Cancún's glitzy resorts at a fraction of the regular cost. Sit and eat a delicious fish dinner under the shade of a palapa (Yucatán's equivalent to the palm tree) at a hard-to-find seaside restaurant where only "insiders" go. Stay in a Spanish colonial hotel with 18-foot-high ceilings and walls more than one foot thick. Sling a hammock in a 200-year-old hacienda where time has stood still. Or sleep in beachfront bungalows so close to the Caribbean that the waves lap gently against the front porch. Enjoy white sandy beaches and turquoise seas, or be thrilled by miles of unbroken rainforest.

It's a countryside whose legacy is intricately involved with the past – including magnificent ruined Maya cities with temples, ballcourts and giant pyramids where humans were once sacrificed. Follow us to deserted antiquarian sites and climb above the jungle canopy with only the ghosts of warrior kings to keep you company.

Visit colonial buildings that housed the barons of the lucrative henequen trade and Spanish forts built to keep away the likes of Blackbeard the pirate. Walk around grand colonial churches and monasteries in tiny towns or enjoy Spanish haciendas and abandoned plantations. The Yucatán is also a nature lover's paradise. Swim in an underground cenote – filled with crystal-clear water –

where the only natural light filters through a hole in the roof of an immense cavern.

Float down a forgotten stream past elegant blue herons, snowy egrets and roseate spoonbills standing guard over a mangrove savanna in one of the largest protected biospheres in the Americas. Dive into the warm Lagoon of Seven Colors where the Maya believed the rainbow began, or take a boat to an *ojo de agua* – an "eye of water." Get close to brilliant pink flamingos by the millions, spider and howler monkeys in the trees and iguanas sunning on the rocks of a deserted beach.

Bike or hike for hours along a shell-covered coastline without meeting another soul. Snorkel a spectacular reef alive with exotic fish that are as curious about you as you are of them. Dive to an underwater cavern where schools of sharks "sleep," suspended in the current, oblivious to your passing. Pilot a boat to a deserted island to see the wild capybara or sail to an island bird sanctuary with Captain Ricardo on the last wooden boat built on Isla Mujeres.

Wrestle a six-foot crocodile into your boat for nighttime tagging and identification by a biologist. Lie back and admire the southern night sky – bright enough to read by and streaked with the traces of falling stars. Shop in local *mercados* and rub shoulders (if you're very short) with Maya women in ancestral huipil dresses. Interested in traditional crafts such as hammocks, wood carvings and pottery? See them being made in villages off the beaten trail. Catch a taxi ride in a Victorian horse-drawn hansom to a renowned local restaurant that serves delicious authentic Yucatecan cuisine. All that and more you'll find here in our new *Adventure Guide to the Yucatán, including Cancún & Cozumel*. We hope you enjoy it.

Happy trails to you...

– Lyrics from theme song of the *Roy Rogers* TV show

How To Use This Guide

Travelers are fantasists, conjurers, seers – and what they
finally discover is that every round object is a crystal ball:
stone, teapot, the marvelous globe of the human eye.

– Cynthia Ozick in *The NY Times*, March 1985

 Nearly everyone who comes to the Yucatán flies into Cancún, a very busy international airport. From Cancún, there are three basic directions *Adventure Guide* readers can take, depending on available time and personal priorities. The first is a "sea and sun" route, south along the Turquoise Coast of Quintana Roo – Playa del Carmen, Cozumel, Tulum, Bacalar, Chetumal. The second is west, direct into Maya and colonial history – Valladolid, Chichén Itzá, Izamal, Mérida, Uxmal. The third way is known among travelers as the "circuit," a complete loop of the peninsula, including Campeche. Our problem in writing about things along the way is our readers' direction of travel in the circuit – clockwise or counterclockwise. If you're traveling north from Chetumal rather than south from Cancún, for example, the beaches will be in reverse order. In that case, try holding the book up to a mirror. No matter, you'll have a wonderful time. Let us know if we goofed, or missed anything, or if we helped make your vacation the best ever!

PRICES

Although we made every effort to be as thorough, complete and as accurate as possible, things change in Mexico – sometimes rapidly. Prices change faster than anything so we tried to build a range that reflects a relative comparison using dollar-sign symbols. Here's how to read them:

Hotels

(usually one shared bed in a room is cheaper than two;
some places include breakfast)

[No $s] = less than US $10 per night for two people.
$ = between US $10 and US $40.
$$ = between US $40 and US $100.
$$$ = between US $100 and US $200.
$$$$ = over US $200 per night

Restaurants

(not including beverage)

$ = less than US $5 for an average meal, per person.
$$ = between US $5 and US $10.
$$$ = over US $10 per person.

P.S. We've included a Maya phonetic phrase glossary at the end to stun your friends and amaze the people you meet in the countryside. Have fun!

WE LOVE TO GET MAIL!

Hunter Publishing makes every effort to ensure that its travel guides are the most current sources of information available to travelers. If you have any information that you feel should be included in the next edition of this guide, please write to us at 130 Campus Drive, Edison, NJ 08818. Feel free to include your opinion or experiences of the places you've visited, as well as price updates and suggestions for ways in which we could improve this book for future readers. If you'd like to contact the authors, Bruce and June Conord, directly, you may e-mail at: brucewrite@aol.com.

Yucatán At A Glance

On a Clear Day You Can See Forever
– Title of 1965 musical

 WHEN TO VISIT/WEATHER: The high season in the Yucatán occurs in the dry winter months from December through April. The peak seasons in Cancún and Cozumel are Christmas and Spring Break. The weather is a comfortable year-round average of 80°F.

MONEY: Mexican money is the peso. It floats against the dollar and can be exchanged at banks and change booths. American dollars are accepted almost everywhere, except in remote areas, at a variable exchange rate. Credit cards are accepted only in bigger cities.

PEOPLE: The population of the Yucatán is a combination of Maya and Spanish/Indian *mestizos*.

VISA: No visas are required, but tourist cards are a must. Stays are good up to 180 days.

CLOTHING: Pack light.

ELECTRICITY: 110 volts.

TIME ZONES: While the rest of Mexico (with the exception of Baja California) sets its clock to Central Standard Time, Cancún, Cozumel and the Yucatán are experimenting with Eastern Time. As of this writing, times are the same as Miami.

FLIGHT TIMES (HOURS) TO CANCUN: New York (3.5); Miami (1.5); Los Angeles (4.5); Vancouver BC (6); Toronto (4.5); Denver (4); and Europe (12).

 HEALTH & SAFETY: No shots are required. Most hotels and restaurants offer purified tap water, but drink bottled or seltzer water (*aqua mineral*) to be sure. Qualified English-speaking doctors are available for health emergencies. Crime in the Yucatán is limited to a rare pick-pocketing or overcharging for drinks.

LANGUAGE: Spanish, Mayan and English are spoken in major cities.

SMOKING: There's far too much. Cuban cigar smokers will be pleased: they're legal here.

 THINGS TO BUY: Silver and gold jewelry, pottery, hammocks, honey, embroidered dresses, Panama hats, men's guayabera shirts, wood carvings and blankets.

DRIVING/CAR RENTAL: Rental cars are expensive, and you should buy all the insurance they offer. Roads are excellent but night driving is very dangerous for a variety of reasons. Buses are a good alternative and very reasonable.

PLACES TO GO: See the Maya ruins at Chichén Itzá, Uxmal, Tulum, Cobá, Dzibanché, Edzná, Calakmul and many other places. Check out the colonial cities of Mérida, Valladolid, Campeche, Izamal and the abandoned and restored haciendas in the north. Visit the nature reserves at Celestún, Rio Lagartios and Sian Ka'an.

 THINGS TO DO & SEE: Swim in cenotes, lie on fabulous beaches, windsurf, get tanned, drink margaritas and beer (not necessarily in that order), read a book, explore the ruins, go down into caves, hike, bike, camp and just generally have a wonderful, exciting vacation.

Land Of The Maya

... For, lo, the winter is past, the rain is over and gone;
The flowers appear on the earth; the time of the singing of
birds is come, and the voice of the turtle is heard in our land.

– *Song of Solomon*, Isaiah 2:10-12

Geography

 The Yucatán Peninsula sticks out of Mexico's land mass and into the Gulf of Mexico like a big hitch-hiking thumb. Its broad width provides a natural division between the warm waters of the Gulf and the Caribbean Sea. Because it borders the Central American countries of Guatemala and Belize, many people think of the area as being Mexico's most southern point. Yet where Mexico narrows at its border with Guatemala, the Yucatán curves north and, geographically, the entire peninsula is actually farther north than Acapulco. The cities of Cancún and Mérida are at more northern latitudes than Mexico City, and Miami is a mere 684 miles (1,102 km) away.

So why is the Yucatán considered so remote? Well, like many regions around the world, its development (or lack thereof) can be traced to its geography. It has been – and in many ways, still is – not easily accessible by land. Thick jungles and high mountains in Chiapas, the southernmost state in Mexico, and swampy lowlands in neighboring Tabasco always limited overland routes. Decent roads into the area were not built until as late as the 1970s. Before that, most commerce and travel was by ship and then later by air. Much of what the Spanish conquistadors found physically on the peninsula in the 1500s you can still find there today. (Sorry, but as they found out the hard way, there's no gold – unless you count the jewelry worn by the guests at Cancún's expensive resorts.)

THUMBNAIL SKETCH: The Yucatán's name may have derived from a classic New World misinterpretation. When Spanish adventurers put ashore and asked the native Maya they met to tell them the name of the land, they replied "*u'y than, u'y than,*" meaning:

"We don't understand, what are you saying?" What resulted is the corrupted pronunciation: "Yucatán."

The three Mexican states that comprise the Yucatán Peninsula – Yucatán, Quintana Roo and Campeche – are part of a huge (84,900-square-mile) limestone platform that also includes the country of Belize and parts of the states of Tabasco and Chiapas. Millions of years ago it rose from the sea bottom like a giant submerged turtle. Ironically, in some myths, the ancient Maya conceived of their land exactly that way – as the back of a turtle. The soil layer is shallow and, because the limestone is porous, there are only a handful of streams, mostly in southern Campeche and several scattered shallow lagoons around the peninsula. But under the sea, the offshore shoals make the Yucatán perfect for watersports, such as snorkeling and diving, and a rich fishing ground. The surrounding seas are clear and sparkle in typical Caribbean turquoise or Gulf blue.

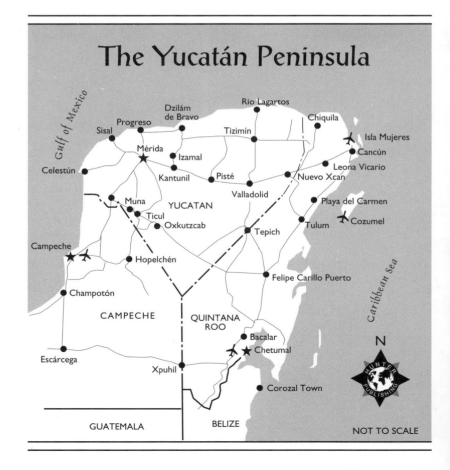

The Yucatán Peninsula

Inland, the terrain is mostly pancake flat and rises to mountains only in Guatemala, southern Belize and in Chiapas. The lowland exceptions are some conical limestone hills in the remote Rio Bec area of Campeche and a series of small rolling ridges, know as the Puuc Hills, which stretch southeastward from just south of Mérida. Because the land is so flat, these hills can provide panoramic views, especially along Yucatán's Highway 184.

CENOTES & THE UNDERWORLD: The Yucatán makes up for its lack of altitude with sinkholes. Deep ones. They form when underground water carves a cavern in the porous limestone. After millions of years the roof collapses, forming a large, steep-walled open well. These are called *cenotes* (say-NO-tays). Cenotes are found in large numbers throughout the peninsula, including the famous Sacred Cenote at the ancient Maya ruins of Chichén Itzá and ones in a wide band around Mérida. Folklore beliefs attribute cenotes as the source of the wind as well as openings into the underworld. The classic Maya civilization grew up around these water sources and even today they provide a source of fresh water to some interior communities. Because of a lack of surface water, irrigation of crops grown by the ancient Maya civilization was not possible in the north. They relied on cenotes for drinking water, and some cities also built cisterns to trap and hold rainwater. The long dry season enhanced the importance of Chac, the rain god. He was an all-important deity who nourished the fields and sustained life. Virtually all towns and small Maya villages throughout the peninsula have a cenote.

In many scattered lagoons, updrafts of fresh water from underwater springs and cenotes bubble to the surface to form an *ojo de aqua* (eye of water). The gently swirling water, as clear as a windowpane, appears a different color because it is sediment free. *Grutas* (GREW-tass) or caves, are another fascinating feature of the Yucatán. Except for three large caverns open for escorted tours – Balankanche, Xtacumbilxunán, near Bolonchén, and Loltún – spelunking and cave exploration is still a largely undeveloped resource for tourism. If you'd like to explore the bowels of the earth for yourself, see the section on *Calcehtok*, page 329. You can hire a private guide there and go spelunking at your own speed. Also undeveloped as a tourist attraction is underwater cenote cave diving, which requires special dive skills and nerves of steel. Clear water and interesting rock formations make this a special thrill for experienced divers. Maps of the underground rivers and cenote tunnels are available for certified cave divers from the National Association of Cave Diving in Florida.

LIFE'S A BEACH: The long peninsula shoreline runs about 1,600 km (1,000 miles) and varies greatly along the way. The eastern Caribbean shore has pure white beaches and boasts three offshore islands: Cozumel, Isla Mujeres and Isla Contoy. The beachside resort city of Cancún didn't even exist until developers in the early 1970s figured out that the location's warm climate and long sandy Caribbean beaches were ideal for tourism. Now it's the most popular tourist destination in all of Mexico, surpassing even the old Pacific coast favorites of Acapulco and Puerto Vallarta. The Quintana Roo shoreline facing the Caribbean is acknowledged to have some of the best beaches in the country, if not the world.

South from Isla Mujeres, a sliver of an island off Cancún, the second longest coral reef in the world stretches down to the Bay of Honduras, over 250 km away (156 miles). Reef diving is spectacular around Cozumel and Xcalak, southeast of Chetumal, and in the quays off the Belize coast.

The entire coastline varies from sandy beach to mangrove to rock. The eastern end of Isla Mujeres has an impressive view of the sunrise from its rocky cliffs into the rough surf below. And between Champotón and Campeche City, along the western Gulf coast, erosion of a natural ridge has produced the only cliffed coast on the Gulf of Mexico. The highest elevation there is approximately 75 meters (246 feet). The southwestern coast of Campeche also has a complex of freshwater marshlands more extensive than the Florida Everglades. Along the rest of the coast up from Campeche and Yucatán and down through Quintana Roo, you'll find mangrove swamps, inviting sandy beaches and brackish lagoons, all of which combine to make a rich and diverse wildlife habitation.

Climate

The extinction of the dinosaurs may have begun in the Yucatán – when the impact of the Chicxulub comet changed the entire world's climate 65 million years ago.

 WEATHER: The Yucatán's weather is why people go south for a vacation. Sunny and warm, the peninsula enjoys a temperate climate year-round. Instead of four seasons, it has only two: a mild dry season in winter (November-April) and a hot rainy season in summer (May-October). The most popular time for vacationers from North America runs from December through March. In Cancún, the Christmas holiday season and spring break are the most heavily booked. But the entire area has much to offer all year. Don't let the words "rainy season" conjure up images of deluges that limit you to watching Mexican soap operas on TV while trapped in your room for days on end. The Yucatán's rains come and go rapidly. And if you're in Progreso, you'll be lucky to see rain at all. Two diverging tradewinds cut the peninsula in two: the northernmost part is much drier than the southern. In July and August, Mexicans on vacation fill Progreso.

The Yucatán's warm temperatures average 29°C (85° F) during the day, but are cooler in evening. Occasionally, however, phenomenons called *nortes* (NOR-tays) occur in the winter. These are cold fronts, dips in Arctic air that come down from Canada and can cool things off considerably for a day or more. Generally, however, the Yucatán has a sunny clime with distinctive high cumulus clouds speckling the sky. The temperature and humidity vary by location – inland and southern are warmer and more humid. On our first trip, we left behind 13 inches of snow and 20° F in New York and were greeted by Cancún's bright sunlight and 80° F . That wasn't hard to take.

HURRICANES: Travel agents sometimes lump Cancún and Cozumel together with other "Caribbean" islands, such as Jamaica and the Virgin Islands, because both Mexican locations are favorite ports of call for cruise ships. So it is fitting that the Yucatán is also subject to the same furious forces of nature that plague other idyllic Caribbean settings farther east – hurricanes.

The peninsula lies smack in the main path of any hurricanes and tropical storms that track through the Gulf of Mexico and the western Caribbean Sea. The entire coast is vulnerable, but the most storm-prone area is the biosphere reserve of Sian Ka'an near Tulum. Compiling records since 1886, meteorologists have found that most hurricanes strike in August through October, with September having the highest probability. On September 13, 1988, Hurricane Gilbert struck just south of Cancún. The damage to the resort area was staggering, totalling over $10 billion US. We met a man on Isla Mujeres who described floating on a wooden door as waves washed away his home. He saved himself by holding onto a neighbor's TV antenna. He later showed us what was left of his house – two walls and a great view of the sea. Tragically, the hurricane also smashed to rubble the ancient lighthouse/temple perched high on the rocky bluffs at the east end of the island. Before that it had survived hundreds of years of use by Maya priests, Spanish conquistadors and camera-toting tourists.

HURRICANE CATEGORIES

Atlantic hurricanes are ranked by the Saffir-Simpson hurricane intensity scale to give an estimate of the potential flooding and damage. Category three and above is considered intense.

Category	Min. Sustained Winds (mph)	Damage
One	74-95	Minimal: Damage primarily to shrubbery, trees and foliage.
Two	96 - 110	Moderate: Considerable damage to shrubbery and foliage; some trees blown down. Some damage to roofing materials.
Three	111 - 130	Extensive: Foliage torn from trees; large trees blown down. Some structural damage to small buildings. Mobile homes destroyed. Flooding along the coastline.
Four	131 - 155	Extreme: Shrubs and trees blown down. Complete failure of roofs on small residences. Major beach erosion. Massive evacuation of all homes within 500 yards of shore possibly required. Hurricane Andrew that smashed into South Florida in 1992 is a good example of a category four.
Five	155+	Catastrophic: Some complete building failures. Small buildings overturned or blown away. Low-lying escape routes inland cut by rising water three to five hours before the hurricane's center arrives. Hurricane Camille, a category five, struck Mississippi and Louisiana in 1969.

The source of a hurricane's devastating power is its winds, which have to be over 74 mph to distinguish it from a tropical storm. Most of the destruction it causes is due to what's called a storm surge, a powerful wall of water forced up by the strong winds.

Hurricanes begin as a cluster of thunderstorms that organize and rotate around a low pressure center. Their potency increases over warm ocean waters, where thermal energy is converted into kinetic energy. The addition of moisture (evaporated from the sea's surface) powers them like giant heat engines. At the center of the storm is an "eye," a cloud-free area of calm around which circulates a wall of its most powerful winds. Amazingly, an average hurricane releases enough power in a single day to supply many industrialized nations with energy for a year.

Hurricanes are nothing to take lightly, so if you're on the Yucatán coast and one is on the way, move inland immediately.

Ecology

The Land of the Pheasant and the Deer
– Mayan name for the Yucatán

 ENVIRONMENT: For a relatively small geographic area, the mostly dry-forested Yucatán Peninsula has an amazing variety of ecosystems that nurture a multiplicity of plants and wildlife. The flat landscape changes from the thorn forest of the northern coast to more luxuriant jungle vegetation in the wetter southern interior. Major tracts of wilderness are now dedicated for preservation (though their management is not always well funded) in the Yucatán, Belize and Guatemala. In the state of Quintana Roo there's the *Reserva de la Biósfera Sian Ka'an*, south of Tulum; *Laguna Chankanab Parque Nacíonal*, on Cozumel; and the Isla Contoy Bird Sanctuary, near Cancún. The state of Yucatán boasts *Rio Lagartos Parque Nacíonal* (and the nearby *San Felipe Parque Nacíonal*) and *Parque Natural del Flamenco Mexicano de Celestún*. All three are known as bird sanctuaries, especially for flamingos. In Campeche there's the *Reserva de la Biósfera de Calakmul*, which extends into Guatemala. Adjoining that to the east is Belize's *Rio Bravo Conservation Area*. The reef that runs down the Quintana Roo coast to Belize is also being protected by new Mexican environmental laws and, in some circumstances, active enforcement. Armed Park Rangers off Isla Contoy in Quintana Roo, for example, guard the delicate reef against vandalism.

Flora

Stingless bees, native to the Yucatán, collect nectar from two million flowers to make one pound of honeycomb.

 FORESTS: The thorn forest of northern Yucatán is similar to others in dry parts of Mexico. For an area with such thin soil cover and so little rainfall you might expect less vegetation than the abundant amount of scrub that grows from every crevice. After the first blush of excitement in seeing a new country, however, the flat Yucatecan landscape can be monotonous, especially on long drives. The scrub is a mixture of thorny leguminous trees and cactus. Greenery is subdued in the dry season, but the landscape comes alive in spring and summer with abundant flowers and green leaves. The profusion of flowers encourages domesticated bee keeping to make honey, or *miel* (me-EL), a vital food source and a major crop since pre-Columbian times. The Maya worshipped Hobnil Bacab, the god of bees and beekeepers, reflecting the importance the liquid gold played in their lives. If you have a sweet tooth, don't go home without having tried Yucatecan honey. We always buy a bottle in the countryside or in a *mercado* and haul it home with us. "Jungle Honey" and "Maya Blossom" are two brand names of the golden-amber nectar available in the United States.

The Yucatán's forests, from north to south, are termed: Thorn (also called scrub), deciduous, evergreen-seasonal and rainforest. The area covering parts of the extreme south of the Yucatán, Chiapas and Tabasco is the only true tropical rainforest in Mexico. Over 1,500 different plant species have been identified to date, even though botanical research has barely scratched the surface. The evergreen and seasonal forests contain large ceiba, breadnut, mahogany and palm trees; plus guaya, papaya, mamey and chico zapotes, all of which bear edible fruit. Zapote sap is called *chicle* and it was the latex originally used for chewing gum. Mamey zapote has a light cocoa-brown skin and soft, sweet, rose-colored fruit pulp, while the chico zapote has a brown potato-colored skin and a fruit described as tasting like "pears with brown sugar."

Thankfully, in some circles, the value of the staggering biodiversity in rainforests is no longer being ignored. Worldwide efforts to halt their destruction have resulted in at least some awareness among governments that the forest has more value standing than cleared. Besides being important watersheds, rainforests hold secrets that can benefit mankind. For example, more than 70% of the plants known to produce compounds with anti-cancerous properties are tropical. Cures for malaria (quinine) and amoebic dysentery (ipecac) are only two of the hundreds of medicines derived from botanical sources. Cortisone is another and so is diosgenin, the active agent in birth control pills, developed from Mexican and Guatemalan wild yams. And there are potentially thousands of new medicines waiting to be found in the rainforest. Since time began, man has used plants as medicine. Indigenous peoples around the world, including the Maya, still use plants and home remedies medicinally with great effect. Not only is the rainforest medically valuable, but it also provides commercial and edible products, such as rubber, vanilla, coconuts, resins, starch, thatch, dyes and bananas.

It's easy, however, to be an ecological advocate in more financially secure regions such as Canada and the US than it is for the people struggling to live in Mexico. Sometimes the exploitation of the rainforest provides subsistence living for the poor. In other cases it's the greed of rich individuals and corporations attempting to get richer. Efforts are in full gear by private organizations and educational institutions to educate the people and the Mexican authorities on the need to care for – and the financial reward of – funding environmental protection. Environmental advocates in the government agree, consequently, "ecopolitical" progress is being made – and ecotourism can take some of the credit. Although, like the word "organic," ecotourism has become a cliché, the responsible use of low-impact tourism can make the difference between preservation and destruction of natural resources.

One of the bigger environmental concerns in the Yucatán is the oil drilling offshore in Campeche. Pemex, the federal monopoly gas and oil behemoth, has a miserable record in other oil-producing states, so the pressure is on to insure a clean and environmentally safe operation. So far, it's comparatively successful.

On a grassroots level there are several organizations working and encouraging ecotourism in the Yucatán. Two private, non-profit groups, *Amigos de Sian Ka'an* and *Pronatura Península de Yucatán*, have worked diligently to preserve the region's precious ecological balance. They have the expertise to share the responsibility for the parks' and biospheres' long- and short-term operations and have raised much needed funds to do so. Other private efforts have also encouraged responsible agricultural land use and a reduction in pesticides and fertilizers.

Unfortunately, as time and "progress" marches on, so does the destruction of the native forests. Since colonial days, lumber harvesting and agricultural clearing have made their mark on the peninsula and now the booming population growth in recent years is accelerating that pressure. But it's also clear that conservation efforts have made inroads in the Yucatán. Besides Sian Ka'an (1.5 million acres), Rio Lagartos (118,000) and Celestún (15,000 acres) nearly two million acres of evergreen jungle forest were set aside in the extreme south of Campeche and Quintana Roo in the new Calakmul Biosphere Reserve. Flowing into neighboring Guatemala, it's the largest rain-forest park in all North America.

ORCHIDS: Exotic blooming orchids are the largest family of flowering plants in the world and they thrive in warm, humid climates. The many varieties have different styles of flowers, from tiny delicate petals running along the stem to bold blossoms and big thick green leaves. The Yucatán claims over 100 different varieties, 75% of which are epiphytes (from the Greek for "upon plants"). Epiphytes attach to host trees and gain their nourishment from airborne dust and rain. These are not parasitic relationships because they do not feed on their hosts. In the amazing world of nature, many tree orchids make use of variety-specific pollinators – bees, ants, hummingbirds, wasps and moths – for their fertilization. Ground-dwelling epiphytes are known as bromeliads, named for Swedish botanist, Olaf Bromel. The most well-known bromeliad is the pineapple.

FLOWERS, FRUIT & FRAGRANCE: It's always intrigued us to find plants that barely survive on our kitchen windowsill at home growing wild and abundant in the jungle. Philodendron and caladium become huge and show stunning colors. Hibiscus thrives here, as do exotic herbs and the fragrant frangipani (plumeria). However, the ubiquitous bougainvillea has to be one of our favorite semi-tropical flowers. Its large red and orange and pink blossoms appear in every garden, framing colonial courtyard arches. They also grow wild along the road.

Bananas, oranges, coconuts and limes are the big fruits of the countryside. Limes, called *limones* (lee-MON-ehz) are an important ingredient in Yucatecan cooking. If you're not aware of what they can do to enhance the taste of food, spend a week in the country and we guarantee you'll become addicted to their unique flavor.

Despite the yellowing disease that has devastated coconut groves throughout Central America, Florida and Mexico, cold coconuts (*cocos frios*) are a popular juice drink. They're sold like lemonade at roadside stands.

Oranges are especially sweet and juicy in the Yucatán. Known as *naranjas* (na-RAHN-hass) in Spanish and *chinas* (chee-nass) in Ma-yan, they are often sold by vendors on the street with the skin already peeled. Antique American hand-crank apple peelers find a new life in Mexico, where they're used to peel the bitter skin of the orange, leaving the white pith to hold in the juice. That cleverly eliminates stinging lips when they're cut and eaten in halves. For an incomparable experience, eat one as the locals do – cut in half and dipped into red chili powder. Wow! Sweet and hot.

A must stop on any adventure itinerary is the town *mercado* (market) for a sampling of regional fruit and vegetables. Check out the red radishes as big as plums, carrots the color of orange crayons, beans and nuts of every size and description and big bunches of fresh flowers. Try *jícama* (HE-cama), a delicious root vegetable that tastes like a cross between an apple and potato. It's peeled and eaten raw sprinkled with lime juice, chili and salt. You'll also find it in the plastic cups of sliced fruit sold by vendors in the square or on street corners.

Since pre-Columbian times, local inhabitants have learned to make the most of their natural resources. Wild and cultivated gourds, for example, are a useful part of rural life. A Maya at work in his field will probably have a hollowed gourd, plugged by a piece of dried corn cob, holding his drinking water. Called a *Chu* (chew) in Mayan, the water slowly seeps through to the exterior surface and evaporates, keeping the inside liquid cool.

The majestic ceiba tree holds a special place in Maya folklore. The tree is the center support that holds up the world's sky. It's rarely cut down even if it takes root in an inconvenient place – like the middle of a farm field. Tall with a thick, arrow-straight trunk and perpendicular branches, immature trees have quite sharp spikes to protect their bark.

Besides commercially harvested hardwoods, such as mahogany, other forest trees offer benefits. The mamey tree provides both pleasing shade and a sweet snack fruit that tastes much like a yam or sweet potato. The fruit of the guaya, a member of the lichi nut family, is also a local favorite. If you are visiting in the summer, the flaming orange-red flowering trees that

Ceiba Tree, the sacred tree of life.

line so many sidewalks are the beautiful *flamboyanes* (royal poinciana).

HENEQUEN: Henequen, or sisal, is the rope fiber produced from one of the more than 300 varieties of the agave plant. Agave plants thrive in warm arid and semiarid regions and have long, stiff evergreen leaves that splay out from the center forming a rosette shape that resembles the top of a gigantic pineapple. Fibers taken from the plant leaf are used primarily to make rope. Other varieties make soap, food and the alcoholic drinks *pulque* and tequila. Sisal changed the course of history in the Yucatán when, in the late 1800s, the peninsula was the sole source of the natural fiber. The invention of synthetic fibers brought a sharp reduction in the demand for natural fiber rope. The word "sisal" (SEE- sal) comes from the name of the old Yucatán port from which the fibers were first shipped.

Fauna

A wonderful bird is the pelican,
His bill will hold more than his belican.
He can take in his beak
Food enough for a week,
But I'm damned if I see how the helican.

– *The Pelican* by Dixon Lanier Merritt, 1879-1954

Until recently, the isolation of the Yucatán has meant that birds and animals continued to thrive here when development pressures pushed them out elsewhere. The "land of the turkey and deer" features such exotic natives as peccaries, tapirs, manatees, iguanas and jaguars. But a huge number of animals use the Yucatán as the tourists do – it's a prime spot for migrating birds and butterflies that rest or winter over in this diverse tropical land. According to *Pronatura Peninsula de Yucatán* environmentalists, almost a third of the bird species in the ancient land of the Maya are migratory – including most of the neotropical species whose sudden declines have caused worldwide alarm. All told, 147 species of vertebrates, not including fish, are native to Yucatán's forests.

LIONS & OCELOTS & JAGUARS, OH MY! Not so very long ago, the wild cats of the jungle could almost be termed "common," especially in Campeche and southern Quintana Roo. No longer.

Civilization has driven them deeper into the shrinking forests. The four species native to the peninsula are jaguar, jaguarundi, ocelot and puma. It's unlikely you'll ever get to see one of these mostly nocturnal carnivores in the wilderness, but they are still out there.

The king of the jungle is the **jaguar,** the largest of the New World cats. It holds a special place in the Maya culture: it is the form taken by the sun when it descends into the underworld at nightfall. Its image symbolizes power and strength. A male jaguar may reach over six feet in length and can weigh in at 300 lbs. Its short coat, spotted much like a leopard, ranges from grayish gold to reddish tan with spots grouped in small circles known as rosettes. Unlike the leopard, however, the jaguars' rosettes surround solid spots. Occasionally they are black all over. Jaguars feed on tapirs, peccaries, foxes, turtle eggs,

The majestic jaguar.

rodents, even deer – but rarely man. They breed once a year with no fixed breeding season. After the birth of one to four kittens, the mother raises them for about a year until the young can hunt on their own. Because of the dwindling habitat, they are vulnerable to extinction in Mexico and Central America. If you're dying to see one up close, see the chapter on Campeche, we'll tell you where you can.

The **jaguarundi** is the smallest cat, with a low-slung long body resembling a weasel. They're solidly colored in ranges from brown to gray. Slightly larger than a household cat, they stand 14 inches at the shoulders and weigh as much as 20 lbs. Nearly half of the cat's 35- to 55-inch length is taken up by its sinuous tail. Already a rare animal, it's becoming more rare as its natural habitat in wild thickets and lowland forests are cut and burned for ranching. We were lucky enough to photograph one outside its den in the brush near the salt mountain of Coloradas.

Ocelots are one of Latin America's most beautiful and rare cats, noted for their creamy tan fur and dark spots with open centers. They usually weigh from 20 to 32 lbs and grow to 33 to 40 inches in length. Like most wild cats, they maintain territories marked by their scents. They're solitary ground hunters but are agile enough to climb trees if threatened. Their main predator is man, who values their fur for coats. They are a protected endangered species so the only hunting is done by poachers.

The **puma,** which is also native to the United States and Canada, is otherwise known as the cougar or mountain lion. A full-grown male puma may be nearly as big as a jaguar and weigh 91 kilograms (200 lbs). Its soft fur coat runs from reddish to gray to brown. This big cat is an amazingly agile climber, able to leap 12 meters (40 feet) in length and an astounding four meters (15 feet) in height. The puma can successfully drop from a height of 18 meters (60 feet).

LAND OF PHEASANT & DEER: Yucatán's **deer** are very much the same as deer found throughout North America, but the pheasant of the old Mayan saying is actually an ocellated **turkey**. They look more like peacocks. If you have it on a menu you'll find it tougher and stronger-tasting than the native bird fatted and consumed in the States for Thanksgiving. According to one theory, turkeys got their common name in England after the birds were picked up in the Colonies and the Yucatán and later transferred to ships returning to England from Turkey and the Near East. Hence the public thought of them as "Turkey" birds.

CROCODILES: An armadillo would win a beauty contest if compared to the authentically prehistoric crocodile. The long leathery-scaled crocodile has beady eyes that stare blankly from its head as it skims the surface of the water hunting for frogs, fish, birds and small mammals. They hunt mainly at night, their eyes glowing red in the beam of a flashlight. During the day they sun themselves along the banks and mangrove swamps. Crocodiles can get as large as six meters (20 feet). Your chance of seeing one during the day in the flesh in the wild is very remote. However, you can see plenty of them at **Croco Cun,** south of Cancún, where the management is devoted to the study and preservation of the species. It makes an interesting side trip from the resort. If you want to get up close and personal, call the Amigos de Sian Ka'an in Cancún and arrange for one of their Thursday night expeditions into the biosphere to tag and count the amphibious reptiles. You get to help pull the beasts into your boat while the biologist tags it. See more details in the section on Sian Ka'an.

PECCARIES, TAPIRS & ARMADILLOS: Some of the strangest looking animal natives are peccaries, tapirs and armadillos. Peccaries are the wild boar of the Yucatán, related to the hog.

Collared peccaries travel in packs of two to 15, while white-lipped peccaries move in herds of as many as 100 or more. The collared variety, found in woodlands and dry forests, gets its name from the strip of white fur around its shoulders. The **white-lipped peccary** has white fur near its mouth and is larger, roaming mainly in the tropical rainforest. They both boast two solid, sharp tusks protruding from their jaws.

Tapirs are shy and nocturnal, so there is little chance of seeing one in the wild. Strictly herbivores, they usually live near water and are very clean animals. Their principal predator is the jaguar. When threatened away from a water escape route (their first choice), tapirs lower their head and blindly crash through the jungle, smashing into bushes and even trees to get away.

Armadillos are common to the southwestern United States and all of Mexico. They're an ugly, armor-plated, dinosaur-like animal with a keen sense of smell and an elongated snout used to root out insects and grubs from underground. Their long sharp claws dig up the grubs or burrow into the ground to make their homes. Found most frequently in the north, they are trapped for food by Maya villagers. Once, while driving near Chichén Itzá, we saw a young boy on the roadside holding one up by its long tail, for sale. We bought the hapless creature and drove a mile or two, then pulled over and released it into the bush. What can we say? We're softies.

Armadillo for sale!

FEATHERED FRIENDS: The Yucatán is prime real estate for birds – and for bird lovers. The peninsula's rich wetlands provide feeding grounds for flocks of both. A pair of good binoculars is worth taking along if you're off into the bush or down the coast. Amateur birdwatchers thrill to the sight of native birds, such as the orange oriole, yellow-lored parrot or the black catbird, as well as a wealth of migratory varieties. Ornithologists working with the Amigos de Sian Ka'an estimate there are 6,000 to 9,000 varieties in the protected wetlands. Even neophytes like us can appreciate the mesmerizing sight of sharp-winged frigates as they float effortlessly on the sea breeze; the unexpected thrill of a flock of bright-green parrots rising from trees; or the spectacular dives of cormorants, who splash in the water in one place only to pop up somewhere else. Stroll in the main plaza in Valladolid at dusk and listen to the loud cacophony of bird calls as a flock settles in for the night. See the majestic flight of a huge white-tipped black bird as it circles and lands – only to realize that up close it is an ugly vulture. Or sit on the beach and watch the animated pelican, gracefully diving into the surf for fish, then bobbing on the water and grinning back at you. Pelicans are fun to observe as they jockey for position to eat scraps alongside the fishing boats on Isla Mujeres, Ciudad de Carmen, Isla Contoy and Champotón.

But it is the flamingo that attracts scores of tourists to the Yucatán. The biospheres at Celestún and Rio Lagartos are home to huge flocks of the one meter (three feet) and taller birds. Large wading birds with long spindly backward-bending legs and thin curved necks and beaks, their colors run from a soft pinkish-white to a stunning salmon-pink. Local guides take tourists out in boats to get close to them at their feeding areas. It's breathtaking to see the huge flocks, which can number as many as a million or more bright pink birds.

Flamingos feed standing on mud banks in estuaries and lagoon shallows. They force muddy water through the serrated edges of their bill, straining the edible animal and vegetable matter for nourishment. The mineral salt content of the muddy water is what affects the coloring of the birds – and the Yucatán's salts make for spectacular colors.

Undersea

The sea has many voices.
– T.S. Eliot, 1888-1965

 REEFS: In some ways, you could say the entire Yucatán Peninsula is one gigantic limestone reef forced up from the bottom of the sea in one of the earth's endless tectonic plate clashes. The material that forms all reefs is essentially the same as the substrata on the peninsula: limestone. On the dry land the limestone is formed by untold generations of tiny sea crustaceans, mollusks and polyps that died eons ago. But on the underwater shelf that runs down Quintana Roo's eastern Caribbean coast, those sea creatures are alive and growing in one of nature's strangest life form combinations: coral.

Coral is the common name for several species of coelenterates, a large group of invertebrate animals. The class has over 6,000 living species and scientists have identified over 6,000 different extinct species. The phylum include jellyfish, hydras, sea cucumbers and sea anemones. What they all have in common is a cylindrical shape, a gastrovasular cavity and a "mouth" surrounded by tentacles. Coral polyps (the living organism) extract calcium from sea water and create calcium carbonate "skeletons" that offers physical support and protection when they're threatened.

Most coral live in colonies, attaching themselves first to limestone on the sea bed, then to each other. As polyps die, leaving hard stony limestone skeletons as a base, new living coral builds upon them. In time, this forms the enormous underwater structures we know as reefs. Coral reproduce either asexually from buds or with a larval polyp, called a *planula*, which floats away and settles elsewhere to begin a new reef colony.

To form and grow, coral reefs need four critical environmental factors; the first is sea water temperature between 23° and 27°C (73 - 80°F). The warmest temperature that coral will endure is 30°C (86°F). Coral also needs water shallow enough to allow sunlight to penetrate. Symbiotic algae, (zooxanthellane) lives in the tissues of the living coral and photosynthesizes nutrients and oxygen that the coral uses. These algae provide "stony," or hard coral, with a brown or yellow color. Other colors found in coral – red, pink, orange, black and purple – come as a result of pigment-colored calcareous spicules. (Got all that? There will be a test at the end of the book.)

Another condition effecting coral growth is salinity, which should be between 30 and 40 parts per thousand. If the sea water is either too saline or not saline enough – perhaps due to freshwater runoff from the mainland or to unusually heavy amounts of rainfall – coral will not grow.

Lastly, coral thrives in areas of strong wave action, which aerates the water. Along the Yucatán coast the Caribbean Sea, unlike the Gulf, has some very active surf. Waves help prevent silt from accumulating in the reef and suffocating the living coral.

In response to environmental stresses – such as higher water temperatures – coral will expel their algae, thus "bleaching" the reef of its color, leaving it ghostly white. Unfortunately, without its beneficial algae the reef begins to die. A reef can come back from occasional mild periods of bleaching, but a sustained warming of the water will kill it completely. Scientists, marine biologists and zoologists are still unsure how global warming is affecting the oceans or whether it is a major contributor to bleaching. However, oil spills, water pollution, damage from ships and attacks of the coral-eating starfish known as the "crown of thorns," has placed many of the world's reefs under additional threat.

The reefs off Quintana Roo, which are known collectively as the Belize Reef, have battled some bleaching in recent years. Another threat comes from divers and snorkelers, usually amateurs, who break off pieces and touch or stand on the reef, killing the fragile living organisms. If you're underwater, look but do not touch.

The Yucatán claims all three of reef types: Fringe reefs, located close to the shore in very shallow water, like El Garrafón Park on Isla Mujeres; barrier reefs, which lie farther offshore and are separated from the land by lagoons or water generally no deeper than 10 meters (about 30 feet), such as at Akumal: and atolls, ring islands that form a natural lagoon in the middle. Atolls are often associated with extinct underwater volcanoes and are found mostly in the South Pacific, but Quintana Roo's Chinchorro coral atoll sits only 22 km (14 miles) off Xcalak. Its inner lagoon varies in depth from two to eight meters. Beyond the reef, the ocean floor drops away to depths of 150 to 200 meters (450-600 feet).

SOMETHING'S FISHY: Since pre-Hispanic times, fishing has been an important economic activity and along the coast entire communities earn their livelihood catching fish, lobster and shrimp. As you might imagine, the seas surrounding the Yucatán teem with life. The reefs and depths of the Caribbean, as well as the warm shallows of the Gulf of Mexico, provide the perfect habitat for hundreds of fish, shellfish, invertebrates, reptiles and amphibians. The beaches from Tulum south and along the stretch from Campeche to Carmen are the breeding grounds for **sea turtles**, who come ashore to lay their eggs in the sand. Loggerhead is the most common type, along with the green, the hawksbill and sometimes the leatherback varieties. Loggerheads, with their massive bird-jawed skulls, have short fins and grow to about four feet in length. Green turtles lay their eggs every two to three years, storming the beach in large groups. The black, narrow-finned leatherback (aptly named because of the leathery hide it has in place of a shell) grow as large as six feet and weigh as much as 1,500 lbs. The hawksbill is one of the smallest marine turtles at about three feet or less and only 200 lbs. Because of its highly valued spindle-shaped tortoise shell, it has been hunted to near extinction.

If you're lucky enough to be in Mexico during summer nesting season, hire an experienced guide to take you out to the see it. It's quite an experience to huddle on a deserted beach late at night with only the brush stroke of the Milky Way to illuminate your world. Any type of unnatural light or noise will disturb the giant lumbering females and can cause them to abort their nest. Turtles return to the same beach each year and lay their precious eggs by digging a shallow hole in the sand with their flippers. Once covered over, the hatchlings emerge about 60 days later and crawl toward the surf. Hopefully. Between wrong turns and predators – sea gulls and other birds, large fish, raccoons, foxes and human poachers – rarely do more than 4 or 5% grow to maturity. Mexican laws severely restrict the harvesting of sea turtles, so if it's ever on a menu, please don't order it. Isla Mujeres has a turtle research station that makes for a pleasant and educational visit.

Walk the beaches of Campeche, Yucatán and Quintana Roo and see some sea shells by the seashore. **Conch**, of course, is the largest (sometimes as big as two feet) and one of the most beautiful of the shells that wash up on the shore. *Caracol*, as the conch is known in Spanish, also provides a delicious meat that Maya people have eaten for hundreds of years. It's commonly served in ceviche. The meat is extracted by drilling a small hole in the top and forcing the muscle out. Vendors line the dock on Isla Mujeres selling conch shells. They're a popular souvenir.

Other shells with great names include whelk, alphabet cone, banded and true tulips, egg cockle, calico scallop, angel wing, sunrise tellin, sunray venus, zebra ark and pearl oyster, among others.

It's said that sea air spurs the appetite. If so, then that may explain the large numbers of restaurants serving delicious lobster and shrimp caught in the Yucatán's waters. Fresh lobster is on the menu nearly everywhere along the shoreline and shrimp is especially popular in Campeche, where they have a particularly delicate variety. What's even better is that they cost a fraction of what restaurants charge in the US and Canada.

But when most people think of the sea they think of fish. So if it's fish you want – to see or to eat – then you've found a home in the Yucatán. Put on a snorkel mask and get into the excitement. **Barracuda**, with their long snouts and razor teeth, grin at you. **Stingrays** bury themselves in the sand and **sand sharks** slide away. And the colors are amazing – Spanish and French grunts, yellowjacks, queen triggerfish, blue tangs, banded butterfish, damselfish, red snappers, sergeant majors, angelfish and spotted drums are just a few of the colorful, edible inhabitants of the Yucatán underwater.

All men are equal before fish.
– Herbert Hoover, 1874-1964

This sketch was drawn by Campeche artist Alejandro Serrano.
© *Alejandro Serrano*

People Of The Yucatán

 The Yucatán is home to some of the friendliest folks in the world. Whether in Cancún's lively restaurants downtown, Mérida's fashionable Paseo de Montejo, Campeche's old walled forts, or Valladolid's *mercado*, you can be sure of a warm welcome from everyone.

The ethnic and cultural make-up of the people who call the Yucatán home is relatively straightforward. A large percentage of the population is Maya, descendants of the original glorious civilization that stretched from the peninsula into the Mexican state of Chiapas, Guatemala, Belize and parts of El Salvador and Honduras. Generally small of stature, with facial structures that resemble the American Indian, most Maya speak their own native tongue as well as Spanish, now required in school.

The largest proportion of inhabitants is *mestizo*, the term used to describe Mexican people whose Spanish-descent bloodline is mixed with that of the indigenous population. An influx of Lebanese merchants into the Yucatán during henequen's heyday also added to the gene pool. Additionally, recent job opportunities in Cancún have attracted many workers from all over Mexico, especially the Federal District (Mexico City). Many of the newcomers have intermarried, blending into the population.

It's the way the Yucatecan people got to where they are today – culturally – that makes the story of the Yucatán so fascinating. Tragedy, peace, bloodlust, sacrifice, gore, romance, glory, pain, triumph, love, ignorance, enlightenment, lost opportunities, treachery, greed, friendship and intrigue fill the history of the Maya, the Spanish and Mexico. And that's just the beginning.

The Maya

Our days upon earth are a shadow.
— The Bible, Job 8:9

MEANING OF MAYA: Astronomers, mathematicians, agronomists, philosophers, artists, architects, sculptors and warriors – the Maya of old were a rich, complex society that continues to fascinate anyone who learns of them. Their stunning accomplishments are still evident today: it was they who first cultivated chocolate, chili peppers, vanilla, papayas and pineapples. The Maya built causeways and reservoirs, created great works of sculpture and art, carved fantastic jade masks and wove rich colorful textiles. They also developed sophisticated mathematical systems; complex, accurate calendars; and perfectly proportioned buildings of immense size and beauty. Much of this while Europe remained in the Dark Ages.

In the modern world, observers continue to comment that Maya culture will soon disappear. Roads and cars have made their world smaller; seaside resorts such as Cancún attract hoards of camera-clicking foreign daytrippers; and television brings cosmopolitan Mexican and North American programs into remote villages. But the Maya have always been resilient. Their history has reinforced a pattern of community-based culture – with pride and respect for tradition. Their communal society has adapted modern means to preserve the Maya culture and language. Besides, they've had nearly 475 years to practice survival skills under pressure – and even longer before that.

THE BEGINNING: The rise of the first civilizations in Mesoamerica took place in what's called the "Preclassic period" (ca. 1500 B.C.-A.D. 250), with several different peoples in several different areas of Mexico and Central America – the Zapotec of Oaxaca, the Olmec on the Gulf coast and the Maya in the lowlands and highlands of Guatemala and Mexico, ideal crossroads on the huge land bridge between the Americas.

Powerful kings who were both rulers and high priests had direct responsibility for the ordered world of the Preclassic Maya. The success and power of their rule was in a direct relation to the kingdom's military strength. Inter-city rivalries were common and, if defeated, the high-living royalty often met ignominious sacrificial ends.

By A.D. 400, complex writing and regional trade had developed and some impressive capital cities had been built. El Tigre, the largest single Maya temple ever built, was constructed at El Mirador, an important Preclassic city a few kilometers south of the Mexican border in the Petén region of Guatemala. The Maya civilization waxed and waned during three periods archeologists have distinguished as Preclassic, Classic and Post Classic.

The end of the Preclassic period may have come about with the eruption of a volcano in 250 A.D. in El Salvador that spewed ash over much of the southern Maya area. Loss of agriculture and commerce in the south increased the importance of the lowlands of the Yucatán in the north, thus begetting new power bases and new glory days of Maya civilization.

CLASSIC SPLENDOR: The apex of Maya growth and prosperity occurred during the time A.D. 250-900. The Early Classic (A.D. 250-600) saw the rise of city states of Tikal and Calakmul – who struggled with each other for control of the lowlands. Calakmul eventually defeated Tikal but was unable to exert power over more territory, losing its chance to rule the world. The Early Classic period gradually slid into the Late Classic period (A.D. 600-800). The Classic age is considered to be the peak of Maya civilization with advanced building styles and carved stone records called stelae. Large ceremonial city centers were built that included massive stone pyramids, ballcourts and platform temples. Tikal reemerged as a powerful city of as many as 40,000 people over six square miles – a population density comparable to an average city in modern Europe or America.

But for reasons not fully understood – drought and overpopulation are two theories – the Classic kingdoms began to lose their luster. The last hundred years of this time are known as "Terminal Classic" and, as the name implies, marked the demise of the era. Maya kings' influence over the population declined, indicated by the halt of ceremonial construction, and by A.D. 900, with no more dated religious stelae carved in Tikal, it was a clear end of the epoch. The great mystery is why. That question lured the Yucatán's first tourists, John Lloyd Stephens, a self-taught American archeologist, and Frederick Catherwood, an English sketch artist experienced in architectural drawing, to explore the ruins of southern Mexico. They set out in the midst of social and civil war and recorded 44 abandoned ruins. Stephens wrote two books, *Incidents of Travel in Central America, Chiapas and Yucatán* (1841) and *Incidents of Travel in Yucatán* (1843), which launched the archeological search for the Maya past.

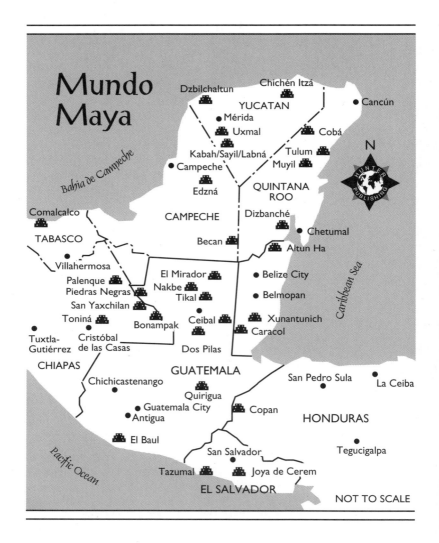

Of his first visit to Uxmal he wrote: *"... emerging suddenly from the woods, to my astonishment came upon a large open field strewed with mounds of ruins and vast buildings on terraces and pyramidal structures, grand and in good preservation, richly ornamented, without a brush to obstruct the view, in picturesque effect almost equal to the ruins of Thebes."* Stephens was one of the first who correctly surmised that the ancient cities of the Maya world were built by the native people still living there and not some mysterious Egyptian or lost European race.

Cities that reached their prime during the Classic period – Palenque, Tikal, Uxmal, Cobá, Edzná and Copan – are often thought of as the cities of the "lost" Maya civilization. No one knows exactly why these great metropolises were suddenly abandoned – forfeited to the jungle – beginning in the ninth century. However, the beginning of the end of the Classic period did not mean the complete end of Maya culture. Other cities rose to take their place.

A HOUSE DIVIDED: Into the vacuum caused by the demise of the Classic kingdoms came outside invaders into the land. The lowland Maya were partly conquered around A.D. 850 by the militaristic Toltec peoples from the highlands of central Mexico and the Itzá, a Mexicanized Chontal-Maya tribe perhaps from Tabasco. The capital they occupied and built in mixed-architectural-style grandeur was centrally located Chichén Itzá in northern Yucatán. The foreigners brought with them their fierce warrior ways, blended religion and influences from central Mexico, such as the cult of the Feathered Serpent (Quetzalcóatl or Kukulcán).

KUKULCAN, IF YOU CAN

No other deity-personage ever created a deeper impression on Mesoamerican people than *Quetzalcóatl* ("Snake of Precious Feathers" or "Plumed Serpent"). The Maya origins of the legend begin with the Toltec civilization in Mexico's central valley around the mid 900s. Topiltzin, a young Toltec prince, entered the priesthood of the ancient god of civilization and fertility, Quetzalcóatl. As was the custom, he assumed the name of the deity. He became a great leader and spurred the Toltec to new heights of civilization. His name became inseparable with the legend. But a power struggle with other lords forced him into exile. Maya records indicate that Quetzalcóatl, or *Kukulcán* as they called him, invaded the Yucatán and may have ruled at Chichén Itzá. Legends of his "death" vary, but all state that he would return to vanquish his enemies. The vague date indicated was 1-Reed, the anniversary of his birth in the cyclical calendar. This was the sword of Damocles that hung over the Aztec, the civilization that had succeeded the Toltec by the time Cortéz landed in 1519 – the year of 1-Reed.

The most beautiful bird of Central America is the Quetzal; very rare, especially in the Yucatán. Its long, brightly colored tail feathers could be worn only by Maya royalty and it was forbidden for anyone to kill one. Their non-flight feathers were plucked and then they were released to grow new ones.

The Yucatecan Maya despised the Itzá Maya and referred to them with such epithets as "foreigners," "tricksters and rascals," "lewd ones," as well as "people without fathers or mothers," in surviving Maya chronicles. The Itzá ruled the Yucatán from their centrally located capital until the city fell to warriors from a rival city, Mayapán, in A.D. 1221. In what may sound like a plot from Shakespeare, the ruler of Chichén kidnapped the wife of the king of Izamal. Izamal's main ally was the opportunistic king, Hunac Ceel, of Mayapán. His warriors drove the Itzá from Chichén and the victorious city of Mayapán became the new center of civilization. But Mayapán was in turn sacked and abandoned in a civil uprising around A.D. 1440 after a later Cocom king apparently tyrannized his people. The revolt, lead by a prince of the Xiú family, slaughtered him and his family. One son, away on a trading mission, survived. In an ironic twist of fate, one of his descendants would wreak terrible revenge on all the Maya people nearly 100 years later.

In 1536, after the Spanish had been initially driven out of most of the Yucatán, the ruler of the Xiú at Maní decided it was a good time to offer thanks to the gods at the Cenote of Sacrifices in Chichén Itzá. Nachi Cocom, the great grandson of the surviving Cocom son, granted the Xiú ruler safe passage through his province on the way. He entertained the 40-man traveling court for four days until a banquet on the last evening, when he and his warriors suddenly turned and butchered their Xiú guests. This treachery caused a civil war between the two most powerful kingdoms in the Yucatán. Luckily for the Spanish, when they returned in 1540 they found a Maya empire divided against itself.

There's an interesting sidelight to the fall of Chichén Itzá in 1221: Surviving Itzás fled south and settled on an island in the middle of Lake Petén in Guatemala. They founded a city known as Tayasal, now named Flores. This isolated Itzá kingdom remained intact until 1697 – over 450 years after their defeat at Chichén and 150 years after the Conquest – when a Spanish naval force finally destroyed the last of over 3,000 years of Maya high civilization.

So much of our future lies in preserving our past.

– Peter Westbrook, manager of London's Waldorf Hotel

HEAVEN HELP US

"God is not all that exists; God is all that does not exist."

– Remy de Gourmont, French philosopher, 1858-1915

The ancient Maya had a large number of gods in their complex religion, each with clearly defined characteristics and purposes. Here's the list of the top five Maya gods of all time:

#1. Itzamná (or Zamná). Itzamná, the big cheese overall and lord of the heavens as well as night and day, could be called upon in hard times or calamities. Who says nice guys finish last? Itzamná was always benevolent.

#2. Chac. Although second in power, Chac was first in importance as the god of rain, and by association, the weather and fertility.

#3. Ah Mun was the corn god and the god of agriculture. He was always represented as a youth, often with a corn ear headdress.

#4. Ah Puch, the god of death, ruled over the ninth and lowest of the Maya underworlds. He was always malevolent.

#5. Ek Chuah. Ek was the god of war, human sacrifice, and violent death. Not the kind of god you'd want to meet in person.

In addition to these, there were patron gods, 13 of the upper world and nine of the lower, plus numerous calendar gods who posed for glyphs. Other deities, such as Kukulcán and Chac Mool, came into the line-up as the society changed in Post Classic times. The religious hierarchy became so bewildering that it was beyond the comprehension of the average Maya, who relied on priests to interpret the religion (so what's new?). To the common man, who lives or dies by the cycle of rain and drought, Chac remains the god most frequently involved in daily life.

The Spanish

Nothing remains but flowers and sad songs,
In Tlatelolco and Mexico,
Where once there were warriors and wise men.

– *Cantares Mexicanos*, Aztec poems (ca. 1523)

 SOMETHING OLD, SOMETHING NEW: The Americas came as a complete surprise to Columbus, who was convinced that he had found a new route from Europe to the Far East. He thought the Caribbean islands he found were barrier islands of India, hence the nomenclature "Indian" to describe Native Americans. His first contact with the Maya came on July 30, 1502 when he encountered sea traders near the Bay Islands off the coast of Honduras. Their canoes were filled with textiles, grains, cacao beans and a fermented liquor. Columbus was soon followed by military expeditions looking to conquer and colonize this "New World."

The first Spanish set foot on Mayn territory in 1511, when 17 passengers from a shipwreck came ashore in the Yucatán. Captured by Maya warriors, most were killed or sacrificed. Two survived, however, and of those two, Brother Gerónimo de Aguilar couldn't wait for his rescue from the heathen barbarians – while Gonzalo Guerrero loved the Maya so much he led their warriors in battle to try to stop the Spanish invasion.

That invasion began in 1517 when Fernando Hernández de Córdoba accidentally "discovered" Mexico when he landed on Cape Catouche near present day Isla Holbox on the tip of the Yucatán. After small skirmishes with the natives, he and one hundred of his men sailed on to Campeche and Champotón, where they were again attacked by Maya warriors. Hernández, mortally wounded, lost half his men in the battle and died shortly after returning to his base in Cuba. The ambush was purportedly arranged by none other than Gonzalo Guerrero. However, Hernández's report of stone houses, cities and gold convinced the Spanish that Mexico might be the India they'd been searching for.

In 1519, a well-armed expedition, led by Hernán Cortéz, landed on Cozumel, a Maya religious and trading center. Hearing of the two Spanish shipwreck survivors, Cortéz bought the clergyman's freedom. Guerrero refused to return and was never heard of again. But Brother Gerónimo had learned the Mayan language and his linguistic skill would be important in the conquest of the rest of Mexico. Sailing around to the Gulf, Cortéz and his men founded the city of Veracruz. The inhabitants there, believing the Spanish to be gods attached to their horses, surrendered, giving Cortéz a valuable lesson he would not forget. In tribute, he received gifts of food and 20 young girls. One of these girls was Malintzin, or Malinche, a captive of the Maya who spoke both their language and Nahuatl – the language of the Aztec. Cortéz, through Malintzin and Brother Gerónimo, could now communicate and negotiate with Mexico's militarily strongest indigenous people – at the height of their civilization – the Aztec. The Aztec ruled all of central Mexico from their floating capital city, Tenochtitlán, where they nervously awaited the return of the avenging god, Quetzalcóatl.

Thus began a quick, two-year conquest of the powerful Aztec empire by Cortéz's small band of battle-hardened soldiers. Superior steel weapons, invaluable alliances with rivals of the Aztecs – and the prophecy that predicted their downfall at the hands of Quetzalcóatl – allowed Cortéz, a consummate warrior and ruthless tactician, to succeed. A thousand-year-old civilization of millions fell to a force of 500 men.

Ironically, the first Indian civilization Columbus encountered – a Maya trading canoe off the Yucatán coast in 1502 – was the last civilization to be conquered.

NEW SPAIN: While Cortéz and Spanish Viceroys exploited Mexico and the lands as far south as Panama, the subjugation of the Maya in the Yucatán was left to Francisco de Montejo, a captain under Cortéz. Employing the medieval concept of the *adelantado* ("one who pushes forward") Montejo had to recruit his own army and pay them in order to subdue the native inhabitants. In return, the Spanish crown offered him the commission of *adelantado* governor and captain general. Marriage to a wealthy widow financed his initial expedition of three ships and 250 men. Unfortunately for Montejo, the Maya were not the Aztec. To conquer the at least 16 autonomous Maya provinces, he began a bloody, cruel and bitter struggle that lasted 20 years. His first forays into the land in 1527 were disastrous. Even in the long run it must have seemed hardly worth the terrible trouble. The Maya had no stores of gold so there was little in the way of booty for conquistadors. And the dry brush and rough terrain of the Yucatán took away the advantage of Spanish fighting methods and weapons. Worst of all for the would-be conquerors, Maya resistance was fierce. After a while, the elder Montejo passed the repulsive work on to his son, also named Francisco de Montejo. Holed up in a narrow enclave in Campeche, the soldiers renewed their attacks in 1540, fighting their way up the peninsula.

Montejo the Younger founded the city of Mérida in 1542 and, in an effective alliance with the Xiú Maya, defeated the last of the large-scale resistance by the Cocom Maya. On the night of November 8th, 1546, the date of "Death and the End" in the traditional Maya calendar, the Maya attacked Mérida, slaughtering not only Spaniards and Indians who had accepted Christianity, but, in a complete rejection of the foreign culture, horses and cattle – anything, even fruit trees that the invaders had brought with them. The final suppression of their five-month-long Great Rebellion probably marks the end date of the Conquest. But Spanish control over the land and its people was incomplete at best and sporadic warfare continued for centuries. In some sense the resistance didn't end until the 1930s when Quintana Roo's Cruzob Maya finally made peace with the Mexican government. The Maya lamented their loss in the book *Chilam Balam de Chumayel*, in which they complain:

> *There was no sin...*
> *No illness afflicted man,*
> *Aches did not hurt the bones,*
> *Fevers were unknown,*
> *There was no smallpox...*
> *All that ended with the* dzules *(strangers)*
> *They taught fear....*

Disease rather than war became the big threat to the Maya now. Smallpox and other illnesses that Europeans had resistance to decimated the native population. In all of Mexico, the indigenous population plummeted from over 11 million in the 1520s to only one million by 1650.

Colonial Days

[The conquest] *was neither a victory nor a defeat; it was the painful birth of the Mexican nation, the Mexico of today.*
  – 1964 Inscription on Tlatelolco Square, Mexico City

 DIRTY BUSINESS: Almost immediately, the Yucatán became a colonial backwater compared to the rest of Mexico and South America. To the great disappointment of the Spanish, there was no gold in its limestone flatlands. The precious metal ornaments they saw when they first landed at Cozumel were all imported from the highlands. The only exploitable economic resource was the land, so Montejo gave large parcels away in exchange for service in battle. As a result, a feudal nobility of prominent families came to control large cattle ranches. The labor pool was the Maya, who were exploited mercilessly.

The clergy – Catholic missionaries hel bent on converting the Maya to Christianity – further consolidated the conquest. Franciscan brothers were key players in the peninsula's political structure. Into the religious-political mix came Friar Diego de Landa, named the first provincial minister in 1559. He was a zealous missionary who, responding to rumors of sacrilege and sacrifice by the Maya, held an inquisition (*auto-de-fé*) where he gained confessions by harsh torture. Some hapless Indians took their own lives rather than suffer torture.

At the same time Landa was determined to rid the Maya of their "books of the devil," burning and destroying Maya books, codices and artifacts, effectively erasing most of their written records. Ironically, Landa went on to write a book called *Relacíon de las cosas de Yucatán*, which may be the most important contemporary single source of Maya culture and history we have today. Despite his torture of Indians accused of pagan rituals, Landa championed an end to their secular abuse by wealthy landowners and crown officials. His mixed legacy includes being a defender of the native Maya.

BUILDING BOOM: Like their Maya predecessors, the Spanish went on a building boom during the long colonial era, this time constructing churches rather than pyramids and temples. Ironically, the Spanish tore down many of the abandoned Maya temples and used the stones in the construction of their own houses of worship. The massive Mannerist-style Cathedral de San Ildefonso was built on the square in Mérida in 1598 with some of the ruins of the Maya pyramids of T'ho. Others followed, including the Franciscan convent, La Mejorada, in 1640 and a church in virtually every village under Spanish control. The architecture is distinctly "colonial."

Eventually, a population boom of non-Indian settlers and a recovery in the number of Maya after the devastating famine of 1769-1774 increased the demand for food. The land holdings of the elite, formerly cattle ranches, now engaged in growing food as prices escalated. Maya left their villages to settle on haciendas, converting the estates into commercial units. These were effectively "company towns" in which the worker was no more than a legalized serf. The haciendas were the financial, political and social base for the privileged class until well into the 20th century. Rigid racial class structures developed among *creoles* (whites born in Mexico), *mestizos* (a racial mix of caucasian and Indian) and the native American Maya.

Despite royal attempts to rein in the abuse of Indian labor, the Yucatán's elite continued their exploitation of the natives. Eventually, in 1761, Jacinto Canek, a Jesuit-educated Indian, called for a rebellion. He declared himself the king that the books of *Chilam Balam* promised would drive the foreigners out. A Spanish force attacked the poorly armed rebels and killed 600 of them. Jacinto was captured, tortured and executed, gruesomely drawn and quartered in the plaza of Mérida. Eight companions were garroted and 200 were flogged and had one ear cut off to mark them as rebels. One result of the crackdown by conservatives was the expulsion of the Jesuit order, who had been rivals of the Franciscans. This impaired the peninsula's educational system, further retarding social progress.

INDEPENDENCE DAY: On September 28, 1821 three centuries of Spanish colonial rule ended and Mexico, the nation, was born. By then, the Yucatán reflected the turmoil that was going on back in Europe, where the French had overthrown the Spanish monarchy; and in Mexico, where elements of liberalism agitated for civil rights. Soon blood spilled. Traditional rivals, Campeche and Mérida fought for power while the entire peninsula ignored the rest of Mexico, which was embroiled in a series of continuing revolutions. Unhappy with centralism and liberal land reforms, the powerful families in the Yucatán declared its independence from Mexico in 1838. Facing economic realities, it came back into the fold in 1843, but that made no difference to the Indian community, which was still under the yoke of Hispanic oppression. In early 1847 the Yucatán seceded again after secessionists armed the Maya to serve as soldiers. With the Mexican federal government preoccupied over the Mexican-American War and Campeche and Mérida still bickering over independence, the Maya rebelled again. This time they were armed.

BLOOD FROM A STONE: In 1847 a seemingly bottomless pit of barbarism opened in the Yucatán – into which the blood of thousands flowed. The chilling precursor of the violence that would soon engulf the land occurred in January when the Maya were called to arms by *creoles* in the name of their Yucatecan independence movement. The revolutionaries stormed Valladolid, an old colonial town laden with aristocratic pretensions and naively confident in its racial superiority. The moment the Maya soldiers entered the city, years of pent up anger exploded and they ran amuck.

Most of the city's non-Indian population who had not yet fled were massacred. The defending garrison's colonel was dragged from his office and hacked to death, a paralyzed curate was attacked with a machete in his hammock and young girls of wealthy families were allegedly raped, then tied to the iron grilles of the windows and mutilated. Aware now that whites were not invincible, a fierce spirit of independence awoke in the native soldiers.

A few months later, when a young Maya was executed in Valladolid for planning an Indian revolt, the Caste War ignited – so called because of the complex racial levels, or "castes," that the Spanish had developed to differentiate the mixed bloodline of the Mexican people. It was an uprising of such magnitude and violence that soon vengeful Maya armies drove the remaining white citizenry behind the thick walls of Campeche and barricades in the narrow streets of Mérida. The fighting devastated the countryside and most haciendas were sacked and destroyed. Except for those desperate pockets, the Yucatán was now back in the hands of its original inhabitants. Poised to push their oppressors back into the sea within a matter of a week or two, what happened next can be explained only by the religious significance of the land – and *maize* – to the Maya. The entire army packed up and went home – to plant corn.

"The day was warm and sultry," recalled Leandro Poot, the son of the Maya leader. "All at once the *sh'mataneheeles* (winged ants, harbingers of the first rain) appeared in great clouds to the north, to the south, to the east and to the west, all over the world. When my father's people saw this they said to themselves and to their brothers; 'The time has come for us to make our planting.'"

The Yucatecan creoles used the reprieve to reinforce themselves with federal soldiers available after the end of the Mexican-American War, offered in exchange for renewed support of a united Mexico. Barbarous counter attacks on the dispersed Maya regained much of the land the Yucatecans had lost.

In 1850, the strange emergence of the "Speaking Cross" occurred in Chan Santa Cruz (current day Felipe Carrillo Puerto) in Quintana Roo. Next to a small dark cenote, superstitious and religious Cruzob Maya worshipped a series of crosses that spoke to them in Mayan and directed a continued campaign against *dzules* (foreigners). Not coincidentally, one of the Cruzob holy men was a ventriloquist. The war dragged on, with the fighters from the cult of the Speaking Cross continually harassing the Yucatecans and defeating any expeditions that tried to tame the wild state, now separated from Yucatán's control and called the "frontier." In one battle, the Maya used biological warfare. By soaking the clothing of a cholera victim in water and leaving hollowed out logs of poisoned water next to a well, they infected the Yucatecan soldiers who drank from it.

The incredibly brutal battles continued through 1855, when a semi-stalemate became apparent: the Yucatecans held the cities and countryside in the west and north, the Maya held the inland eastern province of Quintana Roo. During this time, Yucatecans began the despicable practice of selling captured Maya to Cuba as slaves ($45 a head for men and $25 for women, children free.)

"Whenever I hear anyone arguing for slavery, I feel a strong impulse to see it tried on him personally."

– Abraham Lincoln, 1809-1865

Though sisal production provided a new source of wealth and stability to the whites in the north, anarchy reigned in the east well past the official end of the Caste War in 1855. Skirmishing continued off and on until the very early 1900s when the Maya were finally subdued by repeating rifles and years of starvation and disease. In 1901, the frontier became the Federal Territory of Quintana Roo and official statehood finally came in 1974.

SISAL, THE GREEN GOLD: Though Montejo and the Spanish conquistadors found no gold in the Yucatán, their descendants certainly did. Green gold – henequen, or sisal. The semi-arid tropics of the Yucatán proved to be an ideal area for the plant. Its commercial production began around 1830 in the peninsula with a virtual monopoly on the market. The existing hacienda system, with its built-in labor pool, provided the means to grow and harvest the slow-maturing plant. By the turn of the century, the world's demand for rope fiber had skyrocketed, mainly from its use in agricultural harvesting and baling machines, and Yucatán went from one of Mexico's poorest states to one of its richest. Unfortunately for the *campesinos* (working rural poor) that prosperity remained mostly with those families who had land grants generations before.

Narrow gauge railways carried the tons of leaves from the fields to the hacienda's processing plant where steam engines stripped the fiber for drying. With an insatiable demand spurred by World War I, henequen reached its pinnacle in price and production in 1916-1918. Mérida built its opulent baronial homes on the Paseo de Montejo, paved its streets and installed electric street lights – far in advance of Mexico City – with the proceeds of henequen sales.

Following the Armistice, the price fell precipitously. Aggravating the fact was the wartime introduction of competing sisal plantations in Africa. Richer soils overseas meant a higher quality product could be grown outside the Yucatán. And with the later invention of synthetic fibers, sisal's demand fell further. The green gold that had fueled the peninsula's economy so richly now led it on a long slow decline, from which it has never fully recovered.

Modern Times

Progress, therefore, is not an accident, but a necessity....
It is a part of nature.
– Herbert Spencer, 1820-1903

 LOVE STORY: Alma Reed, an American journalist, gazed into the intense green eyes of the man who sat opposite. The electrical spark between them – she, a 33-year-old tough investigative writer who could hold her own in a man's world; and he, Felipe Carrillo Puerto, the charismatic new revolutionary governor of the Yucatán – could have lit the street lamps of Mérida. The adventuresome Alma was in the Yucatán on assignment for *The New York Times* to cover the Carnegie Institute archeological study of the ruins at Chichén Itzá. Yet the social reforms ushered in by the new Governor Carrillo piqued her reporter's sense for news. The Mexican Revolution had ended only three years before and Carrillo was making an impressive name for himself as a reformer.

There were as many facets to Felipe Carrillo as there were to Alma Reed and both were intrigued by each other's intellect. He claimed to be a descendant of the Mayapán king who drove the Itzás from Chichén 700 years before. Under his liberal leadership he gave women the right to vote, organized Feminist Leagues and placed women in governmental posts. He legalized birth control and estab- lished the first family planning clinics in the Americas. He supported land reform by encouraging *edijos*, communal farming groups. He built schools and roads and encouraged cottage industries for the poor. Most memorably, however, he was a vocal proponent of civil rights for the Maya.

She was an accomplished writer, strong willed, intelligent and very beautiful. At five foot seven, she towered over the Maya men and women among whom she and Felipe walked. When she re- turned to the Gran Hotel in Mérida after that first meeting she wrote in her dairy: *"He is a miracle of goodness and beauty."*

They both knew it was love at first sight, but Carrillo was married, with grown children. Like a modern Romeo and Juliet, they stood watching while Carnegie archeologists poked around the breathtak- ing ruins of Chichén Itzá. When Alma asked, "Why did they build this great city – this fantastic city – only to desert it?"

"Perhaps one day you, little *peregrina*, will discover the answer to that riddle," Felipe replied.

"Peregrina?"

"Pilgrim – is that not what you are? – a wanderer who will all too soon return to your own far off land."

After a brief intense affair, in which the two made no secret of their love for each other, Alma returned to New York with a ground- breaking story about American Edward Thompson's pillage of Maya artifacts from the Sacred Cenote at Chichén, which Harvard University had cached in their Peabody Museum. Her revelation allowed the Mexican government to reclaim some of the stolen treasures – but not until 1958. They are now on display in Mexico City, as well as the Peabody.

Her stories were so insightful that *The Times* decided to make her "their man in Mexico." Once back in Mexico City, Felipe swept her heart away again when he visited with the news that he had made divorce legal in the Yucatán and had become the first to make use of it. He asked her to marry him and surprised her with a love song, *La Peregrina*, written and composed at his request. Its lyrical melody and heartfelt words remain popular to this day in Mexico. He also bestowed on her a Maya name, *"Pixan-Halal"* – *Pixan* meaning soul and *Halal* a word for a water reed. Their love for one another was so strong that it forever changed their lives. In October, Alma returned to her native San Francisco to prepare for their wedding, scheduled for January 1924.

But a power struggle on the federal level gave the powerful hacienda interests, who had bridled under Carrillo's reforms, a chance to get rid of him. Mexico and the Yucatán plunged into a revolutionary bloodbath. Carrillo and his brothers were arrested and imprisoned. His pleas for the lives of his brothers and friends were ignored. On the morning of January 3, 1924, he and his party were marched to the cemetery and lined up against a high stone wall. Felipe gave one of the nervous soldiers the ring that was to be Alma's wedding band. "Please see that *Pixan-Halal* gets it," he asked.

La Peregrina (The Wanderer)
The Ballad Of Alma Reed

Wanderer of the clear and divine eyes,
And cheeks aflame with the redness of the sky,
Little woman of the red lips,
And hair as radiant as the sun,
Traveler who left your own scenes – the fir trees and the snow, the
virginal snow – And came to find refuge in the palm groves,
Under the sky of my land,
My tropic land,
The little singing birds of my fields,
Offer their voices in singing to you – And they look at you
And the flowers of perfumed nectars
Caress you and kiss you on lips and temples.
When you leave my palm groves and my land,
Traveler of the enchanting face,
Don't forget, don't forget, my land,
Don't forget, don't forget, my love.

The first volley from the firing squad hit the wall above their heads. The soldiers refused to kill the brave governor who had acquired the nickname of the "Abraham Lincoln of Mexico" for what he had done to free the Maya from virtual slavery. Incensed, the military commander had the firing squad shot by other soldiers before executing Carrillo and his brothers. Felipe's grave, near the wall that still bears the bullet holes, is a large crescent moon-shaped family monument in the crowded cemetery. A few feet away, under the quiet shade of a cedars of Lebanon pine, the grave containing Alma Reed's ashes watches over the man she remained in love with until her death at age 77 in 1966. Sometimes, in the early evening, visitors to the cemetery can hear the faint strains of *La Peregrina* on the warm breeze.

LIFE STORY: The Yucatán's past – desperate and bloody, rich and grand, glorious and shameful – has been replaced with a present that offers much promise. Sporadic confrontations with the Maya fizzled out by the 1930s after the elections of Governor Felipe Carrillo Puerto and President Carlos Lázaro Cárdenas, who distributed land to the peasants and nationalized the oil companies in 1938. Between the 1930s and the 1970s, socialism had a strong voice in federal government and the worst Indian abuses were addressed. During this time the Maya gradually converted their economy from barter to a monetary base. Those changes accelerated in the 1970s with improved roads, the development of Cancún and the statehood of Quintana Roo – all of which boosted the peninsula's economy. But the Maya do not represent all the workers in Cancún; immigrants have flocked to the city by the thousands in search of work.

Outside of the resort, many Maya still live in thatch-roofed oval huts called a *naj* (pronounced *na* and spelled that way hereafter) or *otoch*. Made of verti-cal sticks tied to-gether, which can then be plastered, a *na* is the timeless house in Maya cul-ture. You can see identical ones de-picted on the bas-reliefs of the 1,000-year-old Nun's Qua-drangle in Uxmal, one of the Yucatán's more famous ar-

Nas, traditional houses, are still seen today.

cheological sites. *Nas* are still seen even in larger towns where modern cement buildings have gone up around them.

In rural areas, the Maya grow their traditional food staples – corn, beans, chilis, tomatoes and squash – using a slash and burn cultivation technique. Individual families often surround their home with lime, orange, banana and papaya trees. The most traditional of the Indian communities on the Yucatán Peninsula are found in the *Zona Maya*, an isolated area of central Quintana Roo – but you'll be able to visit villages on side roads or along the free road from Cancún to Mérida.

Estimates put the total Maya population today at between four and six million; divided into different ethnic groups that speak about 30 distinct indigenous languages. Many of them are bilingual, learning Spanish to communicate with the *ladinos* (the non-Maya inhabitants of the area) especially in the marketplace. It is still possible, however, to venture into villages where not a word of Spanish is spoken by adults, even though Spanish language is now required in school. Although found in every corner of *Mundo Maya*, the majority of the indigenous population is concentrated in the Yucatán Peninsula, Chiapas and the Guatemalan highlands.

On New Year's Day, 1994, Maya in the highlands of Chiapas (calling themselves, *Zapatistas*, after the revolutionary hero, Emiliano Zapata) led an effective and deadly series of armed attacks against the Mexican government. The revolt was ignited by the prospect of further economic hardships as a result of the NAFTA Treaty, a free trade agreement signed among Mexico, the US and Canada. Traditional *edijos*, small plots of communal farming land, are threatened by the need for market efficiencies. The rebellion was not duplicated in Yucatán but the government's attention was drawn again to the plight of all Mexico's indigenous peoples. Tension in Chiapas remains high.

The ups and downs of Mexico over the years include the painful devaluation of the peso in the mid 1990s (which, combined with inflation, cut the average Mexican's buying power nearly in half) and continual scandals at the highest governmental levels concerning election fraud, drug trafficking and corruption. Although not insulated from these problems, sometimes the Yucatán seems a world apart, progressing along at its own pace.

The people of the Yucatán are hard-working and peace loving. We love to stop in small towns and chat with the locals, who are always pleased to meet us and giggle at our bad Spanish and even worse Mayan. In fact, everyone we met in the Yucatán welcomed us with genuine hospitality and eagerness to show the very best of the land they call home. One Maya family, when we stopped and asked to take a photo of their children, invited us into their dirt-poor home to celebrate Christmas dinner. How could we not feel this is a special place?

The Yucatán is a treasure trove of attractions – historical and contemporary, natural and phenomenal. So put away any fears of *banditos*, or getting lost in the wilderness and being eaten by wild animals, and come down for the adventure of a lifetime.

It ended... with his body changed to light,
A star that burns forever in the sky.

– from the Aztec story, *Flight of Quetzacóatl*

Time To Go

For my part, I travel not to go anywhere, but to go.
I travel for travel's sake.

– *Travels with a Donkey* by Robert Louis Stevenson

Travel Essentials

 So you're off to the Yucatán for a vacation adventure. Good choice. You'll be a gringo, a non-offensive term for someone from north of the border, or a *Norteamericano* or *Canadiense* to distinguish from Mexicans, who are "Americans" too. To get general information and brochures about Mexico call the **Mexico Hotline** – in **USA,** ☎ 800/44-MEXICO (800/446-3942), or in **Canada,** ☎ 800/2MEXICO (800/263-9426). Online information about Cancún is available at **http://www.Cancun.com** and email at **welcome@Cancun.com**. Or see the list of Mexican Tourist Offices.

TOURIST OFFICES

MEXICO/Cancún
Mexico Government Tourist Office
Avenida Cobá & Avenida Carlos Nader, Cancún
☎ 98/84-32-38, 4-34-38
Mexico Quintana Roo State Tourism Office
26 Avenida Tulum, Cancún
☎ 98/84-80-73

CANADA
Mexico Government Tourist Offices
☎ 800-2MEXICO, toll-free from anywhere within Canada
Mexico Government Tourist Office
2 Bloor St. West, Suite 1801, Toronto, ON M4W 3E2
☎ 416/925-0704
Mexico Government Tourist Office
1 Place Ville Marie, #2409, Montreal QC, H3B 3M9
☎ 514/871-1052

Mexico Government Tourist Office
999 W. Hastings St., Suite 1610, Vancouver BC
☎ 604/669-2845

ENGLAND
Mexico Government Tourist Office
60161 Trafalgar Square, 3rd Floor London, WCZN 5DS England
☎ 71/859-3177

UNITED STATES
Mexico Government Tourist Offices
☎ 800/44-MEXICO, toll-free from anywhere within USA
Mexico Government Tourist Office
1911 Pennsylvania Ave., Washington, DC 20006
☎ 202/728-1750
Mexico Government Tourist Office
70 E. Lake St., Suite 1413, Chicago, IL 60601
☎ 312-565-2778, fax 312-609-0808
Mexico Government Tourist Office
128 Aragon Ave., Coral Gables, FL 33134
☎ 305/443-9160
Mexico Government Tourist Office
Epcot Center, Ave. of the Stars, Lake Buenavista, FL 32830
☎ 407/827-5315 or 407/827-5110
Mexico Government Tourist Office
405 Park Ave. Suite 1401, New York, NY 10022
☎ 212/755-7261, fax 212/753-2874

The Yucatán remains year-round on Central Standard Time with weights, measures and temperatures in metric. Gasoline is sold by the liter and distances are measured by kilometers. Dates are expressed with the day first, followed by the month. For example, Christmas Day is written 25/12.

If this is your first experience south of the border or if you're planning to leave the Cancún hotel zone to explore the real Yucatán, here's some more practical information you'll find handy for your trip.

WHAT TO TAKE: Everyone does it. It starts with "what if?" *"What if* it rains?" *"What if* it's cold?" *"What if* we go out to a fancy place?"

"*What if* you spill ketchup on your shirt and my dress gets caught in a taxi door?" Then we wind up packing too much. So here's the scoop – pack light, then take all your stuff back out and cut the quantity in half. The idea is to bring only enough clothes and necessities to last until you get to a laundromat or store. Clothing and shoes are inexpensive in Mexico (except in the shopping plazas of Cancún's hotel zone). There's always a laundromat (*lavanderia*) close by that will do it for you inexpensively. Try to take no more than three to four days worth of clothes no matter how long your trip. And take older clothes that you won't miss if the laundry fades or shrinks them. You can always buy what you need. The toiletries needed depend on what you're doing and where. The better hotels have shampoo and soap and just about everything is readily available in stores and supermarkets, so don't bring a gallon. Leave any open toiletries and unwanted clothes in Mexico.

PACKING LIST

Americans have always been eager for travel, that being how they got to the New World in the first place.
– Otto Friedrich, *Time* magazine, April 22, 1985

Clothing

- ☐ comfortable walking shoes with non-skid soles
- ☐ several pair of cotton socks
- ☐ underwear
- ☐ sandals
- ☐ one/two pair of no-iron slacks (slacks are suitable for men and women in towns such as Campeche, Valladolid and Mérida – jeans are too heavy for the weather)
- ☐ one/two pair of shorts
- ☐ women: a modest lightweight dress and/or skirt
- ☐ two shirts or blouses
- ☐ three tee-shirts
- ☐ swimsuit (carry with you everywhere, you never know when a chance for a cool dip might come up)
- ☐ sleepwear
- ☐ light cotton sweater or sport coat
- ☐ water resistant windbreaker
- ☐ hat & sunglasses
- ☐ fanny pack & money belt

Toiletries

- ☐ shampoo
- ☐ toothpaste & toothbrush
- ☐ prescription medicine
- ☐ comb or brush
- ☐ women: make-up as desired
- ☐ personal hygiene products
- ☐ sunscreen lotion (UVA/UVB protection, SBF 30 +) – important, outside Cancún and Mérida it's hard to find. Did you know sunscreen takes 30 minutes to become effective when you first put it on?
- ☐ good insect repellent – another must for back country travel.
- ☐ aloe gel for sunburn
- ☐ Imodium AD and aspirin
- ☐ triple anti-biotic cream
- ☐ band aids
- ☐ facecloth

If you're roughing it:

- ☐ bar soap
- ☐ hand towel
- ☐ bath towel (good for those serendipity dips in blue cenotes or on secluded ocean beaches)
- ☐ toilet paper
- ☐ small size sink stop

Other Items

- ☐ resealable plastic freezer bags
- ☐ antiseptic towelettes in foil packets
- ☐ hand-held calculator
- ☐ small flashlight
- ☐ sharp penknife
- ☐ notebook/pen
- ☐ sun shield, if renting car (such as those stick-on dark plastic or round pop-open sun shields)
- ☐ camera/film & extra batteries
- ☐ compact umbrella – good for the hot sun at the ruins
- ☐ snorkeling equipment (or buy it there)
- ☐ Spanish-English dictionary/phrase book
- ☐ sports watch
- ☐ earplugs
- ☐ passport/ID/license
- ☐ paperback reading book (exchange for others at many hotels)
- ☐ sewing kit/small scissors

☐ laundry bag
☐ address book to send cards telling everyone about your travels
☐ credit cards/travelers checks
☐ phone card
☐ this book

ENTRY REQUIREMENTS: To enter Mexico, Americans and Canadians need **proof of citizenship**, such as a passport or certified birth certificate and a photo ID. (Canadians can use a Canadian Identification Card as proof of citizenship. U.K. citizens need a passport.) A passport carries more authority with bureaucratic Mexican officials, so it pays to have one. Passport applications for United States citizens can be obtained from regional and government authorities at major post offices, courthouses or federal passport offices in larger metropolitan areas. You can also download an application online at **http://travel.state.gov**. Apply two or three months before your trip. The State Department Web site offers tons of additional information, including a very useful Consular Information Sheet that contains special safety or health alerts. You can get the CIS automatically faxed to you by calling ☎ 202/647-3000, or dial 202/647-5225 and press #1. There's also a number that charges about US$5 for the same information at ☎ 900/225-5674. To replace a **lost passport** in Mexico, contact the nearest embassy or consular office. (See "Just in Case" section below.)

I was well acquainted with the gag that if you look like your passport picture you need a trip. But I was unprepared for the preponderance of thug-like pictures that I found in the course of processing them.

– Frances G. Knight, Director US Passport Division

US PASSPORT AGENCIES

If you didn't leave it to the last minute, it might be better to apply for an American passport through a local Clerk of Court or Post Office. Passport Agencies tend to have long lines during the busiest months.

BOSTON Passport Agency
Thomas P. O'Neill Federal Building, 10 Causeway Street, Suite 247, Boston, MA 02222-1094. 9 a.m. - 4 p.m.
Region: Maine, Massachusetts, New Hampshire, Rhode Island, Upstate New York and Vermont

CHICAGO Passport Agency
Kluczynski Federal Building, 230 S. Dearborn Street, Suite 380
Chicago, IL 60604-1564. 9 a.m. - 4 p.m.
Region: Illinois, Indiana, Michigan and Wisconsin

HONOLULU Passport Agency
First Hawaiian Tower, 1132 Bishop Street, Suite 500
Honolulu, HI 96813-2809. 9 a.m. - 4 p.m.
☎ (808) 522-8283
Region: American Samoa, Federated States of Micronesia,
Guam, Hawaii and Northern Mariana Islands

HOUSTON Passport Agency
Mickey Leland Federal Building, 1919 Smith Street, Suite 1100
Houston, TX 77002-8049. 8 a.m. - 3 p.m.
Region: Kansas, Oklahoma, New Mexico and Texas

LOS ANGELES Passport Agency
Federal Building, 11000 Wilshire Blvd., Suite 13100
Los Angeles, CA 90024-3615. 8 a.m. - 3 p.m.
Region: California (all counties south of and including, San Luis
Obispo, Kern and San Bernardino) and Nevada (Clark County
only)

MIAMI Passport Agency
Claude Pepper Federal Office Building, 51 SW First Avenue
3rd Floor, Miami, FL 33120-1680. 9 a.m. - 4 p.m.
Region: Florida, Georgia, Puerto Rico, South Carolina
and US Virgin Islands

NATIONAL Passport Center
31 Rochester Avenue, Portsmouth, NH 03801-2900
9 a.m. - 4 p.m.
Applications Handled: Applications for passport by mail (Form
DSP-82)

NEW ORLEANS Passport Agency
Postal Services Building, 701 Loyola Avenue, Suite T-12005
New Orleans, LA 70113-1931. 9 a.m. - 4 p.m.
Region: Alabama, Arkansas, Iowa, Kentucky, North Carolina,
Louisiana, Mississippi, Missouri, Ohio, Tennessee and Virginia
(except D.C. suburbs)

NEW YORK Passport Agency
Rockefeller Center, 630 Fifth Avenue, Suite 270
New York, NY 10111-0031. 7:30 a.m. - 3 p.m.
☎ (212) 399-5290
Region: New York City and Long Island
Note: New York Passport Agency accepts ONLY EMERGENCY
applications from those leaving within two weeks.

PHILADELPHIA Passport Agency
US Custom House, 200 Chestnut Street, Room 103
Philadelphia, PA 19106-2970. 9 a.m. - 4 p.m.
Region: Delaware, New Jersey, Pennsylvania and West Virginia

SAN FRANCISCO Passport Agency
95 Hawthorne Street, 5th Floor
San Francisco, CA 94105-3901. 9 a.m. - 4 p.m.
Region: Arizona, California (all counties north of and including
Monterey, Kings, Oulare and Inyo), Nevada (except Clark Co.)
and Utah

SEATTLE Passport Agency
Henry Jackson Federal Building, 915 Second Avenue, Suite 992
Seattle, WA 98174-1091. 8 a.m. - 3 p.m.
Region: Alaska, Colorado, Idaho, Minnesota, Montana,
Nebraska, North Dakota, Oregon, South Dakota, Washington
and Wyoming

STAMFORD Passport Agency
One Landmark Square, Broad and Atlantic Streets
Stamford, CT 06901-2667. 9 a.m. - 4 p.m.
Region: Connecticut and Westchester County (New York)

WASHINGTON Passport Agency
1111 19th Street, N.W., Room 300
Washington, D.C. 20522-1705. 8 a.m. - 3 p.m.
Region: Maryland, northern Virginia (including Alexandria,
Arlington County and Fairfax County) and the District of
Columbia

Mexico does not require a visa to enter, but you do need a **Tourist
Card**, usually obtained from the airline before you land or at the
travel agent where you buy your ticket. This is an important
document so look after it. Tourist cards are valid for up to 180 days,
but agents at the airport will only validate 30 days when you enter.
If you plan to stay longer, you'll have to visit an office of *migracíon*
in one of the peninsula's larger cities. (See *Servicios Migratorios* in the
"Just in Case" section below.) Failure to extend your card before the
expiration date results in a lot of aggravation and a fine.

Customs allowances on the way in and out of Mexico are fairly
simple – don't have drugs or firearms, period. Drug possession
penalties in Mexico (even for the smallest amount) include harsh
prison terms and the embassy can do little to help. It's just not worth
it. The Yucatán is making a serious effort to curb drug trafficking so

if you drive in the countryside expect to be stopped several times by Army anti-drug patrols.

You can carry into Mexico two bottles of any liquor and two cartons of your favorite coffin nails. Supposedly, there is a limit of 12 rolls of film, but we've carried in 60 rolls in a clear plastic bag and it never raised an eyebrow. Then again, we were never searched on their green light/red light system. You punch a button at inbound Customs and if the traffic light goes green, you can pass through unhindered. If it flashes red you are subject to either a cursory or complete luggage search.

On your return to the United States you can bring in US$ 400 per person, duty free, including only one litre of alcoholic beverages. Canadians are allowed $300 with a written exemption or $100 without. Unless you're Canadian, Cuban cigars are illegal and for both countries archeological artifacts or items made from endangered species are strictly forbidden.

HONEYMOONS & WEDDINGS

An archeologist is the best husband any woman can have: The older she gets, the more interested he is in her.
– Agatha Christie, English author, 1890-1976

Mexico is now the number one foreign destination for newlywed couples on their honeymoon. It's no wonder, says Geri Bain, travel editor of *Modern Bride* magazine: "Couples nowadays are looking for more than just a nice beach location and good weather. Honeymooners want a romantic and relaxing setting combined with adventure and outdoor activity. Mexico amply satisfies these criteria."

Check with your travel agent for honeymoon packages or try the **Marriott Casa Magna** (☎ 800-223-6388), the **Meliá Cancún** at ☎ 800-336-3542, or the **Krystal Cancún** at ☎ 800-231-9860. Many of the resort hotels also offer wedding ceremony packages, allowing for a romantic tropical affair at your hotel – or you can arrange your own idyllic marriage ceremony anywhere. It's easy to arrange a civil or religious ceremony in Mexico. The legal requirements and regulations are minimal and mirror what a couple would need to provide in the United States.

Marriage Documents

Tourist card
Birth certificate
Blood test certificate

Valid passport or driving license
Divorce certificate (if applicable)
Marriage Application form (available from the civil registry on Calle Margaritas, facing the park)
Four witnesses with details of their name, address, age, nationality and tourist card number.

There are a variety of companies who can help with any Mexican wedding arrangements from the Justice of the Peace to flowers to cake. **Weddings on the Move** is one such organization. They can be reached at ☎ 800/444-6967. **Cancun Weddings** arrange nuptials in the ever-popular honeymoon resort; their number is ☎ 98/84/9522.

Honeymoon Treasure

Sweet, sweet, the memories you gave me.
– *Memories You Gave Me,* sung by Dean Martin 1956

Imagine on your wedding or anniversary, your loved one gets a mysterious pirate map and the promise of exotic treasure buried somewhere near Cancún. Sound like fun? It is. **Honeymoon Treasure Hunters** arranges to bury a hand-written love note from you (and a small gift if you choose) on a deserted beach as a surprise to your partner. The two of you follow authentic-looking parchment treasure maps that give no indication of who is surprising you both. When your hopelessly romantic letter is dug up at the end, it's guaranteed to melt the heart of the one you love. Call them in advance at ☎ 800/890-6341.

GETTING THERE: Cancún has a very busy international airport served by numerous major airlines and a fair number of charters. If you're the kind of person who prefers the security of staying in one hotel, check your newspaper's travel section. Advertised package trips that include airfare can be hard to beat and they offer a choice of accommodations from luxury down to moderate. A good travel agent should be able to offer a selection. They'll also know about bucket shops or wholesalers for airfare-only deals. We once flew Apple Vacations "air only" on a Mexicana flight at a substantial discount. Another big Cancún package vacation company is Friendly Holidays.

ESCORTED TOURS: For organized adventures, **Backroads Tours** (☎ 800/245-3874) has **biking and hiking** escorted tours to the Yucatán and elsewhere in Mexico. So does **Trek America** (☎ 800/221-0596), whose travel packages involve **camping and hiking**.

There are other **cultural, archeological** and **educational** escorted tour packages, without the extra exercise, that also specialize in visits to colonial cities and ruins in *Mundo Maya* (Mayan World), either solely in the Yucatán or including Chiapas, Belize or Guatemala. Some contain naturalist itineraries such as birdwatching or a visit to a cenote and all claim qualified and experienced guides. Noteworthy tour operators include **Far Horizons** (☎ 800/552-4575); **Mayan World Tours** (☎ 800/392-6292, ask for Eva; Mayan World also offers butterfly and whale-watching tours in other parts of Mexico); and **Wild Land Adventures** (☎ 800/345-4453).

The oldest regular day tour operator in the Yucatán is **Mayaland Tours/Barbachano** (☎ 800/327-2254), begun over 150 years ago when Señor Barbachano hauled some visitors on mules from Mérida to Chichén Itzá and Uxmal. A stay at the Mayaland resort at either location includes a free day's car rental. Mayaland's day trip excursions are offered everywhere in Cancún. Another Mérida day tour operator is **Ecoturismo Yucatán** (☎ 99/25-21-87).

You'll also come across numerous free tourist information booths at the airport and in downtown Cancún, as well as booths and storefronts that advertise free trips to Isla Mujeres, discounted tours or car rentals, gifts or free Jungle Tour, etc. These are mostly time-share promotions that require what is euphemistically called "an hour" of your time. It often turns out to be very much longer and there's strong sales pressure to buy at the property you tour. Unless you're an old pro and seriously thinking of an interval ownership, just say "no."

WAY TO GO: Major airlines flying into Cancún or Cozumel from the US include **Aeromexico** (☎ 800/237-6639); **American** (☎ 800/433-7300); **Continental** (☎ 800/231-0856); **Mexicana** (☎ 800/531-7921); **Northwest** (☎ 800/225-2525); **United** (☎ 800/241-6522) and **US Airways** (☎ 800/428-4322). Students and faculty might do well phoning **Council Travel** (☎ 800/226-8624). A ticket consolidator that offers great last-minute deals on charter flights from the NY, NJ and PA area is **Air-Tech, Ltd.** (☎ 212/219-7000). Regional Mexican airlines that to go on to Cozumel, Chichén Itzá, Mérida, Chiapas and other major cities include **AeroCancún** and **Aerocaribe/Aerocozumel**. Any of the numerous travel agents in Cancún can arrange flights for you.

If you're driving from the US, it takes a good four or five days of steady driving from the border to make Campeche. In place of a tourist card you'll get a combination of tourist card/vehicle permit for you and your car. Foreign auto insurance is invalid in Mexico so you'll need to get some from an agency such as **Sanborn's Mexico Insurance**, PO Box 310, 2009 South 10th St., McAllen, TX 78505-0310 (☎ 800/638-9423, fax 210/686-0732). Check with a local Mexican tourism office or Sanborn's and they'll give you all the details of necessary paperwork, which includes a copy of your title, a valid major credit card and a notarized letter from any lease or lien holders. You must be in the car every time it's driven. If you try to leave the country without your vehicle, it will be a bureaucratic and financial nightmare.

CAR RENTALS: The best way to tour the Yucatán is by car – the main roads are in excellent shape – and it's easy to rent one in Cancún or other major cities. The disadvantage is the cost: there are no bargain rates. Shop around the major car companies in the US and be sure to ask if their rates (weekly is cheaper) include insurance, tax and/or mileage. Compare apples to apples. On rare occasions you can negotiate a better deal with the local office rather than the 800 numbers. **Avis** offers a discounted prepaid rate one week in advance during high season, which can save at least 10%. Ask their customer service agent at the 800 number for details.

Mexican driving insurance is required and costs almost as much as the rental rate. Avis is the first to offer a zero deductible insurance policy – a definite plus when driving on foreign soil with foreign rocks kicked up by foreign cars. You must be at least 23 (some require age 25) to rent a car and must have a major credit card. The cheapest cars for rent are VW Beetles with standard shift and no radio or air – and often without the back half of a convertible top. Air-conditioning is cool but not necessary. The highest prices are for four-wheel-drive Jeeps and Suburbans. If you haven't prepaid, ask about paying with cash instead of credit card when you return the car. We put the car rental on the card and saved 10% tax on the insurance by paying for it in cash. One friend claims he received a 20% discount by paying the whole thing in cash.

International car rentals with offices in Cancún are **Avis** (☎ 800/331-1084 or 98/86-02-22); **Budget** (☎ 800/472-3325 or 98/84-46-12); **Dollar** (☎ 800/800-4000); **Hertz** (☎ 800/654-3001); **Kemwell** (☎ 800/678-0678); **National** (☎ 800/227-7368 or 98/86-44-90); **Payless** (☎ 800/729-5377); and **Thrifty** (☎ 800/367-2277). These and other local renters, such as **Royal Caribe** (☎ 98/84-01-41) and **Top** (☎ 98/85-00-94), have offices either at the airport, in the hotel zone, downtown or in travel agencies. One tip: check your car thoroughly for all its parts and condition. Rental cars are required by law to have a good spare tire, jack, seatbelts and a fire extinguisher.

DRIVING IN MEXICO: With some cautions, driving in the Yucatán is a breeze. Cancún is a big city and anyone experienced driving in heavy traffic will feel right at home. Parking, however, is another thing: spaces are very limited downtown and if you're only renting to have a car locally, don't bother; the bus service is excellent. The other congested city is Mérida. Most of its streets in the center are alternating one-way and there's a vigilant traffic cop on every corner.

The peninsula's main roads are surprisingly straight, level and well marked. Intrepid travelers may run into some rough pavement – or none at all – only on the tertiary roads, especially in the wet season. All-in-all, very few people have problems driving in the Yucatán. If you do have a flat or break-down, Mexico has an amazing road patrol known as the **Green Angels** that regularly patrols main roads. And it's a free service (tips greatly appreciated). A pile of branches or brush in the road indicates a disabled car ahead. If you break down, try to do this so cars will pass with caution. Use the emergency flashers and keep to the side of the road. To signal for help, raise the hood. You can dial "06," similar to our 911, for **emergencies**. Fortunately, we never had to test this service.

Magna sin is the name for unleaded gasoline in Mexico, sold from the green pump.

CALLING ALL GREEN ANGELS

Cancún	☎ 98/84-32-38 or 84-34-38
Puerto Juárez	☎ 98/87-29-13
Campeche	☎ 981/6-60-68 or 6-09-34
Mérida	☎ 99/24-95-42 or 25-69-29
Valladolid	☎ 985/6-20-65 or 6-28-34

DRIVING TIPS: Check your car thoroughly before you leave the rental agency, especially the windscreen fluid, wipers, spare tire and jack. Bugs and dust (*polvo*) just love to hang out on windshields. Check the signals, windows, lights, seat belts, brakes and fire extinguisher. If you don't have a 100% deductible policy, mark every little nick and ding on your inspection sheet before you rent it. Make sure you have a gas cap and check it again when you fill up just before returning the car. We were in the office once when they charged a tourist US $45 for a missing gas cap. As he left he grumbled about the possibility that the station and the rent-a-car agency were in collusion. If you're not satisfied with your car ask for one in better condition.

Don't drive in the countryside at night – it's dangerous. Roads are relatively narrow, totally dark, and have wild animals, bicyclists and pedestrians wandering around on them. In addition, oncoming trucks and buses with high-beam headlights are a real pain.

Left turn signals are used constantly but their meaning varies dramatically. They can mean the car, bus or truck in front of you is turning left – but that would be too obvious. They could also mean that it's OK for you to pass because there is no oncoming traffic ahead. Or they're saying hello to the oncoming traffic, another truck or bus approaching in the other direction. Or their right signal is out and it's half of their emergency lights signifying they are slowing down. Or else they just forgot to turn them off. Take your pick but proceed with lots of caution. The other problem is that many automobiles on the road don't have working directional signals or sometimes not even working brake lights. Always **drive defensively** and **slow down**; you're on vacation.

Left turns are not too common in Mexico unless it's into a small road. At busier intersections, left turns are made from a right-hand pull over, much like a jug-handle. Cross only when traffic is clear.

Topes. Remember that name. If you see it on a sign, slow down or you may leave your car's undercarriage behind you in the road. *Topes* (toe-PAYS) are concrete speed bumps that slow traffic to a crawl before every school building, bus stop and before entering and exiting each small town. Your first experience may be in downtown Cancún, where pedestrian crossings are giant *topes*. They litter the free road to Mérida, so be patient and enjoy the scenery. Frequently, little refreshment stands or people selling fruit or handicrafts sprout up at the *topes.*

It's a good idea to **fill your gas tank** every chance you get when traveling in rural areas. In some remote villages, your tank is filled from a gas can or siphoned directly from a barrel. If you're running low and you come into a tiny village, tell someone you need a few liters of gasoline (*necessito gasolina*) and most places have someone who can help.

Carry a cleaning rag or paper towels with you, and if you're doing much traveling, buy a small bottle of window cleaner. Young boys will clean your windshield at most gas stations; the meager tips you give are often split with the pump attendant.

Since one peso is worth (at 8 pesos per dollar) less than 12¢, any fraction of a peso when you fill up your tank is customarily rounded up to the next peso. You can tip the attendant a few pesos if you wish. **Pedestrians** have the right of way, so stop for them in crosswalks. **Never drink and drive,** anywhere. Gas stations do not **repair** cars in Mexico, so if you're having mechanical problems ask for a "*taller mecanico*," an auto repair shop. **Parking** in the cities can be a problem. If your hotel doesn't have secured parking, look for signs that read "*Estacionmiento*," which translates as parking lot. Don't leave valuables in plain sight, even though many lots are guarded 24 hours. Parking prices are reasonable and a tip to the attendant when you leave is customary.

Ask the rental agent how many liters it takes to fill the takn (our Bug took about 40). It's an unfortunate truth that some gas station attendants try to cheat you. See our section on "scams," below.

ARRIVAL/GETTING AROUND: Pick up a copy of *Cancun Tips* and any other magazines or brochures at Cancún's modern airport and look for discount coupons and offers. They can save you money.

The choice of transportation upon arrival is either taxi or combi (*colectivo*) bus. **Taxis** are the quickest, the most comfortable and the most expensive. They're probably the best bet into the downtown because they bypass the hotel zone; perhaps you can share a ride with fellow travelers. **Combi buses** cram eight people plus baggage and a knowledgeable driver into an air-conditioned van. If you're going downtown rather than to the hotel zone, relax. The combi will work its way along the resort-lined beach first. A one or two dollar tip is reasonable.

If you're staying downtown, on Isla Mujeres, or pushing on to Playa del Carmen or Mérida, **buses** are an excellent alternative to the high price of renting a car. Cancún's bus terminal is behind the circle (*glorieta*) of Av. Tulum and Av. Uxmal. They are reliable and surprisingly inexpensive. Mexico has two classes of bus service: first class offers the more modern, comfortable and air-conditioned buses that make fewer, or even no, stops between points. Second class offers more of a local route, often with well-worn buses, and takes more time. From Cancún you can get frequent service on either, south to Playa del Carmen and Chetumal, or west to Valladolid, Chichén Itzá and Mérida. Long distance buses can also carry you direct to Campeche, Villahermosa, Veracruz or even Mexico City. The principal inter-city long distance carrier in Mexico is ADO (Autobuses del Oriente). The companies that cover the peninsula from Cancún are ATS (first class) and Oriente, Noreste, Dorado, Mayab and Playa Express, all second class.

Service within Cancún is excellent. Buses marked *Zona Hoteles* or "Hotel Zone" ply up and down the strip and run frequently between the downtown and hotel area. Bus fare is about 40¢. A change on Av. Tulum will take you up to Puerto Juárez and the ferry to Isla Mujeres – much more fun than taking the hotel zone's expensive shuttle boat.

If your itinerary is reasonably set, completely flexible, or your budget is limited, seriously consider travel by bus. It will save money and is a great way to meet fellow travelers as well as local people.

HITCHHIKING: A thing of the past in the States, hitchhiking is alive in the Yucatán, given the long, lonely distances. If you're thinking of hitching, take all the precautions you would at home, such as not accepting a ride with someone who has been drinking or, if you're female, not accepting a ride from a carload of guys. It's always best to travel in pairs, but expect a wait: gringos are in the habit of passing you up and some Yucatecans might think you're rich enough to take the bus – which, given the low cost and safety, is probably a much better idea.

Picking up locals is another thing. If you drive extensively, you may see people sitting in the shade along the side of a road as if they're waiting for a bus. They may hold up a hand as if to say hi. Chances are they'd like a ride. If you're not comfortable with stopping, wave hello and keep driving. We'll sometimes pick up people to practice our Spanish or Mayan until the next village. When you let them off, it's a custom – at least among older folk, who may be as poor as church mice – to dig their hand into a well-worn pocket and ask, "*Cuanto cuesta?*" How much?

Simply smile and reply, "*Por nada.*" For nothing.

What To Expect

If you reject the food, ignore the customs, fear the religion and avoid the people – you might better stay home.
– James A. Michener, American author

CULTURE & CUSTOMS: The *siesta* is still a part of Mexico's lifestyle and one of the reasons impatient North Americans talk of a Mexican "mañana attitude." While it's true that the lifestyle in Mexico is slower, why would you go on vacation to a place that requires more work from you than you do at home? The image of a lazy Mexican asleep under a sombrero is just not true, especially not in the Yucatán. For example, you'll see men working in the blazing sun with machetes clearing the sides of highways of the encroaching brush. We watched welders and construction workers labor all day and into the following morning to finish the roof of the Flamingo Plaza Sanborn's restaurant in Cancún, which was due to open soon. Things may proceed at their own pace in Mexico, but it's not from lack of effort.

Because the heat of the day comes in the afternoon, it is customary to close shops and offices for long lunches or naps, then open again at four or five in the afternoon and remain open until seven or eight at night. Because of the pressure of tourists who, like mad dogs and Englishmen, go out in the noon day sun, not as many shops or restaurants close down in Cancún. But *siestas* are still a part of the countryside, so pace yourself accordingly.

Cancún differs from the rest of the Yucatán because of the overwhelming influence of North American culture. People speak English everywhere and the city's Mexican hotels, stores, restaurants and workers cater to American tastes. Two embarrassed patrolmen walk the north beach of Isla Mujeres once or twice a day and ask women to please not go topless. That particular beach is mostly *extranjeros* (foreigners) so they're really just going through the motions. It's definitely not acceptable to sunbathe topless where local families go, nor to wear revealing clothes or bathing suits in the shopping malls, on the bus or in the streets downtown. Mexicans are mostly Catholic and conservative, but they can party with the best of them too. We'd like to think that users of this guide would be sensitive to local mores.

One of the not-so-good things about Mexican culture is *machismo*. Women have doors opened for them, seats held and, in general, are put on a pedestal. Then again, attractive young women are also treated to little sounds, whistles, calls and veiled propositions in public. The good thing is that it happens much less in Cancún than in the rest of Mexico and even less outside the resort city. It should not be a big problem to you, even if you're a woman traveling alone. However, you might handle it the way Mexican women do by avoiding eye contact on the street, ignoring the occasional harmless strutting and by walking or sitting with other women. Because of limited opportunities in Mexico's male-oriented society, more and more Mexican businesses are women-owned, especially in the hospitality and service industry in the Yucatán. A high percentage of the hotels and restaurants we reviewed are owned and operated by women.

What's very positive about the society south of the border is its emphasis on the family. It's a real pleasure to stroll in a public park on Sundays and holidays and see so many families out enjoying themselves – a valuable example to take back home.

SPORTS: The ancient Maya played a kind of basketball/soccer game in which the players could not touch the ball with their hands or feet, but propelled it instead with their hips. You'll see stone rings that were goals on the ceremonial ballcourt at Chichén Itzá. Losers (or maybe the winners) lost their lives in sacrifice. Today's Yucatecans enjoy organized sports such as baseball, basketball and soccer. **Bullfighting** goes on year-round in Cancún

The winter bullfight season is often the highlight of town fiestas.

every Wednesday in the bull ring downtown. Be forewarned that they slay bulls in the course of the fight. During small town or village festivals in the countryside, bullfights are an entirely different experience, with matadors that travel a circuit. In the smaller venues, bulls are not always killed. **Pancho Villa's Ranch**, near Playa del Carmen, offers a bloodless bullfight and cowboy show.

The resort sport activities include diving, snorkeling, windsurfing and swimming. Cancún has a new international **marathon race** in December, attracting world-class runners as well as amateurs. There are several **fishing tournaments** and you can also take a fishing trip any day of the week.

HOLIDAYS, FESTIVALS & LOCAL CULTURAL EVENTS: Most of Mexico's festivals and holidays have religious significance as Catholicism is the country's predominant religion (although evangelist faiths have made some inroads). Local villages have annual bashes tied to the patron saint of their town. These aren't solemn occasions but spirited celebrations that, in some cases, blend Maya rituals and culture with the Catholic religion. Local people dress up and enjoy dancing, music, feasts and fireworks. If you're planning to attend any large special events, it might pay to make hotel reservations in advance.

To many, holidays are not voyages of discovery,
but a ritual of reassurance.

– Philip Andrew Adams, Australian writer

Jan 1: New Year's Day. Agricultural fairs in the country. In the Yucatán look for scarecrows on porches and roofs, holding a bottle of booze. These represent *burrachos*, drunks celebrating a new year.

Jan 6: Día de los Reyes Magos: Day of Three Kings. Christmas gifts are exchanged in memory of the three wise men who brought gifts to the infant Jesus. At many parties a ring-shaped cake with a miniature doll is baked. The person whose slice contains the doll must throw another party on February 2, Candlemas. In Campeche there's a religious ceremony called a "Cock Dance," where 12 men dance a complicated ritual dance known as the Olk Kekén.

Jan 21: Fiesta in Dzitás, Yucatán.

Jan 25 - Feb 2: Town Fair in Candelaria, Campeche, includes the blessing of long wax candles used when someone dies.

Last Sunday in Jan: Día de la Immaculada Concepcíon. A lively festival is held after nine days of religious services, highlighted by a dance that features a pig's head covered with offerings of ribbons and flowers – even cigarettes and liquor.

Feb 1-5: San Felipe Festival in San Felipe (near Rio Largartos).

Feb 2: Candeleria. Many villages celebrate Candlemas with candlelight processions. Corn Fair in Tzucacab, Yucatán.

Feb 5: Flag Day/Constitution Day. Legal holiday.

Feb/Mar: Carnival. Festive Carnivals are held in Mérida, Chetumal, Isla Mujeres, Cozumel, Campeche and many towns around the countryside the week before Ash Wednesday. It's a last blast before the somber season of Lent. Parades with decorated floats, fancy costumes, fiestas and sporting events are featured throughout the Yucatán. Mérida has parades, floats and traditional dancing. Chetumal hosts a wild Caribbean-style affair with folk dancers from all over *Mundo Maya*. Carnival's festivities end on Fat Tuesday, the day before Ash Wednesday and the first of the 40 days of Lent before Easter.

Mar 16-21: Spring Fair in José Maria Morelos, a small town about 85 km east of Felipe Carrillo Puerto, Quintana Roo.

ca. Mar 21: Vernal Spring Equinox. The shadow of a serpent appears to undulate down the steps of the pyramid of Kukulcán at Chichén Itzá. The Maya perfectly positioned the pyramid so that as the sun strikes the steps during the two times of the Equinox a unique pattern of light and shadow creates the allusion of a slithering serpent. Packed with spectators.

Mar 21: Birthday of Benito Juárez (1806). The first Indian-blood President of Mexico and leader of the reform movement, *La Reforma.*

Mar/Apr: Easter Sunday. Perhaps the most holy day in Mexico. Religious processions are held throughout the countryside. The week preceding is called *La Semana Santa* (Holy Week). Dramatizations of the crucifixion of Christ occur on Good Friday in Mérida and Anaceh, among other towns in Yucatán.

Apr 3: San Ildefonso in Izamal.

Apr 13-17: Honey Fair held in Hopelchén, Campeche. Bees and honey have their own diety in the ancient Maya religion.

End of Apr/beginning of May: International Yacht Races are held in the Bahia off Isla Mujeres. There's a **Deep Sea Fishing Tournament** there around the same time. In Cozumel, the **El Cedral Fair** occurs at the end of the April and lasts for one week.

May 1: Labor Day. Legal holiday.

May 1-7: Theater Festival in Mérida.

May 2-3: An International Deep Sea Fishing Tournament is held on Cozumel.

Seybaplaya, Campeche, celebrates its **patron saint.**

May 3: Day of the Holy Cross. Fiestas at Celestún, Felipe Carrillo Puerto and Hopelchén.

May 5: Cinco de Mayo. This holiday – also celebrated in Mexican restaurants and bars throughout the States – commemorates the Battle of the Puebla (1862), in which the Mexican Army defeated invading French troops. The victory proved temporary as the naive Austrian Archduke, Maximilian, was installed as the ill-fated "Emperor of Mexico." He was left to his own devices when the French withdrew their troops at the demand of the US. In Cancún, tourists celebrate by drinking yards of beer.

May 12-18: Immaculate Conception. Maya music, bullfights and religious processions honor the Virgin in Chankah Veracruz (near Felipe Carrillo Puerto).

May17-27: Jazz Festival. Cancún's jazz festival attracts some big names and not-so-well-knowns to a popular celebration of music.

May 20: Hammock Fair. A good time to buy a hammock in Tekom, south of Valladolid on Higway 295.

May 20-30: Jipi Festival is held in honor of the palm plant *jipijapa* (HEE-pee-HAA-pah), from which Panama hats are made. Held in Becal, Campeche.

June 4: Festivities in Valladolid. Music and dance as well as historic recreations.

June 22-Aug 4: Saint John the Baptist in Campeche.

June 24-Aug 9: Saints Peter and Paul get their due in Cozumel and Campeche.

June 29: Day of San Pedro. Towns with the name of San Pedro (and some without) celebrate with festivals.

Traditional dancers.

Early July: Ticul Festival. A week-long fiesta celebrates the founding of Ticul, Yucatán.

July 16-31: Festival in Ciudad del Carmen includes nautical events and cattle drives. These festivities are repeated for Carnival when the town fills up.

July 25: Saint James the Apostle is celebrated in Rio Lagartos.

Aug 15: Our Lady of Izamal. This is the scheduled festival day in a town known for its religious parties, but friends who were there on the 15th were told that it was the following week – or the week before.

Aug 16: Chetumal and Bacalar sponsor a motorboat race and regatta, to honor Saint Joaquín on the Chaac Inlet on and around this date.

Aug 17: Cruz de la Bahia celebrates the founding of Isla Mujeres in 1854. A bronze cross weighing about a ton (39 feet in height and nearly 10 feet wide) was set into the Manchones Reef between Isla Mujeres and the coastline in 1994. The "Cross of the Bay" is the island's tribute to all the men and women of the sea. Scuba divers celebrate with a mass dive.

Aug 20: Traditional Fair occurs in Maní, Yucatán.

Sept 15: Independence Day. Legal holiday.

ca. Sept 23: Autumnal Fall Equinox at Chichén Itzá's archeological zone. Reenactments of Maya rituals and dancing. The two equinoxes occur when the sun is vertically above the earth's equator. Less crowded than the first equinox.

Sept 27-first two weeks in Oct: Procession de Cristo de las Ampollas (Christ of the Blisters), a religious holiday, occurs in Mérida. This statue of Christ was carved from a tree struck by lightning that, legend has it, burned all night without any sign of fire damage. Its fiesta includes fireworks, music and folk dances.

Sept 29-Oct 9: Saint Miguel Archangel gets his own celebration in San Miguel, Cozumel.

Oct 4: Feast Day of San Francisco de Asis. Maya villages near Mérida (Conkal, Hocaba, Pueblo, Telchac Puerto and Uman) celebrate a week-long fiesta that ends on this day.

2nd weekend Oct: Isla Mujeres Music Festival. An eclectic array of talented musicians rock the island.

Oct 12: Columbus Day. Legal holiday.

Oct 18-28: A fiesta honoring **El Cristo de Stilpech** features a procession with the image of Christ carried on foot from Stilpech to Izamal. Religious services, fireworks and a grand fiesta on the 25th. Spirited *jaranas* (regional folk) dances are featured.

Oct 31: All Souls' Eve. Beginning of an eight-day memorial observance. Flowers and candles are placed on graves of relatives. Boo!

Last week Oct-first week Nov: Orange Festival in Oxkutzcab, Yucatán.

Nov 1-2: All Souls' Day/All Saint's Day/Day of the Dead. Graveside and church ceremonies honor the memory of departed loved ones. Instead of a somber occasion, the Day of the Dead is a happy celebration with a fiesta atmosphere high-lighted by sugar skulls and candy skeletons. A family meal is eaten at the gravesites and favorite food is left for the departed souls. A haunt-ing experience.

1st week Nov: X'matkuil Fair is hosted at a former

Gift shop skeletons.

henequen hacienda eight kms (five miles) north of Mérida. Local arts and crafts, bullfights, rodeo competitions and lots of food.

Nov 20: Día de la Revolucíon commemorates the Revolution of 1910.

End of Nov/beginning of Dec: Expo-Cancún is a big city fair held outdoors near the bullring downtown. Arts and crafts, exhibits and folk dancing.

Dec 4-8: A **fair** occurs in Campeche and Champotón.

Dec 8: Feast of the Immaculate Conception. Festivities are held in many locations in the Yucatán but there's a particularly notable fiesta in Izamal. In Celestún and Champotón boat processions carry a statue of the Virgin Mary in the lead. Champotón also features a waterskiing show and other aquatic events and a fair.

Dec 12: Our Lady of Guadalupe. Mexico's patron saint and a big holiday. All over the Yucatán young people run from town to town with a torch in her honor. Children begin their Christmas caroling carrying a decorated tree of ribbons and plastic flowers. Contributions are graciously accepted.

Dec 15: International Marathon is run in Cancún. Begun in 1996.

Dec 16-24: The Mexican custom of **Posadas**, celebrated by parties and restaurant meals with friends, family and co-workers. There are processions and children break *piñatas*. Christmas Eve is an important family night.

Dec 25: Christmas Day.

Dec 31: New Year's Eve. Partytime. In the Yucatán look for stuffed dummy people on porches and roofs, holding a bottle of booze. These are *burrachos*, drunks celebrating a new year.

FOOD & DRINK: Another way the Yucatán is different from the rest of Mexico is in its food. Two types of *comidas tipicas*, typical food specialties, are seafood or meat flavored with a spicy (but not hot) anchiote paste; and meats, marinated in a rich sauce then steam-baked in earthen pits.

Despite their *habanero* pepper, 20 times hotter than the jalapeño of northern Mexico, Yucatecans prefer their heat on the side, rather than cooked into the food. Always ask if the dish of salsa offered contains *habanero* before scooping some up on a chip. Otherwise you'll be drinking liquids and eating tortillas till the cows come home.

Each Yucatecan state has its own culinary claim to fame – as well as the old stand-by of tacos and burritos. Thinly sliced pork, marinated in sour orange and vinegar then grilled and served topped by pickled onion, is *poc chuc,* a dish made famous by Los Almendros restaurants. *Sopa de limon* is a chicken soup with tortillas and a squeeze of lime juice; *cochinita pibil* and *pollo pibil* are flaky, tender pieces of pork or chicken, spiced and marinated in a rich sauce and baked in banana leaves; and anything called *"a la Yucateca,"* is spiced in a wonderful anchiote paste and grilled. Valladolid has its own sausages, Campeche invented fresh shrimp cocktails and Mérida has incorporated Lebanese cooking into its cuisine. In addition, Cancún boasts some of the best international cooking around. One thing you may want to remember is that waiters consider it rude to offer you your bill before you ask for it, so be sure to say *"la cuenta, por favor."*

A *comida corrida* is a fixed price complete meal that includes everything but your drink. It's low priced and not necessarily the best dish on the menu, but generally tasty and filling. Another dish that fills you up without costing much is *molletes,* grilled open-faced rolls with refried beans and melted cheese. And the soups in Mexico are very flavorful.

As for **bebidas** (drinks), favorite alcoholic national drinks include margaritas and tequila – and nothing beats Mexican tequila. You can buy Heineken or American beer in Cancún, but why would you? Mexico's beers are excellent. Sol, Dos Equis and Corona brands may be familiar to you, but **Superior** and **Victoria** are superior Mexican beers. Two great local brews from Mérida are **Montejo** (our all-time favorite) and **Leon Negra**, a dark amber brew. A refreshing light-alcohol drink is *chelada,* a glass of limeade with a little beer added. Tourists and residents alike should appreciate the connection between "trouble" and alcohol. Stay out of situations where you or other people drink too much; Mexico is not the place to lose control.

Coca-Cola is ubiquitous, of course, but other flavors in Mexico's soda (*refrescos*) line-up include orange, grapefruit and apple. *Licuados,* fresh fruit juice drinks, are available plain or mixed with milk. Our favorite is *horchata,* a refreshingly delicious drink made from rice and milk and flavored with cinnamon and cane sugar. Or try *Jamaica* (ha-micka), a fruity drink made from flowers.

SHOPPING & BARGAINING: There are plenty of designer clothes and gift stores in the three large shopping malls of the hotel zone. Prices are lower but sales pressure is higher in downtown Cancún where two indoor markets are located on Av. Tulum. "*Señora, Señor,* where are you from?" "Like to look at some blankets?" "Best price, cheaper than K-Mart," vendors call out to entice you into shopping at their stalls. This constant come-on is a source of irritation to those more accustomed to searching for sales help at home. In Cancún they never leave you alone. It may help if you realize just how hard things are economically for people in Mexico. Most of the vendors can't afford to stock the stalls they sell from, so most have their goods on consignment, which can be tough, especially in a country where the wage averages only US $25 per week and gringo dollars can mean the difference between just being poor and abject poverty. And with hundreds of competing places to shop, perhaps you could be a bit tolerant of the high pressure and accept it gracefully as part of the shopping ritual. Usually a firm, *"no, gracias"* discourages further patter.

We're less inclined to be hard bargainers because much of what we buy is already cheaper than it would be at home. A seasoned negotiator offers about half of what's asked and settles for a price somewhere in between. We still bargain in the markets and even at hotels, but our realization of the economic inequities between most tourists and the average worker in the Yucatán tempers our desire to bicker for a quarter of an hour just to save a dollar. But we never allow vendors or taxi drivers to cheat us. Always shop around or ask the tariffs first – a good habit anywhere.

What we do buy in the Yucatán are things not readily available at home. We'll buy some ground chili powder, anchiote paste and a bottle of honey on every trip. There are also unique gift items we can't pass up. **Silver** and **gold jewelry** are cheaper in Mexico so we always look for the unusual. Large **hammocks**, hand woven of string, are the traditional bed, couch and crib in the Yucatán. Made of nylon, cotton, silk or sisal, mostly in the state of Yucatán, they are extremely comfortable once you get used to sleeping in them. In Campeche, **wooden model ships** are hand-crafted, featured in a great Maya arts and crafts store in the Centro. Chetumal has an **artisans'** shop with carvings and crafts that combine Maya and Caribbean influences from Belize. **Pottery** is always a good bet, the Maya were known for their skills. **Tree of Life** candelabras, made in central Mexico, are elaborate and beautiful. Frequently used at Christmas, they depict the fall of Adam and Eve and are decorated with a snake, angels, leaves and flowers in bright colors. Also check out hand-painted **laquerware** and **woven baskets**.

Once you leave Cancún you will see Maya women dressed in their traditional white cotton shift dresses called *huipiles* (WE-peels). They're colorfully embroidered around a square neckline and hem. A white cotton lace-trimmed underskirt (*ternos*) peeks out demurely below the hemline. The embroidery on the *huipiles* of Quintana Roo is geometric and abstract, while in the Yucatán it is done in cross-stitched floral. Silk or cotton shawls (*rebozos*) are also part of the traditional dress.

Men's business dress includes short-sleeved embroidered and pleated light shirts, called *guayaberas* (guy-ya-bearas), that are worn outside the pants. This traditional shirt is common throughout the Hispanic Americas, where it's generally too warm to wear ties or jackets. They usually come in pastel colors and white. A good place to buy these are in the *mercados* and stores in Valladolid and Mérida. There are several shops along Calle 59 in Mérida, including the well-known **Jack Guayaberas**, where you can also have them made to order.

Panama hats are made in the state of Campeche from the fibers of the jipijapa palm. They offer good protection against the strong Yucatecan sun and their fibers breathe, allowing the air to keep your head cool. Types of fiber, closeness of weave and suppleness determine the quality. The best ones are *fino* – a fine weave of thin palm fibers. The middle and fine grades are durable, pliable hats that, once flattened, tightly rolled and stuffed in a suitcase, can be ready to wear again with a sprinkle of water. If you're going to Campeche, street vendors and shops in Mérida and Isla Mujeres will be happy to sell you one. Buy the best you can afford for both comfort and long life.

MONEY, ATMs & TRAVELERS CHECKS: The Mexican money is the peso, sometimes called the new peso after a drastic devaluation late in 1994. It floats against the dollar at the rate of 7.5 to 8 pesos to the dollar, as of this writing. The more pesos per dollar, the better the rate of exchange for you. Throughout Mexico, most prices (written as NP$ or N$) are quoted in pesos – but make sure beforehand. A careless Mexican businessman took one of the glamorous suites in Casa Turquesa in Cancún thinking that the 3,200 price was in pesos. The next day he was presented with a NP$24,000 bill – 3,200 US dollars. Good morning *Señor*.

Don't count on using credit cards anywhere but in the cities – and even then only in the larger establishments. Banks exchange cash or traveler's checks, usually without commission, during limited hours everywhere but the smallest towns. In Cancún and tourist destinations, such as Playa del Carmen, exchange booths will change cash or traveler's checks at a slightly lower rate, but they are open longer hours and offer more convenience. You'll need a copy of your passport and sometimes another ID.

Shop around because the rates vary between change booths and even banks – and they change daily. Make sure and ask about the rate before you commit. The worst place to convert money is your hotel, where the rate is generally lower than anywhere else. The change booths with the best rates in Cancún are downtown, as opposed to the hotel zone, and of those, the best rates are found at one of the two on the south side of Av. Cobá, before you get to Av. Tulum, near the Plaza America. Furtive types also exchange money at a good rate during the day outside the Banamex bank downtown on Av. Tulum. It's perfectly legal and safe (though don't flash your money around) and saves the time and aggravation of waiting in line.

Be sure to tell your credit card company and bank that you'll be in Mexico. That way they'll not be suspicious of any overseas use and will approve your bank card for Automatic Teller Machine withdrawals. Big cities have ATMs in shopping malls and banks. Any credit card charges or ATM withdrawals go through at the official exchange rate. Watch those decimal places when you sign your charge slip.

SAFETY & CRIME: In the many times we've been to the Yucatán we've rarely had a problem and are completely comfortable traveling everywhere there. But because it's a new environment, it's important to be aware of the possibility of danger. Safe traveling involves basic common sense. Inform yourself about where you're going and what to expect.

Pedestrian beware seems to be the unofficial slogan when it comes to walking on the streets and sidewalks of Mexico. Cancún's hotel zone is an exception, of course, but elsewhere potholes, broken curbs or head-bashing sidewalk awnings are the norm. Be careful too, climbing around the thousand-year-old Maya ruins. Don't be embarrassed to use your hands or the rope aid and go slowly. Always think safety first. Be sure to wear good non-slip sandals or walking shoes and carry a flashlight after dark. Be aware of your surroundings. As Carl Franz, another Mexico aficionado, put it: "Expect the unexpected underfoot, overhead, from ahead or behind."

Ever wake up in the middle of the night and not know which hotel you are in or where the bathroom is located? Imagine if there were a fire. As any frequent traveler should do – at home or abroad – make sure you familiarize yourself with the emergency exits and escape routes at each of your hotels.

Besides charging too much for the drinks in the hotel zone restaurants, crime in the Yucatán is mostly limited to pickpocketing or lifting of things left unattended or in an unlocked automobile. Simple precautions lessen your chances of being victimized and if you are, your vacation is not completely ruined. Carry only enough money with you to cover the day and leave the rest with your valuables in the hotel's safe. Leave your expensive watch and gold jewelry home.

It's rare that valuables or cash left in your hotel room are ever stolen, but it does happen. If your hotel offers a **lock box safe** it's worth making use of, but don't lose the key – it can cost up to US $50 to replace. Keep travelers check numbers separate from the checks in case they're lost or stolen. We've become addicted to **fanny packs** as a secure way to carry a wallet. They're difficult to pickpocket and, in addition, relieve the pain of sitting with a lumpy wallet in the back of your pants.

We once fell prey to the old "drop some coins in front of a naive tourist so they watch you – or even help – pick them up while your accomplice nicks their camera" routine. Though we've never had another instance and have returned several times, we were suckers for that one in a crowded *mercado* a few years ago. Be aware of getting bumped or distracted by anything unusual. If you have a camera, keep your camera bag closed and secured between pictures.

BRIBES & SCAMS: Although we're giving this section much coverage because people worry about it, problems involving bribes or being scammed happen infrequently in the Yucatán. When it does happen it's annoying but seldom serious. If it should happen to you, try not to let it spoil your vacation.

Tipping taken to its extreme in Mexico is the *mordida*, a small **bribe** paid to an official to "expedite" matters. Tourists rarely encounter the "bite," as it translates, because they rarely have to deal with Mexican authorities. There is no need, for example, to bribe anyone at the *migración* office to extend your tourist card. The most common instances involve driving and the police. When you're stopped for a minor traffic violation, as we were once in Mérida and once in Chetumal, both times for driving the wrong way on an unmarked one-way street, you can expect a stern lecture and perhaps a fine. Don't be cowed or intimidated but maintain a respectful attitude. Wait to hear his lecture before you apologize for your honest mistake. If you're not sure, make him explain exactly what it is he thinks you've done wrong.

In Chetumal the policeman gave us an on-the-spot lecture about paying attention to signs that weren't there and the need to be law-abiding tourists. He must have known how basically honest we are because after carefully explaining all the laws in Mexico in great detail, he let us go. The two policemen in Mérida who stopped us one Easter Sunday were not as accommodating. We had turned right, realized it was a one-way and immediately made a U-turn. Not fast enough. The policeman signalled us over and got out of his car when we parked. We waited patiently through a lecture about the severity of the transgression until the subject of a fine came up.

When it did, it came with an invitation to go to the stationhouse. It was a cue to say something like "Officer, we're on our way to (wherever) so would it be possible for you to pay our fine for us?" (Usually US $5 or less.) It's the fastest and easiest way to handle things and, unlike in the States or Canada, acceptable.

Policemen must know what terror it strikes in the heart of tourists to think they have to go to a stationhouse to resolve such a simple matter. If you're adamant about not having done anything wrong, you can agree to follow him there, at which point he may backtrack and let you go with a warning. Always allow him to save face – this is not a one-upsmanship contest. No matter which course you choose, you can chalk the experience up to a complete appreciation of the idiosyncrasies of travel in Mexico.

An alternative angle is to feign total ignorance of even the most obvious words in the Spanish language. Never be impolite or snicker or you'll find yourself regretting the indiscretion. An attentive face that struggles to understand the complete depth of all your wrong-doings, as related in your lecture, followed by a "*lo siento pero no entiendo*" (I'm sorry, I don't understand) may exasperate the officer until he finally gives up in disgust at your ignorance. This is a delicate game and you don't want to aggravate or insult him. If you're somewhat fluent in Spanish you could try not quite getting his point. We told the officer a long involved story about another policeman who directed us up that wrong way in our effort to find a store to buy flowers to put on the grave of Felipe Carrillo, a national hero. We were going the wrong way? Which way should we go? Was he now directing us on the correct route? Where was the graveyard that everyone told us was so beautiful in his wonderful city?

If the officer is on foot and waves you over for something minor you could always develop instant cataracts and keep driving. Few foot patrolmen have radios to call ahead so high-tailing it out of there avoids the inconvenience of a traffic stop. Good luck. Don't try that in a crowded area like Mérida's *mercado* where the traffic crawls and the policeman's whistle alerts the cop on the next corner. Nor at any of the numerous Army or agricultural checkpoints along the highway or side roads. You're usually waived through these stops, although you may also be questioned and asked to open your trunk. The Army is making an effort to control any drug or arms smuggling that may pass through the Yucatán's many miles of deserted coastline. If you try to outrun an Army checkpoint there's a soldier down the road in a sand bag foxhole who might shoot you. In rural areas you may see an open truck on the side of the road filled with soldiers dozing against their weapons. Just south of Cancún, there's even a semi-permanent checkpoint, complete with armed soldiers. Don't worry. Besides drug and arms eradication, this is Mexico's way of reassuring tourists that they are safe and secure.

Americans just want to be liked – it's part of their psychological make up. Unless you're a paranoid schizophrenic, chances are you travel, as we do, in wide-eyed wonder and complete openness. It brings out the best in us as well as the people we meet. But there's always the one person who looks at your innocence and says, "sucker." The only time anyone ever tried to take advantage of us with a **"scam"** (other than the distraction ploy used to lift our camera) was at two gasoline stations. Considering the number of times we've been in the Yucatán, that's not a bad average.

The simplest "fill 'er up" scam happened to us on the western outskirts of Valladolid, where the city's one-way road joins with Highway 180. At Pemex (on the left heading west), several boys stood in front of the pump as we pulled up. As the overly attentive attendant quickly pushed the nozzle into our tank, two boys came to our windows with questions about how we liked Mexico and so forth. We chatted away until it came time to pay the bill – twice what it should have cost. The scam works by having someone screen your view of the pump to keep you from noticing that it was not cleared back to zero before pumping your gas. The solution? Make sure you have a clear view of the pump before saying how much gas you want. Especially effective is to step out of the car and look. If in doubt, wave him away as if you don't want gas, just directions. If you want to avoid this particular station (though this happened to us many years ago), there's a new and better Pemex in town. To find it as you head east: after 180 becomes Calle 41, it's on your left. If you're heading west on Calle 39 toward Chichén, look for the Pemex sign on the side of a building with a driveway on your left, near the Super Maz shopping center.

It's hard to avoid the Pemex station on the Chetumal-Escárcega highway, near Xpuhil, just east of the Calakmul biosphere's border. It's a long run between cities and most cars need to fill up here. The pump is the old-fashioned kind that registers only liters, not the total peso amount. We got out of the car to make sure the pump was cleared and were engaged in a friendly conversation with two other men and the attendant. When the tank was full the attendant showed us the price on his hand held calculator, about twice what it should have been. Since we knew we needed half a tank in our Bug, about 20 liters, the 25 liters the pump showed was probably correct. So we took out our calculator and punched in the pump's 25 liters, then multiplied that by the cost per liter we had paid in Chetumal. "There must be something wrong with your calculator, here's what it should be," we told him. Realizing we weren't going to fall for his sleight of hand he responded: "Gasoline is more expensive this far from the city." It was, but only by a peso or so, so we agreed on our price. Later we met a Canadian couple who had felt intimidated by the men hovering around them as they discussed the high price. They paid it without arguing.

Perhaps before filling up there, take out your calculator and confirm the price per liter. That should send a message to the attendant that you know what you're doing and will scrutinize the transaction closely. Know how many liters your car should take! Don't feel intimidated.

TELEPHONES: We've made it easy for you to call Mexico. Dial 011 for an international line, then 52 for Mexico and then the number. We've listed the area or city code first separated from the phone number by a slash (/). Calls within different areas of Mexico are preceded by 91. Local calls do not need the area code. If you're in Cancún, for example, and the number we list is 98/88-88-88, simply drop the 98 when you dial.

Except in larger cities, international telephone service is not as convenient, accessible or inexpensive as we'd like. When you call home from your room (dial 95 to reach the States) make sure hotel surcharges aren't exorbitant. You can call through Telemex and charge your call to an AT&T card, but it's more costly than dealing direct with a USA-based server. Small towns have a central location for telephone service called a *larga distancia*, where you can reach an English-speaking Telemex operator. The phone offices are also good for local calls within the Yucatán, especially if you don't have a pre-paid phone card, because you can pay in cash.

Public telephones marked "Ladatel" can also be used to call the states directly. Unfortunately, the only way to reach the operator or a direct service from a pay phone is by using a Ladatel phone card. Buy a card from any of the vendors that display the blue and yellow Ladatel logo. They're commonly sold in values of 30, 50 or 100 pesos. With them you can direct dial or reach the overseas operator.

Call collect or charge your call to an AT&T card by dialing 090 and speaking with the operator. To reach **AT&T Direct Service**, dial either 01/800/462-4240 or 95/800/462-4240. **MCI WorldPhone** is at 95/800/674-7000. **Sprint International** are at 001/800/877-8000 or 95/800/877-8000. We had trouble getting through, so good luck.

If you can help it, do not place your call home on the phones that say you can call the US or Canada directly by punching *01 (or similar prefix) to charge it on a major credit card. These phones are everywhere in Cancún and although convenient, charges are upwards of US $25 for the first minute! It's a rip-off aimed at young vacationers who might not have major phone company cards.

Few public phones accept coins, but most use a prepaid calling card, available in many stores, and a good cheap way to make local calls within Mexico.

HEALTH & HAPPINESS: The first time we came back from Yucatán, we extolled the virtues of Cancún to a friend who was getting married. "Did you get sick?" he worried. "No, not at all," we replied honestly. "We spent two weeks wandering around the interior, eating what and where we pleased. The only precaution we took was to drink *aqua mineral* or *aqua purificada*." It figures that Rich and Gail, ever the cautious ones, honeymooned in Cancún – never left the hotel zone; drank only bottled water; and ate only in the fancy restaurants in their hotel. Regardless of their precautions, both of them got sick with *tourista*, a digestive disorder caused by bacteria foreign to your system. Since that time Cancún has improved its purified drinking water system, but discretion is always advised. Most ice in bigger restaurants is made from purified water, but if you're in doubt, ask for your drink *sin hielo* (without ice).

We eventually learned, firsthand, that drinking bottled water does not offer fail-safe prevention – nothing does. Some medical sources even suggest *tourista* can be caused by a combination of other factors. Its symptoms, which mimic salmonella poisoning, may include any or all the following: nausea, diarrhea, vomiting, stomach cramps and low-grade fever. Purists suggest waiting it out for three or four days, but that's hardly realistic if you've got only a week's vacation and a gazillion things to do. So here's our tried and true treatment.

If we're in a budget hotel, the first thing we do when we start feeling bad (and it comes on *very* quickly) is upgrade to a hotel with air-conditioning – maybe cable TV – and a comfortable bed. A couple of aspirin and plenty of sleep is called for. If we suffer frequent diarrhea and stomach cramps, we take the recommended dose of Imodium AD. Pepto Bismol relieves the symptoms as well, but takes longer. It's necessary to drink plenty of bottled water or Coca-Cola with lime or, in severe cases, rehydration fluids such as Pedialyte, available at a local drugstore. We sometimes also drink *manzanilla* (chamomile) tea, without milk, a helpful folk remedy. Then we crank up the air-conditioner, curl up and go to sleep. We repeat the Imodium if the diarrhea returns. In about 24 hours we're usually feeling well enough to get back out and enjoy the sunshine – with some reservations. If you've had a bout, you may still feel a little weak so take it easy; and don't over-exert. For a few days you may also experience mild stomach cramps after eating. Eat light and cut out liquor and hot spices.

The US Public Health Service does not recommend taking any prophylactic medicines beforehand, but there are other ways to aid in prevention. Besides drinking bottled water, use it when you clean your teeth. Peel fruit before consuming and avoid salads outside large towns (or at least ask if it was washed in purified water). In addition, we theorize that much of the bacteria that gives problems can be eliminated with frequent hand washings. The sensory delights of the Yucatán include touching new things, so a good hand scrub every chance you get is a good idea. You should have a fair number of chances because many restaurants offer a sink right in the dining room and it's considered polite to wash before eating. Alternatively, use the antiseptic towelettes we recommended or consider taking along one of the new anti-bacterial **sanitizing liquids**, such as Purelle, available in the US.

One tends to be preoccupied with one's bowels in Mexico, with entire conversations revolving about whether they have or haven't yet moved. That's because the other side of the coin is "travelers constipation." Our "killer" cure is plenty of fresh fruit in our diet and tons of liquid. Just relax; what goes around, comes around.

If you should have a severe medical problem, most hotels will arrange for an English-speaking doctor to make a house call. Mexico's doctors are well trained so if you're really sick don't wait until you get home to have someone look at you. Go to a hospital, rather than a private *"clinica"* for treatment. Malaria and cholera are extremely rare in the Yucatán, but they're not to be fooled with if you display symptoms. Use mosquito repellent to aid in malaria prevention. If you're traveling on to more remote sections of Central America, such as Guatemala, El Salvador or Honduras, a vaccination against hepatitis A is recommended. (A shot of immune globulin gives temporary protection.) It is thought to be contracted through contaminated water. A doctor friend of ours, who has vacationed in Mexico for the past 20 years, recommends a hepatitis vaccine for all travelers regardless of where they go, Paris or Escárcega.

TIPPING & BEGGING: Many restaurants add a 10% tip, *"propina,"* to your bill along with the tax. If you have good service don't hesitate to leave another 5-10% on the table. Tips are often the major source of income for service workers, as their salaries are well below North American standards and sometimes even below Mexican standards. **Tipping is customary** in situations where a service is given; otherwise it's at your discretion. We drove to a remote Maya village to find a ruined hacienda. When we stopped to ask directions of a man on a bicycle, he insisted on leading us there (although it was only one block more). Despite telling him we didn't need a guide, he led – or was it followed – us around and in the end provided details about the history and family that we would never have known without his help. So we tipped him US $2. In Campeche, every time we parked, men would come out from the shade of a tree and wash our car. It didn't seem necessary to have our rental car washed, although it got dusty every day, but it provided them with meager employment so we paid US $1-2, every time it happened. Tip rates for maid service in hotel rooms should be about US $2 per day.

When you buy things in larger stores that charge a sales tax for convenience they sometimes round up or down any fractions of a peso (remember, one peso is less than 12¢). Children (12 years old or older) bag your groceries or purchases and it's customary to tip them a peso or two plus any fractions that come as change.

If you drive in Cancún, you'll see men with rags near every parking area or lot. They'll direct you into your space, signal you when you're backing out – sometimes conveniently blocking traffic for you – and reasonably guard the cars in their territory. A tip is called for. It's probably worth bringing a big stash of dollar bills and an understanding attitude just for gratuities. That way, if you're at all confused over the value of pesos or don't have the right change, a dollar or two is always handy.

Begging is a problem that vexes us in New York as well as in Mexico. A number of old Maya women and men will beg on the street in the larger cities of the interior, especially on Sundays at the churches. They may have obvious infirmities but many are just old and somehow out of the traditional Maya family care. Sometimes we give, sometimes we don't.

In Valladolid, signs caution tourists not to tolerate children begging or asking to "watch your car," which they pronounce in English as "wash your car." Instead, refuse and encourage them to go to school. This seems to be the only town where this happens, but children selling handicrafts, such as hand-embroidered hankies, Barbie doll *huipiles* and woven friendship bracelets, are everywhere in the Yucatán. Some are up late at night working the outdoor restaurants. It's an unfortunate fact of life.

We try to make a habit of taking along something (because we pack light and have the room) such as small gifts and/or something to contribute to countries where we travel. We bought new and used baseball caps at flea markets and garage sales for 50¢ to US $2 and used them as additional "thank-yous" to our guides or anyone who was helpful to us. We also carried a big bag of pens that we gave out to children and even stopped at a rural school and gave a supply to the teacher. Other easy-to-carry gifts are packets of seeds, especially vegetables, that you can give to adults in rural areas.

Being There

Poor Mexico, so far from God, so close to the United States.
– Porfirio Diáz, 1830-1915

HANDY HINTS: Here's an assortment of hints and ideas – culled from years of trial-and-error experience and in no particular order – to make your travel easier, safer and more fun.

We make much use of **resealable plastic bags** to carry or store things in.

We've twice taken immersible heaters and bought cups and instant coffee in Mexico, but they seem to stop working after one use so we've given up.

Don't bring much **jewelry** – if any at all – and especially don't pack it in checked luggage. Why not wear one and buy a second or third pair of earrings in Mexico?

We met an intrepid couple with backpacks who used plastic pull-tight **seals**, insuring that their bags couldn't be opened without cutting the seals. They kept a supply and resealed the luggage after each packing.

If you're a water-lover and have packed light, consider taking a tube and face mask for **snorkeling** rather than paying US $6 rental each time you go. We actually bought a fairly good set at Chedraui in downtown Cancún for about US $10.

Lost documents can be a hassle, so make a **photocopy of your tourist card** in a hotel or copy shop as soon as you can and put it with your passport. A copy will help in replacing it if it's lost or stolen. If you haven't already, **copy your passport** and carry the photocopy, rather than the passport, with you. Leave your passport in the hotel.

Colorful woven plastic mesh **shopping bags**, sold inexpensively in *mercados*, make a great carry-on bag for all those gifts you swore you weren't going to bring back. You can reuse them to do grocery shopping at home.

Handles on faucets marked "C" mean *caliente*: Hot – not cold, even when the other one reads "H." **Bathrooms** are usually marked *Caballeros* (Men) and *Damas* (Women).

Speaking of feeling foolish, we discovered the hard way that the plastic bucket next to the toilet in hotels is for used **toilet paper**. A problem occurs outside of the resort hotels, where the plumbing can not handle paper and could get blocked. The maid will empty and wash the bucket daily.

Creases in slacks, jackets and tops can sometimes be lessened by carefully folding and placing them under your mattress at night. Whenever you drop off **laundry** (saves buying soap) be sure to specify that you want your whites and colors "*separado*," washed separately.

Free refills of your **coffee** are uncommon in Mexico and not automatic when your cup is empty. Sanborn's is a notable exception. A drink in a bar or restaurant should be accompanied by *bocas*, **appetizers** such as tostadas or ceviche. These are sometimes not automatically given to gringos, so you might have to ask.

Find a **skink** (*iguanita*) in your room in the countryside, most often posing on a wall, and find good luck. People-shy skinks eat mosquitos.

If you live in a cold-weather city such as Minneapolis, there may be some **low-priced specials** on charters or regular airlines to get you down to Mexico in the middle of winter. We met more Minnesotans in Cancún than there are in St. Paul. Ask your travel agent to watch out for you.

Prices are lower in the **off season**, that's obvious. But there's a bit of a lull in Cancún and Cozumel in early January so there's more room to negotiate. It never hurts to ask for a discount or a promotional rate.

No need to gloat about avoiding eateries that say "**Restaurante Turistico**." That simply means they are appropriate for travelers – it does not mean they're for gringo tourists only. They tend to have a pleasing ambiance and a somewhat higher standard. On the other hand, just because a restaurant doesn't say that it is "*turistico*" doesn't mean that it's not good. Follow your instincts.

Hotels just a block off the waterfront are generally cheaper than those right on it. Because electricity is expensive, rooms with **air-conditioners** (*con clima*) frequently cost more. Try a night or two with a ceiling fan and see how you like it.

Bakeries (*panaderias*) are a good resource for inexpensive snacks or breakfasts and a great place to try new taste sensations. Many of the pastries and breads are dry so get a coffee or tea somewhere to wash them down. Things to go are sold "*para llevar*" (para yea-bar) and if it's a soda or beer in a recyclable bottle you'll pay a little extra.

Free concerts are common on weekends and holidays in city parks and plazas. Special events abound. Stop in the tourist office at each new city and ask what's happening. Mérida, a cultural gem, has events nearly every night. **Museums and archeological sights** are free of charge on Sundays, but many close on Mondays. Most of the Maya sites have a flat fee of 10 pesos, or about US $1.50. **Flash photography** is almost never allowed and **tripods** are also forbidden without a permit bought in advance from INAH (*Instituto de Historia y Antropología*). All sites charge extra if you want to use a video camera.

It's a good idea to **ask permission to photograph** the Yucatán's indigenous people. More often than not a smile or nod allows an absolutely perfect memory to be captured on your film. Sometimes a tip afterward is welcome. We give out pens or a packet of seeds. If a person refuses permission, please respect his or her wishes.

Always **count your change** – it's good practice while you get used to the different monetary system and it prevents misunderstandings. A good way to know what a taxi should cost is ask someone at your hotel. Agree on a price before you drive away.

If you need some more time on your tourist card and you're in the south and not able to find Chetumal's obscure *migracíon* office, take a quick trip into **Belize**. When you return you automatically get a new 30-day tourist card!

Several of the hotels we mention are in fairly remote areas of the countryside, beyond telephone – and in some cases electric – lines. Most hotels have either cellular phones or at least **shortwave radios** in case of emergencies.

If a Mexican mentions Mexico, chances are they're speaking of the capital city (*Districto Federal*), not the country. The term **gringo** is not derogatory. "PB" means *Planta Baja*, the first floor in Mexico. In an elevator, what we think of as the second floor is considered the first floor and is marked "one."

The crowded little VW **combi,** or *colectivo*, buses you see running around take passengers for a slightly higher price than regular buses. They can be flagged down anywhere but it's hard to know if they're going your way. They also cover some areas that regular buses don't. Unlike the States, regular local buses will **stop or pick up** at almost any corner.

If you're wandering the Yucatán, many hotels have **storage lockers** where you can leave your extra stuff rather than lugging it around. If not, they may hold it for you.

A special edition of *The Miami Herald* is published for Mexico daily and many Cancún hotels have *USA Today*. Newsboys ply the morning restaurants on Isla Mujeres, Playa del Carmen, Cozumel and Cancún. The *Mexico City Times* publishes an English-language edition Monday through Friday. It is also found in Mérida.

JUST IN CASE: If you lose your passport or have need of consular services such as lists of qualified medical doctors or *abogados* (lawyers), or you just need advice and empathy, you can turn to your **embassy.** They won't, however, give you money, fly you home or get you out of jail.

Canadians can reach their embassy in Mexico City, Monday through Friday, from 9 a.m. to 5 p.m. (closed for lunch from 1-2) at ☎ 5/724-7900. In Cancún there's a Canadian consul in the Plaza México 312, 2nd floor, Monday-Friday, 10-2, ☎ 98/84-37-16. Reach the **Embassy of the** United Kingdom in Mexico City by dialing ☎ 5/207-2569 between 9 a.m. and 2 p.m., or in Mérida the consul is at ☎ 99/21-67-99.

The **Embassy of the United States** is also in Mexico City at ☎ 5/211-0042. There is a US Consulate in Mérida on Paseo Montejo near the Fiesta Americana Hotel, ☎ 99/25-63-66. Another US Consular Agency is in Plaza Caracol, 3rd floor, in Cancún, ☎ 98/84-24-11. There's another downtown on Av. Nader north of Av. Uxmal.

Her are other consulate representatives with a location in Cancún: **Austria** (☎ 98/84-75-05), **France** (☎ 98/84-60-78), **Germany** (☎ 98/84-18-98), **Great Britain** (☎ 98/85-11-66, ext 462), **Italy** (☎ 98/84-12-61), **Spain** (☎ 98/83-24-66), **Switzerland** (☎ 98/81-80-00) and the **Netherlands** (☎ 98/83-02-00).

There's a Mexico Tourism-sponsored 24-hour **Traveler's Help Line** in Mexico City at ☎ 91/800/9-03-92. **Police** in Cancún are at ☎ 98/84-19-13 or 84-23-42. Dial "06," similar to our "911," for **emergencies.** In major medical emergencies **jet evacuation services** for a fee are available from Air Ambulance America of Mexico (☎ 95/800/222-3546) and Air Evac in San Diego and Mexico City. In San Diego, ☎ 619/278-3822.

To extend your tourist card for longer than your original 30 days you'll need to visit the *Servicios Migratorios*, who control extensions up to a total of 180 days. Wait four days after arrival before going into the office; the paperwork takes a while to get from the airport into the system. In Cancún the office is open from 9 a.m. until noon daily downtown at the corner of Av. Uxmal and Nader, (☎ 98/84-16-58). Get there early, take a ticket and commiserate with your fellow travelers. It's a great place to pick up tidbits of first-hand information and personal recommendations.

Other regional offices are: in Cozumel, ☎ 987/2-00-71; Mérida, ☎ 99/28-58-23; Campeche, ☎ 981/6-28-68; and in Ciudad del Carmen, ☎ 938/2-13-30.

The big hospital in **Cancún** is **Hospital Americano** (☎ 98/84-61-33). **Total Assist**, with an English-speaking staff, is on Av. Tulum (☎ 98/84-10-58). In Mérida there is the **Hospital General O'Horan,**

☎ 99/24-41-11 or the **Instituto Médico Qurúgico del Sureste,** ☎ 99/25-81-64.

> *Exit according to rule, first leg and then head. Remove high heels and synthetic stockings before evacuation. Open the door, take out the recovery line and throw it away.*

– Emergency instructions of the
Rumanian National Airlines, 1984

HOLLYWOOD vs. MEXICO

The country due south of La-La Land was never ignored by Tinsel Town's movie mogols, although their portrayal of Mexican culture and history should be taken with a grain of salt. In fact, take several grains of salt on the rim of your margarita as you sit back and enjoy one of these videos.

Night of the Iguana: Ava Gardner and Richard Burton slither around in Puerto Vallarta. Directed by John Huston. The movie transformed the sleepy fishing village into a jet-set getaway.

Under the Volcano: Albert Finney drinks his way down, in and through 1930's Cuernavaca.

Like Water for Chocolate: A dreamy tale of delicious love and romantic food, from Laura Esquivel's best seller. Good movie – great book.

Treasure of the Sierra Madre: Bogie and Huston feud over gold in steamy Tampico. In Gold We Trust.

Juárez: Paul Muni as Benito Juárez with Bette Davis as Carlota and Mexico as itself.

Revenge: Kevin Costner and Anthony Quinn get bloody revenge in Puerto Vallarta and Durango. Neither's best effort.

Born in East LA: Cheech Marin proves he's no dope as he struggles to get back to the US after being mistakenly deported to Tijuana as an illegal alien.

Against All Odds: Jeff Bridges and James Woods chase Rachel Ward around Cozúmel and the Maya ruins of Chichén Itzá.

Captain from Castille: Stars Cesar Romero as Hernan Cortés, with Tyrone Power and Jean Peters in an epic recreation of the Spanish Conquest of Mexico. Somewhat true to history, *mas o menos.*

Villa Rides: Yul Brenner – with hair – as Pancho Villa. Charles Bronson and Robert Mitchum also have hair.

Viva Zapata: Marlon Brando portrays Emiliano Zapata as Marlon Brando.

10: Dudley Moore, Julie Andrews and Bo Derek. Bo started a craze for beachside beaded hair and undulating pectorals.

Fun in Acapulco: Elvis Presley dives off the cliffs at La Quebrada in Acapulco and still lives!

Old Gringo: Carlos Fuentes' novel about Ambrose Bierce was filmed in Zacatecas. Gregory Peck plays the crusty old gringo who gets the young girl. Lucky stiff.

Mexico Movie Settings Depicting Other Areas

Clear and Present Danger: Tom Clancy's best seller about drug-crazed South American bad guys was filmed in the Mexican States of Veracruz and Morelos. *Predator:* Arnie fights a slippery illegal alien outside Puerto Vallarta. *Medicine Man:* The Amazon flows through Veracruz. *Romancing the Stone:* This romantic gem set in Columbia was filmed in Veracruz City and the surrounding countryside. *African Queen:* Some scenes were filmed at Coyuca Lagoon outside Acapulco. *Herbie Goes Bananas:* Walt Disney's Puerto Vallarta-filmed movie about a loveable Volkswagen may explain why the Beetle is still manufactured in Mexico to this day.

Quintana Roo

*The Maya of interior Quintana Roo live much as
their forefathers did – still preserving many of
their ancient traditions.*

At A Glance

NAME: The state of Quintana Roo (keen-TANA ROE) was
named after Andrés Quintana Roo, Yucatán's first poet.
Born in Mérida on November 30, 1787, he died in Mexico
City in 1851. In a fateful paradox, this was the first landfall
of the Spanish conquistadors (1517), but the last land in Mexico to
be conquered. Once a part of the states of Yucatán and Campeche,
it became a federal territory on November 24, 1902. It was not until
October 8, 1974 that it became a full-fledged Mexican State – just in
time to build the Cancún resort.

CAPITAL: Chetumal.

MAJOR CITIES: Cancún, Chetumal, San Miguel Cozumel, Felipe
Puerto Carrillo, Isla Mujeres and Playa del Carmen.

POPULATION: 495,000 – indigenous Maya and Spanish descent.

CLIMATE: Hot and humid inland, the coastline is cooled
by ocean breezes. Rain in the summer.

VEGETATION: Jungle, mangroves and some savanna.

GEOGRAPHY: Lowland, cenotes, Caribbean beaches,
islands.

SIZE: 20,337 square miles (50,843 square kilometers).

WILDLIFE: Spider monkeys, deer, jaguars, tapirs,
water birds, crocodiles and armadillos.

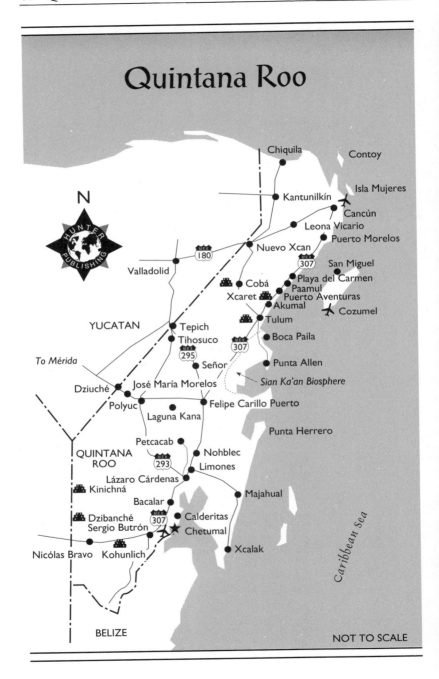

Quintana Roo

N

Chiquila

Contoy

Isla Mujeres

Kantunilkín

Cancún

Leona Vicario

Puerto Morelos

Nuevo Xcan

180

307 San Miguel

Valladolid

Cobá Playa del Carmen

Xcaret Paamul

Puerto Aventuras

Akumal

Cozumel

YUCATAN Tepich Tulum

Tihosuco Boca Paila

295 307

To Mérida Señor Punta Allen

Sian Ka'an Biosphere

Dziuché José María Morelos

Polyuc Felipe Carillo Puerto

Laguna Kana

Punta Herrero

Petcacab

QUINTANA Nohblec

ROO 293 Limones

Lázaro Cárdenas

Kinichná Majahual

Bacalar

Dzibanché 307 Calderitas

Sergio Butrón Chetumal

Nicólas Bravo Kohunlich Xcalak

Caribbean Sea

BELIZE NOT TO SCALE

ECOLOGICAL RESERVES: Sian Ka'an, Punta Laguna, Cozumel Reefs National Park, Isla Contoy.

MAJOR ARCHEOLOGICAL SITES: Tulum, Cobá, Rio Bec, Kohunlich, Muyil, Dzibanché (also spelled Tzibanché), San Gervasio.

Cancún & Isla Mujeres

I never expected to see the day when girls would get sunburned in the places they do now.

– Will Rogers, American humorist, 1879-1935

The sandy strip of Cancún's hotel zone, packed with luxury hotels hugging the shore, forms the shape of a lucky number seven, wedged between the turquoise surf of the Caribbean and the calm waters of the Nichupté Lagoon. The name Cancún in Mayan means "Golden Snake" and it aptly describes the slender slither of its powdery golden sand beaches. Squeezed along the 27-km (43.5-mile) causeway are 20,000 hotel rooms in a mix of architectural styles, which welcome sun-worshippers and vacationers from all over the world. Last year, some 2.5 million visitors touched down at the modern airport, most bound for the luxury and pampering of the famous hotel zone.

Cancún

Unlike Acapulco or Puerto Vallarta, which were idyllic little villages until tourism replaced fishing as the major source of income, Cancún is a made-to-order resort, built specifically for tourism where the wild jungle met a deserted shore. One creation story claims that around 1968 a computer program churned out the Cancún location after being fed vital statistics from all over Mexico. The statistical parameters included climate, beach conditions and proximity to the United States. Whether the legend is true or not, we know that before the bankers and government officials realized that Cancún's reliable sunshine (240 days per year), warm weather and sparkling waters provided the perfect place to build a new world-class seaside resort, nothing much was here. Just some small ruins of the ancient Maya civilization out on the barren dunes and in what is now the ferry and fishing town of Puerto Juárez and scrub brush. Only Puerto Juárez and the tiny island of Isla Mujeres supported minor Mexican fishing villages. John Stephens, the American adventurer who toured the world of the Maya in the 19th century, mentioned that *"In the afternoon we steered for the mainland, passing the island of Kancune, a barren strip of land with sand hills and stone buildings visible upon it."* What's left of those stone buildings can be seen at **El Rey**, near the southern end of the hotel zone, **San Miguelito**, half a km north of El Rey, and **Yamil Lu'um**, on a hill next to the Sheraton.

The other Cancún – inland from the waterfront – is the Mexican town built to supply housing and community for the hospitality workers in the hotel zone. While some of it is not of particular interest, the downtown (*El Centro*) has become a tourist destination all its own. We suspect that if the hotels in the hotel zone sank into the sea, Cancún downtown would stay on, living and working much as it does now – a gumbo of Yucatecan, Maya, Mexican and North American lifestyles. It's a pleasant and lively place to be, close enough to the shore and the diversions of the hotel zone, but far enough away so that it doesn't feel like you're in Kansas anymore.

No matter what your vacation needs, between the two Cancúns you can satisfy them. Get-away-and-relax-on-the-beach vacationers will find Cancún is all it's cracked up to be. More adventuresome, lower-budget travelers can find the best of both worlds downtown. Cancún's laid-back but cosmopolitan ways make it an easy transition to a Mexican "vacation mode." And Cancún makes a good base from which to begin your exploration and enjoyment of adventures in the Yucatán.

Orientation

 GETTING AROUND: The international airport is outside the city in the dry jungle, but most flights pass over the brilliant sand beaches and bright blue water of the shoreline before setting down. It whets your appetite for getting right to the beach. **Tickets** for the *colectivo* buses and taxis into town may be purchased at a booth in the airport. This method sets the prices and prevents any rip-offs.

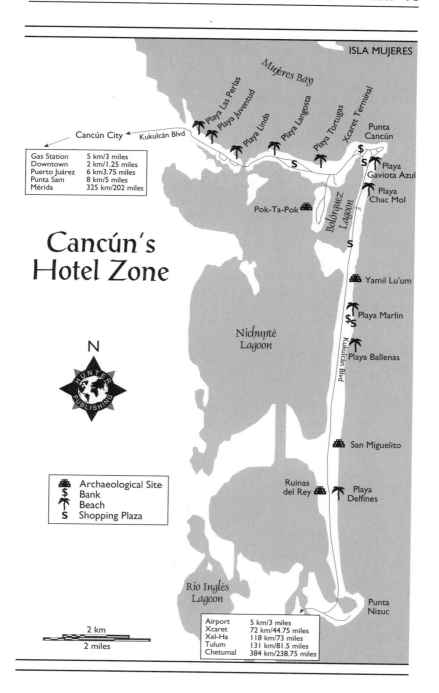

ISLA MUJERES

Mujeres Bay

Playa Las Perlas
Playa Juventud
Playa Linda
Playa Langosta
Playa Tortugas
Xcaret Terminal

Punta Cancún

Cancún City ← Kukulcán Blvd

Gas Station	5 km/3 miles
Downtown	2 km/1.25 miles
Puerto Juárez	6 km3.75 miles
Punta Sam	8 km/5 miles
Mérida	325 km/202 miles

Playa Gaviota Azul

Playa Chac Mol

Pok-Ta-Pok

Bolórquez Lagoon

Cancún's Hotel Zone

Yamil Lu'um

Playa Marlin

N

Playa Ballenas

Kukulcán Blvd

Nichupté Lagoon

San Miguelito

Ruinas del Rey

Playa Delfines

Archaeological Site
$ Bank
Beach
S Shopping Plaza

Río Inglés Lagoon

Punta Nizuc

2 km

2 miles

Airport	5 km/3 miles
Xcaret	72 km/44.75 miles
Xel-Ha	118 km/73 miles
Tulum	131 km/81.5 miles
Chetumal	384 km/238.75 miles

Cancún (population 300,000) is divided into two zones, the **downtown** and the **hotel zone**. The hotel zone is along the clear Caribbean and is the Cancún you see in all the brochures and ads. More expensive than downtown, the beaches have it all for sun and fun vacations. The downtown is inland, connected to the hotel zone by the Paseo Kukulcán and reached by inexpensive (40¢) public buses or taxis. Clearly marked *Zona Hoteles*, the Ruta (Route) 1 and 2 buses take you downtown and back (Ruta 1 turns up Tulum, Ruta 2 passes it on Av. Cobá). For the Isla Mujeres ferry, catch the bus marked *Puerto Juárez*, north of Av. Uxmal on Av. Tulum near the supermarket, *Comercial Mexicana* (look for the pelican logo).

The main drag downtown is Av. Tulum, which runs north and south perpendicular to Av. Cobá. Cobá becomes Paseo Kukulcán (also spelled Kukulkán) in the hotel zone. Most of the downtown attractions – stores, hotels and restaurants – are clustered around the three parallel avenues of Nader, Tulum and Yaxchilán. The bus station is behind the circle of Av. Tulum and Av. Uxmal. City blocks in Spanish are *manzanas* and groups of blocks are *super-manzanas* or S.M. The heart of the downtown is in a rhomboid-shaped block surrounded by Av. Tulum and Yaxchilán, Uxmal and Cobá.

Beachfront, Cancún.

BEACHES: There is a series of 11 **public beaches** along the Paseo. All beaches in Mexico are free, although some hotels are not anxious for you to know it. The beaches on the windward side (the top part of the number seven), protected by Isla Mujeres, are better for swimming. The leeward beaches are more picturesque, with broad sand, warm waters and strong surf. The south beach farthest from the downtown, Playa Delfines, is a favorite of locals partly because this stretch of sand against the brilliant turquoise sea is free of hotels. Playa Tortugas, with its soft sand and gentle surf, is the most popular spot for tourists staying downtown. Among all of Cancún's fabulous beaches, we think Playa Chac-Mool may be the prettiest.

SEASONAL TEMPERATURES

Month	High (°F/°C)	Low (°F/°C)
Jan	80/27	64/18
Feb	86/30	68/20
Mar	90/32	72/22
Apr	95/35	77/25
May	99/37	81/25
Jun	99/37	77/25
Jul	99/37	77/25
Aug	99/37	77/25
Sep	91/35	73/23
Oct	95/35	73/23
Nov	88/31	72/22
Dec	80/27	65/19

Practicalities

 Tourist information is found in a kiosk building next to the Multibanco Comerex, near the Municipal Palace in the middle of Av. Tulum (☎ 98/84-80-73). The **Quintana Roo State Tourism** office is in the FONATOUR building on Av. Cobá at Av. Nader (☎ 98/84-32-38).

A **laundromat** that does a good job of washing, drying and folding clothes is **Lavanderia Tulum**, between the Comercial Mexicana and the big McDonalds on Av. Tulum. It's open Monday through Saturday, 7 a.m. to 8 p.m., and on Sunday from 9 a.m. to 6 p.m. Full service laundry runs about 80¢ per kilo.

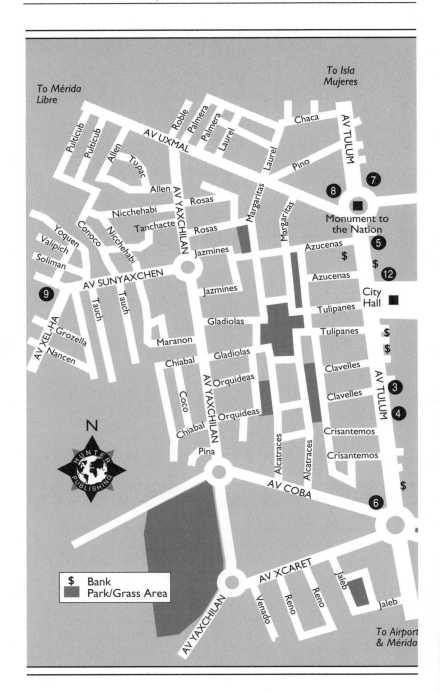

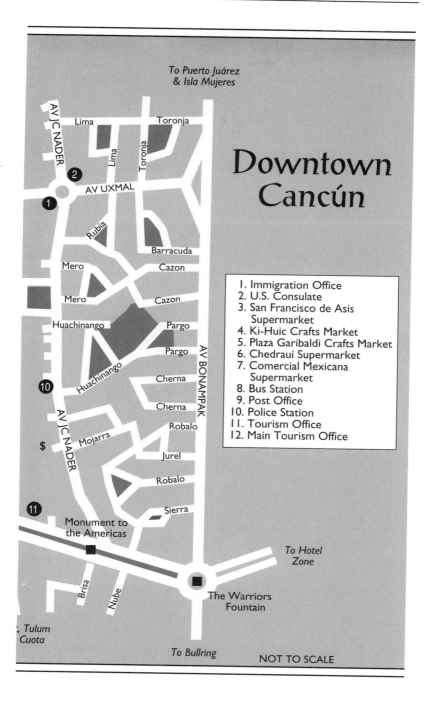

Downtown Cancún

To Puerto Juárez
& Isla Mujeres

1. Immigration Office
2. U.S. Consulate
3. San Francisco de Asis
   Supermarket
4. Ki-Huic Crafts Market
5. Plaza Garibaldi Crafts Market
6. Chedraui Supermarket
7. Comercial Mexicana
   Supermarket
8. Bus Station
9. Post Office
10. Police Station
11. Tourism Office
12. Main Tourism Office

NOT TO SCALE

Papelería de Cancún is a large office supply and gift store tucked up Calle Margarita in SM 22. It sells good maps of the Yucatán's states, makes copies and has an impressive line of clay products and gifts. The **Post Office** is on the corner of Av. Sunyaxchen and Av. Xel-Há and is open Monday through Friday, 8 a.m. to 7 p.m., and Sunday 9 a.m. to 1 p.m. The **Red Cross** is open 24 hours a day on Av. Labna No. 2 (☎ 98/84-11-16). **Hospital Americano** (15 Calle Viento, ☎ 98/84-61-33) and **Total Assist** (5 Claveles), both with English-speakers on staff, are each just off Av. Tulum (☎ 98/84-10-58).

The **Police** in Cancún are at ☎ 98/84-19-13 or 84-23-42. A **US Consular Agency** is located in Plaza Caracol, 3rd floor, in the hotel zone, ☎ 98/84-24-11. The downtown office is on Av. Nader, just north of Av. Uxmal. In the case of an emergency, ☎ 99/25-63-66 in Mérida or 5/211-0042 in Mexico City. **Canadians** will find their consul in the Plaza México 312, 2nd floor (open Monday-Friday, 10-2, ☎ 98/84-37-16). Contact the Canadian Embassy in Mexico City at ☎ 5/724-7900. See page 83 for other countries' consular representatives in Cancún.

The **American Express** office (☎ 98/84-19-99) is open weekdays 9-6 and Saturdays 9-1 on Av. Tulum near the Hotel America. There are several **pharmacies** in the hotel zone malls and plazas, two in Plaza Caracol and several downtown. The **Farmacia Canto** (☎ 98/84-40-83), a **drugstore** on Av. Yaxchilán and Sunyaxchen, is open 24 hours. There's a **Narcotics Anonymous meeting** in Spanish every night from 8:30 to 10 p.m. at Parque Margaritas (41 Norte between 50 and 51) and one in English every Monday, downtown at 7:30 p.m. at Plaza Centro (3rd floor) on Av. Nader. English meetings of the **Friends of Bill W** also assemble at Plaza Centro, 3rd floor, on Av. Nader – daily from 6:15 p.m. for an hour. They can be reached at ☎ 98/84-33-75 or an emergency group number at ☎ 98/74-30-82.

EVENTS: Bullfights abound at Avs. Bonampak and Sayil each Wednesday at 3:30 p.m. Get your tickets through travel agents or downtown in front of the San Francisco Asis supermarket on Av. Tulum. Look for the big plaster bull. **Carnival** festivities take place before Lent and there's a respected **Jazz Festival** over the Memorial Day Weekend (☎ 98/84-58-95). July hosts a **Country Western Fest** and a **Rockfest** is held in October. **Expo Cancún**, a crafts and exhibits fair and festival, is held at the end of October. Call the Cancún tourism office for more information. ☎ 98/84-80-73.

HEALTH CLUBS: Most hotels contain their own health clubs exclusive to guests. However, there are two public gyms: **Gold's Gym** is open Monday through Friday, 7 a.m.-9 p.m. and Sunday

from 9 a.m.-9 p.m. at the Plaza Flamingo in the hotel zone. **Michaels'
Gym** (☎ 98/84-23-94) is on Av. Sayil No. 66. S.M. 4 (near the
bullring).

Shopping

DOWNTOWN

Plaza Garibaldi. This market on Av. Tulum, at corner of
Av. Uxmal, contains stalls of serapes, tablecloths and
traditional clothing, gifts and crafts.
   Plaza Mexico. The market at Av. Tulum No. 200 is a
cluster of 50 handicraft shops.
   Ki-Huic. The biggest market downtown is in the center of Av.
Tulum between two banks. Open daily from 9 a.m. to 10 p.m. (some
take a siesta), this streetfront and indoor labyrinth of stalls is the
city's oldest with 100 vendors of gifts and crafts. Good bargains can
be struck here but be prepared to haggle if you like what you see.
You'll be "eagerly invited" to enter each shop.
   Plaza Bonita, Av. Xel-Há, near the post office, is a attractive
outdoor mall that looks like a little village street, right next to a
Mercado Municipal. This is a favorite shopping and eating area of
local residents. Upscale goods but low prices.
   Mercado in SM 23. The large triangular block behind the bus
station at Av. Uxmal and Av. Tulum houses a market that local
workers frequent. Gringos are scarce here but bargains are not. Gifts
and clothing.
   Supermarkets downtown are the **San Francisco de Asis,** in the
middle of Av. Tulum; the **Comercial Mexicana,** at the circle of Av.
Tulum and Uxmal; and the **Chedraui,** at the corner of Av. Tulum
and Cobá. They're good places to stock up on water, food and
miscellaneous necessities. All three double as department stores, but
Chedraui has the largest selection and a good bakery called La
Hogaza. Take an aluminum pizza tray and some tongs and pick
what you desire from the open racks. The sales clerk will add it up
and bag it at the register. Bakery goods are very inexpensive. Another notable bakery is La Baguette, on Av. Uxmal.
   There's a large **Ace Hardware** on Av. Tulum south of the city
center (☎ 98/87-68-00) and a **Sam's Club** (the US-based membership
club) is tucked behind Av. Yaxchilán and Av. Labna, near the
Telemex microwave towers. If your annual membership is expiring

soon, think about renewing here – it's cheaper. They offer a list of stores and restaurants that discount with a Sam's card.

The hotel zone has a tiny convenience store on the lagoon side before you reach Club Med.

HOTEL ZONE

Plaza Flamingo, Km 11 Paseo Kukulcán, is a pleasant mall with a good variety of shops. This was our favorite in the hotel zone, with the best fast food.

Plaza Kukulkán, Km 13, is an American-style shopping mall. Expensive but with a large choice. Food court and good restaurants.

Plaza Caracol, Km 8.5 across from the Convention Center. The largest mall in Cancún with over 200 shops, including designer specialty stores.

Plaza Mayfair, across from Hotel Americana, features more restaurants than stores in its open courtyard setting. Food prices are reasonable but check the drink prices. We felt cheated big time by having to pay US $2 for a glass of water and US $3 for a beer that costs 65¢ downtown. There were lots of two-for-one drink specials at a price that's twice what it should be. Sidewalk spray paint artists draw a big crowd in several of the outdoor malls. Their paintings are quite clever and very cheap.

Coral Negro Mercado de Artesanias, Km 9 across from the All Star Café, is a Mexican-style artesians' *mercado* with a fancier outdoor handicraft gift section that imitates a village square.

Plaza Nautilus, located at Km 3.5 on the lagoon, is a favorite of American shoppers with 70 assorted stores.

Isla Mujeres. If you take one of the party boats or hotel-zone cruisers over for shopping, rumor has it that the boat owners have an interest in some of the stores and restaurants they "recommend." We've heard that some guides on the way over even caution gringos to stay or shop only in a certain area at what the say are the "best" places. If they say this – it's a lie. La Isla is virtually crime free and all the shops are cheaper than most on the mainland. If food is included in your cruise price, you'll miss some inexpensive and delicious dining opportunities in town.

Night Spots

As always on this boulevard, the faces were young, coming annually in an endless migration from every country, every continent, to alight here once in a long journey of their lives.
– Brian Moore, author

 Péricos on Av. Yaxchilán No. 61, is one of the last "happening" places downtown. It's an eatery and bar with live Mexican music from 7:30 p.m. to midnight. Its party atmosphere makes a festive night out. Bar stools here are saddles. **Carlos O'Brien's** on Av. Tulum is a late-night hangout.

In the hotel zone, **Mexico Magico**, at Km 12, has dinner shows with live music and dancing. **Ballet Folklórico Nacional de Mexico** features traditional Mexican music and folk dancing at the new Convention Center at the turn opposite Punta Cancún. Dinner and show or just show tickets available (☎ 98/83-01-99). Several posh hotels also do a dinner show with a different Ballet Folklórico performance.

Dady'O, Km 9.5, is the "in" disco in town, with long lines, especially on the weekends. This place throbs with nightlife. The sister bar and grill is **Dady Rock**. Across the street is the **Official All-Star Café** restaurant where you might see one of the famous owners – Monica Seles, Shaquille O'Neal, Wayne Gretzky, André Agassig, Ken Griffey Jr. and Joe Montana – but then again, you might not.

The **Hard Rock Café** is in Plaza Lagunas and **Planet Hollywood** is in Plaza Flamingo. **La Boom** booms out at Km 3.5 and **Christine** rocks the Krystal Cancún Hotel. **Rock Lobster Garage** at Plaza Terramar is a restaurant with a party atmosphere and a karaoke bar with a DJ. **Pat O'Brien's** in Plaza Flamingo, **La Palapa** outside the Club Lagoon Hotel, **Tequila's Boom** at Km 3.5, **Señor Frog's** in Plaza Caracol and Plaza Kukulkán and **Mango Tango**, Km 14.2 opposite the Ritz Carlton, are all restaurants with rocking bar areas and live music. Young adults can warm up for action at the **laser combat center** located in Plaza Kukulkán and romantic types can check out some of the night-time dinner cruises, of which there are several. On the **Asterix** party fishing cruise (☎ 98/86-48-47) you catch your own dinner and the crew cooks it for you. If you're not lucky, they provide for you while you drown your sorrows at their open bar.

GAMBLING: Luckily, there are no gambling casinos in Cancún. Sports betting is allowed in the **L.F. Caliente** restaurant-bar, open

11 a.m. to midnight in the Fiesta Americana Hotel in the hotel zone and in the Plaza Caribe Hotel, downtown. Also in Cozumel.

FLICKS: There is an American movie theater in Plaza Kukulkán called **The New Telecines**. There are three more downtown: **Espectaculos del Caribe** on Av. Tulum No. 44, with dialog in English and subtitles in Spanish; **Cinemas Tulum** has five screens on northern Av. Tulum; and **Cines Cancún** on Av. Cobá, No. 112.

Adventures

There was a young lady named Bright,
Whose speed was far faster than light;
She set out one day in a relative way,
And returned home the previous night.
– Professor Arthur Buller, 1874-1944

If you're based in Cancún or Isla Mujeres and want to see it all in **day trips** or short overnight jaunts, there's no lack of ways to get wherever you're going. A "must see" is **Tulum**, a Post-Classic ruined walled city, set high upon a bluff with spectacular views of the turquoise Caribbean below. Tulum is now the most visited archeological site in all of Mexico, with 107.5 million visitors in 1996. **Chichén Itzá** is a more impressive sight, because of its size and architecture. The giant pyramid El Castillo, where human sacrifices occurred, dominates the fascinating abandoned city. On the way, a stop or overnight stay in the historic colonial city of **Valladolid** gives a sense of the Yucatán not found in the modern streets of Cancún. Visit the **Xke'ken** cenote near Dzitnup or the **Balankanché Caves** near Chichén. The ancient lost city of **Cobá** is also within reach, as is the **Gran Cenote** near Tulum Pueblo. Exciting educational trips into the **Sian Ka'an Biosphere**, a 1.3-million-acre nature reserve, are arranged by Amigos de Sian Ka'an, headquartered in Plaza America (☎ 98/84-95-83).

Of course, **Isla Mujeres** should be more than a quick shopping trip. Its quaint personality survives the hordes of daytrippers that shuttle over from the mainland. A great snorkel and nature trip from there is to **Isla Contoy**, a bird sanctuary.

Croco Cun, about 45 minutes south of Cancún near Puerto Morelos, is a crocodile research zoo that offers a fascinating glimpse of the prehistoric beasts up close. Good kid spot. Nearby is Dr. Alfredo

Barrera Marín's **Jardín Botánico** (botanical garden), 150 acres with three km of walking trails though plants and trees. Open daily from 9-5, a guide is available. Five miles north of Tulum, **Xel-Há** (ishell-HA) is a natural aquarium in a lagoon that offers commercialized snorkeling and swimming in an attractive park-like setting. The clear lagoon is lined with coral caves and a sunken Maya altar. A cool snorkel and swim after visiting Tulum is their big selling point.

Xcaret (ish-car-et) could be owned by the Disney Company or Six Flags (it's not). The large-scale "eco-archeological" park has walking and horseback riding trails, authentic Maya ruins, a recreation of a Maya village, an underground river that runs through a sacred cave and beaches with soft white sand. It attracts busloads of water-lovers and fun-seekers. Dolphins perform in the lagoon and there's an aquarium, an aviary and a zoo. Brightly painted buses leave from the Xcaret terminal building Plaza Caracol, next to the Coral Beach Hotel, at 9 and 10 a.m. everyday. No reservations are needed, but be there at least 30 minutes before departure.

Playa del Carmen is the haunt of European travelers and **Cozumel** is a diver's and snorkeler's paradise. Both are much different experiences than Cancún, especially Playa.

AUTHORS' NOTE: For some people, just going to Mexico – much less leaving the hotel zone on a strange bus – is an adventure. Our definition of "adventure" is inclusive of the first-timer because every journey begins with the first step. That's why we mention golf (yes, even miniature golf) in the same breath as we tell of tagging crocodiles in the biosphere or visiting the deserted jungle cities of the Classic Maya culture. Excitement should be as much who you are as what you do. As you'll see, we're always on the lookout for unusual, non-touristy activities and sports, as well as exploring life off the beaten trail. So kick back and enjoy – you're going to love Mexico.

ON WATER

Swimming offers year-round fun, whether it's in the warm waters of the Caribbean or the languid hotel pools. Some beachfront hotels offer **parasailing**, an activity in which you are pulled by a motorboat above the sea or the lagoon attached to a parachute. If yours doesn't, inquire at Lorenzillo's Restaurant (☎ 98/83-30-07). Be aware that this is a dangerous sport and injuries are not unheard of. **Sailboarding**, or **windsurfing**, also has its fans here. At Playa Tortugas, Km 7 (distances are marked along the 27-Km Paseo Kukulcán in the hotel zone beginning in the downtown), there's the **International**

Windsurfer Sailing School (☎ 98/84-20-23) that features rental equipment and lessons. A local **National Windsurfing Tournament** (☎ 98/84-32-12) is held here every year. And Pedro Silvera organized an **International Windsurfing Tournament** in Progreso in May of 1997 that he hopes will become an annual stop on the world tour (☎ 99/44-35-37 or e-mail: pedros@sureste.com).

You can **sail** from any number of lagoon marinas. A Sunfish is ideal for the calm lagoon. **Fly-fishing** and **deep-sea fishing** lure many Cancún sportsmen. April through September draws the best varieties of fish to local waters, but the sport is good year-round. There's a **Cancún Billfish Tournament** from late April through June. Several marinas in Cancún and over on Isla Mujeres will arrange charters of four, six or eight hours. Charters include captain, first mate, gear, bait and beverages. And a boat.

MARINAS

Marina Aqua Rey, Km 10.5 Paseo Kukulkán, at Lorenzillo's Restaurant. They offer Jungle Tours and their own floating sports center as well as SubseaExplorer, a boat for underwater viewing (☎ 98/83-30-07).

Marina Aqua Tours, Km 6.25 by Fat Tuesdays Restaurant. Chartered fishing, waterskiing, snorkeling, jungle tours and lobster dinner cruises (☎ 98/83-04-00).

Royal Yacht Club, Km 16.5 by Captain's Cove Restaurant and Royal Mayan Hotel. Watersports and canoe rentals with showers and lockers (☎ 98/85-03-91).

Aqua Fun, Km 16.5 by the Omni and Royal Mayan Hotels. Canoes, sailing, snorkeling, diving, etc. (☎ 98/85-32-60).

Pelican Pier, Km 5.5, has an air-taxi and sportfishing (☎ 98/83-03-15).

Mundo Marina, Km 5.5, offers snorkeling and diving trips, fishing and a cruise.

Marina Playa Langosta, Playa Langosta (☎ 98/83-28-02) has trips and rentals.

Aqua World, Km 15.2 in front of the Melia Cancún Hotel. "Sub See Explorer" viewing ship and "Paradise Island," a private watersports island in the lagoon (☎ 98/85-22-88).

The **Jungle Tour** that you'll be offered everywhere is actually a guided foray. Boarding either a one- or two-person personal watercraft, such as a jet ski, or small speedboat, you'll head into the mangrove lagoon. This is less the tour of a jungle than a chance to zoom around and get wet. Some offer snorkel stops. **AquaWorld** is a big supplier of the jungle tour and it also offers underwater sightseeing tours in a nautical bus. **Nautibus** (☎ 98/83-35-52) does a similar underwater sightseeing adventure in a vessel they describe as a floating submarine. **Destination Atlantis** (☎ 98/83-30-21) shuttles you over to Isla Mujeres for their unique real submarine expeditions. **Dolphin Discovery** ships you over to La Isla to swim with dolphins (☎ 98/83-07-79). These tours and others are available from travel agents and can include **diving** and **snorkeling** – as close as Isla Mujeres or as far away as Isla Contoy. Snorkeling is best at Punta Nizuc, Punta Cancún and Playa Tortugas (watch the strong currents here). Also offshore at Chital, Cuevones and Manchones Reefs. American-owned **Blue Water Divers** (☎ 98/83-03-27), at Km 15.6 Paseo Kukulkán, take smaller groups for dive and snorkel adventures up and down the coast. **Scuba Cancún** (☎ 83-10-11) also trains novice divers. Local dive spots are **Chital**, north of Hotel Presidente, with shallow depths and clear visibility to 33 meters; **Cuevones Reef**, three km north of Punta Cancún, with a 45-meter visibility; and **Manchones Reef** off Isla Mujeres. **Playa Linda** is the headquarters of many of the specialty cruises, fishing and sightseeing boats.

You can catch any of many cruises to **Isla Mujeres** (from US $15 & up) from the hotel zone. A more adventuresome (and cheaper) way is to take the bus on Av. Tulum (north of Av. Uxmal) to Puerto Juárez and catch one of the speedy cruisers (15 minutes; US $3) or the slower people ferry (40 minutes; US $1).

Waterskiing is available with other watersports at **Club Lagoon** (☎ 98/83-11-11) and **Marina del Rey** (☎ 98/83-17-48).

Romantic evening **lobster dinner cruises** are popular. The *Cancún Queen* is a stern-wheel paddle steamer decorated in twinkly lights (☎ 98/85-22-88); the *Columbus* is a pirate galleon (☎ 98/83-14-88); and the *Excellence* is billed as the "Island Love Boat" (☎ 98/83-04-00). Less romantic but more exciting is the 17-acre, US $20 million **Wet n' Wild** amusement park with huge new water rides. It is south of the hotel zone, past Rio Nizuc (Km 25). The 1997 admission prices were US $21 adults, US $16 for children.

There are just too many suppliers of identical services in Cancún to list each one. Any travel agent or hotel can arrange these activities.

ON WHEELS

A smooth 14-km (8.7-mile) serpentine path for bicycling, inline skating, jogging and walking weaves among flowers, topiary bushes and trees along the hotel zone's Paseo Kukulcán from downtown to Punta Cancún. With so many young vacationers and hard bodies the path gets a workout, especially in the morning hours before the heat of the day. **Cancún Bicycle Club** has two locations: Plaza las Glorias at Km 3.5, Paseo Kukulcán; and the Radisson Sierra Plaza. Rental bikes (about US $6/hour) are also available at the big Xcaret terminal at Playa Caracol and numerous hotels. You can rent inline skates (about US $7/hour) from any of several kiosks along the pink brick path. Multi-hour rentals get a discount.

Go-kart racing is very popular. Cartwheel over to **Karting International Cancún**, open daily from 10 a.m. to 11 p.m., south of town. Some special vehicles reach the scary speeds of 80 mph on a competition standard track. Other karts putter along at 15 mph maximum. When we passed they were advertising free taxi rides from downtown (one-way).

ON FOOT

Golfers can enjoy the **Pok-Ta-Pok Club**, open 6 a.m.-6 p.m., along the lagoon at Km 7.5 (☎ 98/83-12-77). Designed by Robert Trent Jones, the 18-hole course incorporates Maya ruins and sand traps, restaurant, bar, pro shop, equipment rental, swimming pool, tennis courts and driving range. The **Melia Cancún** (☎ 98/85-11-60) offers an 18-hole, par 54 executive course and pro shop. The new **Caesar Park Cancún Beach and Golf Resort** (☎ 98/81-80-00) boasts its own championship 18-hole, par 72 course, designed around the Ruinas del Rey archeological site on the Nichupté Lagoon.

There's a **Mini Golf Palace** for the sacrilegious at the Cancún Palace, Km 14.5, featuring 36 holes of mini-golf around pyramids, waterfalls, a river and a lagoon. There's a **bowling** alley in Kukulkán Plaza, open from 10 a.m. to 1:30 a.m. (☎ 98/85-34-25).

Many hotels offer tennis courts for their guests as there are no public courts in Cancún. Either sneak on to one of the hotels or take a temporary membership at Pok-Ta-Pok Club, whose courts are well maintained.

Horseback riding is a popular pastime for visitors. The largest ranch, **Rancho Loma Bonita** (☎ 98/87-54-65), Km 49.5 on Highway 307, is opening a second location somewhat closer to Cancún. Rides on the American owners' 987 acres can be booked through travel agents, or you can save 10% by calling and arranging the trip yourself. **Rancho Grande**, Km 41.5 Hwy 307 near Puerto Morelos, features beach rides (☎ 98/87-54-65). **Rancho de Pancho Villa** (☎ 98/74-72-01) at Km 54 Hwy 307, near Playa del Carmen, is also owned by an American and offers less formal riding trips into the jungle. Owner Mark Meyers plans on cabaña rentals or camping that could include a half-day of horseback riding.

IN THE AIR

Non-US citizens can fly direct from Cancún to **Havana, Cuba** for one-night shopping sprees or longer vacations without having their passport stamped by Cuban officials (it's not legal for US citizens to go there). Contact any travel agency to find out about the pricey junkets. Although parasailing could almost apply here, **Pegaso Air Tours**, at Plaza Caracol, offers helicopter flights over the hotel zone, as well as the archeological sites of Tulum, Chichén Itzá and Cobá. **Trans Caribe** (☎ 98/87-15-99) offers a regular shuttle to Cozumel as well as island-hopping and sightseeing fly-overs in a twin-engine seaplane. Licensed, current pilots might have some luck renting general aviation planes from **Cancún Air** (☎ 98/86-01-83) at the airport.

Accommodations

When you compare hotel and restaurant prices in Cancún's hotel zone with those found in major North American metropolitan areas, you can see what a bargain Mexico is. Not because it's cheaper in Cancún – you'll pay about the same price as you would in New York – but when you walk out the door you're on a magnificent beach. And you're on vacation! That being said, there's no sense in paying more than you have to. Find a little freebie called the *Hotel Guide* (☎ 98/80-16-45) or the *Cancún Tips* magazine and look for some good discount coupons, including some for hotels. They're available at the airport in shops and booths. Be wary of the "free info" booths, where they'll offer you a free trip to Isla or something if you visit a time-share or similar property. Just get the "Tips" – free – and go.

If you're planning to stay only in Cancún's beachfront hotel zone, a good travel agent in your hometown should be able find several inexpensive package prices to fit your budget – ones that include air and hotel. Even adventure travelers can begin or end a Yucatán adventure in comfort. (See page 3 for price chart.) Here are a couple of our personal favorites in the hotel zone, two of which are "all-inclusive."

CANCUN'S HOTEL ZONE

Casa Turquesa (*Kukulkán Km 13.5,* ☎ *98/85-29-24 or 85-29-25, fax 98/85-29-22, 31 suites with air, big pool, cable TV, ensuite jacuzzi, 2 restaurants, tennis court, fitness center, safe, mini-bar, wet bar, massage, free in-room musical CDs and VCR movies*). Walk to your room along a warren of marble-floor hallways and sitting areas, past original works of art, and you may just run into Bruce Willis or Demi Moore. Or perhaps Sly Stallone or Reba McEntire. That's because the Casa's small number of opulent suites and its renowned restaurant – appropriately named Celebrity – attract notables (including the President of Mexico) who cherish their privacy and their comfort. It's a member of "Small Luxury Hotels of the World." Rooms are very large, with king-size beds, couch, cocktail table, dining table with chairs and private balcony or patio facing the beach, complete with a two-person jacuzzi and built-in day bed. The honeymoon suite sits high above the hotel with panoramic private balconies. Just below is the huge Presidential Suite; the palapa-covered mansion next door is the getaway of the President of Mexico. As long as you're "roughing it" in the hotel zone – why not go deluxe? **$$$$**

Hotel Flamingo (*Kukulkán Km 11, in US:* ☎ *800-544-3005, in Mexico: 98/98-83-1544, fax 98/98-83-1029, 220 rooms and jr. suites with air, 2 pools, balconies, safe deposit, wet bar*). The Flamingo is ideally located on a white Caribbean beach in the center of the *Zona Hoteles,* midway from the airport to the center of town, across from the Flamingo Plaza shopping mall. Its large rooms all have balconies; the odd-numbered rooms face the ocean. The rooms, beds and decor are attractive and comfortable. The hotel restaurant, La Frente, is open to the poolside with sliding glass windows overlooking the sea. The all-you-can-eat buffet is US $10 per person and offers a different theme every night: Yucatecan, Mexican, Italian, etc. Relax near the pool with an American masseuse who helps get the kinks out for about US $10. Across the street, the Flamingo Plaza is a good source of inexpensive hotel zone food. It has Sanborn's, Dunkin' Donuts, McDonald's and our Mexican food favorite, Checándole. **$$$**

Calinda Beach (*Kukulkán Km 8.5, in US:* ☎ *800-228-5151, in Mexico: 98/83-16-00, 470 rooms with air, telephones, pool, hot tub, restaurant, watersports, cable TV*). This Quality Hotel property, one of two in the hotel zone, is situated on one of the hotel zone's prettiest and best swimming beaches, adjacent to the inlet of the lagoon. The rooms all have balconies facing the soft surf. This was one of the rare hotels that offered a better deal from the United States on their 800 number than they did in person – more than $50 less per night less, including breakfast! Ask for their "Mexican Package." **$$-$$$**

Club Lagoon (*Kukulkán Km 5.8,* ☎ *98/83-11-11, fax 98/83-49-59, 89 rooms with air, 2 restaurants, nautical center, TV*). An all-inclusive resort facing the picturesque Laguna Nichupté, the rooms and two-level suites here are in white adobe-style buildings scattered around colorful garden-filled courtyards. Quiet and secluded, it's a taste of Mexico. $$$$

El Pueblito Beach Hotel (*Kukulkán Km 17.5,* ☎ *98/85-04-22, fax 98/85-07-31, 240 rooms with air, 3 restaurants, 5 pools, safe, TV, golf, tennis court*). A few all-inclusive hotels in the "zone" try to create their own Mexican atmosphere and El Pueblito – which means "small village" – does that very well. Twenty-one guest houses cluster around courtyards that are woven with greenery and flowers along the Caribbean. The rooms are large with simple furnishings that invoke an "Old Mexico" feeling. Small terraced pools cascade down to the seafront. $$$$

CREA Youth Hostel (*Kukulkán Km 3.2,* ☎ *98/83-13-37, pool, restaurant, beach*). The only "hotel" that qualifies as budget in the hotel zone is this youth hostel, which sleeps men and women in dormitories. Although it's a hostel, it sleeps up to 600 so it looks more like a fancy hotel from the outside. Tent camping spaces are available and sometimes they allow RVs. Look for the sign with its official name, "Villa Deportiva Juvenil." $

CANCUN CITY

The downtown area of Cancún provides the best opportunity for bargains in hotels and restaurants, but also for experience. Unfortunately, too many tourists believe the rumors – willingly retold by tour operators – about the dangers and rip-offs and all kinds of trouble outside of the protected cocoon of the hotel zone. It's not true. The crime rate is no more and probably less than that of many US cities . We've selected a series of hotels in safe areas of the downtown with reputations of customer satisfaction.

Budget Hotels

Novotel (*Av. Tulum,* ☎ *98/84-29-99, fax 98/84-31-62, 41 rooms with air or fans, pool, restaurant, TV*). Located near the circle of Av. Tulum and Uxmal, the modern Novotel is reminiscent of an old colonial building. There's heavy wood furniture in the sitting area and an indoor courtyard garden. The "superior" rooms are in this building and are so-called because they offer cable TV, air-conditioning and a tiny balcony. Out back, next to the tiny pool, there are two

Caribbean-style wooden buildings that house the "standard" rooms. Except for television and air-conditioning, these rooms are the same and are even slightly larger than the superiors. We think these newer, quieter rooms are the better buy. $

Hotel Handall (*Av. Tulum,* ☎ *98/84-11-22 or 84-14-12, fax 98/84-19-76, 50 rooms with air, TV, swimming pool, telephones*). This south-end-of-Tulum Avenue hotel has an Art Deco feel with very wide hallways and framed doorways leading to comfortable rooms. Each has both a queen and twin bed. Around back there's a small pool and tiled patio and the second floor boasts a solarium. Budget restaurant "Super Deli" will deliver to your room. $

Hotel Alux (*Av. Uxmal No. 21,* ☎ *98/84-66-13 or 84-05-56, 30 rooms with air or fans, TV, travel agency*). Close to buses and downtown attractions. Some rooms are a little dark but they're all quite clean and pleasing. And the price is right for well-furnished, agreeable bedrooms, but ask for one that doesn't face Av. Uxmal. $

Punta Allen Guest House (*Calle Punta Allen,* ☎ *98/84-02-25 or 84-10-01, 18 rooms with air*). The Punta Allen, an intimate, family-owned hotel, has a large salon for sitting and dining that was once the downstairs of this three-story former private home. Rooms facing the sidestreet have balconies and there's a secure locked entrance gate of wrought iron. The Punta Allen will appeal to travelers who appreciate their privacy and security, as well as a friendly atmosphere. Its low price, charm and location – on a quiet street only two blocks from downtown – make this colonial-styled gem a genuine best value. $

Maria de Lourdes Hotel (*Av. Yaxchilan,* ☎ *98/84-40-09, fax 98/84-12-42, 51 rooms with air, TV, phones, pool*). The Maria is a perennial good value in "close-to-it-all" downtown hotels. Pleasant and friendly, it has an outdoor patio, pool and small restaurant open Monday-Saturday, 7-11 for *desayuno* (breakfast) and 4-8 p.m. for *cena* (dinner). Each respectable-size room has two queen-size beds. $

Hotel Tulum (*Av. Tulum at the corner of Claveles,* ☎ *98/84-18-90, 25 rooms with air*). Not as nice or as fancy as the Antillano across the street (see listing below, under "Moderate Hotels"), but basic and affordable. Ask for a room near the back. $

Parador (*Av. Tulum No. 26,* ☎ *98/84-10-43 or 84-13-10, fax 98/84-97-12, 66 rooms with air, pool, TV, private parking*). Although the common areas of this well-known budget hotel were not clean when we visited, the rooms were. However, in the medium-size bedrooms hints of another light color peeked through the white paint on the walls making them appear blotchy. The hotel has a small, oddly shaped swimming pool and a children's wading pool in the back. Located right in the heart of the downtown. $

Hotel Coral (*Av. Sunyaxchen,* ☎ *98/84-20-97, 27 rooms with air or fans, pool*). Ask to see the room before checking in to be sure you're satisfied with this clean but very basic budget hotel. The accommodations are adequate, and it even has bedside table lamps (missing in some other higher-priced hotels). But the toilets lacked seats and several tiles were broken in the bathrooms. A good buy, but not as good as the Hacienda, across the street. **$**

Hotel Hacienda (*Av. Sunyaxchen,* ☎ *98/84-36-72, fax 98/84-12-08, 35 rooms with air, pool, restaurant, TV*). This family owned hotel has a small restaurant for breakfast and lunch next to its sparkling swimming pool in a quiet center courtyard. The rooms are relatively small but on a quiet street only two blocks from the downtown. Some rooms are higher priced because, according to the manager, the mattresses are newer and more comfortable and the TV is larger and comes with a remote control (but since the channels are all in Spanish, we're not sure it's worth the extra). Otherwise, the rooms are identical. Limited private parking in front. **$**

Hotel Colonial (*Tulepanes,* ☎ *98/84-15-35, fax 98/84-48-61, 46 rooms with air or fans*). Recently reconditioned, but the fresh paint did not cover blotchy walls. The rooms, surrounding a large and airy courtyard, boast new beds, tile floors and big bathrooms. **$**

Hotel Maria Isabel (*Palmera,* ☎ *& fax 98/84-90-15, 10 rooms with air, TV, overhead lights, 3 floors*). On a quiet sidestreet off of Av. Uxmal, the Maria Isabel is a small hotel popular with budget travelers. Smallish rooms have good clean bathrooms, with tiles in place. Not all toilets have seats, common to budget accommodations. **$**

Hotel Villa Rossana (*Av. Yaxchilan,* ☎ *98/84-19-43, 14 rooms with air or fans*). These economy-style rooms are on the second floor over some stores on Av. Yaxchilan. The rooms are in relatively good condition. Bathrooms are clean, but have broken tiles and not all rooms have toilet seats. The Pasteleria Italiana Café, downstairs, is a good place to have cappuccino and some fine pastries. **$**

Hotel Cotty (*Av. Uxmal No. 44,* ☎ *98/84-05-59, fax 98/84-13-19, 38 rooms with air*). One block from the bus terminal, this hotel is not as attractive as it once was, despite its low price. There are two beds per room, television and a secured parking area around back. Front lobby hosts the Shalom restaurant. **$**

Hotel Posada Lucy (*Calle Gladiolas No. 25,* ☎ *98/84-41-65, TV, 19 rooms with air, 1 with fan only – 5 have little kitchens*). The *posada* is a well-known stop among bargain travelers to Cancún. It has very attractive cool rooms, a little dark but comfortable. Getting a room with a kitchenette is worthwhile, especially if you're spending some time in town. There's a restaurant/bar next door, which becomes a church for two hours on Sunday mornings. **$**

Villa Maya Cancún (*Av. Uxmal No. 20 on the corner of Rubia,* ☎ *98/84-28-29, fax 98/84-17-62, 13 rooms with air, TV, pool*). Nestled on the corner of a dead-end street (Rubia) and across from the Howard Johnson, the Villa Maya is quiet and clean with comfortable rooms and a friendly staff. This is a good choice for an inexpensive stay in town without sacrificing comfort or cleanliness. Upstairs rooms are brighter. It has a helpful travel agency in the lobby. **$**

Hotel Canto (*Yaxchilán and Tanchate,* ☎ *& fax 98/84-12-67, 23 rooms with air, TV, telephone*). Small quiet rooms, some with tiny balconies and linoleum floors, mark this bargain hotel one block off the downtown area. There are no toilet seats in some bathrooms and the rooms have overhead lights instead of table lamps. But the rooms were clean and those on the third floor have attractive new wooden doors. **$**

Hotel Cancún Rosa (*Margaritas No. 2,* ☎ *98/84-06-23, fax 98/84-12-94, 33 rooms with air, TV, telephones, bedside lamps, attractive figure-eight swimming pool*). Stretched over sidewalk storefronts, including an aerobics and dance studio as well as their own little café/lunch-eonette called Bugambilias, the Rosa is an appealing family-owned hotel. Inside the café it's diner-like, but walk through into the enclosed courtyard garden for a pleasurable environment.

Ivy-covered walls and carts full of flowers enhance the quiet peace of their inexpensive eatery under the red umbrellas of the outdoor tables. The courtyard has a lovely garden with a trellis of bougain-villea and an abundance of portulacas and other flowers. The rooms are not too fancy but pleasant, with a homey, comfortable atmosphere. Room 20 has a sitting area and wet bar (tile counter and sink, but no fridge or stove) and two king-size beds. Room 12 has four beds. **$**

Mecoloco Trailer Park (*between Puerto Juárez and Punta Sam, showers, laundry and food store*). The Meco has full hook-ups for RV's or trailers and spaces to pitch a tent, most of them out in the open, but if you catch it right there are some shaded spots. The beach across the street isn't that great, but there is a very good one about 500 feet down the road. Close to both ferries to Isla Mujeres. Surprisingly good rates combined with regular, inexpensive bus service to downtown or the beaches make this a real bargain. **$**

Moderate Hotels

Hotel Antillano (*Av. Tulum and Claveles,* ☎ *98/84-15-32 or 84-11-32, fax 98/84-18-78, 48 rooms with air, TV, pool, telephones*). The hotel is as bright and fresh and spotlessly clean as it was the first time we stayed here many years ago. But the price has gone up to a point that makes it hard to call this a real bargain anymore – unless you compare it to the hotel zone prices. Still, it's an excellent choice in downtown for quality and a perennial favorite. The floors are all polished terra-cotta tile and the rooms are stucco-white with rosewood trim. In larger rooms the feeling is intimate, with curved walls and bathrooms and closets set back into niches. Smaller rooms are a little small. Free lockers are available to store your stuff while you wander the peninsula. $$

El Rey del Caribe (*Av. Uxmal near the corner of Nader,* ☎ *98/84-20-28, fax 98/84-98-57, 25 rooms with air, pool, jacuzzi, parking, TV, kitchenettes*). The Rey del Caribe is a white hacienda-styled building with a green central courtyard garden and red terra-cotta tile floors. Just off the busiest part of town, the Rey is the best value in moderate hotels. The rooms are clean and bright and have something of a colonial feel. They are modern and well equipped, with kitchenettes. A jacuzzi and tiny pool are nestled among the flowering plants. There are seven rooms around the back that don't face the street. Number 25 offers the best of both worlds with size and brightness. On the third floor in the front are two very appealing rooms – if you're not carrying a lot of luggage. One is a single and the other, #18, has a balcony with a good city view. $$

Suites Cancún (*Calle Alcatraces No. 32 opposite Palapas Park,* ☎ *98/84-23-01, fax 98/84-72-70, 13 suites with air, 30 suites with air or fans, pool, TV*). Suites and rooms in this hotel, tucked away in a quiet section of town, rent by the day, week or month. Each suite, facing a central outdoor courtyard, features tiled floors, small but pleasant bathrooms, open fully equipped kitchen area, dining and sitting sections, bedrooms with two twin and one king bed each and generous closets. Rooms are also modestly priced. Except for the high season of December and January, these suites are available by the month for about US $335, which is an outstanding value. Call early if you're thinking long term. $-$$

Backpacker Hotels

There are a few hotels in Cancún whose main claim to fame is their low price – even cheaper than the youth hostel. These three had acceptable standards of cleanliness (more or less), but we would *not* leave valuables in the rooms. This is not because of a specific incident, but simply because some of the doors could be easily forced. These places do attract young backpackers, especially

Europeans, so you can practice your German. All three are off the north end of Tulum.

Hotel Jerusalem (*Av. Tulum heading towards Puerto Juárez,* ☎ *98/84-43-33, fax 98/84-42-99, 18 rooms with fans*). On the edge of the downtown, the Jerusalem is a typical backpackers' hotel – spartan but clean. If you're a student on a very tight budget and can tolerate bare light bulbs, doors that don't secure well and an elevator that stops either higher or lower than the floor, depending on its mood, you could do worse. It's close to a McDonald's, a movie cinema and a *mercado*. On the sidestreet is a little lunch stand that offers a daily special for about $1.50.

Hotel Tropical Caribe (*Calle Cedro No. 30 around the corner on sidestreet next to the Jerusalem,* ☎ *98/84-14-42*). There's an old photo on the wall that shows the hotel when it was new. It would seem nothing has been done to it since. If you're a student with extremely low expectations you could suffer a night here because of its super-low rate.

Hotel San Carlos (*Calle Cedro next to the mercado off of Av. Tulum,* ☎ *98/84-06-02*). Windows are painted over here, which avoids the expense of curtains. Its clientele are mostly young Europeans spending one night – which is more than enough. Good bargains in the surrounding market.

Dining

Part of the secret of success in life is to eat what you like and let the food fight it out inside.
– Mark Twain, 1835-1910

 What's a vacation for if not to eat out? In Cancún, there's a whole range of choices for meals – Mexican, continental, Italian, Chinese, Japanese, seafood, fast food, BBQ. It's all there and in every price range. Naturally, the hotel zone's prices are higher, but so are the service and ambiance. See page 4 for price chart.

CANCUN HOTEL ZONE

La Dolce Vita (*Av. Kukulkán Km 14.6,* ☎ *98/84-13-84*). There is no argument that this is Cancún's best Italian restaurant. After years of luring customers downtown to its pretty garden setting, La Dolce now sits on the water's edge of the lagoon in the hotel zone. They retained the same attentive staff, and the superb regional cuisine comes at prices much lower than you might expect. One of the house specialties is beautifully presented lobster medallions and shrimp simmered in white wine and herbs over green tagliolini (about US $15).

The manager, Juan, has been with the restaurant for over 10 years and he stops and greets customers at every table. With terrace dining, soft lighting, romantic live music played by a Cuban horn player and luxurious table settings, La Dolce reeks of casual elegance. We never miss dinner here on a trip to Cancún. Reservations are suggested. $$$

Hacienda El Mortero (*Kukulkán Km 9.5, across from Dady Rock* ☎ *98/83-11-33*). The ambiance of El Mortero is one of the most intriguing in Cancún. Built in the style of its 18th-century namesake, the hacienda displays curved arches, hanging plants, soft lighting, adobe walls, Spanish tile and beveled glass windows.

The traditional menu features steak, prime rib, and authentic Mexican dishes with such touches as homemade tortillas and home-made sauces. The bar offers 15 types of tequila and there's a cocktail "on the house."

Mariachis play nightly at 7:30, 9 and 10 p.m. and a romantic guitar trio serenades on Saturday. Non-smoking section. A definite dining experience. Open from 6:30 to 11:30 p.m. $$$

Rio Nizuc (*south end of the Zona Hoteleria*). There's a small sign among the mangroves, easily missed, that announces the location of the Rio Nizuc restaurant. Fortunately, hardly any tourists find it, despite hundreds of them passing by on jet skis as they enter the Laguna Nichupté on a Jungle Tour. You can sit in the cool shade and watch them watch you with envy as you enjoy this very special seafood-only restaurant. To get here, pass the Club Med and turn left just over the bridge on the edge of the

Local families come for lunch
And a swim at Rio Nizuc

Hotel Zone. You can park your car in the dirt lot. Follow the path among the mangroves to this rustic, water's edge afternoon rendezvous restaurant. One of the dishes they're famous for is *Tikin-xic*, fresh fish cooked in Maya anchiote spice and limes. Absolutely delicious. Bring your swim suit and snorkel too. Have a beer or two and spend the day. Open for lunch 11 a.m.-5 p.m. **$$**

Sanborn's (*Mayfair and Flamingo Plazas*). See Hotel Flamingo's review, page 20. Great value in the hotel zone. **$$**

Ty-Coz (*on Kukulkán, angled across the street from El Presidente hotel*). With only three patio tables beneath umbrellas, this little place may not last in the "bigger-is-better" Cancún hotel zone. That would be a shame, because it serves deliciously strong cappuccino and fresh-brewed coffee and makes great sandwiches on crusty French bread. Daily specials. **$**

Checándole (*Flamingo Plaza*). A fast-food offshoot of a popular Mexican restaurant in Cancún City, the food here is tasty and well prepared. Hot spices are on the side. Specials often offer two-for-one beers. Right next to **Dunkin' Donuts,** which offers two donuts and a cup of coffee for one dollar. The Flamingo Plaza's cheap fast food eateries are the hotel zone's best kept secret. **$**

CANCUN CITY

The experience of eating downtown is very different than eating in the hotel zone, perhaps because the atmosphere is more authentically Mexican, or maybe because it's so much cheaper. Take a bus into town and look around. We reviewed a wide range of dining delights in our list.

Budget

Los Huaraches de Alcatraces (*Claveles No. 31, open Tuesday through Saturday, 7 a.m. to 10 p.m.*). Ever wonder where the locals eat in a resort town like Cancún? Many of them eat here, only one block off touristy Tulum Ave. Inexpensive food is offered à la carte cafeteria style in this clean walk-through restaurant. The name Huaraches (oua-RACHES) means "sandals" and the food item with the same name is a oval-shaped tortilla filled with refried beans (*frijoles*) that you can have topped with chicken, beef, more beans or anything that catches your fancy. It's an excellent value, with fairly generous servings. If you're not sure about the food the staff will patiently explain the dishes, even as the line builds in back of you. Evening meals are served tableside. **$**

Los Amigos Restaurant (*Av. Tulum*). Colorful painted ladder-back chairs fill the sidewalk under tables with umbrellas, next to several similar downtown restaurants. All Tulum Ave. restaurants have barkers to lure in customers with a free drink, and Los Amigos is no exception. If it sounds too good to be true – it isn't. For dinner they display plates of grilled steaks and fresh seafood that they guarantee will be just as appetizing and generous when served to you. We paid under $7 for a large filet mignon, potato, green salad, *and* a margarita. With prices like that it's hard to go back to the hotel zone and spend the same or more for a sandwich and soda. **$$**

Santa Maria (*Azucenas at Parque Palapas*). Between this charming dinner-only restaurant (5-11 p.m.) and the nearby La Habichuela, this corner of Palapas Park is a dining delight. The Santa Maria has a big menu of typical Mexican cuisine and the servings are both generous and tasty. **$-$$**

Gory Tacos (*Tulipanes No. 26*). Simple decor and cheap fast food make Gory a popular spot with young tourists and locals as well. The Mexican menu includes quesadillas, tortas and, of course, tacos. Or you can order complete meals of chicken, beef or fish that come with ample portions of side dishes. Daily specials. **$**

La Tabasqueña Restaurant (*in the mercado in the center of the triangle formed by Av. Uxmal and Tulum*). One of several outdoor eateries under a roof in the *mercado* of SM 23, this restaurant is spotlessly clean and inviting. The *mercado* is a good place to find low-priced bargains. La Tabasqueña serves a generous and delicious complete *comida corrida* (daily special) for about $3 US. Great prices and good food combine well here. **$**

La Antigua Heladeria (*Av. Alcatraces No. 32*). If you're hot and bothered shopping downtown, sneak over to this wonderful little ice cream parlor one block off Tulum for super smooth and delicious Italian-style ice cream. Stroll in Parque Palapas opposite or sit inside in the cool shade. **$**

La Cocina de Rosy (*Claveles, off Av. Tulum*). In a tiny sidestreet shopping center under a yellow tarp, this cute little lunch place offers a *comida corrida* for about $2 US. **$**

Chiffer's Restaurant (*Av. Tulum, next to San Francisco Asis supermarket*). In the middle of the shopping strip next to the San Francisco supermarket, this diner-like café offers a basic, reasonably priced Mexican menu. There's excellent air-conditioning when it's hot, but the bathrooms are in constant use by both clients and the general public. **$-$$**

Navajo's (*Calle Alcatraces on the south end of the Parque de las Palapas*). Bigger mixed juice drinks ($1 US for fresh squeezed) and a good selection of "health foods" distinguish Navajo's from the more famous "100% Natural" restaurant chain. Whole wheat tortillas and tasty preparations of "natural" chicken and beef are served with fresh vegetables. **$$**

Meson de Vecindario "La Baguette" (*corner of Av. Uxmal and Nader*). Open from 7 a.m. to midnight, this neat and tidy French sandwich shop, coffee shop and bakery combination has some of the best prices in Cancún – without sacrificing any atmosphere. Set back from the road under a palm tree wrapped in romantic twinkling white lights, its outdoor tables have green canvas market umbrellas. Inside, you can pick from their pastries, croissants and cakes, then order wine, cappuccino or espresso and sit at brightly hand-painted tables. Their delicious sandwiches come on crusty French bread that they bake themselves. If you're tired of Mexican food, try their lean corned beef and add some hot pickled peppers. *C'est magnifique!* **$**

Tlaquepaque Restaurant (*Av. Yaxchilán*). If traffic is not too busy, this is a pleasant place to sit and eat good Mexican food outdoors at one of their four tables set under a palapa roof. Inside is air-conditioned. Great little spot for breakfast or lunch. Next door to Perico's restaurant (see below). **$-$$**

El Café (*Av. Nader No. 5*). Only one block from crowded Av. Tulum, the local business people escape to this clean and cool outdoor café that serves up coffee or tea and fresh-baked *pan dulce* (sweet rolls) both mornings and afternoons. They offer a varied menu from breakfast through dinner under drooping *flamboyán* trees. Unusually fast service, good food and reasonable prices are why those in the know go here. **$-$$**

Sanborn's Café (*Av. Uxmal and Tulum across the street from the bus terminal*). Sanborn's is a chain of restaurants similar to Denny's, perhaps with a touch of pancake house thrown in. In fact, they serve breakfast 24 hours a day on linen tablecloths, with generous cups of good coffee and free refills. For lunch and dinner they feature Mexican cooking at reasonable prices. The waitresses dress in colorful long cotton skirts and give prompt attentive service. The restaurant also offers one of the few non-smoking areas. There's a dining area out on a homey front porch; inside it has a diner look, complete with lunch counter. Other locations are in the Mayfair and Flamingo Plazas in the *Zona Hoteles*. **$-$$**

Moderate

Perico's Restaurant (*Av. Yaxchilán*). Perico's continues to attract diners with an extensive menu of Mexican food, steaks and seafood. The colorful bar, with huge murals of Mexican heroes and American movie stars, also features saddles as its bar stools. There's always a party atmosphere here from 1 p.m. to closing at 1 a.m., with lots of music and an infectious conga line. This is one of the downtown's most festive places; happy hour here is just that. Worth a visit just to see. **$$**

Pizza Rolandi (*Av. Coba & Tulum*). Cool and private, this out-of-the way sister to the one on Isla Mujeres and Plaza Caracol in the hotel zone is less crowded but still features excellent brick oven pizza and Italian food in a romantic setting. **$$**

El Pescador (*Tulipanes*, ☎ 98/84-26-73). Since its opening in 1980, the Pescador has steadily competed with **Carrillo's Lobster House**, the other premier seafood restaurant downtown on Claveles. Carrillo's still serves great seafood, but the lines of customers at El Pescador crown the newcomer as champ. The open-air patio is particularly popular. **$$-$$$**

La Habichuela (*Av. Margarita No. 25*, ☎ 98/84-31-58). Capturing a quiet corner of old Yucatán with its lush garden and Maya artifacts, the *Habichuela* (Stringbean) is a legend among locals and select tourists. Since 1977, the Pezzotti family has run this almost secret seafood restaurant with a Caribbean flavor and fine cuts of meat.

Their specialty is *cocobichuela*, lobster and shrimp cooked in a mild curry sauce and served in a coconut shell with fruit (US $22). The romantic ambiance includes beautiful table settings of linen and crystal, soft lighting and outdoor dining to the gentle sound of a fountain. Not very easy to find, but worth the effort. Moderate to expensive. **$$$**

Leaving Town

 For **Isla Mujeres** take any bus marked "Puerto Juárez" or "Punta Sam" north on Av. Tulum from in front of the *Comercial Mexicana* supermarket. It's a short ride to Av. Lopez Portillo to the ferries. Driving from the hotel zone, turn right on Av. Bonampak and go straight. Failing that, take one of the cruises from Playa Linda.

If you're making the grand **circuit** (Cancún, Mérida, Campeche, Chetumal, Cancún), you can do so either clockwise or counterclockwise. Either way has its advantages. Not that ambitious? Then go for either a sea and sun trip along the southern leg or head west into Maya history and a colonial past. To go south for **Playa** or **Tulum** from the hotel zone, drive south on Paeso Kukulcán and take the marked exit over the bridge. This is Highway 307 South that goes all the way to Chetumal. As soon as you start on the road, you'll come to the military anti-drug checkpoint, where you'll probably be waved through. The highway is now a divided highway that replaces the old two-lane road, at least as far as the new construction has finished (about 96 km or 60 miles down when we were last on it). Traffic travels rather fast. To return to the **airport**, stay on Kukulcán over the 307 bridge and go straight. If you're downtown, go south on Av. Tulum – it turns into 307 South.

DISTANCES FROM CANCUN

Akumal	105 km/65 miles
Campeche	494 km/307 miles
Chemuyil	109 km/68 miles
Chetumal	379 km/236 miles
Chichén Itzá	192 km/119 miles
Cobá	96 km/60 miles
Cozumel	93 km/58 miles
Isla Mujeres	10 km/6 miles
Mérida	306 km/190 miles
Playa Del Carmen	68 km/42 miles
Paamul	92 km/57 miles
Progreso	341 km/212 miles
Puerto Aventuras	98 km/61 miles
Puerto Juárez	2 km/1.2 miles
Puerto Morelos	36 km/22 miles
Punta Sam	7 km/4 miles
Tulum	131 km/81 miles
Uxmal	382 km/237 miles
Valladolid	152 km/94 miles
Xcaret	72 km/45 miles
Xel-Há	122 km/76 miles

Heading **west** for the Yucatán offers a choice of two routes, both shown on maps as Highway 180. The first is the *Mérida Cuota*, the only road west made easy to find from Cancún. It's a toll road with very limited exits and two collection booths, one east of Valladolid and one west of Piste. Although it's relatively expensive (US $8 Cancún to Chichén Itzá, US $13 total Cancún to Mérida), the road is new and built to allow cars to zip along at a fast clip. If you're going from one place to another – such as Valladolid, Chichén Itzá, or Mérida – the Cuota's shortcut through the jungle makes life much easier. The Cuota is accessed from Highway 307 south. Simply follow the signs for Mérida and Valladolid.

The alternative is *Mérida Libre*, a two-lane route through the heart of Maya country. It offers the great advantage of being able to see the "real" Yucatán and we've had a special adventure of one sort or another every time we've been on it. The road is always interesting, wandering through villages passed by time, but it does require some patience. *Topes* (speed bumps) guard each village from speeding cars and they make for a slower journey. But there's more to life than driving fast, especially in the Yucatán. Handicrafts, gifts and bottles of honey are sold from private homes along the way.

*Maya children in front of white-washed stone walls,
which are often seen in small villages.*

To find *Mérida Libre* from downtown, take Av. Uxmal west for a few blocks and turn left at the Mérida sign on Av. Lopez Portillo, Route 180. From the hotel zone, if you're closer to town follow the directions above. Otherwise, head south on 307 (toward Playa/Tulum) and turn right at the big Pemex station on your right. Follow that to a left turn (Av. Lopez Portillo) marked for Mérida. That becomes Route 180 and you're on your way. See the chapter titled East - Red (*Lakin Chac*), in Yucatán state, for information on the route.

Not all those that wander are lost.

– J.R.R. Tolkien, *Fellowship of the Ring*

Isla Mujeres

*A woman is a citizen who works for Mexico. We must not
treat her differently from a man, except to honor her more.*

– Adolpho López Mateos, former President of Mexico

 If your fantasy is a vacation on a small peaceful island
where time passes at its own slow pace, then we have the
place for you. Eleven km (6.8 miles) off the Cancún
shoreline rests an island with a name right out of a 1950's
grade-B movie – the "Island of Women" – Isla Mujeres. It's close
enough to Cancún to provide easy access but far enough away to
offer a taste of real Mexico. The sandy slip of land – only 1½ km (one
mile) at its widest and eight km (five miles) end to end – is a
lower-priced, low-key alternative to the shopping-mall atmosphere
of Cancún itself. While many Cancún-based tourists take advantage
of the lower shopping prices by commuting from the mainland on
party boats, by the late afternoon they've upped anchor and the
island comes alive.

No bikini-clad Amazons here, the Spanish coined the name "Isla
Mujeres" after they found some stone idols of bare-breasted women,
believed to be *Ixchel*, goddess of fertility. If the conquistadors returned today, they could find live women with bare breasts on the
North Beach. The Maya temple-lighthouse on the rocky southeastern tip provided an important link in the chain of lookout signals
around the peninsula. Sadly, after a thousand years of guard duty,
the structure was reduced to rubble in 1988 by Hurricane Gilbert.
But there's still a working lighthouse here, and if the keeper is in a
good mood (and gets a big *propina*, or tip) he may let you go up to
the top. From the dramatic rock cliff headlands, early risers can
watch the sun come up over the Caribbean. You'll be standing on
one of Mexico's most easterly points – the place where the first warm
morning rays of sunlight strike the land – a special place to the Maya.

Washed by the Caribbean Sea on one side and cradled by the
turquoise Bahia de Mujeres on the other, Isla Mujeres is casual and
relaxed with a blended Mexican-Caribbean feel. Its only town is the
fishing village where the island's shops and low-rise hotels are
located in a basket weave of narrow streets of cobblestone and sand.
During the day those streets fill with daytrippers and shoppers, but
in the early morning and evening the local population comes out to
play – along with a sizable number of expatriate North Americans
and Europeans who run funky little cafés and trendy eateries. De-

spite the inevitable conversion from fishing to tourism as its main income, *la Isla* has managed to retain much of its native charm. A white and red lighthouse rises above the palms to welcome home fishermen and the island's clapboard and stucco houses – painted in whites and blues and pinks and turquoise – lean helter-skelter in an easy-going tropical attitude. It's a fantastic place to enjoy the sea, around which life on this ancient fishing island still revolves.

Orientation

GETTING AROUND: Our favorite method of arriving on Isla Mujeres is via the old "people" ferry (US $1), a rickety-looking but brightly painted wooden boat. *Beatriz Blanca* looks much like Humphrey Bogart's *African Queen*. Our shipmates, passengers too poor to pay the extra few pesos for the faster cruiser ferries that also serve the island, are good-natured and chat away in Spanish. On our last journey (40 minutes), a broad-faced Maya woman, dressed in a traditional *huipil* (a cotton dress embroidered around the collar and hem) held a live chicken that poked its head out from her shopping bag. It looked right at us, questioning our future enjoyment of chicken *fajitas*. Laden with a load of timber and cinderblock someone brought aboard as baggage, our little boat chugged across the strait while we acclimated ourselves to a slower lifestyle.

Yet even troglodytes like us see the advantage in the new high-speed boats that zip across the blue-green waters between Puerto Juárez and *la Isla* in only 15 minutes (about US $3) every half-hour or so. Unless you're patient or just lucky, chances are you'll take the faster boat, which departs more frequently from the same dock.

There is also an even larger car ferry that leaves and returns to Punta Sam, only a kilometer or two north of Puerto Juárez. There's no sense in taking a car over to the island unless you're living there. To get to either ferry from Cancún take cab or catch a bus marked "Puerto Juárez" from in front of the *Comercial Mexicana* supermarket (look for its Pelican logo) on Av. Tulum, north of the *glorieta* (circle) with Av. Uxmal.

When you arrive on Isla Mujeres you'll be docking at a wooden pier in a quaint harbor, home to fisherman, yachtsmen and pirates for generations. Pink colonial-style arches straddle the ends of narrow streets facing the waterfront. This is the north end of town, where all the shops, the best beaches and most of the hotels on the half-mile-wide island are situated. There's a taxi stand to the right of the pier, although most of the hotels are within walking distance.

People mill about the pier as each boat arrives, some selling handicrafts, offering rides, or just hanging out people-watching. On the street are some yellow tricycles (*triciclos*), large bicycles built with one wheel in back and a freight cage and/or seats over the two front wheels. They are common in the Yucatán and offer an interesting way to arrive at your island hotel – like Sydney Greenstreet in a rickshaw. Have them carry your luggage; the rates are inexpensive.

The preferred mode of island transportation is by foot; you can easily walk the entire downtown. The town's youth and energetic visitors can be found at the basketball court in the plaza near the end of the *malecón*, a red brick pedestrian walkway along the Caribbean, built after the havoc wrecked by Gilbert. The commercial heart of the city clusters in the north, but most residents live in the suburbs in the center of the island. To go somewhere on the south end, such as Garrafón or Maria's, take a cab. But to see the entire island with the wind in your hair and the sun on your back, rent a motor bike or a golf cart. Wave to the policeman directing non-existent traffic and head south for El Garrafón (the jug), a coral reef underwater National Park. The Caribbean island's southern end is less populated and its rolling hills are covered by scrub brush and punctuated by an occasional house.

Perhaps less thrilling or romantic transportation – but much cheaper – is a rented bicycle for exploring the mostly flat, lightly traveled streets. The main road follows the southern shoreline in a big loop past a Naval base, small airport, the pirate Mundaca's place, El Garrafón National Park, Ixchel lighthouse and then back along the rocky deserted Caribbean side. The road takes several sharp turns, and at one there's a soccer pitch of white limestone dirt rather than grass – kind of a soccer *Sacbé*. At Mundaca's house a road to Sac Bajo branches off along the peninsula between the *bahia* and the lagoon.

BEACHES: Calm water and gentle surf mark the idyllic western and northern beaches, while clashing Caribbean currents make swimming dangerous on the spectacular eastern shore. **Playa Cocoteros** or Playa del Norte (North Beach) is a pristine white sandy beach with a warm shallow surf. **Playa Lancheros** has a more secluded location toward the southern end near Garrafón, whose waters are good for beginning snorkelers. A tranquil beach across the street from the pirate Mundaca's hacienda is **Playa Paraiso**, complete with a good restaurant and palapa gift shops. Local families favor the beach near the dock downtown. All the major beaches have a beachchair and/or umbrella rental concession (starting at about US $5 per day). The best beach for young children is the inlet past the **Na Balam Hotel**, where the water is warm and shallow and there are no people, except for the ones who wander across the wooden bridge to the sand island of the now-defunct and deserted Presidente Hotel.

North Beach.

Practicalities

Tourist information is found on Av. Hidalgo No. 6 (☎ 987/7-03-16). Pick up a copy of the free *Islander* magazine in Cancún or at the info booths at the ferry docks and many stores and hotels in Isla Mujeres. It contains a wealth of information and a good map. It's edited by long-time resident Enriqueta M. de Avila (known as "Henrietta" to her fellow Americans).

If you're returning to Cancún airport from the island, the taxi fare (US $10) is posted outside the terminal at the taxi stand, along with the set prices to downtown or the hotel zone. Don't agree to a ride from the guys that hang out on the dock and offer a taxi. They count on your not knowing the posted fares.

Places for **changing money** (9 a.m. to 2:30 p.m., Monday through Friday) are Banco Serfin, Bancomer, an American Express office and

Banco Atlantico, all near the docks downtown. The **post office** is on Av. Guerrero at Lopez Mateos. Two **laundromats** compete in town, but there's no question that Wash Express is hands-down cheaper than the more established Tim Phó's, both on Av. Abasolo. Both do a good job washing and folding, but Tim charges double to separate whites and colors.

Police headquarters are near the basketball court in the main *zócalo* (☎ 987/7-00-82). There is a **decompression chamber** at the Hospital de la Armada on Medina (☎ 987/7-00-01). Several **doctors** on the island speak English: Dr. Antonio Torres Garcia (☎ 987/7-00-50) makes house calls and is available 24 hours for emergencies. He's located on Matamoros at the corner of Guerrero. Dr. Antonio Salas does general medicine and emergencies on Calle Hidalgo No. 8 (☎ 987/7-04-77), next to the **pharmacy**, Farmacia Lilly.

The **Cultural Center** on Av. Guerrero hosts frequent activities for children and also has a paperback library where you can trade English-language books from the open shelves.

EVENTS: Boating and **sailing regattas** are organized by the Club de Yates the last week of April or first week of May. For specific information, ☎ 987/7-01-73. The 12-day Isla Mujeres **International Music Festival** is the second weekend in October. There's a **fishing tournament** February through May, and the waters surrounding *la Isla* are good year-round for bonito, grouper, mackerel, kingfish and amberjack.

HEALTH CLUBS: Good living is good health. Discover **Isleños' Gym** on Av. Hidalgo, north end. After a hard work-out (without air-conditioning) *los Isleños* head for the showers – or in this case the beach, as the street-front gym has no running water.

Shopping

 The shops of *la Isla* offer better deals than those in the hotel zone and that's why boatloads of sunburned shoppers descend on the island daily. There are many to choose from, but noteworthy are the following:

Casa Isleño, a custom-painted T-shirt and shell shop run by Henrietta Morris de Avila on Guerrero across from el Cuba Ron Restaurant. **¡Qué Bárbara!** (How Barbara!) is a designer and manufacturer of comfortable custom tropical clothing, located on Matamoros No. 18 (☎ 987/7-07-05).

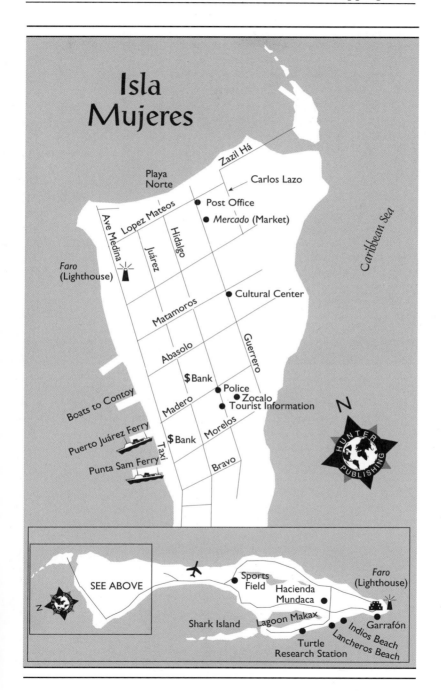

Van Cleef & Arpels jewelery is on Av. Morelos at Juárez. Another prominent jeweler is **Rachat & Rome** in the pink building on Av. Medina across from the ferry dock.

Paulita's, on Av. Morelos in front of the police station, will lure you in with their large collection of arts and crafts and wide variety of incredible collector's masks. Across the street is **Valentina Arte-sanias,** owned and operated by native islander Blanca Rosa Schmied de Ramos. On Juárez, the owner of **Artesanias Arco Iris,** Alejandro Trejo, comes from an area in central Mexico that is known for its hand-woven blankets. He features some unique weavings.

Artesanias El Nopal sells Mexican folk art and women's co-op crafts at the corner of Guerrero and Matamoros. **Boutique Elenita,** on Av. Hidalgo No. 13, has nice gifts and crafts but their ad in the *Islander* loses something in translation: "Wallets and Bags of Skin."

There are several **mini-supermarkets**, the largest of which, Benitos, also has a small inexpensive eating area on the *zócalo*. Others are **Capricornio** on Matamoros near Rueda Medina and **Ciro's** on Guerrero. Besides some trendy cafés that offer delicious baked goods, the island's only regular **bakery** is on Madero near the corner of Juárez.

Night Spots

 Isla Mujeres' nightlife pales in comparison to Cancún's, except when the whole island has a celebration. Then, it can be like Carnival in the streets. The **Casablanca Disco,** upstairs in a hurricane-damaged building, shakes the foundations every Friday and Saturday night with no cover charge. Otherwise it's bar action with dancing. **Las Palapas** on the north end beach kicks up some sand. You could also try **Buho's** at Cabañas Maria del Mar or the nearby **Zazil-Ha** bar at the Na-Balam Hotel. **Sunset Bar** and **Pinguino's** on Medina also have some action.

Adventures

I collect experiences the way others like to collect coins... "
– Michael McGuire, adventurer

 La Isla's laid-back attitude doesn't mean there isn't plenty to do, it just means you *can* do nothing at all. When you're ready to get up and go, read on.

ON WATER

How could you not go **swimming** on an island? Check out the beaches we listed above, but avoid the strong undertow on the eastern shore. We took Captain Ricardo Gaitán's six-hour cruise to the uninhabited **Isla Contoy** (US $50) for a day of nature hiking and birdwatching, plus snorkeling and beachcombing. His boat, the *Estrella del Norte*, a 36-foot motor sailboat, was the last one to be built on the island in 1968. The coral island is a bird sanctuary to 70 species, including some large nesting colonies. During the summer, female sea turtles lay their eggs along its sandy bays. After snorkeling on a colorful coral reef on the way over, we spent lots of our time beachcombing among the rock pools while the others sunbathed and swam. There's a small museum and a lookout tower to climb for a panoramic view. Gear and lunch are included – grilled grouper, deliciously spiced *à la Yucateca*, caught by the mate on the way over. Just in case you don't catch a fish, they bring one along. Buy your tickets at the *Cooperativa* (the shack along the waterfront, north of the ferry dock) or phone **el Capitan** at ☎ 987/7-04-34. You can take a fisherman's launch. They are faster, but can't beat the romance of a journey under a red sail in a wooden hull. Another trip offered by Capt. Gaitán is an exciting but rugged **explorer's adventure** to **Boca Iglesia**. The ghostly church (*iglesia*) is all that stands in a colony established by the earliest Spanish conquistadors in the mangrove jungle north of Contoy. It was wiped out in a massacre by the Maya in the early 1500s. You'll be walking in historic footsteps near Cabo Catoche, the first land fall of the Spanish in 1517, where there's also a little explored Maya ruin, **Ecab** (Gran Cairo).

Underwater **Destination Atlantis**, (☎ 98/83-30-21) out past Playa Lancheros, puts you in a real submarine for undersea viewing trips. Farther along is **El Garrafón National Undersea Park**, a great place for beginning snorkelers to float over a colorful reef teeming with fish. It also teems with daytrippers from Cancún, so time your visits for the early morning or late afternoons to avoid the crowds.

To go fishing or snorkeling is easy, just visit the *Cooperativa* and ask to be set up with a **qualified fisherman**. Captain Francisco Sosa and first mate Pedro Rodriquez run two of the smartest bigger boats for fishing charters, dive charters and snorkel runs. A two-hour snorkel trip costs about US $32 for two, or US $40 for four. They offer a three-hour fishing trip and one all-day, with guaranteed fish, for US $400. Get a group together and it's a good deal.

About 50 years ago Carlos Garcia, a young island lobster diver, discovered a deep-sea cave where some sharks went in, but didn't come out the other side. Curious, he entered the cave to find sharks

asleep in the current with their eyes wide open. Now known as the
"Cave of the Sleeping Sharks," dive shops, such as the one at **El
Garrafón** (☎ 987/7-0-572), **Bahia Dive Shop** (☎ 987/7-03-40) and
Buzos de Mexico (☎ 987/7-02-74) near the dock, will take certified
divers on this popular professional 65' scuba dive. The slumbering
sharks became world-famous when Jacques Cousteau and his crew
filmed them for one of his television specials.

Other snorkel and dive spots are the **Cuevones Reef** at 10.5 meters
(35 feet) deep and the **Manchones** and **Banderas Reefs**, coral reefs
one kilometer long by 700 meters wide, at a depth of about 10 meters.
A bronze cross weighing approx. one ton, 39 feet in height and 9.75
feet wide, was planted into the **Manchones Reef** between Isla Mujeres and the coastline in 1994. The *"Cruz de la Bahia"* is the island's
tribute to the men and women of the sea. Divers celebrate the
founding of Isla Mujeres in 1854 with a mass dive on August 17.
Snorkelers can float among the fish that swim around the lighthouse
at the entrance to the harbor.

ON WHEELS

To putter around town, rent a **golf cart** or **motorscooter**, but if there
are two of you make sure it's a two-person model. Of late, some
rental places are only offering single seaters and they're damn
uncomfortable for two. There are plenty of vendors to choose from,
the slightly cheaper ones are back away from the dock area. Try
Motorenta Kankin on Calle Abasolo, **Pepe's** on Hidalgo, **Ciro's** on
Guerrero or **Zorro's**, also on Guerrero.

Bicycles are for rent at several hotels. Zorro also offers them, but
the best on the island (mountain bikes) are at **KoKo Nuts** on Av.
Hidalgo. They run about US $10 per day, but bargain for longer term.

ON FOOT

The western shore north of Playa Paraiso is home to **Centro de
Investigaciones**, a turtle research station funded by the government
and private donations. This is a fascinating and popular educational
stop for some of the party boats from Cancún, who walk along the
beach to reach it. Isla Mujeres was an ancestral hatching ground for
giant sea turtles, who lumbered ashore from May through
September to lay their eggs in the silky sand. Many turtles were
captured by local fishermen and killed for their meat and shell; the
eggs were dug up for food. Finally, a concerned fisherman
convinced his brethren to spare the eggs. His efforts lead to the

founding of the research station where turtles are now bred for release. To educate and sensitize local school children, they participate in the annual releases. Take the guided tour. Recommended donation: US $1.

From the Garrafón Underwater Park it's a short walk up to Ixchel and the **rock headlands** of the island. Check out the spectacular dawn! At the other end, crowds gather for the sunset on the northern beach. The deserted Caribbean eastern shore makes a great walk for **beachcombers** into exploring rocky pools and washed up coral and shells. **Hoopsters** can join in pick-up basketball games at the Municipal Court in the main plaza (**volleyball** is also played here) and **soccer heads** can show off their skills at the sports field south of the airport.

Mundaca's Hacienda (see below) has some redundant cement paths that weave through his former gardens, but one of our favorite stops is the **cemetery** along the north beach on Av. Lopez Mateos. Mexicans build shrines to their dead and leave personal objects on them as a celebration of their life. We wept over a little girl's tiny pink slippers left on her grave. Find **Mundaca's grave marker** there too, complete with skull and crossbones. He died in Mérida and he's not supposed to be under there, but we searched unsuccessfully for his grave in the crowded Mérida cemetery. The caretaker had never heard of him.

Skull and crossbones decorate Mundaca's grave marker.

PIRATE'S TREASURE

"As you are, I was. As I am, you will be."
– words of encouragement carved on Mundaca's grave

Fermin Mundaca de Marechaja lived life as a pirate and slave trader, getting rich at the expense of others who paid with their lives for his greed. For many years he plied the seas from Africa to Cuba with human cargo destined to labor as slaves and die in the sugarcane fields. By 1860 the British Navy's campaign against slavery cramped his style, so he furled his sails and retired to the sheltered harbor of Isla Mujeres. Once there, he fell in love with an 18-year-old girl, famous on the island for her beauty, called *La Trigueña*, the "brunette." But the young girl rejected the former slaver. Determined to win her love, he built a whimsical hacienda surrounded by gardens filled with exotic plants, entered by arches carved with her name. But instead of changing her mind, *La Trigueña* married a young island fisherman whom she loved. She bore her husband child after child while Mundaca slowly went insane. He died in Mérida but the grave marker he had carved for himself is located in the island's sandy cemetery (approximately in the front center to the right of the gate). His ruined hacienda and former gardens – a tragic example of "love's labor lost" – makes an interesting short visit.

Accommodations

 La Isla's hotels run the gamut from budget to moderate and plain to fancy. Because of the laid-back lifestyle and proximity to the beach, staying anywhere on the island is a delight. We have always gloated in our ability to find good valued bargains here. The jewels of the island for most travelers are the moderately priced hotels on or near the beach. Some have impressive accommodations or locations even by Cancún resort standards, yet they would be termed "budget" if they were in the hotel zone. See page 3 for price chart.

Budget Hotels

Poc-Na (*Matamoros, ☎ 987/7-00-90, fax 987/7-00-59, 6 dorm rooms with fans, 1 exclusively for women*). Poc Na is the only "youth hostel" around. It's a great place to meet other people from around the world. In Mayan, the name means "destroyed house," but the hostel is actually in good shape and relatively clean. Sleeping is on bunk beds, dormitory style, although each bedroom has a bathroom and two smaller niches with a bunk bed in each. Or you can sleep cooler upstairs in hammocks, which are included in the price. Dormitories are co-ed except for one, which is exclusively for women. Camping or outdoor hammock sleeping is also available next to the communal dining/lounging room. Each space includes a wooden locker (locks may be rented or you can bring your own). Showers and bathrooms for the hammock swingers are co-ed and are located next to the lounge. The restaurant serves an inexpensive but limited menu from 7 a.m. to 10 p.m. There's a big, often-used message board.

Vistalmar (*Medina, ☎ 987/7-02-09, fax 987/7-00-96, 43 rooms with air or fans*). The best rooms – the three back apartments around a friendly little terrace – at this perennially popular place are next to impossible to get. They are rented long term during the winter. But the front rooms' balconies and the hotel roof are a favorite hang-out for regular guests to watch the beach-goers across the street or the crowd that comes off the ferry. Ideally located both downtown and near the waterfront, the rooms here are simple and clean. $

Hotel Carmelina (*Guerrero, ☎ 987/7-00-06, 20 rooms, most with fans*) is a favorite with very budget-minded travelers because each large room has two queen-size bed, one single bed, good-size closets and hot water. It's also clean. On the down side there are no dressers and the small bathrooms show some heavy wear. They rent bicycles, a good way to see the island. $

Caribe Maya (*Madero, ☎ 987/1-05-23, 25 rooms with air or fans*). The air-conditioned rooms here have two queen-size beds against a hardwood paneled wall. All the rooms are the same size, but those with fans have two twin beds and no fancy walls. They're all clean and neat, but there are no dressers and the closets are open. Directly across the street from La Casita, a popular inexpensive café. $

Hotel Isleño (*Guerrero and Madero, ☎ 987/7-03-02, 20 rooms with air, 12 rooms share bathrooms*). A basic and serviceable hotel, this is not a bad choice for bargain hunters and students. Twelve low-ceilinged rooms have two single beds in each and share several bathrooms. The baths have showers and two toilets each, with doors and shower curtains. Other rooms have private baths. There are also four mini-suites with two queen-size beds and one single, a sink, table and chairs. $

Las Palmas (*Guerrero across from the mercado, no phone, 14 rooms with fans*). This is a very basic hotel with two beds and a low ceiling in each room. It's nice and clean but an overhang above the windows makes the rooms feel a little dark. Upstairs rooms may be more appealing. Only a block from the north beach and across the street from the local *mercado* and several inexpensive luncheonettes. $

Xul-Ha (*Hidalgo, ☎ 987/7-00-75, 11 rooms with fans*). The common area of this plain-on-the-inside hotel leaves something to be desired, although the rooms were adequately clean. The owner was expanding when she ran out of money, so the hotel remains unfinished at 11 rooms. It's usually filled with European tourists. $

Hotel Gomar (*Medina, ☎ & fax 987/7-05-41, 16 rooms with air or fans*). Up a hallway behind a gift store is the surprising lobby of this modern hotel across the street from the ferry dock. There's a large wall mirror and plants and new overstuffed furniture that's tastefully color-coordinated. However, the bedrooms have rough cement walls that are impossible to keep clean of handprints and furniture marks. The bathrooms are new, large and well lit and the housekeeping seemed satisfactory. **$**

Marcianito (*Abasolo*, ☎ 987/7-01-11). This eight-room hotel is easy to miss because it's squeezed between two storefronts. Each freshly painted, average-size room comes with a fan, closet and one queen-size and one single mattress. The bathroom tiles are a bit worn but they, like the rooms, are clean. **$**

San Jorge (*Juárez, near the north beach, no phone*). A basic Mexican hotel, the San Jorge was recently painted on the outside and is well lit at night to help attract lodgers. Choose an upstairs room; the downstairs ones are dim. **$**

Maria José (*Madero near the ferry dock*, ☎ 987/7-02-44). Only the third floor has a view of the sea from the hallway, but the older rooms in this well-known budget hotel are medium in size, clean and simple. A friendly staff and a good location. The lobby offers local and long-distance phone calls. **$**

Hotel Osorio (*Juárez*, ☎ 987/7-02-94, *34 rooms with fans*). You can't miss the color scheme of cream walls and brick red trim on this venerable hotel that conveniently lines both sides of Avenida Juárez. The housekeeping was not especially good in the public areas and some of the rooms felt somewhat close inside, especially when the wooden window shutters were closed. Still, it remains popular in its price range. **$**

El Caracol (*Matamoros*, ☎ 987/7-01-50). They installed new box springs and mattresses in 1997 in this tidy hotel with ample size rooms, two of which have kitchens. Downstairs the six-table restaurant with the same name is open 8 a.m. until noon and 6 p.m. till 10 p.m. It features excellent breakfast prices and claims to serve the best coffee on the island. **$**

Janet McCammon, a delightfully deep-tanned woman, is one of the pirate island's secret treasures. She lives life to its fullest most of the year on Isla Mujeres, but when she gets bored she hops a cargo ship for exotic ports around the world. When she's in town she rents out small housekeeping studios on a good swimming beach just south of Playa Lancheros but before Atlantis, heading out toward Garrafón (*fax only 987/7-07-11*). The weekly rent averages only US $20 per day and an unbelievable US $900 for three months. **$**

Moderate Hotels

Casa Isleño II Apartments (*Guerrero*, ☎ & *fax 987/7-02-65*). These are owned by long-time *Isla* resident Henrietta Morris de Avila, who edits the *Islander* magazine, a free monthly publication that extols the virtues of life on the island. In her home, one street from the Caribbean, she has made small apartments with fans and complete kitchens that rent by the week or month. Very small and quiet, the rooms have a "built-above-the-garage-at-a-beach-house" feel to them. We found them homey and appealing. The *Islander* magazine is a must-have for any visit and is available at the ferry or in lots of places downtown. **$$**

Na Balam (*at the end of the north beach,* ☎ *987/7-02-79, fax 987/7-04-46, email: nabalam@cancun.rce.com.mx, 31 rooms with air, pool, dive shop, master suite with jacuzzi, restaurant and bar, optional meal plans*). All the attractive rooms here are luxurious – with terraces or balconies, large beds and baths and all decorated in Maya motif. The deluxe Na Balam has expanded in recent years to include new cabañas, a small pool and yoga meetings, which attract a gentle crowd of cosmic-conscious travelers. Peeking out from along the paths through carefully tended gardens, owner Judith Fernandez has situated some of the most artistic and creative pottery we've seen. Second-floor beachside rooms are vine covered and look over palm trees to the fine sand *playa*, where topless sunbathing is common. The happy hour's two-for-one drinks pack the beach bar with friendly folks who chat while the sun sets and the adjacent indoor-outdoor Zazil-Ha restaurant is one of the island's finest. **$$**

Roca Mar (*Bravo,* ☎ *& fax 987/7-01-01, pool and patio, 22 rooms with fans plus a suite*). Perched on the edge of the Caribbean where it meets the town center, the Roca Mar hotel is one of the island's oldest, but doesn't look it. Smallish rooms with two queen-size beds each and windows with thick wooden shutters have been remodeled; each has a spectacular ocean view from its balcony. The lone suite has two bedrooms (a single and a double) and a kitchenette so it's a good value for families. They offer "stay four nights, pay for three" – which means an eight-day stay gets two free nights, bringing the cost down to about US $45 per night. Perfect for roar-of-the-surf sleepers and those who love the sea. **$$**

Martita Apartments (*Bravo and Juárez, 5 apartments: 4 have 2 bedrooms*). Other long-time island residents, Arlene and her husband – who profess they're known on the island as "Mom" and "Pop" – manage this white apartment building near the town square. Arlene will rent the plain but large apartments by the day or week at a price she claims is as low or lower than many hotels. **$$**

Garrafón del Castilla (*next to Garrafón Park,* ☎ *& fax 987/7-00-19 or 7-05-08, 12 rooms with air or fans plus 2 bungalows*). Small but pleasant hotel rooms here look out to the bay from the steep bluff next to Garrafón Park. Each has a balcony, big closet, dresser with mirror, in-room refrigerator and a marble bathroom counter. You can negotiate rates if they're not full. Better yet, check out the bungalow rooms, which are separate from the newer hotel building – they're nearly as nice and also cheaper. **$$**

Francis Arlene (*Guerrero*, ☎ *& fax 987/7-03-10, 22 rooms with air or fans*). This soft peach-colored family-run establishment has guests who return each year for its homey atmosphere. It's no wonder: the beds are comfortable and the showers hot. Completely remodeled and redecorated within the last few years, all the rooms have small terraces or balconies, with limited views of the Caribbean, one block in from the sea. Three rooms have kitchenettes and a "suite" on the top floor has a king-size bed. A good value with high standards. **$$**

Perla del Caribe (*Madero*, ☎ *987/7-03-06, fax 987/7-00-11, 90 rooms, restaurant, pool, telephone, air*). In the middle of the *malecón*, this modern hotel faces the Caribbean. All rooms have terraces. **$$**

Cielito Lindo Apartments (*Av. Medina, 2 studio apartments with air or fans*) are worth a look. This three-night minimum apartment house is owned by a former New York advertising executive (she dropped out of the rat race after falling in love with the lifestyle of Isla Mujeres). Pull the bell cord behind the iron grate to gain access to the two second-floor studios. The rooms have cable TV, good closets, pretty tiles, tiny bathrooms and easily rearrangable furniture. The shared balcony faces the beach and *la Isla's* sunset. **$$**

Hotel Belmar (*Hidalgo*, ☎ *987/7-04-30, fax 987/7-04-29, 11 rooms with air, 1 suite with jacuzzi, TV, telephones*). You might think that a hotel over a busy restaurant right in the center of the shopping area would not be a pleasant stay. But the Belmar proves that wrong – it is directly above Pizza Rolandi, *la Isla's* most popular restaurant. We found the rooms very inviting: colonial-style with thick terra-cotta tile floors and white walls. Big closets with shelves were a plus, as were the king-size beds. Very classic Spanish feeling with all modern comforts and amenities. **$$**

Meson del Bucanero (*Hidalgo*, ☎ *987/2-02-10*). Upstairs from the popular restaurant of the same name – and across the street from the Belmar – this hotel is also clean and bright with 14 attractive small rooms with fans. When we were there they were completing an additional eight new rooms that will have air-conditioning, TV and fan. Colonial style, with stained glass windows in some of the bathrooms, the bedrooms are a soft cream color with natural wood trim. The bathrooms also boast rare full-size bathtubs and white tile floors. The restaurant serves very good food at moderate prices. Between it and the Pizza Rolandi across the street, this portion of Av. Hidalgo is tough to pass if you're hungry. **$$**

Casa Maya Guest House & Cabañas (*Punta Norte at Zazil-Ha*, ☎ *& fax 987/7-00-45, 12 rooms, including 8 in a palapa building*). Jose

Lima's guest house is nestled next to the north beach inlet, behind a dive shop near the larger Na Balam Hotel. There are signs around the island advertising a US $29 rate, but that's either low season or the daily rate for weekly stays. Still, the four rooms in the large beach house are attractive and well furnished. There's a communal kitchen and sitting room with a library, TV and videos. The eight rooms in the cabañas each have private baths and either two queen-size or one king-size bed in each. **$$**

Maria del Mar (*Lazo, ☎ 987/7-01-79 or 7-02-13, fax 987/7-02-13, 56 rooms with air or fans, pool, restaurant, bar*) is also on the north beach of the island. There are 18 newer rooms over the restaurant/bar which the hotel calls the "castle" and a main hotel building styled like a hacienda. Upstairs rooms with dressers, wardrobes and balconies are better than those on the ground floor. Near the ho-hum little pool there are 15 cabañas whose rooms are large (but low ceilinged) with big palapa-covered front terraces – great for shade when it's hot or to entertain on the odd rainy day. The hotel is stingy with their beach chairs, which can't leave a fenced-in area in front of the hotel. Otherwise it costs US $3 to rent one. **$$**

Posada del Mar (*Medina, ☎ 987/7-00-44, fax 987/7-02-66, 28 rooms and 15 bungalows, pool, restaurant, bar*). Across the street from the beach and close to all the shops and the ferry, the *posada* is a long-time favorite. It was one of the island's first hotels. Each room in the main building faces the shore and has a balcony and air-conditioning. Upstairs rooms are much better than those downstairs. After a recent cosmetic face-lift they raised prices, so it's not the same value it once was. Penguinos is the hotel's palapa-covered restaurant and bar. It got its name many years ago when a slightly inebriated customer happily remarked that his beer was "as cold as a penguin." Order a "penguin" today and you'll get an ice cold Superior beer. **$$**

Cristalmar (*Laguna Mar Macax, Sac Bajo, ☎ 987/7-03-90, fax 987/70-00-07, 38 suites with air and kitchenettes, very large pool, restaurant*). One of the few hotels on the slender slip of land between the lagoon and protected waters of the Bahia Mujeres – along a road populated with the private homes of wealthy North Americans – is the all-suite Cristalmar. Each large suite has a kitchenette, one or two bedrooms, dining room and sitting area. Inviting and pleasantly apportioned, the hotel is worth considering because of its lovely beach (right next to a sea turtle research area), large pool and the advantage of kitchenettes. It's under US $2 for a taxi ride into town, or even less to Garrafón. Offers full or partial meal plans. **$$-$$$**

Maria's Kankin (*next to Garrafón Park, ☎ 987/7-00-15, fax 987/7-03-95, 8 rooms with air, including 3 suites*). You can walk to Garrafón from Maria's, which was the "in-spot" for the jet set yachting crowd when

Cancún, whose lights are visible across the bay at night, was still a swamp. Nowadays, her palapa-covered French restaurant, down the flowered walk to the beach, is the most exclusive place to eat. The hotel rooms have high windows, which make them somewhat dark, and a decorative scheme heavy on bamboo for tropical ambiance. The best rooms are in the cabañas or the suite upstairs from the terrace restaurant. The excellent (but pricey) restaurant is open from 8 a.m. to 9 p.m. and serves huge drinks. This is a sentimental favorite, so even if we're not staying there, we often buy a Margarita or Mai Tai and swim all afternoon at their soft sand beach. The first time we stopped here it was quite intriguing to wonder what strange romantic tragedy, nearly 20 years before, brought a Frenchwoman to this tiny island so far from her home. For years we tried to catch a glimpse of the mysterious Maria. She had a long and hearty laugh at our vivid imaginations when we finally met and told her of our theories. Say hello if she's around when you're there – she's a character. $$-$$$

Dining

The tiny island has nowhere near the huge variety of restaurants that feed Cancún's appetite. But because there are fewer choices, that doesn't mean the dining here is of a lower quality; it's just lower priced. Naturally, fresh seafood is the specialty of most restaurants in the village, where residents have always been seafarers. Some island women joke that their sons could sail before they could walk. See page 4 for price chart.

Miramar (*next to the ferry dock*). This small and personal restaurant sits beneath a palapa roof, unchanged and undiscovered by the crowds of tourists that disembark on the nearby ferry and charter boats from Cancún. Open for breakfast through dinner with a complete menu that includes beef, chicken and pork as well as fresh fish, the Miramar is an idyllic spot to spend hours over a beer or a delicious meal while watching the local fishing launches bring in their catch. Close your eyes and listen to

A pelican awaits a snack.

the melodic sound of the fisherman talking or the hypnotic rhythm of boat owners who scrape barnacles from their beached boats with handfuls of sand. Sit and watch the daily pelican show as the fisherman throw scraps from their cleaned catch. If you have a room with a kitchenette, you can buy fish here as the boats come in. **$$**

Café Cito (*Matamoros*). The influx of residents who have chucked the rat race for the slow pace of the island has spawned many new restaurants that combine an artistic ambiance with creative cuisine. One of these surviving the test of time is Café Cito. A black and white cat purrs lazily on one of the open-shuttered, streetside windows, beckoning you into this neat breakfast and dinner café. Painted blue and white, it has a custom-made, stained glass wave separating the connected dining areas, and   there are beach scenes under each small, glass-topped table. The ice cream sundaes here are outrageous and, thankfully, this is also one of Mexico's rare no-smoking eateries. The owner, Sabrina, is into New Age soul searching. If you'd like, you can arrange to have a "reading." **$$**

La Casita Bakery and Restaurant (*Madero*). The continental breakfast here features a toasted loaf of their home-made bread (US $1.50) instead of sliced "Bimbo," the brand name of Mexican commercial white bread. La Casita is open for all three meals and they have good coffee (a bit overpriced at US $1.60). They have discovered the pleasures of soft lighting (you'd be surprised at the number of restaurants in Mexico that light their dining rooms with harsh fluorescents), which creates a romantic atmosphere at night. **$$**

Bistro Francais (*Matamoros*). Open from 8 a.m. till noon, then again from 6 to 10 p.m. for dinner, the Bistro is one of the island's larger charming storefront restaurants. It does a good business because of the reasonable prices, colorful ambiance – the menu is painted on the walls – and excellent presentation. The restaurant's rare-in-Mexico bottomless cup of coffee is delicious and refilled often. The French toast for breakfast is "oo-la-la" and includes a fresh fruit plate. With a friendly and relaxed atmosphere, it's also surprisingly economical. **$$**

Café El Nopalito is nearby at the corner of Matamoros and Guerrero. This breakfast and dinner (6 a.m. to 9 p.m.) health food restaurant is combined with a folk-art gift shop called El Nopal. Homemade breads, granola and good service makes this a popular spot to sit and chat. The gift store carries !Qué Bárbara! clothes – produced and designed by an American expatriate who lives on the island – and many local women's co-op crafts. **$$**

*People, like wines, have their moods and no restaurant
is suited to every mood and every occasion... There are
days when one does not feel like making love. There are days
when I don't like to shave and I have a favorite
restaurant for these non-shaving days,
which are not necessarily nonlove-making days.*

– David Schoebruen, *Esquire*, February 1961

Los Portales (*Juárez*). Brand new in 1997, this restaurant opens and closes like a yo-yo for breakfast, lunch and dinner. But the all-you-can-eat buffet lunch (12:30 - 2:30 p.m.) is worth sampling at about US $5. **$$**

Pizza Rolandi (*Hidalgo*). Across the street from Meson del Bucanero is Rolandi's, the island's most popular eatery. Its open dining porch extends out into the shopping avenue in front. Good-time atmosphere, it can be warm and inviting. Excellent brick oven pizza. See also the one in Cancún. **$$**

Martita's Restaurant and Bar (*Medina, across from the Punta Sam ferry dock*). A local watering hole for fisherman and islanders. Good prices make up for its plain atmosphere. **$$**

Cazuela M&J (*Bravo*). The Cazuela is a little treasure of a restaurant tucked into a corner behind the Roca Mar hotel with a great view of the pounding surf. Owners Marco and Julie named it after the popular egg dish they developed, cooked in a ceramic chafing dish called a *cazuela*. The dish comes with a variety of fillings and is a cross between an omelet and soufflé. The hand-colored menus reflect the care and consideration that makes the M&J popular with both expatriates and visitors. **$$**

Bar Fredy's (*Hidalgo*). Fred bought the old Mano de Dios restaurant – which was kind of a local bar but still one of our favorite cheap eateries on Isla Mujeres – and brightened it up both inside and out. With a new and improved menu, Fredy's is a bargain restaurant that offers good homemade Mexican cooking and fresh fish tastefully prepared. Next door to the Red Eye Café, it's also across the street from a Crystal stand that sells cold water, soda and beer. **$$**

KoKo Nuts (*Hidalgo*). A bar and restaurant that plays reggae and salsa music at night and during the day rents the best mountain bikes in town at US $10 per day or US $2 per hour (more than other retail places but the bikes are better). **$$**

Tonyno's (*Hidalgo*). Exposed brick walls covered by clay suns and moons and masks creates the atmosphere in this narrow storefront restaurant down the street from the fancier and pricier Pizza Rolandi's. Tonyno's offers delicious Italian food – such as a meat lasagna with a béchamel sauce – or wood-oven baked pizza at very reasonable prices. If you're enjoying the nightly live music you may be handed a bongo or tambourine and invited to join in. Free tequilas arrive at your table as they deliver your bill. **$-$$**

Red Eye Café (*Hidalgo; closed Tuesdays*). Beneath a large red awning, Inge and Gus Kasulke own this little corner breakfast and lunch café on a quiet sidestreet near the north beach. It's the first place open in the morning (6 a.m.), so it's often crowded with early birds. Lunch is traditional German food such as bratwurst, and there are daily specials, like fish, hamburgers, or roast turkey. Needless to say their home-baked breads and potato salad are excellent. **$**

Carmelita's (*Juárez, south*). Dining in this three-table restaurant is like dining in someone's home. That's because the Martinez family converted their living room into a dining area that serves evening meals. The ambiance is plain but the platters are generous and delicious and the least expensive on the island (under US $4) – so bring your friends. The best price for lobster in town. **$**

Loncheria El Poc Chuc (*Juárez*). Six tables rest against two long walls painted with primitive art murals in this narrow little restaurant. The Mexican menu offers some of the best prices in town from breakfast to dinner. Sandwiches come on toasted kaiser rolls. Try the "Torta Loca," or crazy sandwich, for about US $2. It's filled with chicken, ham, eggs, sausage, refried beans, salad – just about anything but the kitchen sink. **$**

Maria's Kan Kin. Beachfront French restaurant, see entry under hotels, above. **$$$**

Zazil-Ha (*at the Na-Balam hotel*). When islanders and tourists are up for a fancy night out with friends, an intimate dinner, or just a great meal, they often choose the Zazil-Ha. Actually three separate restaurant/bars, the outdoor/air-conditioned indoor restaurant "Zazil-Ha" has a superb atmosphere and gourmet cooking at relatively moderate prices. The Palapa restaurant and bar is open from 10 a.m. until 4 p.m. and serves light meals and snacks. The beachfront bar, packed with people to its palm-topped rafters around sunset, serves bar food and drinks all day. **$$-$$$**

The sky broke like an egg into full sunset and the water caught fire.

– *The Unspeakable Skipton*, Pamela H. Johnson, 1981

Isla Holbox

Isla Holbox (ol-bosh), like Cancún, isn't really an island, it's a sand-bar peninsula that forms a barrier between the mainland and the Caribbean well north of the Isla Contoy Bird Sanctuary. The city of Holbox is tiny a fishing community on the northernmost tip of the Yucatán Peninsula. The attraction of the area involves fishing, long deserted beaches and a remote untamed natural wilderness. Unfortunately for campers and explorers, the tip of Isla Holbox is aptly named Punta Mosquito. Biting bugs are a pain, except during dry season, when there is a steady breeze. Pack plenty of insect repellent. Beachcombers rejoice: the beaches here are packed with sea shells of incredible beauty.

Accommodations

Fish should smell like the tide.
Once they smell like fish, it's too late.

– Oscar Gizelt, food & beverage manager,
Delmonico's restaurant, NY

There are two hotels in the city. Both are clean and offer private bathrooms, screens and ceiling fans, but are otherwise modest. **Hotel Holbox** is near the pier and **Posada Amapola**, a pink house, is on the east side of the plaza. Restaurants in town serve – you guessed it – delicious fresh fish.

Events & Daytrips

Fiesta week, celebrating San Telmo, is April 6th through the 14th. You could visit Holbox in a day trip from the Cancún area. By boat, it's a long three hours from Isla Mujeres. By car, head west on Mérida Libre, Rt. 180, to Nuevo Xcan and turn right for **Chiquila**, a tiny fishing village with a twice-a-day ferry (8 a.m. & 2 p.m., more or less) that runs across the large lagoon out to Holbox. The are few facilities in Chiquila, so don't miss the ferry. Also, don't bother to take your car over. If you do miss the last ferry to Holbox, you can either hire someone with a launch or retreat back to **Kantunil Kin**, 44 km back south. Stay in the **Posada Letí** and, if you have time, explore the unexcavated Maya ruins nearby.

Cozumel

Not bound to swear allegiance to any master, wherever the wind takes me I travel as a visitor.

– Horace 65 - 8 B.C.

 The kaleidoscope of colors here is amazing. Sergeant major fish striped in bright yellow and black. Parrot fish shine as if under a dayglow lamp. French grunts with blue-green shimmering stripes dart among white angelfish as the two schools mingle to avoid the human swimmers ogling them. The garlands of reef around Cozumel were discovered many years ago by divers and snorkelers who flocked here for the indescribable beauty of life undersea and a visibility reaching 250 feet. Later, cruise ships began an annual migration like huge pregnant white ducks to the docks of Cozumel. Now both the reefs and the seafront downtown become crowded with divers and cruise passengers making the most of their time here.

Positioned somewhere between the resort atmosphere of Cancún and the laissez-faire attitude of Isla Mujeres, Cozumel casts a magical spell over anyone who sets foot on shore. The island somehow manages to absorb a daily dose of tourists and still maintain a charm all its own. Only about 5% developed, beyond the tourist mecca are spectacular natural wonders and a relaxed lifestyle.

The ancient Mayan called the island *Ah-Cuzamil-Peten*, "Place of Swallows," and it was an important pilgrimage for Maya women to the temple honoring Ixchel, goddess of fertility and the moon. It was here that Spanish warrior, Hernan Cortéz, landed in 1518 in an expedition that would develop into the conquest of the continent. He found friendly natives – and so do tourists who disembark nearly 500 years later.

Cozumel became a port of call for Caribbean cruise ships after Jacques Cousteau dove its amazing reefs in the 1950s. Now, an average of 600 cruise ships visit the island annually. It's also a favorite hop-over for tourists from Cancún. After diseases brought by Europeans decimated the Maya population, Cozumel was virtually abandoned except by pirates, such as Jean Lafitte, who used its shelter of as a base to attack cargo ships. Refugees from the Caste War repopulated the island in the 1800s.

You can "do" Cozumel in a day or spend a month and still not "do" everything. The reasons for the island's popularity are obvious: sparkling emerald waters that hold a coral coat of many colors and a population of warm and friendly *Cozumeleños* make the island a natural place to be.

Orientation

 GETTING AROUND: San Miguel (population 60,000) is the only city on Mexico's largest island at 47 km (28 miles) long and 15 km (11 miles) wide. With a maximum elevation of 45 feet, the island sits 18 km (11 miles) offshore from Playa del Carmen. Two ferry services – a car ferry from Puerto Morelos and a people ferry from Playa del Carmen – serve Cozumel from the Yucatán mainland. The ferry service from Playa (US $7) changes schedule as often as we change underwear so check at one of the ticket booths. San Miguel also has an international airport with some direct flights landing from the States and numerous 15-minute connecting flights from Cancún (call Aerocozumel, ☎ 98/84-20-00).

The scrub brush jungle covers the northern half of the island, which is virtually uninhabited. The southern portions, the interior and the entire windward east coast also have few inhabitants. A road loops the entire southern part along the sea, then cuts back into town, dividing the island in half, while a coastal road follows the northern shore to its end. The concentration of population in San Miguel makes for some interesting expeditions and explorations far from the madding crowd.

The **Chankanaab National Park**, south of town, may have some crowds but is a great place to snorkel, sun and see a botanical garden. The western shore beaches – both north and south of the main pier – are very beautiful. The northern section is mostly hotels and private homes of the wealthy; to the south are the "public" beaches.

Besides taxis (a good choice when going direct from one place to another), three types of personal transportation are available: **motorbikes, bicycles** and **cars** – especially four-wheel-drives. Many major hotels rent motorbikes or cars and every street corner downtown near the dock has men hawking rentals. Cozumel's excellent roads combined with long stretches of wilderness make a motorbike ideal – and they even have automatic shifts. The prices on vehicles are pretty much the same between individual renters, especially near the dock, but you could try going direct to some of the shops in town or waiting until the ferry is empty and the crowd disbursed before negotiating. It's illegal to ride without a helmet and a rental may *not* come with insurance, so check first.

If you are already a crowd, or want to really see every detail of Cozumel's wilderness, try getting a good deal on a Jeep. Only a **four-wheel-drive** vehicle can handle the arduous northeast coast road (in the dry season only) to El Real ruin, a minor Maya ruin overlooking a good snorkeling spot. Farther along is the dramatic picturesque Punta Molas lighthouse warning ships of the reefs – then you have to turn around and bounce back. Take note, Jeeps carrying more than five people are subject to a moving violation ticket and impound of the car. The rest of Cozumel has excellent roads and enough to see and do to keep occupied, even if it's nothing more than floating around in the warm Caribbean waters.

If you're staying in town, a bicycle is handy on the more lightly traveled sidestreets. For longer hauls down to southern beaches or to do the island "loop" you'd have to be very fit. Bikes are rented at several of the car rental agencies.

RENTALS
(a partial list)
M=motorcycles/B=bikes/J=jeeps/C=cars

Aguila Jeep & Moto Calle 11 # 101	☎ 987/2-07-29	M/B/J/C
Budget Jeep & Auto Av. 5 x Calle 2	☎ 987/2-09-03	J/C
Masha 5ta Av. x 3 Sur	☎ 987/2-10-96	M/B
Popoy 3 Sur #3	☎ 987/2-10-96	M/B
Avis airport	☎ 987/2-00-99	C
Rentador Cozumel 10 Av. x Calle	☎ 987/2-11-20	1 M/B
Less Pay Hotel Barracuda	☎ 987/2-47-44	J/C
Auto Rent La Ceiba Hotel	☎ 987/2-08-44	J/C

The streets in Cozumel make it easy to know where you are... once you get used to them. **Av. Rafael Melgar** is the main road running along the western waterfront. Roads running north and south, parallel to the water, are *avenidas* and those running perpendicular to the sea, east and west, are *calles*. The sole exception to this is **Av. Benito Juárez**, which cuts San Miguel and the island into northern and southern halves and should be a "*calle*," but is not. The streets north of Juárez are marked "*norte*" and have even numbers (i.e. 2, 4, 6, etc.). All the *calles* south of Juárez are "*sur*" and are given odd numbers (3, 5, 7...). Vehicles traveling north and south are *supposed* to have the right of way, while those traveling east and west are required to stop on every corner. Drive carefully and look before you go.

Parking can sometimes be scare in town so be careful of NO PARKING zones. Your car or *moto* could be towed or the license plate removed so that you pay a fine at the rental agency.

Practicalities

The **police** are reached at ☎ 987/2-00-92 in the Palacio Municipal on Calle 11 Sur. For English service, ☎ 987/2-04-09 and ask for James Garcia. The **post office** is on Av. Rafael Melgar at Calle 7 Sur. **Tourism information** can be obtained at the Plaza del Sol building facing the central square (☎ 987/2-09-72) or at the *Consejo de Promocion Turistica* on Av. Rafael Melgar at Calle 11 Sur (☎ 987/2-43-79), open weekdays only 8-1 and 4-7. The **American Express** representative is at the Fiesta Cozumel, Av. Melgar No. 27 (☎ 987/2-08-31).

A **bookstore** with English-language titles is the Agencia de Publicaciones Gracia on the east side of the plaza. **Laundromat Margarita** is on Av. 20, near Calle 3 Sur. Phone home from the **Calling Station** on Av. Melgar at Calle 3 Sur, open till at least 10 p.m. daily. English-language **A.A.** group meetings are held Sunday, Monday, Wednesday and Friday at 6 p.m. on the corner of Av. 5 and Calle 7 Sur (☎ 987/2-10-07). There's no **consulate** on Cozumel, but if you've got troubles (and who hasn't?) contact the Cancún office (see Cancún chapter for details).

There are several **pharmacies** in town, including one on the plaza, another at the *zócalo* near the Hotel Lopez and a 24-hour one at the Medical Center on Av. 20 Norte No. 425 (☎ 987/2-29-29). There's a tourist **Medical Service**, open 24 hours, on Av. 50 between Calles 11

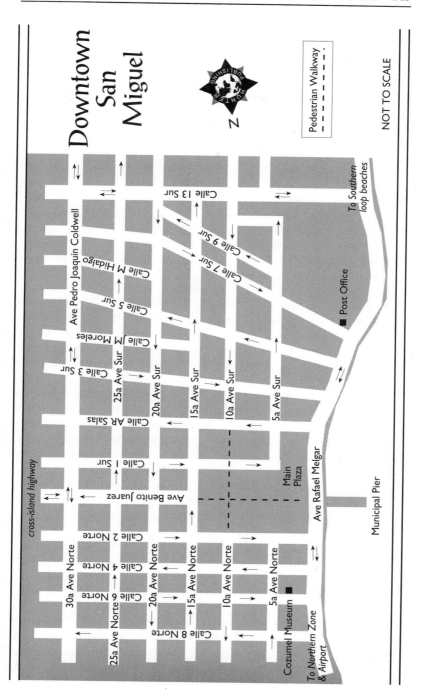

Downtown San Miguel

N

HUNTER PUBLISHING

Pedestrian Walkway

NOT TO SCALE

To Southern loop beaches

Calle 13 Sur

Calle 9 Sur

Calle 7 Sur

Ave Pedro Joaquín Coldwell

Calle M Hidalgo

Calle 5 Sur

Calle JM Moreles

Post Office

25a Ave Sur

20a Ave Sur

15a Ave Sur

10a Ave Sur

5a Ave Sur

Calle 3 Sur

Calle AR Salas

Calle 1 Sur

cross-island highway

Ave Benito Juarez

Main Plaza

Ave Rafael Melgar

Municipal Pier

30a Ave Norte

25a Ave Norte

Calle 2 Norte

Calle 4 Norte

Calle 6 Norte

Calle 8 Norte

20a Ave Norte

15a Ave Norte

10a Ave Norte

5a Ave Norte

Cozumel Museum

To Northern Zone & Airport

and 13 Sur (☎ 987/2-09-12). Call an **ambulance** at ☎ 987/2-06-39. There are also several English-speaking **doctors** on the island. Try Dr. Lewis on Av. 50 (☎ 987/2-16-16). A diver's **compression chamber** is on Calle 5 Sur off Melgar, ☎ 987/2-23-87. There are several banks around to change money (usually mornings).

EVENTS: Carnival, the Sunday before Ash Wednesday, is a festive holiday with masquerades and dances. A free open-air **concert** is held every Sunday from 7-10 p.m. in the main square.

BEACHES: The **windward eastern beaches** are rocky, dramatic, impressive, gorgeous and – with a few exceptions – are too rough and dangerous for swimming. These are best suited to beachcombing and shell collecting. The **leeward western beaches** feature picture-book white sand, gentle lapping waves, warm emerald green water and a series of vibrant living reefs. Good swimming, snorkeling and diving.

Following the leeward loop about nine km (5.5 miles) south of town brings you to **Chankanaab National Park**, a lagoon and an over-400-species botanical garden along the shoreline (admission US $7). The lagoon used to be connected to the sea through underground passages (now collapsed) and it created a living aquarium of over 60 different aquatic species. A research project precludes going into the lagoon now but swimming and snorkeling on the seashore is still sensational. The fish in the Caribbean hang out waiting for food scraps, the snorkeling is wonderful. It's also a marvelous place to relax in the sun or shade in picnic areas. Swimming beaches, restaurants, a museum, plus snorkel and dive areas with rental and lessons are available. Fills up with cruisers midday.

The beach just before Chankanaab is **Playa Corona**, with a fresh fish and Mexican food restaurant and snorkel rental. **Playa San Francisco**, the beach south of Chankanaab, is very popular with cruise tourists who stop for lunch and a swim. It's one of the best beaches in Cozumel. At **Playa Sol** there are gift shacks, a little zoo and a wide swimming beach with recreations of Maya idols sunken in the sea for snorkelers. The large palapa restaurant is slightly more reasonable than the one at San Francisco, but this is also a cruise-ship tourist magnet. **Playa del Cedral** is opposite the turn for the small **El Cedral** ruins (small). It's a public park with a tiny seafood restaurant (see below). **Playa Palancar** is opposite the famous reef of the same name. It features a restaurant and good swimming.

After a long ride through the jungle bush you come to the **Paradise Café**, a reggae bar along the rough windward side. A right leads to secluded beaches of **Punta Celerain Lighthouse**, reached by four-

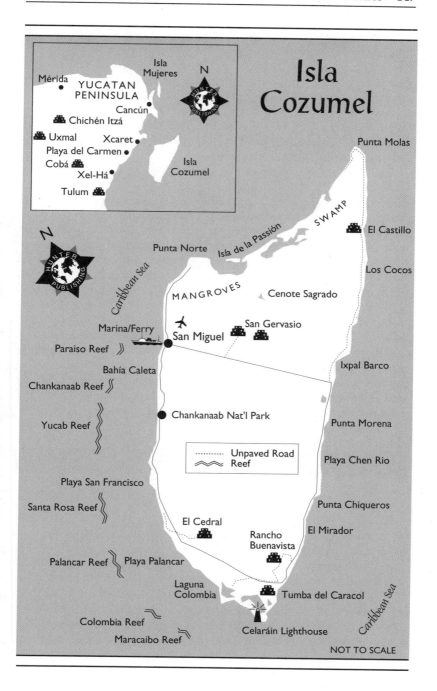

Isla
Cozumel

Punta Molas

El Castillo

Los Cocos

Isla de la Passión

SWAMP

Punta Norte

Cenote Sagrado

MANGROVES

Ixpal Barco

Punta Morena

Playa Chen Rio

Punta Chiqueros

El Mirador

Tumba del Caracol

YUCATAN PENINSULA inset:
Mérida
YUCATAN PENINSULA
Isla Mujeres
Cancún
Chichén Itzá
Uxmal   Xcaret
Playa del Carmen
Cobá
Xel-Há
Tulum
Isla Cozumel

Caribbean Sea

Marina/Ferry
San Miguel
San Gervasio
Paraiso Reef
Bahía Caleta
Chankanaab Reef
Yucab Reef
Chankanaab Nat'l Park

---------- Unpaved Road
〰〰 Reef

Playa San Francisco
Santa Rosa Reef

El Cedral
Rancho Buenavista

Palancar Reef   Playa Palancar
Laguna Colombia
Colombia Reef
Maracaibo Reef   Celaráin Lighthouse

Caribbean Sea

NOT TO SCALE

wheel-drive along a four-km (2.5-mile) dirt road. On Sundays the lighthouse keepers sell fried fish and soft drinks. A nearby lagoon contains alligators so don't swim there. Soldiers from a beach post guard the beaches during turtle egg-laying season in a conservation effort. The Late Postclassic Maya ruins at the southernmost tip, **El Caracol**, while small, are quite charming. Embedded with rows of conch shells that call in the wind, the diminutive building is one-of-a-kind in Maya architecture. Heading north from the Paradise again is a blowhole in the rock, a great place to get wet and a fun photo op.

Farther north is **El Mirador** snack bar, a tiny place with outdoor tables among the dunes. Sometimes there's a guy with a huge iguana who hopes to get a US $1 tip for photos. As you drive the road there are plenty of herons, pelicans and iguanas to be seen in the wild. Pretty **Playa Bonita** can be camped on and the **Chen Rio beach**, with its little seafood restaurant, is shielded by rock formations that break up the waves and form a cove. It's excellent for swimming and snorkeling and a peaceful place to hang a hammock. The paved road north ends in the center of the east coast, so to continue on to Puntas Molas requires a four-wheel-drive and stamina. Turn left on the paved road to return to San Miguel, past the San Gervasio ruins. The beaches north of the pier on the leeward side are also sublime, especially around Playa Azul, but there's less access to them because of all the private homes. The strange unfinished lighthouse-looking structure near the marina is part of a mansion, connected with the main house by a tunnel under the road. Rumor has it the eccentric owner killed his family and himself there.

Adventures

"There is a third dimension to traveling, the longing
for what is beyond."

– The Silk Road, Jan Myrdal

 It's a no-brainer to guess that adventure activities on Cozumel center around the water. If you're an experienced diver with PADI certification, there is no end to the number of dive trip operators to the 11 big dive spots offshore, which include a sunken airplane near the La Ceiba Hotel. Snorkelers can find paradise at Chankanaab National Park or La Ceiba and El Presidente hotels (where you can snorkel without staying there). Hikers and bikers might also like to go to the main Maya ruins, **San Gervasio**. The trails between the sites follow the ancient *sacbeob* (plural of *sacbé*) and the shade of trees gives it a natural ambiance. As much fun to walk around as it is to see the ruins.

The **Cozumel Museum** opened in 1987 in an airy building along the seafront, 2½ blocks north of the main plaza. It presents local archeological history in four *salas*, exhibition halls, on two floors. The well-arranged museum is open 10 a.m. to 6 or 7 p.m. weekdays and 1 to 6 p.m. on Saturdays. No flash photograhy is permitted.

There are several **horseback riding** ranches offering guided trips into the bush. Our favorite was the one at the very end of the north coast road along the western shore, after the last of the condos and hotels. Rides into the undeveloped jungle, and along the beach and lagoons are available; this stable is less expensive than those near the southern hotels. We skipped the *caballero's* offer of a visit to his ranch to see a caged lion and concentrated on looking for wildlife in the wild.

Accommodations

 The areas north and south of the town of San Miguel house the more expensive but generally gorgeous beachfront hotels. If you're on a budget, don't despair – the island is small enough that everywhere is close to the beach. Staying in one of the downtown hotels is a good way to save money, but we've also found some excellent values beachside too. There's a central phone number that will make reservations at many of the island's hotels, ☎ 800/327-2254. See page 3 for price chart.

Budget

Hotel Del Centro (*Av. Juárez and 25th Av. Norte,* ☎ *987/2-54-71, fax 987/2-02-99, TV, air, attractive courtyard and pool, friendly staff*). This is a new "old-fashioned" downtown hotel on a busy corner, not close to the beach. Inside it's attractively adorned with a colorful mural. Each door lintel of the guest rooms is also hand-painted. They plan to open a small restaurant, and room prices will include breakfast. The lone suite is a one-bedroom plus a pull-out sofa bed in the sitting area. Ask for rooms that face the courtyard in the back. An excellent value. $

Hotel Flores (*Calle Rosado Salas No. 72,* ☎ *987/2-14-29, fax 987/2-24-75, 33 rooms with fans or air*). Situated above dive shops and car rental places, the Flores is an exceptionally clean and economical place to stay in the downtown center. Half a block east of the waterfront, up the street from Pepe's Grill. **$**

Maya Cozumel (*Calle 5 Sur,* ☎ *987/2-07-81, 38 rooms with air, small pool, telephones*). Neat and attractive, this pleasant hotel's lovely gardens, rooms and lobby are filled with Maya statues, paintings and artifacts. Definitely worth checking out. We find it to be a comfortable, popular place to stay. **$**

Hotel Flamingo (*Calle 6 Norte,* ☎ *987/2-12-64, 22 rooms with fan*). Relatively modern, the Flamingo is a three-story budget hotel with aspirations of luxury. Bright-white tile floors and street-view balconies in the larger second- and third-floor rooms enhance the value. Often considered as offering the most for the money in the downtown. **$**

Hotel Pepita (*Av. 15 corner of Calle 1 Sur,* ☎ *987/2-00-98, fax 987/2-02-01, 30 rooms with fan or air*). Located in a tranquil area of San Miguel, the Pepita is a economical little hotel with a narrow courtyard garden. Some rooms have refrigerators, two double beds, tiled baths and screened windows. **$**

Paraiso Caribe (*Av. 15 North between 12th and 10th,* ☎ *& fax 987/2-07-40, 36 rooms, pool, fans*). When we were here the large open courtyard was suffering from overgrown grass and the big pool was "being cleaned." The atmosphere is definitely "Mexican motel" with a woman hanging laundry off the palapa bar, which opens only to serve parties. Overhead lights aside, this is a very inexpensive two-story hotel in a quiet semi-rural section of town. **$**

Tamarindo B&B (*Calle 4 between 20th & 25th,* ☎ *& fax 987/2-36-14, 5 rooms, security safe*). Native Frenchwoman and former language teacher Elaine Godement met her husband, Mexican architect Jorge Ruiz Esparza, in San Francisco before settling in Cozumel and opening this magnificent but hard to find bed & breakfast. Two bright and airy upstairs rooms are in the white stucco main building. These inviting rooms have French doors, narrow balconies, a circular staircase to a little patio, hidden skylights in the bathrooms and Elaine's continental decorating touch. Two brand new attractive rooms with air-conditioning and kitchenettes are located in a separate stucco building at the back of the fruit-tree garden. Then there's one palapa Maya hut, with a private bath, also in the garden. The separate palapa room is the best value at the same price as the upstairs rooms. With a shared kitchen off the upstairs patio and a generous European-style breakfast included in the price, the Tamarindo is worth   finding. Child care and French-lessons are also available, so indulge. **$-$$**

Moderate

B & B Caribo (*Av. Juárez,* ☎ *in US: 800-830-5558 or in Mexico: 987/2-31-95, 10 rooms with air, including 3 kitchenette suites*). The American owners of this bed & breakfast know what pleases *norteamericanos* – pleasant, spotlessly clean rooms and a welcoming, very American atmosphere. There's a shady screened-in porch and cable TV in the communal sitting room and dining area. A former doctor's residence, it's no surprise that his bedroom at the back of the first floor is the best. In addition to two beds, each guest room has a hammock and hooks for those who want to try the Yucatecan sleeping style. The plain white doors upstairs are being replaced by solid mahogany doors hand carved with images of Maya gods and symbols. Innkeepers Harold Mondol and Cindy Cooper found a Maya artisan near Uxmal who is carving each door panel individually. Check with them for upcoming special week-long events – such as painting, learning to dive, dream analysis, even a clown school – led by educators or other expert guests. Weekly and monthly rates. A meatless breakfast is included. Mention ecology and Harold will invite you to the roof to see his home-made solar works. **$$**

Hotel Barracuda (*Av. Melgar,* ☎ *987/2-00-02, fax 987/2-12-43, 51 rooms with private terraces*). This is an old favorite of scuba divers who flock to the island for the incredible dives available in the surrounding waters. Despite an energetic clientele, the rooms themselves are somewhat tired. **$$**

Suites Elizabeth (*Calle Rosado Salas No. 44,* ☎ *987/2-03-30, fax 987/2-07-81, 19 rooms with air, TV*). Dated furnishings don't detract from the convenience of this functional accommodation only a hundred feet or so from the downtown waterfront. The large upstairs balconies don't offer much of a view, but if they did, you'd pay more. Comfortable and clean. **$$**

Safari Inn (*Av. Melgar south of the ferry dock,* ☎ *987/2-01-01, fax 987/2-06-61, 12 rooms with air*). Facing the busy street that runs along the sea, this second- and third-floor hotel is a downtown divers' favorite. The attraction is the excellent dive shop downstairs and very large rooms with built-in couches. If you're on the island to dive, ask about their package deals. **$$**

Club Del Sol (*Southern Coastal Road Km 6.8,* ☎ *987/2-37-77, 41 rooms with air*). The Club Del Sol – not nearly as pretentious as its name – is painted a deep sunflower gold. It sits across the street from tiny beach that rents scuba and snorkel gear. Each room in the two-story building that runs back from the road has a table with two chairs and faces a pretty garden. Some rooms are available with kitchenettes ($7 US extra) that include fridge, stove, pots and plates. Some rooms are occasionally plagued by a slight mildew smell. Aside from that, this is an excellent value for so close to the beach. **$$**

Caribe Hotel (*Calle 2 between 15th & 20th,* ☎ *987/2-02-25, fax 987/2-19-13, pool, 14 rooms with fan*). This 1992 pink motel has a small L-shaped pool. Medium-sized rooms center around a pretty garden and are painted bright Caribbean blue, which makes them slightly dark with the door closed, but they're very clean and appealing. **$$**

Luxury

Sol Cabañas Del Caribe (*Northern Coast Rd Km 5.1,* ☎ *2-01-61, fax 987/2-15-99, 40 rooms plus 8 beachfront cabañas*). This attractive luxury hotel is made much more so at the low-season price (September through mid-December, under $90.) Excellent beach. **$$$**

Playa Azul Hotel (*Northern Coast Rd Km 4,* ☎ *987/2-01-99, fax 987/2-01-10, balconies, restaurant/bar, safety deposit box, telephone*). There's an idyllic beach here and a helpful divemaster, Thierry. With spacious rooms, the hotel has an intimate feeling. Negotiate rates if not full. Overly friendly staff. **$$$**

La Ceiba (*Coastal Rd South, near the Cruise ship dock,* ☎ *in US: 800-877-4383, in Mexico: 987/2-08-44, fax 987/2-00-65, big pool, jacuzzi, tennis, gym, sauna, restaurant and bar, 113 rooms with air*). La Ceiba, named for a type of tree indigenous to the Yucatán and sacred to the Maya, is a resort hotel very popular with divers. There's a small beach – with optional topless sunbathing – within sight of the giant cruise ships anchored offshore. Just off the wooden pier, a large Convair 40-passenger plane was sunk in the crystal-clear water for a disaster movie by a Mexican film company. Now it's a frequent dive and snorkel spot that you can swim to even if you're not staying here. Del Mar aquatic shop on the beach runs frequent trips to the wreck and the reefs and the hotel offers dive packages. **$$$**

Presidente Inter-Continental (*Southern Coast Rd Km 6.5,* ☎ *in US: 800-447-6147 or in Mexico: 987/2-03-22, fax 987/2-13-60, pool with jacuzzi, 2 tennis courts, scuba and snorkel rental, 2 restaurants and bar, 253 rooms and suites with air, cable TV, telephones*). We can't think of a hotel in the Yucatán we enjoyed more than the fabulous El Presidente. Yes, it's expensive, but its location on 100 acres along the crescent-shaped beach is absolutely perfect for swimming and snorkeling. Schools of colorful fish provide great photo ops. With gardens everywhere, the most expensive rooms (other than suites) are beachfront. We loved ours, a superior (#2125), whose patio – surrounded by a flowering hibiscus hedge – faced the beach and the sunset. If you can, spend the extra $50 to get a superior. **$$$$**

Dining

Virtually everything on an island costs more than it does on the mainland. Even fish – go figure. But there are still plenty of places where you can get a good bargain meal. If you're broke, the absolute cheapest places to eat are the *loncherias* near the *mercado* and the central plaza. We've also listed some sit-down restaurants. See page 4 for price chart.

Alfalfa's Restaurant (*Calle 1 just west of pedestrian mall*). Clean and neat with large windows, this vegetarian and health food restaurant (with a/c) has a reputation for tasty veggie food and reasonable prices. $

El Moro (*75 Bis Norte #124 between Calle 2 & 4*, ☎ 987/2-30-29, *closed Thursday*). Most tourists find this place difficult to locate. Get a cab or go west on Av. Juárez to the large new Pemex station on the left. Make a left just before it, then take the first right and the first left onto a bumpy dirt street. This is a very popular place with diners in the know. El Moro, or the Moor, offers an extensive menu (in both English and Spanish) of regional dishes and fresh seafood. Once you try the food here, you'll wonder why you bothered to eat anywhere else on the island. Giant drinks, excellent food. It's an unbeatable value. $

Comida Casera Toñita (*Calle Rosado Salas between 10 and 15 Norte, closed Sundays*) is great for low-priced *comida corrida*. It's a former living room in a private home that's been converted into a fairly nice dining area. Outstanding Yucatecan dishes. Daily specials. $

Jeanie's Waffle Houses (*oceanfront in Hotel Vista del Mar & the Days Inn on Calle 11 Sur, breakfast and lunch only in the Days Inn, till 10 p.m. in the Vista*). Relax your "going native" facade and chow down on what you haven't had for awhile – feel-good food such as hotcakes and ice cream. Besides waffles and crêpes, the dinners feature excellent steak and regional dishes. Try a big home-style breakfast for dinner. $-$$

Playa Paso del Cedral (*on the southern beach opposite the turn for the Cedral Maya ruins*). This little palapa restaurant with a sand floor and plastic tables serves fresh seafood. Fishermen pull their boats up in front to unload. It's set in a public park with palm trees and a white sand beach perfect for swimming/snorkeling. You can spend an entire afternoon here watching the dive boats or practicing your Spanish with the agreeable staff. This is one of the most "primitive" in a series of intriguing beachfront restaurants that attract day-trippers and cruise ship crowds for long pleasurable lunches. $$

La Choza (*Calle Rosado Salas at Av. 10 Sur*). La Choza has a big palapa roof over its dining area with large, open windows. It has reputation is for the best *comida tipica*, typical Yucatecan-Mexican food on the island. We can't argue; our pork stew and beefsteak in pepper sauce was well prepared and quite tasty. $$

Casa Denis (*Calle 1 Sur*). The yellow wooden house on the right as you walk up Calle Uno is Casa Denis. A few tables are set out front in the pedestrians-only street. There are two small dining parlors inside and some more tables in the shady back garden patio. It offers tasty light or full Mexican home-style meals. $$

Las Palmeras (*at the ferry pier*). Certainly not the cheapest nor even the best restaurant on Cozumel, this cool and breezy palm-planted open-air corner spot is nevertheless very tempting. Its decor is appealing, it's right at the ferry dock and the food smells good. We find it hard to pass by without at least a look at their menu. Sea breezes and oversized awnings keep it cool. Best time is off hours and the best seats are those that allow gawking at the crowds. $$

Morgan's (*Av. Juárez on the north side of the plaza, live music in the evening*). There's enough polished wood in this Caribbean-style restaurant to make a pirate ship. The distinguished building, with a large wrap-around dining porch, is the harbor's former customs house. Its international and seafood menu, impeccable service and nautical ambiance make it a place for a refined night out or a celebratory lunch after striking shopping bargains in the *mercado*. $$-$$$

Café del Puerto (*Av. Melgar near the ferry pier, 987/2-03-16*). Despite the name "Café," this is a strictly upscale, dinner-only establishment with a commendable international cuisine. The steaks here are as tender as they get and the preparation and presentation top notch. Two levels up a spiral staircase is a good view of the harbor activity at sunset. It's a growing competitor for the well-heeled cruise ship crowd at the better known Pepe's Grill down the street. $$$

Los Almendros (*Calle 2 North No. 101*). Cozumel hosts the newest branch (1998) of the Yucatecan restaurant chain that had its beginnings in the market town of Ticul in the 1960s. The chef created a dish called Poc Chuc, thin fillets of pork marinated in sour orange and grilled with onions, which has now become synonymous with Yucatecan cuisine. Dining is on checked cotton tablecloths with attractive china. There is seating on a pretty garden terrace as well as the pleasant indoor dining rooms. Traditional Yucatecan cooking, Los Almendros specialty, is less spicy than what you may know as Mexican. Very high standards. We love the Maya anchiote paste that gives the regional food its distinctive flavor. $$-$$$

Panchos Backyard (*corner of Av. Melgar and Calle 8, behind Los Cinco Soles mall*). In the rear of Los Cinco Soles, Cozumel's most famous shopping store, hides this lovely courtyard restaurant under colonial arches and loads of greenery. In the early 1900s the building was a warehouse that stored dried resin from the zaptote tree. In 1960, it became a hotel. In 1990, after four years of extensive renovation, it opened as a large store, art gallery, and restaurant. The charming atmosphere is matched by delicious food – generous servings of Mexican and seafood, cappuccino and expresso coffees, and "awesome margaritas." The custom hand-painted dinnerware and hand-blown glassware (certified lead-free) are sold in the store. You can also buy metal works from Jalisco, enameled painted animals, table-cloths, onyx and silver jewelry, embroidered clothing, paper mâché fruit, high quality reproductions of Maya artifacts, and gift items from all over Mexico. The store is kind enough to supply public restrooms, thank you! **$$-$$$**

Turquoise Coast Of Quintana Roo

Good travel books are novels at heart.
– Jonathan Raban, author

 Known as the "Turquoise Coast" because of its brilliant blue Caribbean Sea colors and fine white sand, the coastline south from Cancún rates among the world's best beaches. The craggy limestone shoreline is speckled with stunning mixes of long stretches of sugar-white, palm-fringed beaches, secret grottos, tropical coves, Maya ruins and deep clear cenotes.

Puerto Morelos

Puerto Morelos is the embarkation point for the car ferry to Cozumel island. The town suffered a fair amount of damage from Hurricane Gilbert in 1988 but has since rebuilt. Visitors who stay are more likely to be here for a month than a week. The beaches are fine and the town is very low-key, a little like the older suburban development that it is. Fortunately, the high-volume building and tourism frenzy bypassed this location for Playa del Carmen and resorts south. It offers a good quiet vacation only 30 minutes south of Cancún. Two major attractions nearby are **Croco Cun crocodile farm** preserve and the **Jardín Botánico**, a botanical garden featuring identification signs in

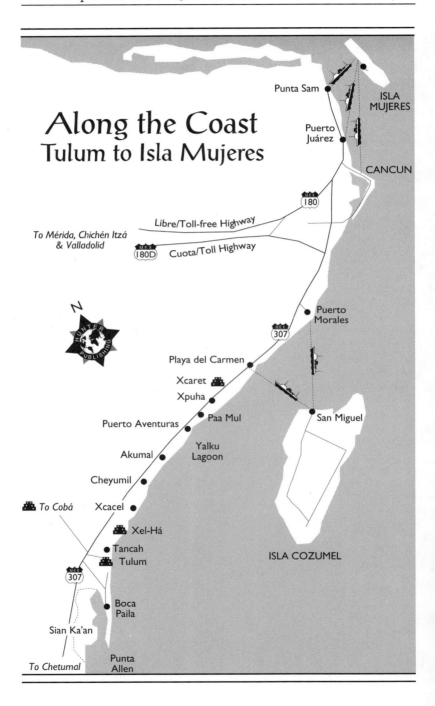

Along the Coast
Tulum to Isla Mujeres

Punta Sam

ISLA MUJERES

Puerto Juárez

CANCUN

MEX 180

Libre/Toll-free Highway

To Mérida, Chichén Itzá & Valladolid

MEX 180D   Cuota/Toll Highway

N
HUNTER PUBLISHING

Puerto Morales

MEX 307

Playa del Carmen

Xcaret

Xpuha

Puerto Aventuras

Paa Mul

San Miguel

Akumal

Yalku Lagoon

Cheyumil

To Cobá   Xcacel

Xel-Há

Tancah
Tulum

ISLA COZUMEL

MEX 307

Boca Paila

Sian Ka'an

To Chetumal

Punta Allen

English and Spanish, an epiphyte and orchid area, and a recreation of a *chiclero* camp. Chicle, the sap from the native *chicozapote* tree, provided the original base for chewing gum. Quintana Roo saw a boom then bust in chicle in the 1920s. You might see trees along the roadway with crisscrossing marks, as if a strangler vine once wrapped the trunk. These are marks of chicle tapping.

Orientation

There's a mini-bus every two hours between Cancún and Puerto Morelos that departs from the Cancún bus terminal. To get to the **car ferry to Cozumel** (it's not really worth taking your car there – US $45 plus US $7 per person on a three- to four-hour trip) turn right as you enter town; it's one kilometer or less down the road.

Adventures

Two adventure providers are **Wet Set Water Adventures**, ☎ 98/71-01-98, a dive and snorkel shop run by gringo Paul Hensley, located across the street from Los Pelicanos restaurant. Opposite is the **Secret Reef Eco Center**, set in a small booth on the ocean side of the square. It offers deep-sea fishing, diving and snorkeling. ☎ 98/71-02-44. **Sea kayak** and **mountain bike** rentals are available at Rancho Libertad Hotel.

Accommodations

The development rush ignored the little port town of Puerto Morelos. Consequently, it attracts laid-back tourists who stay longer, often in rooms with kitchenettes. Puerto Morelos' great appeal – besides its wonderful beach – is that it's quiet, both day and night. See page 3 for price chart.

Budget Hotels

Posada Amor (*one block in from the beach,* ☎ *in Canada and the US: 819-562-7556, or in Mexico: 987/1-00-33, fax 987/1-01-78, 16 rooms with* *fans but only 8 have private bathrooms, travel agency across the street, restaurant).* This eclectic jumble of rustic bungalow cabañas became known as "House of Love" after two children in the Fernandez family – who own and manage the hotel – married Canadian guests they had met there. The hotel's "typical" Maya accommodations run from modern plain to rustic primitive. The Robinson Crusoe adventure atmosphere and the friendly Fernandez family make this a popular stay, but check the rooms to make sure this is your kind of quarters. Definitely not for everyone. Mosquito repellent required. See the restaurant of the same name, below. **$**

Motel Eden (*Av. Andres Quintana Roo, no phone, reservations at the owner's house:* ☎ *987/1-00-15, 19 rooms with fans, kitchenettes*). With its back to the mangrove savanna and three blocks from the beach, the Eden is the best bargain in town. The two stories of white cement contain rooms that are almost suite-like. The kitchen and dining areas are separated from the bedroom by partition walls. The bedroom has one queen-size and one twin-size bed with big closets and bathrooms. Friendly fellow guests and decent rooms invite longer stays, but remember to keep some mosquito repellent handy if you're out on the terrace. **$**

Amar Inn (*Av. Javier Rojo Gomez, beachfront,* ☎ *987/1-00-26, 3 bungalows, 3 rooms with fans*). Funky and strange, the Amar is an experience as much as a hotel. The three rooms that face the beach are large and clean with one queen-size and one twin-size mattress (or you can ask for a different configuration). An iron stairway spirals to the second floor, seemingly around a tree. Three bungalows attach to each other and face a jungle-like center courtyard with statues randomly placed among the banana and palm trees. The rustic cabaña quarters have thatched palapa and stick and plaster construction, but come with all the necessities, including hot water. Sleeping lofts save space and each has simple cooking facilities. This is a family hotel and one can feel quite at home here. Ask for a discount on weekly stays. **$**

Acamaya Camping (*beachfront, 5 cabañas and 2 more being built with private bath, full hook-ups,* ☎ *987/1-00-81*). The husband and wife team of Daisy and Denis Urbain – he's French, she's Mexican – own this tiny campground/cabaña combination hard against some modern condos and an old fishing port. Trees shade the spots available to trailers and RV's or tenters. From the outside, the cabañas are primitive looking, but they have bright and cheerful bedspreads, kitchenettes and a couch that could be used as a bed for a child or small adult. Shared bathroom and showers. Intimate and pleasant – and far away from the madding crowd – this is a great place to do nothing. The restaurant serves inexpensive and very generous portions, family style. To get here, make the turn just before Croco Cun along the highway or snake your way back north from Puerto Morelos along the beach road that passes Motel Eden. Deserted beach. $-$$

Moderate Hotels

Rancho Libertad (*beachfront, south of the car ferry,* ☎ *in US and Canada: 800-305-5225, in Mexico: 987/1-01-81, 12 rooms with fans, prices include breakfast*). Six duplex, palapa-roofed, octagonal-shaped cabañas are set back among the palms here on a broad, bright-white sand beach. The airy second-floor guest rooms cost more, but all the rooms have comfortable beds suspended from the ceiling and spacious bathrooms. A huge sand-floor, beachside palapa, with a tiled dining area and kitchen, serves as a common room for guests. The kitchen dishes up a big buffet breakfast (included in the room price) and guests can use the facility to store food or cook. The unusually large common room is like a giant screened-in sand box with such toys as a swing, stereo, lounge chairs and books to read. Co-owner and manager Ginny Hill, a certified dive instructor, claims the Rancho is "New-Age" friendly, but don't bring the kids, it's adults only. They rent sea kayaks and mountain bikes. Good karma. $$

Villas Latinas (*Av. Javier Rojo Gomez, beachfront,* ☎ *& fax 987/1-01-18, 14 rooms with fans, pool*). Large rooms with kitchenettes and a pleasing beach distinguish this family-run hotel. The white-and-blue trimmed cement rooms face the beach, only 150 feet away. $$

Hacienda Morelos (*beachfront,* ☎ *987/1-00-15, pool, restaurant*). A block south of the main square is the sparkling clean Hacienda hotel, overlooking the water, where the upstairs rooms have an especially pleasing view of the Caribbean. Each fair-size room comes with a small kitchenette with refrigerator. Daisy's restaurant downstairs (formerly Muelle 8) offers fine oceanview dining and specializes in seafood. $$

Ojo de Aqua (*Av. Javier Rojo Gomez, beachfront,* ☎ *& fax 987/1-00-27, 24 rooms with air or fans, pool, restaurant, dive shop*). Ojo de aqua means "eye of the water," a phenomenon caused by underground water rising into a lagoon or shallow sea and causing a change of water color. This popular spot hasn't changed since its opening in 1970 – it's still a great place. The Ojo boasts a charming odd-shaped small swimming pool, a sundeck lined with flowers and a restaurant that overlooks the sea. The rooms are large and all have kitchenettes, good-size closets and modern bathrooms. $$

Cabañas Puerto Morelos (*Av. Javier Rojo Gomez,* ☎ *in US: 612-441-7630 or in Mexico:* ☎ *& fax 987/1-00-04, 3 rooms with fans and kitchenette,* *very large 1-bedroom apartment, 4-bedroom house, 2-bedroom house*). Bill and Connie Butcher have lived in Puerto Morelos since 1987. Their apartment and three one-bedroom suites that they call "cabañas" are completely furnished with all the amenities North Americans are used to. A home away from home, the three downstairs suite/rooms have complete kitchens (plus a personal coffee brewer, a rarity in Mexico) and sleeping couches with either one king-size, one queen, or two twins. The upstairs apartment used to be their home and offers a huge amount of living space with one master bedroom. Next door they manage Villa Miguel, a four-bedroom, four-bath house (US $1,400/week, high season), and down the street they have Casa Dos Amigos, a large two-bedroom house (US $750/week, high season). **$$-$$$**

Casita Del Mar (*Av. Javier Rojo Gomez, beachfront, 19 rooms with air, pool, restaurant*). This Caribbean-colored, hacienda-like beachfront hotel opened in January 1997, next to Arrecifes (see below). Small handsome rooms with either one king-size or two twin beds face the pretty beach. The custom-made stick furniture is very appealing, as are the color-matched drapes and bed spreads. Cuban-American manager Pablo Gonzalez wants to make people feel at home so he doesn't put numbers on the doors – a nice touch. But the hotel's prices are, we think, a tad too high for the market. Check to see if they're a good value now that the hotel is in full swing. The hotel's lovely little poolside restaurant, however, is inexpensive. **$$-$$$**

Expensive Hotels

Arrecifes (*Av. Javier Rojo Gomez, beachfront,* ☎ *987/1-01-96, fax 987/1-01-40, 9 rooms with kitchenettes*). Next door to the new Casita del Mar, the formerly low-priced one-bedroom condo suites at Arrecifes are now relatively pricey. They're on a gorgeous beach and the large rooms are clean, though a little worn. If there's no one at the site, go up the street to the multicolored condos across from the military base and look for manager Beatriz Canto's information sign. If they're not full, haggle. **$$$**

Caribbean Reef Club at Villa Marina (*south of the ferry dock, in US:* ☎ *800-322-6286, 30 studios or suites with air, pool, TV, restaurant, watersports*). The best and most expensive hotel in Puerto Morelos, it boasts a beautiful figure-eight-shaped pool with two islands. Isolated beach, large rooms and guarded entrance. **$$$**

Dining

Pelicanos (*beachfront opposite the park*). Pelicanos has the best location, atmosphere, service and menu in Puerto Morelos. You'll find it opposite the park, under a huge palapa dome roof, overlooking the beach. Ocean breezes keep it cool and comfortable. The restaurant serves up Mexican food, fresh fish and seafood at moderate prices. **$$**

Gringo's Café (*Av. Javier Rojo Gomez*). Paul Hensley took over this appealing eatery, which used to be called Doña Zenaida's, one block in from the waterfront. A capable staff runs it, and Paul spends most of his time at his other business, Wet Set Water Adventure Tours, across the street from Pelicanos restaurant. The Wet Set agency offers good dive and snorkel trips at a better rate than its competitors. The little Gringo's Café has three seating areas – an inside dining room, three tables out front under umbrellas and a serene backyard terrace with individual palapa umbrellas and palm trees. Try the grilled vegetarian special for about US $4. **$**

Posada Amor (*Av. Javier Rojo Gomez*). This family-run restaurant in front of the hotel of the same name is the favorite meeting and eating place for Americans and Canadians staying in Puerto Morelos. The service is impeccable, the food is very good and the prices are reasonable. Worth a stop. **$**

See page 4 for price chart.

Playa Paraiso

The sign for Playa Paraiso is on your left, going south, past Puerto Morelos at about Km 49, just before you come to Rancho Loma Bonita, a horseback riding ranch, on your right.

Carrousel (*on the beach of Playa Paraiso, 50 rooms with air, pool, cable TV, safes, restaurant, watersports, all-inclusive*). The Carrousel (whose sister hotel is in the hotel zone in Cancún) is an all-inclusive resort that opened in 1997. It sits alone on the Playa Paraiso well south of Puerto Morelos. It's worth mentioning because it uses solar panel-assisted hot water and each unit has a windmill on the roof to help generate electricity. You can see them from the highway, twisting in the wind at the end of a well-paved road to a fine beach. **$$$**

Punta Bete

 This isn't a town but rather a superb beach about three miles long, stretching north from Playa del Carmen. With the explosive growth of Playa there will soon be no distinction between it and Punta Bete. Punta Bete features a series of three rustic camping and cabaña beachfront hotels about 1½ hours' walk along the sea north of Playa. One of them, **Playa Xcalacoco**, was sold in early 1997 and will reopen as a foreign language school sometime soon. In the meantime, the Swiss couple who bought it plan to keep their restaurant open and rent camping spots only.

Frederico's (*on the beach at Playa Xcalacoco, Km 52,* ☎ *987/45-09-05, 7 cabañas, 5 with hot water*). German-born and bred Frederico Vatter first emigrated to Canada, then discovered this Mexican niche of paradise here at Playa Xcalacoco. Adequate rooms set back from the beach make this a popular stop with Europeans, Canadians and Americans. Don't expect too many amenities, but the prices are fair. He runs a good little restaurant, and the beach here is nothing less than wonderful. **$**

Los Pinos (*on the beach at Playa Xcalacoco, Km 52, 4 rooms with fans*). The serene beach at Xcalacoco was named after the coconut plantation that was there when Juan Fernando Rejon Cardana's grandfather started this little campground and restaurant in 1971. New rooms have just been built back from the beach. They are big and comfortable with tiled bathrooms, closets and screened windows. Toilet seats are lacking and the electric is solar powered (so expect a car bulb hung from the ceiling). Camping is beachfront under palapa huts. The tiny restaurant's specialty is *tikinchik*, Maya-spiced fish. Breakfast runs about US $6. Daily snorkel tours cost US $20; five-hour deep-sea fishing trips are US $130. **$**

Playa del Carmen

*You don't watch for potholes around here, you watch for
the little roadway between them.*

– Raza Manji quoted in a *NY Times* article,
The Pothole: A Source of Civic Pride

The once sleepy village of Playa del Carmen doubled twice in
population in the last few years, mainly due to Europeans who
discovered the alabaster-white beaches, gentle surf, coral reefs and
slow lifestyle were the equal of the more expensive island of
Cozumel just across the straits. Playa's dock is the pier for the
"people ferry" to Cozumel, so it's only a short trip over to snorkel
or dive on Cozumel's incredible coral reefs.

The strong Italian (and German) influence has created a unique
vagabond traveler ambiance. Numerous outrageously delicious
Italian restaurants provide sustenance and several German-owned
hotels raise the standards of service to exacting levels. Combine that
with a relaxed Mexican-Caribbean feeling and a sprinkling of
American free-spirits and you've got Playa. It's definitely not the
place to "get away," but it is a place to enjoy marvelous beaches by
day and a lively nightlife in the evening. The mix of backpackers,
archeological buffs and New Age sun worshippers makes Playa very
interesting and worth some time.

Orientation

 GETTING AROUND: To get to Playa, 68 km (42 miles)
south of Cancún, take a bus from the station downtown
(about 1½ hours). If you're in the hotel zone, you could
negotiate a fare with a Cancún taxi driver to scoot you
down. We did and paid only about US $10 more than the bus.

The main road into town, Av. Juárez or Av. Principal, depending
on whom you ask, leads you right to the ferry dock and the pedestrian-only 5th Avenue, running perpendicular to the beach. It boasts
many of the town's hotels, stores and restaurants. The **bus station** is
right there at Av. 5 and Juárez and is a hub for further journeys down
to Tulum, Chetumal and Belize. Most hotels are within easy walking
distance from the bus and the street in front of the station is full of
men on large yellow tricycles (*triciclos*), who will ride you and/or

your luggage cheaply to your hotel in a Mexican version of a rickshaw. If your hotel isn't close or you have to go on the back streets of Playa, get a cab right there. In 1994, in response to the growing popularity of the town, the streets were torn up for sewer and water lines. Unfortunately, there wasn't enough money left to repave them. Consequently, many of the new streets look as if the American Air Force has been using them as target practice with 500 lb smart bombs. The water-filled potholes in the unpaved roads outside of the oldest part of town make traffic crawl and require zig-zagging to the max.

Playa's unusual lighthouse.

A stroll on the beach leads to Playa's attractive lighthouse (*faro*), where you can climb its exterior circular cement staircase to the top. The view is excellent and provides a great photo op.

Practicalities

The **post office** is three blocks back from the beach on Av. Principal, as is a **pharmacy** and the **Centro de Salud Medical Center**. The **police** (☎ 987/3-02-91) have set up a tourist help table on 5th Ave (Av. 5) in front of the Hotel Delfin near the park plaza. You'll find **Tourism information** on Av. 5 near the central plaza. Several hotels rent **bicycles**, but get a mountain bike to dodge the water-filled cenote-like potholes and sandy streets.

There are two **banks** downtown on Juárez and the *Bancomer* has an **ATM**. Reasonably priced **Spanish lessons** are advertised from a language school, ☎ 987/3-05-50. The **ferry to Cozumel** has a schedule that changes constantly. If you're going over, just ask about times at any of the ticket booths scattered around the plaza. Try to get a ticket on the *WJ Mexico*, a fast waterjet (25 minutes). The *Xel-Há* or *Cozumeleño* takes 45 minutes.

For **shopping**, the stores of Playa's Av. 5 and surrounding sidestreets offer an eclectic assortment of hand-made pottery, arts and crafts both local and from all over Mexico, gifts and New Age paraphernalia.

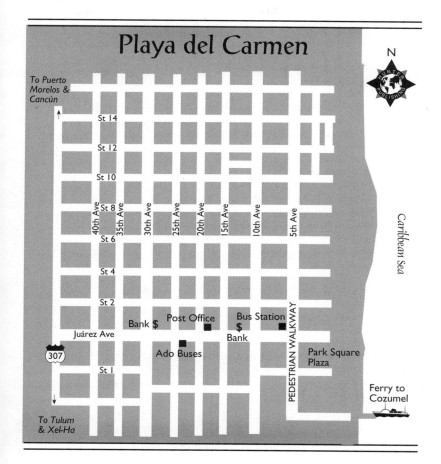

Playa del Carmen

N

To Puerto Morelos & Cancún

St 14
St 12
St 10
40th Ave
35th Ave
St 8
30th Ave
25th Ave
20th Ave
15th Ave
10th Ave
5th Ave
St 6
St 4
St 2

Juárez Ave

Bank $ Post Office   Bus Station $
Bank
Ado Buses

307

St 1

PEDESTRIAN WALKWAY

Park Square Plaza

Ferry to Cozumel

To Tulum & Xel-Ha

Caribbean Sea

Adventures

Most of Playa's activities involve the water – the beaches are fabulous for **swimming**, **snorkeling**, or **diving**. There are numerous dive shops around. Try the **Tank Ha** (*Ha* means water in Mayan) dive shop at the Maya Bric Hotel (no phone). The **El Albatroz** (no phone; on the beach, downtown) rents dive and snorkel equipment, as does **El Oasis**, on Calle 4 between Av. 5 and 10 (no phone).

Golf is available in Playacar on an 18-hole course designed by Robert Von Hagge. Beachcombers could **hike** north and make a whole day of it, relaxing in one or two beachside restaurants along the way. Wear a hat and much sunscreen.

Accommodations

 Between the time you plan your trip and the time you arrive in Playa del Carmen, chances are there will be another new hotel or restaurant to choose from. The former sleepy little fishing village is seeing phenomenal growth, thanks mostly to European vacationers who discovered that Playa is more laid back than Cozumel – and totally unlike Cancún. Although it's not the same village it was only a few years ago, tourism has created a busy atmosphere that still caters to an off-beat, almost bohemian crowd. This is a fun place to stay. See page 3 for price chart.

Budget

Hotel Lolita (*Calle 8, no phone, 12 rooms with fan*). With a Moorish look and ingenue name, the Lolita still looks unfinished after two years of construction. Only a half-block from the beach and surrounded by fancier, more pricey hotels, its small rooms feel a little close, but at this low price it may be worth it. **$**

Hotel Maya Bric (*Av. 5 between Calles 8 and 10,* ☎ *987/3-00-11, 29 rooms with air or fans, pool, dive shop, restaurant*). This is everyone's favorite budget hotel in Playa. Well, perhaps not everyone – it's a little too reserved for the party-animal crowd. The pleasing and airy rooms cluster around a landscaped flower garden and small pool. Each plain guest room has two queen-size beds and the reputable beachside dive shop runs snorkel and dive trips daily. The family-run hotel is very quiet and locks its gates at night, so it's also private and secure. **$**

CREA Youth Hostel (*Calle 4, no phone, snack bar, basketball court*). It's a long, long walk to the beach from the officially named Villa Deportiva Juvenil, but it's the cheapest place in town. Although the prospect of single sex bunk beds can be unsexy, the hostel also has a couple of cabañas with private baths.

Cabañas Las Ruinas (*beachfront north of the ferry,* ☎ *987/3-04-05*). If you're camping, this is the only authorized beach campground in Playa. As the name implies, it's not exactly high living, but the name actually refers to a tiny Maya ruin nearby. You have a choice of small cabañas with bath, tent spaces, hammock sleeping under a palapa, or small RV and trailer parking. Lockers and safety boxes, available for rent, are strongly recommended.

Hotel Delfin (*Av. 5 at Calle 6,* ☎ *in US: 800-601-7285,* ☎ *& fax in Mexico: 987/3-01-76, 14 rooms with fans, surf shop, refrigerators*). Americans Dan and Miriam Shore built the Delfin on the pedestrian walkway overlooking the sea. The ivy-covered hotel, with an intriguing French look, is not as special inside as the interesting exterior promises. It does have good-size rooms, some with an ocean view, and is reasonably priced. Stay here and you don't have to go far with any problems that may arise – directly outside the local police set up a daily "help table" to aid tourists. **$-$$**

Mom's (*Av. 30 at Calle 4,* ☎ *& fax 987/3-03-15, 20 rooms with air or fans, 3 apartments, bar/restaurant with satellite TV, room rates include breakfast*). Nothing to look at from the outside, Mom's is quite an attractive, colonial-style hotel inside. There's a small pool tucked into the corner of the open center courtyard and a bulletin board near the entrance that's frequently used as a communal message center. They rent bicycles here, a good way to get around the town. American owner Ricco Merkle is a jovial host and experienced travelers flock to his comfortable medium-size rooms with bedside table lamps and original artwork on the walls. Plans are in the works to expand with more apartments and private parking. Five blocks off the beach. **$-$$**

Hotel Trinidad Faces (*Av. 5 Norte, at corner of 12th St., no phone, pool*). Owned by the same artist as both Trinidad hotels in Mérida, Faces promises to be a unique experience in the already eclectic Playa. Relax in their refreshing pool set in a tranquil tropical patio. Definitely worth a look. One block from the beach. **$-$$**

Moderate

Hotel Maranatha (*Av. Juárez between Calles 30 and 35,* ☎ *987/3-01-43, fax 987/3-00-38, big pool, satellite TV, 36 rooms and suites with air, private parking, kitchenettes, restaurant, MC/V*). As you enter Playa Del Carmen, heading toward the dock, the Maranatha is on the left, set back from the main drag. A modern colonial-style hotel, it offers a good value, especially for long term. Ask about their weekly or monthly rates. The large rooms and suites on two stories have attractive wooden doors and center around an open courtyard with a very large pool. **$$**

Suites Las Quintas (*Av. Juárez,* ☎ *987-3-01-20, air-conditioning, tiny pool, satellite TV, private parking*). The rooms here are okay, but the suites are huge, almost apartment-like. The hotel, located directly across the street from the Maranatha, is very clean with a celery and white color scheme and attractive big wooden closets plus modern baths in each bedroom. With only a tiny garden courtyard and pool, the big attraction here is the beach, three long blocks away. Negotiate if you're staying longer. **$$**

Tree Tops Hotel (*Calle 8,* ☎ *& fax 987/3-03-51, 6 private bungalows and 5 rooms in a modern hotel building*). Imagine if someone built a wall around virgin jungle while a city grew around it, unaware of the life within. That's pretty much what Tree Tops is: a cabaña hotel in a piece of jungle sealed off before Playa grew from 3,000 to 30,000 people. Behind its wall and squeezed between two neighboring hotels the land drops down under tall trees and heavy tropical vegetation. Owners Bill and Sandy Dillon built six rustic bungalows that are not quite primitive, but close. Under the trees, this has to be the coolest place in town. It even has its own miniature cenote. A small restaurant and tiny pool have been added, as well as five modern rooms in two new stucco buildings. Their dark and intimate Safari Bar is a popular hang-out. Prices include continental breakfast. **$$**

Hotel Molcas (*Av., 5 next to the Town Square,* ☎ *987/3-00-70, pool, 36 rooms with fan and hammock hooks*). Others who have stayed at this venerable mainstay right at the ferry dock to Cozumel have been pleased, but we found it somewhat tired with better values nearby. Worn Astro-turf carpeting covers the patio lounge area in the center and some of the public areas are showing their age. The big draw here is its location in the heart of it all. **$$**

Hotel Casa Blanca (*Calle 8,* ☎ *987/3-07-35, 15 rooms with fan*). Owner Alberto Hedding Aranda is currently building even more rooms behind his new three-story beachfront hotel. The pure white Moorish-style hotel offers balconies with the ocean view rooms but it's somewhat overpriced. Restaurant and tiny bar on beach. **$$**

Balcones Del Caribe (*Calle 34,* ☎ *987/3-08-30, fax 987/3-08-31, 72 2-bedroom, 2-bath suites plus hotel rooms with air, refrigerator, pool, private parking with security*). North of town on Playa's rough roads, Balcones is just up the street from Shangri-La, a well-known bungalow hotel on an incredible beach. Also on the beach is a bar called El Arrecife, where the swimming and snorkeling are excellent because of the reef's proximity to the shore. Balcones rents bicycles and has a bus for its own restaurant, Los Terraces, closer to town. The hotel, very popular with Europeans who buy packages, is well priced but out of the loop in terms of location. It's a hike to the beach. **$$**

El Sol Del Caribe (*Av. 5 between Calles 4 and 6,* ☎ *987/3-09-58, air-conditioning and fans, kitchenettes with microwave, cable TV*). Each room here has an ocean view from its balcony. Situated right in the middle of the pedestrian-only walkway, it may be somewhat noisy in the early evening. Friendly staff, European managed. **$$**

Hotel Alejari (*Calle 6 beachfront,* ☎ *987/3-03-72, fax 987/3-00-05, 28 rooms and studios with air or fans, restaurant*). The garden path weaves through a labyrinth of hibiscus bushes and flowers and leads to duplex rooms and studios, some with air and some with kitchenettes. Choose a good room and you'll never want to leave. Reasonable prices in the beachfront restaurant where you can eat in the dining room or under individual palapa shades. **$$**

Jungla Caribe (*Calle 8 near Av. 5,* ☎ *987/3-06-50, 25 rooms and suites with air, TV, pool, restaurant/bar*). This four-story corner hotel houses a fine bar and restaurant on the second floor called Jaguar, whose tables overlook either the street or the lush jungle garden. The hotel entrance is inviting and the service is impeccable. In the middle of the courtyard there's an attractive narrow figure-eight swimming pool. The rooms are all very large with a fancy Spanish Mediterranean decor. The ultra-modern tiled bathrooms even have a bidet, a rare luxury in Mexico. High quality throughout. Ask for a discount for stays of more than one night. **$$**

Albatros Royale (*Calle 8 beachfront,* ☎ *in US: 800-538-6802, in Mexico: 987/3-00-01, 35 rooms with fans, safety boxes surf shop, rates include breakfast*). These modern interpretations of Maya *na* homes are romantic, absolutely clean and pleasant. Rooms on the top have palapa roofs and balconies; downstairs all have porches and all come with hammocks for lounging or sleeping outside. A stone walkway leads from the white-tiled rooms and winds through lush flowering bushes out to the beach. This is a well-designed hotel. It's also one of several Turquoise Reef properties in Playa, the others being the Pelicano Inn, Chican Baal Kah apartments and Quinta Mija efficiencies. Turquoise also handles Apartmentos Jacques in nearby ritzy Playacar. **$$**

Pelicano Inn (*Calle 8 beachfront,* ☎ *in US: 800-538-6802, in Mexico: 987/3-09-97, 38 rooms with fans, restaurant, rates include breakfast*). The rooms of this appealing Pueblo-styled hotel have red-tiled roofs and private balconies or patios that surround a private village-like courtyard. Completely rebuilt within the last two years, the hotel knows what guests like and offers it. The rooms are either beachfront, garden-view or ocean-view and the ambiance is more like that of a small apartment in the center of town, than of a hotel. Behind huge glass windows facing the beach, Ronny's Steakhouse specializes in fine cuts of beef. **$$-$$$**

Hotel Colonial (*Calle 8, near 20th,* ☎ *& fax 987/3-04-56, 16 rooms with air*). Local builder Peter Kaufmann, a German-trained engineer who has been the contractor on buildings for other developers in this rapidly growing town, decided to build his own hotel and has spared no expense in doing so. Under construction when we visited, it is a large coral-colored stucco structure with Spanish-styled wrought-iron balconies and tall front columns. The Colonial promises to be quite luxurious with a penthouse suite ($220 US) five blocks from beach. **$$-$$$**

Luxury

Las Palapas (*beachfront in back of Balconies Del Caribe,* ☎ *987/3-05-84, fax 987/3-04-58, 49 rooms plus 6 cabañas*). Delightfully beautiful inside and out but very upscale European, the cabañas on the beach (#1, 2 and 3; #26, 27 and 28) have a US $13 surcharge. Super-special place to get away from the downtown. About 15 blocks north of the ferry on the beach of Punta Bete, next to Shangri-La. **$$$**

Mayan Paradise Hotel (*Av. 10,* ☎ *987/3-09-33, 40 rooms with air, 4 suites, kitchenettes, TV, restaurant, pool, bicycle rental, rates include breakfast*). Expensive and off the beach, this is nevertheless the best place to splurge in Playa del Carmen. The small hotel is probably the most attractive and luxurious of anything in town, with high palapa roofs and polished woods that give its cabaña rooms an almost Polynesian feel. The luxurious quarters all have kitchenettes and lovely shaded terraces. With an owner named "Palacio," how could you not expect royal accommodations? And they are. One-bedroom suites have a jacuzzi and steam bath. The pretty pool is figure-eight shaped but if you prefer the sand, the hotel offers their own beach club. You'll find this gem three blocks off the beach to the north of the ferry dock. **$$$**

South of the ferry are some very luxurious resorts in a complex known as **Playacar**. The only real adventure there is trying to find a place you can afford. You can't miss the pink, colonial design, 188-room **Continental Plaza Playacar**, (in the US, ☎ 800/882-6684) next to the dock.

New hotels constantly spring up north of the pier where Playa's beautiful beach wanders off to the seclusion of Punta Bete.

Dining

 Restaurants and gift shops jostle each other for space along the pedestrian walkway part of 5th Avenue (as even many locals call Avenida Cinco). There are so many places here – beachside, or within a few blocks – that we selected only a sampling of delicious restaurants in the lower price range and a few exceptional eateries in the moderate range. Eat well and enjoy. See page 4 for price chart.

Red Eye Café, El Alternativo (*Av. 10 and Constituyentes, open 4 p.m.-midnight*). They call their menu "medicinal food for body and soul" and it's just what the doctor ordered. With well priced and tasty dishes, the restaurant has a bohemian following and, despite being outside the main tourist area, it can fill up at night with diners who linger at their tables. Asian and Afro-Brazilian specialties and a large selection of natural juices and salads. **$**

Daily Donuts (*Av. 5 between Calles 8 and 10*). There's a big choice of donuts in this tiny donut shop that has a small inviting eating area under a tree. Good coffee and heavy donuts make filling snack. **$**

Restaurant La Tarraya (*beachfront between Calles 2 and 4*). This little seafood restaurant and bar claims to be "Born with the Town." Its more important claim to fame is that it serves the best fresh fish and seafood around. Not much in the way of ambiance – except for the Caribbean sea a few feet away – it offers delicious fish at excellent prices. **$**

Sabor (*Av. 5 between Calles 2 and 4*). This people-watching bakery is in the midst it all. Popular spot for light snacks, coffee, cakes and juice drinks. Pull up a chair on their patio and watch the world go by – Playa style. **$**

Mr. Baguette (*Av. 5*). Of all the eateries that line 5th Avenue, we found Mr. Baguette to be just right. Large meat or vegetarian sandwiches are served on crisp, toasted French bread. Enjoy a cold beer while you wait under one of their six umbrella-covered, streetside patio tables. A nice change. **$**

Karen's Grill & Pizzas (*Av. 5 between Calles 2 and 4*). More fun than gourmet, Karen's fills up with a boisterous crowd watching TV, music videos, or listening to live music. Italian and Mexican menu. Don't bother to ask for Karen – she ain't here. **$**

Limones Restaurant (*Av. 5 at Calle 6*). This highly romantic restaurant set down in a hollow right on the pedestrian mall features international and French cuisine. Soft candlelight, numerous plants – even old wine bottles hanging from the ceiling – enhance the amorous atmosphere here. There's live music in their "Red & Black" Bar. Daily specials help make this a special night out. **$$**

Da Gabi Hotel & Restaurant (*Calle 12 at Av. 5,* ☎ *987/3-00-48, fax 987/3-0198*). This is one of the best – if not *the* best – in the plethora of Italian restaurants in Playa. We had a delicious gourmet meal for only a few dollars more than we would have spent at a less-interesting sidewalk café on the pedestrian walkway. The evening ambiance is romantic in a giant palapa decorated in twinkly lights. It's an excellent value with great Italian and Mexican cooking.

Worth considering is the Maya-styled **Da Gabi Hotel** next door. Reasonably priced rooms with fans sit near the beach. **$$**

I have a trunk containing continents.

– Beryl Markham in a PBS interview, 1986

Xcaret

 Promoted as an "eco-archeological" park, Xcaret (ish-car-et), ☎ 98/83-31-43, is a resort playground that combines Maya ruins with tranquil coves, inlets, grottos, natural wells and an underground river. Originally known as *Polé*, meaning "place of trade," it was the pre-Hispanic port for Maya canoes to the sacred island of Cozumel. Excellent swimming (available with dolphins for US $50 extra), good but crowded restaurants, snorkeling and sunbathing. There's a wild bird aviary, gift shops, a small museum, scale models of some of the Yucatán's more famous Maya ruins, a botanical garden and a saltwater aquarium. You can horseback ride or enjoy the shade of palm trees in one of their hammocks.

Xcaret is a few miles south of Playa and 72 km (45 miles) south of Cancún. Colorful funky buses run from the hotel zone every morning and return late in the day. It has no lodging but allegedly offers **camping** (no phone) near the ruins. They've also added a night-time light show (starts at 5 p.m.) with festive dancing and folk activities, all included in the admission price of about US $30 (under 11 years, US $18) for the day. For an extra fee, qualified divers can dive to a sunken 90-foot shrimp boat, the *Mama Viña* (at a depth of 27 meters, 90 feet), and explore the cabin and living quarters complete with a full bar built of fine wood.

Bring your snorkel equipment or rent it at the park. Don't bother renting flippers for the underground river snorkel, they only kick people and a strong current pulls you along anyway. The underground river is an interesting trip but is not for the claustrophobic and is not recommended when it's crowded. When there are a lot of people it may be better to take the above ground Maya river run, which is less jammed and offers more fish to see.

Paa Mul

Paa Mul, which means "Destroyed Ruin" in Mayan, has a crescent-shaped beach and a storybook location on the Caribbean south of Xcaret.

Paa Mul Cabañas and RV Park (*Highway 307, Km 85, ☎ 987/4-13-87, 10 rooms with fans, restaurant, bar, dive shop*). About 10 km south of Xcaret lies this simple little gem of a place on an isolated bay that only Canadians seem to have discovered. Step out of one of the 10 bungalows and you're nearly in the surf. Each large room, completely remodeled in 1997, has two queen-size beds with bent wood headboards, clean tiled bathrooms, hooks for hammocks and broad front porches. The sound of the waves lapping against the shore will rock you to sleep. The half-moon swimming beach is about 50 meters (165 feet) away. The oceanfront bar and restaurant, under a round palapa roof, overlooks the beach and the exposed reef. Many of the RV's are here long term under giant, custom-built shade palapas. Annual space rental is $2,400 US, and they'll move your rig inland if there's a hurricane. The **Scuba Max** dive shop (no phone) features computer dives that give you more time in the water. Their snorkel or dive trips run US $25-35. Located just north of the fancy Puerto Adventuras resorts, Paa Mul has been around since 1961. $$

CENOTES: As you continue south on 307 there is a series of gift shops and cenotes along the road managed by local Maya families. Cenote Crystallino, Kantun-Chi and Cenote Azul all offer swimming. Azul and Crystallino are best for swimming, Kantun - Chi's cenotes are in four caves with a small Maya ruin at one. Wash off any sunscreen before swimming in any cenote; it damages the marine life.

Puerto Adventuras

 A complete Cancún-like, self-contained 90-acre resort around a protected bay. The **Museo CEDAM**, a diving museum, is the one redeeming adventuresome attraction in Puerto Aventuras.

Xpuha

 Another of the Turquoise Coast's hidden hideaways is Xpuha Beach, with separate driveways through the brush to each of its four secluded properties.

Accommodations

 Villas Xpuha (*Highway 307 Km 88, beachfront, 4 rooms with fans, no phone*). Spartan accommodations in a block building high up on a fabulous beach, Villas offers two twin beds in each room, hammock hooks and hot water in the bathrooms. **$**

Villas del Caribe (*Highway 307 Km 88, beachfront, 24 rooms with fans, no phone*). This brightly painted new-in-1997 hotel faces the Caribbean Sea on a lovely stretch of lonely white sand beach. With the same owner as the Hotel Flores in Cozumel (☎ 987/2-24-75), this hotel attracts a fair number of scuba divers. Big airy rooms with king-size or two queen-size beds open onto balconies on the second floor, or patios on the first. The Villas is an ideal spot to combine comfort with seclusion. Twelve rooms are in the two-story hotel and 12 are in bungalows. **$$**

Manatí Xpuha (*Highway 307 Km 85, beachfront*). Camping is excellent here where there's a tall rolling sand dune that rises up to some scattered palm trees. Also facing the idyllic beach are some primitive cabañas that share a bath. Ruggedly rustic. **$**

Bonanza Xpuha (*Highway 307 Km 85, beachfront, no phone*). Same deal as the Manatí. **$**

See page 3 for price chart.

Akumal

The fame that Cozumel and the Mexican Caribbean has for incredible dive spots first spread from Akumal in 1958 when a group of ex-WW II Mexican frogmen salvaged the Spanish galleon, *Mantanceros*, sunk against the Palancar Reef in 1741. They called their group **CEDAM**, the *Club de Exploración y Deporte Acuáticos de Mexico*. In 1968 they donated Xel-Há and over 5,000 acres of their coconut-palmed land around Akumal as a national park. Before Cancún, Akumal (Mayan for "Land of Turtles") was the only resort along the Quintana Roo coast. Since then the shoreline has been built up to a point where condos, villas and hotels line the formerly deserted half-moon bay beach. It's a fine place to stay if you're after the amenities of the Cancún hotel zone without the crowds. Not our style, but still a big dive spot.

Our pick is nearby **Yal-Ku**, a seldom-visited lagoon where canals of fish-filled emerald water provide wonderful snorkeling. It's an 800-meter (half-mile) stroll north of the road that loops Half Moon Bay in Akumal, or there's an unmarked road on the left (opposite Rancho San Miguel) before the resort at about the 98 Km marker. There's also a teeny tiny Maya building there.

Playa Chemuyil

A very intriguing concept for this part of the peninsula, Playa Chemuyil is a snorkeling and swimming beach that charges an admission (US $2 – even though all beaches in Mexico are free). What you're paying for are amenities and the care of the powder-white beach area. Protected by a reef across the entrance to the horseshoe-shaped cove, Chemuyil claims to be the "most beautiful beach in the world." We might agree if it were not for the devastation the lethal yellowing disease has inflicted on the coconut palm trees in the area. Playa Chemuyil features restrooms and showers, a medical clinic and a palapa-covered restaurant, **Marco Polo** (no phone), that serves delicious low-priced Mexican and Yucatecan seafood cuisine.

On the south end of the beach there's a camping area that includes thatched hut cabañas for hanging hammocks and spaces for trailers (there is no electric). Very clean and well run. There's a six-kilometer dirt road along the old coconut plantation good for hiking as far as Xel-Há.

South of Chemuyil and north of Tulum is a primitive beachfront campground called **Xcacel** (no phone). It offers good swimming behind the reef and a sinkhole with underwater rock formations in crystal-clear water. Xcacel is another camper's paradise, with spread-out locations under palm trees on a marvelous sparkling white beach. It has a small restaurant, bathrooms and showers. Trailers and tenters seem equally at home here as there is no electricity. This campground also participates in the turtle protection program when the turtles come ashore to lay their eggs in October. If you're camping, hang a hammock here; it's a good deal. $

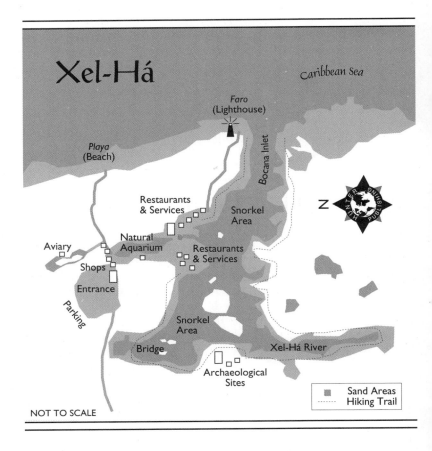

Xel-Há

Mayan for "Clear Water," Xel-Há (ishel-ha) is aptly named. The park (☎ 98/84-94-22) is a series of interconnected clear-water lagoons that form a natural aquarium for angelfish, lobster, barracuda, parrot fish, French grunts and many others. Wash off your suntan lotion before entering the water, as it harms the marine life.

Snorkeling and swimming are the predictable big pastimes here, or you can drop into one of the comfortable Yucatecan hammocks strung in a sandy grove of coconut palms. The park features five restaurants, 11 different shops, lockers, showers and changing rooms.

A few hundred feet before the inlet entrance are some small Classic and Post-Classic Maya ruins with painted murals and several cenotes. A good walking path through the jungle offers a close-up of the typical vegetation, including bromeliads, orchids and ferns, while swallows swing by overhead. The park is a common stop with bus tours heading to Tulum from Cancún so it can become crowded. Still, it's a big place. There is no lodging but some cabins are being planned. Admission is US $10.

Tancah Cenote

The only sign for this magical sinkhole, nine km (5.5 miles) south of Xel-Há at Km 127, is for the **Casa Cenote Restaurant** ($$). In real estate there's an expression, "location, location, location," and Casa Cenote is a restaurant that's got it, got, got it. Perched on a rise above a gorgeous beach, the Casa serves up California-style Mexican food.

It's great place to while away hours, stopping occasionally to sunbathe (ocean swimming is best a short walk up the beach) or dip in the clear blue-green cenote across the street. This is a great swimming and snorkeling cenote and scuba divers love to explore its deep caves. The Tancah cenote is one of the largest underground cenotes in the Yucatán. Stand on the edge and look straight down where the walls slip deep into the abyss. The shallowest part looks to be about 15 feet deep. So many fish swimming by in the clear water make the snorkeling superb.

Beyond the restaurant there's a small Maya fishing settlement and some small pre-Hispanic ruins hidden in the scrub forest. Before you come to the restaurant and unmarked cenote, there are a few houses scattered along the beach, one of which is a hotel.

Tulum, Punta Allen & Sian Ka'an

The end of the human race will be that it will
eventually die of civilization.

– Ralph Waldo Emerson, 1803-1882

 Tulum, like Cancún, is actually two cities: the ancient abandoned Tulum ruins and Tulum Pueblo, two km (1.25 miles) south of the archeological zone. In addition, Boca Paila and the Punta Allen peninsula, as well as the Sian Ka'an Biosphere are all accessed through Tulum. The **Gran Cenote** is not far outside Tulum Pueblo, four km (2½ miles) down the road toward Cobá. A small admission fee (US $3) entitles you to climb down some steep steps into an open sinkhole, where the bright blue water of the Gran Cenote flows under a cave to an open area beyond. Fabulous place for snorkeling. On the other side of the cavern is deep water where only the brave can dive from the rock ledge. Do not wear suntan lotion when going into the water. Another cenote worth a visit is **Cenote Crystal**, a short distance south of Tulum Pueblo on 307. This cool clear languid cenote, surrounded by trees, is great for swimming and snorkeling and is a hot spot for cave divers. It has an extensive network of underwater caves, including one that leads under the road to a cenote on the other side.

Tulum Ruins

Civilization is a movement and not a condition,
a voyage and not a harbor.

– Arnold Toynbee, historian, 1889 -1975

 For a bunch of old stone buildings, Tulum is a particularly impressive site, perched as it is high on top of limestone cliffs that spill down to the turquoise waters of the Caribbean below. The first time we entered the modest walled city, it took our breath away. El Castillo, a large temple, is the site's biggest structure. Regrettably, it was off limits to climb this last time we were there. But the nearby Temple of the Descending God is accessible. If there are not too many people around it's a wonderful feeling to sit in the sun on the temple's platform with the waves crashing below and imagine what it must have been like years ago. If you time your visit for early morning or late afternoon you'll be blessed with fewer crowds.

Tulum above a turquoise sea.

Tulum is not a particularly important city to archeologists. A Late Post-Classic city, the style of architecture is nowhere near the complexity of the Classic period. By that time in history the building arts and stone cutting skills of the Maya had degraded and much use was made of heavy stucco to cover any rough spots. But what Tulum lacks in architectural style it more than makes up for in location. It is now the most visited archeological site in all of Mexico, with busloads of tourists coming from Cancún and cruise ships docked at Cozumel or Playa. Even its first tourist, John Lloyd Stephens, American author and adventurer who toured the Yucatán in the early 1840s, was impressed: *"Besides the deep and exciting interest of the ruins themselves, we had around us what we wanted at all the other places, the magnificence of nature.... We had found this one of the most interesting places we had seen in our whole exploration of ruins."*

The walls on three sides enclosing the city may have been defensive, as they average 18 feet thick and are between nine and 15 feet high. Entrance is via one of the original five tunnels through the wall. Guides are available outside at the new visitor's center that's complete with snack bars and gift shops. A troop of brightly dressed *Los Olmecas Ototonacos de Veracruz* Native Americans perform ceremonial twirling dances while hanging upside-down from a huge flagpole. (Nothing to do with Tulum or the Maya, but entertaining and worth the US $1 tip they ask for.) A word of caution if you're driving a car: The parking lot has odd-angled stone walls that, if you're not careful, can scrape the body as you maneuver.

If you're serious about appreciating many of the Maya ruins in your journeys around the Yucatán, we recommend *An Archeological Guide to Mexico's Yucatán Peninsula*, by Joyce Kelly (University of Oklahoma Press), available in paperback.

Tulum Pueblo

Tulum Pueblo is an undistinguished community that straddles Highway 307 before it's swallowed up by the jungle along the long southern portion down to Chetumal. We call it "Pollo Town" because of the many grills either side of the divided road that grill chickens, *pollo asado* or *pollo carbon*. The thick mouth-watering smoke hovers across the road, making it impossible to drive through without getting hungry. Furthermore, it's a very long haul down to the next major town, Puerto Felipe Carrillo.

There's been an influx of European immigrants, mostly Italian, who have discovered Tulum Pueblo's proximity to the fabulous beaches of the Punta Allen peninsula and the convenience of its 24-hour electric and low living costs. As a consequence, there are several new eateries and the town may be sprucing itself up in anticipation of increased tourism. Tulum is improving so much that a dive center, **Ak-Tún** (no phone as of press time) has opened on the main drag.

The hotel and restaurant choices near the Tulum ruins are in three close but distinct areas: the pueblo of Tulum itself, including a few hotels near the ruins; a stretch of the Boca Paila Road along the beach south from the ruins; and the Boca Paila Road farther along the shore south into the Punta Allen peninsula. They offer very different experiences, so your choice may depend on what you like and what your plans are. See page 3 for price chart.

IN TOWN ACCOMMODATIONS

Hotel Acuario (*Hotel Zone, 26 rooms with air, pool, TV, restaurant*). The Acuario is a bulky pink hotel along Highway 307 at the beginning of the old road to the Tulum ruins, now a dead-end. It's a colonial-style hotel centered around a deep swimming pool in the courtyard. The rooms have stone-tile floors and modern bathrooms, comfortable beds but paper-thin sheets. Our TV got two hazy channels. Its redeeming features are a good restaurant and a small convenience store. Within walking distance of the ruins. **$$**

Christine's Palapas (*Hotel Zone, restaurant*). Christine's consists of five big adjoining rooms in a large rectangular building, each one clean but spartan. We're tempted to call it a "backpacker," but it's really a cut above that, with private bathrooms and showers. High ceilings and big screened windows diminish the darkness of the black tar-paper roof. Christine's Restaurant out front is good and quite economical.

El Crucero Motel & Restaurant (*Hotel Zone, 16 rooms with fans, restaurant*). Huge split-leaf philodendrons climb the columns that hold up the front porch of this corner restaurant on the old road to ruin. The shady overhang is a good place to sit and watch the world while you enjoy some excellent Mexican cooking from the varied menu. Friendly owners Patricia Zapata and Mario Murello worked in the Akumal resort before opening their own place here in Tulum 21 years ago. Back off the road is their wooden two-story motel. Its rooms, with two queen-size beds, are somewhat spartan but nice and clean. A good budget value. **$**

Mary's Palapas (*Hwy. 307 at the southern edge of town*). Mary is the American owner of these very rustic cabañas set back from the highway among some broad-leafed banana trees. Without the advantage of a beach and having to share bathrooms, they're a little too primitive for our taste. **$**

Punta Allen Peninsula

If you close your eyes and imagine paradise – complete with blindingly white sand beaches, warm deep blue water, swaying palms and romantic palapa cabañas – you're imagining the northern coast of the Punta Allen peninsula. Beginning at the Tulum ruins, the coast curves east until a narrow causeway breaks away at Boca Paila to serve as a barrier between land and sea. At the end of that long peninsula, with its bone-jarring rutted road, lies the undisturbed Maya fishing village of Punta Allen. No longer as remote as it once was, the shores north of Boca Paila are sprouting new beachside accommodations. Fortunately, future development is limited thanks to the Sian Ka'an Biosphere, the 1.3 million-acre nature reserve that begins along the road and continues for 95 km (60 miles) south. Development is also limited by the lack of electricity, generated during the day only. Despite its natural beauty, this is not for everyone.

We've divided our review by either left turns north, or right turns south, when you reach the Tulum Ruins-Boca Paila Road.

Accommodations

TULUM RUINS ROAD

 A series of rustic and not-so-rustic beachfront cabañas have been attracting adventuresome tourists for a good number of years. The road to them is unmarked; you'll find it opposite the turn for Cobá, just south of the Tulum ruins. Go east for a few miles to where the road ends in a "T." A left there will take you back north along the beach toward the ruins. A right leads to the Sian Ka'an Biosphere and eventually to the fishing village of Punta Allen at the end of a long peninsula. The beaches both ways are some of the most beautiful in the Yucatán. All the cabañas' electricity comes from generators. These are turned off at 10 p.m., which suits both hotel owners and guests alike because it limits new construction – at least for now.

If you make a left on what we're calling the "Tulum Ruins Road," here's what you'll find:

Gatos Restaurant y Cabañas (*Tulum Ruins Road, 6 cabañas and building more, also hammock dormitories*). The coffee-house setting of this popular European student destination gives it a laissez-faire feeling. The shady restaurant and communal area has overstuffed furniture and is a hang-out for young intellectuals and vagabonds – kind of a Karl Marx meets Timothy Leary in paradise. On a rough rocky seafront, walk a few hundred feet to a long flat sandy beach. Fifteen dollars and up for cabañas, much less to rent a hammock and get into the swing of things. Eclectic without electric. **$**

El Paraiso (*Tulum Ruins Road*). Motel-style rooms with double beds set back from the beach on a rolling bluff. Not too clean, not very agreeable. See if they've got any new cabañas on the beach. **$**

Un-named (*Tulum Ruins Road, identified by a broken off cement sign on the right, 10 cabañas, communal bath and showers*). We know it sounds foolish, but no one could tell us the name of this large and open beachfront establishment (not even the family who run it). But we do know that it is owned by the *Collectivo de Pescadores* (Fishing Cooperative) in Tulum Pueblo. That means the local fishermen beach their boats and unload their catch here. There is a hammock-hung open dormitory and several very "natural" *na* palapas – natural as in primitive. We met a young French-Canadian woman, uniquely named Laurence Panama Lippins Carom, who raved over its simple pleasures and planned to stay for a month.

Cabañas Don Armandos - Zazil Kin (*Tulum Ruins Road, 30-something cabañas*). Don Armandos has long been a favorite place to stay near the Tulum ruins. We found the spartan rooms on the fabulous flat beach only for the hardy and suggest you bring your own soap, towels, candles and bottled water. Within walking distance of the ruins. The English-speaking owner runs a good family-style restaurant serving from 7 a.m. to 9:30 p.m.

Santa Fe and El Mirador (*Tulum Ruins Road*). The road north to the Tulum ruins is blocked to cars just past this sandy, primitive camping crash pad. Beautiful broad Caribbean beachfront, but bring your own everything. The ruins are a 10-minute walk.

Beach along Boca Paila Road.

BOCA PAILA ROAD

A right turn back at that "T" intersection leads south toward the Sian Ka'an Biosphere, the Boca Paila Bridge and finally to Punta Allen. Almost immediately you'll encounter paradise. The accommodations listed below are in order as you will pass them heading south. See page 3 for price chart. By the way, your vehicle may be stopped and lightly searched on this road by anti-drug military patrols.

Cabañas Front the Sea (*Boca Paila Road, 3 cabañas, small restaurant, no phone*). A great place for a romantic, secluded, get-away-from-it-all escape to a magnificent beach along this part of the Punta Allen peninsula. Opened in December of 1996, this should do very well, especially if Marlon Brando discovers he doesn't need to go all the way to Tahiti for this kind of experience. The cabañas are large and cheery and feature floor-to-ceiling wooden doors with louvers that swing vertically to open to the breeze. Set down in a tiled drain area, one room's shower hangs from a tall piece of driftwood, mounted upright to make it look like a tree. Safe, shallow swimming is down the bluff on a sandy, white, deserted beach. First cabañas on the left after turning south. **$$**

Cabañas La Conchita (*Boca Paila Road, no phone*). Somewhat dark and rustic but appealing *na*s with thatched roofs, mosquito netting over a double bed and a small table and mirror. Clean, white sand beach. Collective showers and bathrooms. **$**

Cabañas Punta Piedra (*Boca Paila Road, no phone*). Basic accommodations with traditional *na* construction and dark corrugated roofs, but there's a new communal bath and shower building. The large rock formation that juts into the water along the beach is great for sunbathing and watching the iguanas. They rent snorkeling equipment and bicycles. New money exchange building along the road in front. **$**

Cabañas Nohoch-Tunich (*Boca Paila Road, no phone, 10 rooms, restaurant*). An attractive two-story pink stucco building offers new rooms with two queen-size beds each. The upstairs rooms are more appealing because they have a wrap-around balcony that overlooks the big rock crowding the beach. Three new cabañas with bathrooms and showers have been built back against the rock formation. Three other cabañas, without private bathrooms, front the playa. All-in-all, a good value. At the entrance is Piedra Escondida, an inviting Mexican, Italian and fresh seafood restaurant and bar with good food at reasonable prices. **$-$$**

Cabañas La Perla (*Boca Paila Road, no phone, 2 cabañas and 6 rooms, restaurant*). Lazy hammocks hang in a small grove of palms nearby

La Perla's bar and new palapa restaurant overlooking the beach. The cabañas are ugly, but a new stucco-and-stone two-story building is very attractive and worth a look. Spanish-styled and nicely decorated, including curtains. The best room is number four with its tiny balcony and sea view. **$-$$**

Zamas Cabañas (*on a bend in the Boca Paila Road, ☎ in US: 800-538-6802 or 303-674-9615, 11 cabañas total, 5 directly on the beach, the rest are 40 paces west, dive shop*). Watch pelicans dive-bomb for fish in the surf at this bend-in-the-road beachfront cabaña complex. American owners, Susan Bohlken and Dan McGettigan, bought a part of deserted paradise in 1986 and built beachfront bungalows in 1993. Across the street from the beach, they recently built two (and are planning a third) large palapa-roofed buildings that house two suites in each. The huge bathrooms are a special treat, larger than most hotel bedrooms. The hotel's restaurant, Qué Fresco! (How Fresh!) is well respected locally and, not surprisingly, features fresh seafood. Some of the beachfront cabañas share a bath. The name Zamas was the original name of the ruined city of Tulum, meaning "City of New Dawn." **$$**

Osho Oasis (*Boca Paila Road, ☎ 987/4-27-72, dive shop, honeymoon suite, vegetarian restaurant*). This retreat offers accommodations from budget to deluxe and is well known among beachcombing travelers. If the isolated seaside life isn't enough to soothe the wild beast in you, they offer yoga, meditation and massage. Very attractive cabañas and lovely communal areas decorated with Japanese simplicity. The paved road ends in front of Osho at the official entrance to Sian Ka'an Biosphere Preserve. Anything farther is slower going over pot-holed packed earth as the road bumps and grinds. There's no need for concern because it's not that bad all the way to the bridge – well past Cabañas Tulum – but gets rougher past Boca Paila. Every once in a while the holes are filled, but that doesn't last. **$$**

Los Arrecifes (*Boca Paila Road, 20 cabañas, only 2 with private bathrooms, restaurant*). Pull the rope on a sea-bell to attract the manager from somewhere among the palms on this flat-beach part of paradise. The cabañas, with two queen-size beds, white-washed walls and mosquito netting, are pleasant, but the bathrooms are old. The attraction for beach bums of all types are Los Arrecifes' round, very primitive *nas* (sand floors and hanging beds) right on the beach. This is so back-to-nature that you'll find the patterned tracks of tiny sand crabs around the sand floor in the morning. **$**

Restaurant y Cabañas Ana y José (*Boca Paila Road, ☎ 988/0-60-22, 16 rooms with fans, restaurant*). Extremely popular, Ana y José's is a landmark along the rough road to Punta Allen. It continues to be the standard by which other places are measured. Picturesque white stucco two-story buildings, set back from the stunning beach, house well-decorated rooms on both floors. Upstairs rooms with their palapa roofs, are naturally more in demand. Ana and José offer an excellent, comfortable restaurant overlooking the water with inside or outside dining. Guided trips into the Biosphere, led by a naturalist from the Amigos de Sian Ka'an, depart from here daily, except Friday and Sunday. You can sign up and pay in the restaurant (US $40 if you drive yourself with the group to Boca Paila; if you take their van, it's US $ 50). Departs around 9 a.m. and lasts about six hours. See details in the Sian Ka'an section. **$$**

Cabañas Tulum (*7 km down the Boca Paila Road, 28 rooms, restaurant, no phone*). This is the last of the cabaña hotels that line the upper part of the Sian Ka'an Biosphere until you near the Boca Paila Bridge, where there is the very expensive – but equally rustic – Boca Paila and Casa Blanca fishing lodges. Cabañas Tulum's stucco bungalows, with a design reminiscent of a New Jersey shore motel, line the high ground above a long gorgeous beach shaded by palm trees. Painted in bright Caribbean colors, each has a tiled front porch with wooden chairs. Private baths but cold-water showers. Informal, relaxed atmosphere prevails. Wide wonderful beach. **$$**

Cruzan Guest House (*Punta Allen,* ☎ *983/4-03-58 in Felipe Carrillo Puerto, 8 rooms, 6 with bathrooms, restaurant*). This is the only hotel in the sleepy little Maya fishing village of Punta Allen. One room and some rustic cabañas. We met some people who were renting a private home, who complained that the beaches up the coast from Punta Allen were strewn with plastic and garbage that they believed was illegally dumped from cruise ships. Transplanted Californian owner, Sonja Lilvik, can arrange deep-sea fishing trips, diving, boat tours, or naturalist birdwatching excursions from the Cruzan. **$$**

Dining

 Besides the restaurants mentioned in the hotels above, where they have somewhat of a captive audience on the Boca Paila Road, there are some good eateries in the little village of Tulum Pueblo. It's hard to even drive through the town without getting hungry – the smoky smell of delicious *pollo carbon*, grilled chicken, drifts across the road from the many charcoal grills on both sides of the street. Try some, you'll like it. But an increasing *extranjero* population here and on the Boca Paila Road has meant there are a few more cosmopolitan restaurants available to choose from. See page 4 for price chart. Here's what we especially liked:

Il Giardino di Toni y Simone (*up a side*
road divider begins). To get to Il Giardino, w
make the first right at the beginning of tow
bit of road so, just in case your muffler f
breakdown shop on the corner. Only two b
lovely garden restaurant run by Toni and Ca
mela's daughter) that features fine Italian cu
large kitchen is behind stone walls and dinin
overhang on the porch, or you can eat under
umbrellas on an artificial beach. Very welcome a ....essly
clean bathrooms. Pricier than one would normally ....pect in a town
like Tulum, the food here is beautifully presented and absolutely
delicious. If you've just discovered the ruins nearby, this is a good
place to celebrate the experience. Don't leave without having cap-
puccino with cream. **$$**

La Isla (*side road near where the concrete divider ends*). This is a little
hard to find; make the last right-hand turn (at Doña Tina's restau-
rant) when heading south in Tulum Pueblo and it's one block in.
Appearances can be deceiving as this perennially popular but out-
wardly shacky-looking restaurant is cool and attractive inside and
serves up excellent home-made pasta, pizza, vegetarian dishes and
fresh fish. A huge philodendron plant nearly covers the front so look
hard. It's worth finding. **$-$$**

Captain Gemini's (*middle of town*). The Captain's is a cool
thatched-roofed place for lunch on a hot day and a popular spot at
night for dinner. The bar fills up in the evening. Sit at their high tables
in bar chairs and enjoy good food at reasonable prices. High standard of cleanliness. Right next door there's a new arts and crafts shop
called **Utzi Ché**, which means precious wood, featuring beautiful
useful and decorative pieces made by local artists. **$-$$**

Don Cafeio (*middle of town*). Mexican diner popular with locals
and bus patrons. Clean and cheap. **$**

Doña Tina's (*at the southern edge of town*). Right at the end of the
divided road through downtown Tulum Pueblo, Doña Tina has
been running this little restaurant since 1979. Her Poc-Chuc was
better than the one we had at Los Almendros and less than half the
price. There's not much atmosphere in her palapa-covered, stick-
walled open dining area, but it's just a good place to get home-made
Mexican food at a price that's below your budget. **$**

El Crucero (*Hotel Zone*). See the reference in "In Town Accommodations." Excellent food within walking distance of the ruins. **$**

Sian Ka'an Biosphere

*People into eco-tourism really don't want things made
too easy for them, they are generally travelers who
eschew anything like mass tourism.*

– Barbara MacKinnon, one of the founders of
Amigos de Sian Ka'an

 The bus we catch for the wilderness area known as Sian Ka'an leaves the Cancún terminal at 6 a.m. By Tulum Pueblo the tourist contingent is down to the two of us and an American doctor, who is kicking around Quintana Roo on a two-week vacation. At 9 a.m. we catch a cab down the beautiful beach along the Boca Paila Road to Ana y José's cabañas where our biologist guide, Manuel Galindo, greets us enthusiastically. "The Sian Ka'an Biosphere was set aside as a protected natural reserve in January 1986," he tells us. From the Mayan, *Ziyan Caán*, meaning "birth of the sky," the biosphere was the first large-scale attempt by the Mexican government to actively safeguard the fragile ecology in one of Mexico's last undeveloped areas.

The unique reserve covers 1.3 million acres of land, savannas, salt marshes, beaches and three lagoons. The protected area also includes 110 km (69 miles) of coral reef. Less than 1,000 people live in the zone, most of them lobster fishermen in Punta Allen. Manuel drives us to Boca Paila while he tells us about the exceptional flora and fauna of the area – 1,200 species of animals in 17 different classifications. We join with other tourists for a boat ride into two of the large lagoons. The best part comes when we enter twisting channels lined with reed and mangrove that connect lagoons. The banks are alive with birds – roseate spoonbills, blue and white herons, wood storks, kingfishers, diving cormorants, king vultures – and we're on the lookout for any of the two species of crocodile, 12 kinds of snake, five types of iguana, wild pheasants, pelicans, flamingoes, jungle cats, manatees, several kinds of marine turtles and Amazonian dolphins that make their home here. Birdwatchers should pick up Barbara MacKinnon's book, *100 Common Birds of the Yucatán*, published by Amigos de Sian Ka'an. Helpful descriptions and even more helpful color photos aid in identification.

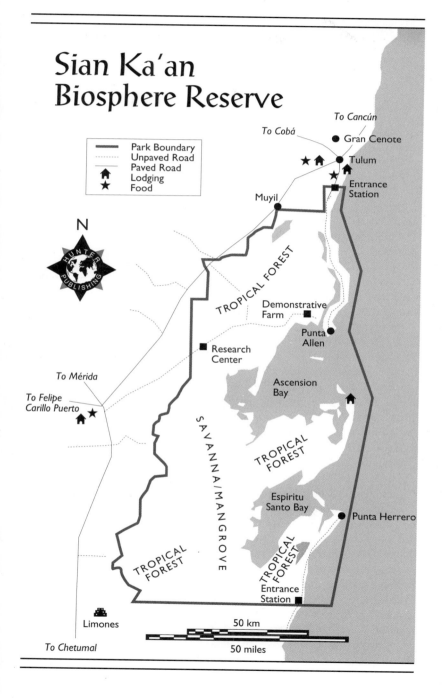

Sian Ka'an Biosphere Reserve

Legend:
- Park Boundary
- Unpaved Road
- Paved Road
- Lodging
- Food

N

To Cancún
To Cobá
Gran Cenote
Tulum
Entrance Station
Muyil
TROPICAL FOREST
Demonstrative Farm
Punta Allen
Research Center
To Mérida
To Felipe Carillo Puerto
Ascension Bay
TROPICAL FOREST
Espiritu Santo Bay
Punta Herrero
TROPICAL FOREST
SAVANNA/MANGROVE
TROPICAL FOREST
Entrance Station
Limones
To Chetumal
50 km
50 miles

After seeing some *ojos de aqua* in the lake, we re-enter the canal and dock at an overgrown Maya ruin, a customs house that checked cargo and collected fees from trading canoes nearly 1,000 years ago. The highlight of the trip occurs when Manuel goes ahead in the boat while we jump in the strong current of the channel and float downstream, joking about the two types of crocodiles.

Trips into the Biosphere run daily, except for Fridays and Sundays, sponsored by the Amigos de Sian Ka'an, a private non-profit environmental group that works closely with the government to promote sustainable resource management in the zone. To insure the lowest possible impact, usually no more than 18 visitors per day are allowed in the preserve.

Our second venture into the wilderness comes on a Thursday night when we take a cab from Tulum Pueblo to the Muyil ruins to meet Carlos, a working biologist. We pile into a launch with several Austrian tourists and set out into the black lagoon, led only by the glare from Carlos' coal miner's helmet and the light of a billion stars. The lagoon's water is warm and shallow, ideal territory for the prehistoric nocturnal-hunting crocodile. Carlos explains the counting and tagging research is to assertain if the crocodile population can be sustained with selective harvesting by the local Maya families. If it can – and they can make money at it – it will take some of the ecological pressure off other resources and lessen the need for slash and burn agriculture.

When Carlos sees the tell-tale red dots of a croc's eyes, he turns on a car-battery-powered spotlight that eerily illuminates the mangrove trees along the bank. The crocodiles slide back farther into the tangled web of roots; it's a little too cool this evening to lure them out. We miss out on the thrashing and rolling of the beasts along the boat as they're marked with metal tags. It will be for someone else, another week. Meanwhile the southern sky puts on a show of twinkley lights and shooting stars that boggles the senses, while little fish jump in front of Carlos' light in a dance of silver and shine. We lay back in the boat, hands dangling in the warm water and pretend we're Maya traders, slicing across the trackless world of the night lagoon. Never to be forgotten.

Both trips (approximately US $50 per person) can be arranged by calling the Amigos de Sian Ka'an in Cancún, ☎ 98/84-95-83. Their offices are in the Plaza America on Av. Cobá, upstairs rear. They sell books and gift items that benefit the preserve. Impulsive people can just show up for the 9 a.m. trip by asking for Manuel or at least informing the Ana y José restaurant staff that they're there for the trip. You run a slight risk of it being fully booked. Wear adequate insect repellent.

Cobá

What is a ruin but time easing itself of endurance?

— *Selected Works*, Djuna Barnes, 1962

 The Maya civilization may have grown around Cobá due to its group of five lakes (rare in the Yucatán), scattered as if by chance around the nearby jungle. Cobá, meaning "Ruffled Waters," was mentioned in the *Chilam Balam de Chumayel*, a chronicle of Maya history told in Mayan but written down in Spanish. Occupied from the Classic through the Post-Classic periods, it was a rival of Chichén Itzá during the latter's apex. The large site spreads out over several square miles, but in general the ruins are not well preserved. The most interesting of the structures are the massive Nohoch Mul temple and the Iglesia, a nine-tiered pyramid with broad steps. From the base of the tall Nohoch Mul pyramid, a *sacbé*, a sacred white road, runs some 100 km (62 miles) to the minor city of Yaxuná, near Chichén Itzá. Cobá is also the place to see standing steles, carved with incredibly long date glyphs. Most are badly weathered. Climbing any of the structures takes you above the tree line, where a cooling breeze may provide relief from the hot and humid jungle. If you need a break, check to see whether you can use the Villas' pool (see below) if you buy a drink at their bar.

The little town has improved itself on the east side of the lake near the bus station and several restaurants. The other side of the lake is the residential village, without services except for a small **local crafts** store and **gasoline** that is dispensed from steel drums.

Cobá can be included in your itinerary from either Tulum or Nuevo Xcan, a town halfway between Cancún and Valladolid on Highway 180. North of Cobá on the road to Nuevo Xcan is the Reserva de Areania Mono, a **spider monkey reserve**. It was organized a number of years ago by Serapio Canul Tep, a Maya elder who realized the population of local monkeys was endangered by fellow villagers who hunted them for food. His efforts led to the reserve, now managed by local families from the town of Punta Laguna. A US $2 admission gets you a guide (in Spanish or Mayan) on paths into the thick jungle. In addition to spider monkeys, the reserve also houses the howler monkey, a cousin of the spider monkeys who can swell its larynx to form a natural amplifier – allowing its cry to be heard as far as 9-10 km (5-6 miles) away. You may also see wild turkeys or deer on the path past a small Maya ruin to the cave where the monkey colony lives. A couple of hundred feet down a dirt road is a large natural lake, Lago Punta Laguna. Wear plenty of insect repellent.

Accommodations & Dining

 Villas Arqueológicas (*Cobá,* ☎ & *fax 987/4-20-87, 40 rooms with air, pool, restaurant, tennis courts*). A mirror image, approximately, of its sister hotels in Uxmal and Chichén, Villas is on the lake, a few minute's walk from the ruins. The sunset over the water and into the jungle is quite beautiful here. See our review of Chichén Itzá's property. **$$**

Nichte Ha (*next to Villas*). Open at 6 a.m., this little restaurant on a hill overlooking the lake offers relief from the high price of Villas dining. Mexican and Yucatecan cooking. **$**

Posada Bocadito (*next to the bus stop, 12 rooms with fans*). Cold water and basic rooms. **$**

Rumor has it that there will be another *posada* in town by press time so ask around. The Bocadito is located next to the quiet bus station, which has a restaurant of the same name. It's a popular spot with bus travelers but we were disappointed with the food. Try the cute little restaurant, **La Susan Mexicana**, across the street. La Susan drapes lavender tablecloths and puts fresh flowers on each table.

At the end of town, to the left along the road around the lake to the ruins, there are several **gift shops** and **restaurants** that cater to visitors.

Muyil

 South from Tulum Pueblo one   enters a sparsely inhabited 98-km stretch (61 miles) of jungle bordered on the east by the Sian Ka'an Biosphere and on the west by a trackless jungle. But it wasn't always without big cities. The rather geographically large Maya ruin of Muyil, "Place of Rabbits," is hidden on the left as you pass through the minuscule village of Chunyaxche. Most of the ruins, covered by brush, are badly weathered and only archeological freaks will find more than a quick look worthwhile. However, birdwatching is reported to be excellent here. The ancient Classic-age city is connected to the Caribbean through a series of lagoons and canals but is not thought to have been a shipping port. Today, that water route is in Sian Ka'an and it is from the grass parking lot of the ruins that a weekly Thursday **night expedition** to tag and count wild crocodiles is made by a biologist (either Carlos or Gonzalo) into Laguna Chunyaxche. You can arrange to go with the Amigos de Sian Ka'an in Cancún (about US $50). Most of the few people who make this run stay at the expensive **Robinson Club Resort**, (☎ 98/81-10-34; fax 98/81-10-04) south of Tulum. We stayed more cheaply in Tulum and, even though we had a car, we hired a taxi driver to take us down and pick us up again at 11 p.m. This is an adventure of a lifetime. See details in the Sian Ka'an section, above. Even if you don't catch crocodiles and wrestle them alongside the boat, the southern sky at night is unbelievable! We counted more shooting stars in the pitch black abyss above than we counted red beady eyes of crocks in the shallow lagoon.

Felipe Carrillo Puerto

 A dusty crossroads market town, Felipe Carrillo was named for the assassinated hero who governed the Yucatán and worked for the liberation of the grossly exploited Maya. Ironically, the city was one of the last bastions of the Maya independence movement and is still the unofficial capital of *Zona Maya*. The brutal War of the Castes (see page 38) drove the Maya into the remote Quintana Roo countryside. A settlement grew here called *Chan Santa Cruz* (Small Holy Cross) after a wooden cross was erected at a cenote and "spoke" in a native tongue, extolling the Cruzob Maya Indians to renew their resistance to the oppressive Spanish-Yucatecan rulers. The cross, in a mix of ancient Maya religion and Christianity, directed Maya holy men to run a campaign against the "foreigners." Perhaps it is no surprise that one of the leaders of the bizarre cult of the talking cross was a ventriloquist.

To visit the muddy little cenote that started it all, head five blocks west from the Pemex station and ask someone to point out the **Sanctuario del Cruz Parlante**. You'll find the cenote, a tiny museum and a brick shrine with a painted cross in the small park steeped in the Yucatán's bloody history. With almost no attractions in town, very few tourists spend the night. If it's late the **Faisán y Venado Hotel and Restaurant** is acceptable. In the town's main square there's a "whipping fountain" used by the Cruzob elders as a place of punishment. Next to it is the Balam Nah temple (looks like a colonial church) built to hold the cross by white prisoners of the Maya. The *mercado* near the crossroads is very lively and a good place to check out if you're not in a hurry.

Two roads to the right in the center of town lead into the heart of the Mayan world. The first, Route 295, takes you back north through the most traditional Maya area past Tixacal and on to Valladolid. A Maya general and supreme council still possess a sister cross to the original in a Tixaxal sanctuary. Every two years the *Quich Kelen Yum Tata*, a celebration offered to the Trinity, takes place there. This is a solemn occasion that ends with the Holy Cross procession on May 3. In an attempt to preserve traditions, tourists are sometimes turned away. If you photograph or wish to speak with an elder, ask permission. Farther north is Tihosuco, the historic hometown of Jacinto Pat, one of the Caste War leaders, where you can find the **Caste War Museum**.

Two km (1.25 miles) south of Tixcacalcupul and 22 km (14 miles) south of Valladolid you'll cross the Cobá to Yaxuná *sacbé*. A sign says "Mirador," meaning a sight, but there really isn't much to see. The ancient raised white roadway looks like a clearing in the trees, but if you look closely in the weeds you'll see the outline of the *sacbé*, made of limestone boulders.

The second way inland from Purto is northwest along Ruta Maya, Highway 184, along the Puuc Hills through the historical Maya communities of Tzucacab, Ticul, Muna and finally Mérida. It's a fascinating trip back through time. If you're continuing to Bacalar and Chetumal, keep straight on 307. Fill up with gasoline in Felipe Carrillo, no matter where you're going from there.

Dining

For dining, the **Mayob Turquesa Restaurant,** less than a mile north of downtown on 307, is our choice. The impressive paintings hanging on the wall are by local artist Marcelo Jimenez, who is the director of the Cultural Center in town. Master painter Jorge Corona once lived in the center's colonial building and the art school he founded there for Maya artists has made an impact on local and regional arts. Beneath the Mayob Turquesa's big cool palapa you can stop for a rest and have a good inexpensive meal under one of their six overhead fans. If it's hot, take a dip in one of their two swimming pools before passing through the crowded town ahead. Generous servings and inexpensive prices. In town, besides the *Faisán y Venado*, there's

Restaurant 24 Horas, across from the bus station. Two doors away is **Hamburger Maya,** worth a stop just for its name. Both places are clean, tasty and cheap.

Xcalak Peninsula

 The land mass south of the Sian Ka'an boundary and east of Highway 307 inland contains a flat limestone shelf of mangrove, savanna and low rainforest, long accessible only by sea. A paved road now makes a tedious ride to **Majahual.** The small village there has become popular with Chetumal families as a vacation spot and summer homes dot the shore. A federal Naval post guards the area against smuggling. South from Majahual to **Xcalak,** the rutted and bumpy dirt road runs past spectacular beaches and boring dead palm trees in the former plantations. It ends at the fishing village of Xcalak, where most of the tourists are die-hard divers or fishers. The divers are here for the **Chinchorro Banks,** a 42-km (26-mile) atoll two hours offshore by boat. Strewn with shipwrecks and crowded with colorful coral, it's protected as a no-fishing National Park. You're a short boat ride from the better-known cayes of Belize, namely Ambergris Caye, and there are enough underwater sights nearby to wrinkle your skin for weeks.

The few hotels here are mostly high-priced dive resorts, the most prominent of which is **Costa de Cocos,** with 12 beachside cabañas (no phone). Other are **Sanwood Villas** and **Villa Caracol,** both beachside, and **Hotel Caracol,** in town. There are two minor Maya sites on the peninsula, Rio Uach and Xcalak.

Bacalar

*Blue color is everlastingly appointed by the Deity
to be a source of delight.*

– John Ruskin, English art critic, 1819-1900

 Located 38 km (24 miles) northwest of Chetumal, the historic town of Bacalar overlooks Lake Bacalar, also known as the *Laguna de Siete Colores,* the "Lagoon of Seven Colors." The Maya name, *Bak Halal,* means "Place

Surrounded by Canes." It boasts magnificent water with hues of mauves and blues and greens, great for swimming and lined on its elevated west bank with summer homes and a few small hotels. The 42-km-long (26 miles) lake is linked to the Hondo River that separates Mexico and Belize by the Chaac Inlet, where traditional regattas are held on and around August 16 each year.

Laguna Bacalar, the lagoon of seven colors.

The town of Bacalar itself is not geared for tourists, although the one-story buildings are all of great antiquity. The first Spanish colony settled here in 1545, but by 1652 it was destroyed and abandoned. In 1726, Canary Islanders resettled it, building the thick stone **Fort San Felipe** in 1729 to fend off English pirates who scourged the town. The fort protected the town from attack by water, only to have the city ravaged twice – the second time in one of the most bloody and brutal massacres of the Caste War. Today, Fort San Felipe is commanded by Ofelia Casa Madrid, a strong woman with a Masters Degree in Social Anthropology and history teacher in a local high school who works part-time as the fort's caretaker. Be sure to stop and say hello and give her a chance to practice her English. She'll direct you to a good family restaurant, **La Esperanza**, two blocks away.

There are no in-town hotels, but there is a **boat rental** along the waterfront. There's an immigration road stop near Bacalar, but nine times out of 10 you'll be waved through.

Accommodations & Dining

Many tourists bypass the multi-cultural Chetumal downtown and stay outside along the picturesque Laguna Bacalar, 20 km (12.5 miles) north of the city on Route 307, where the choices are fewer but more appealing. There's a large resort being built south of Cenote Azul, but it was not yet open when we passed. This is a good base to explore the ruins of southern Quintana Roo or to nip into Belize. The following hotels are as you pass them from north to south along the lagoon. See pages 3 and 4 for price charts.

Rancho Encontado (*Hwy 307,* ☎ *US, 800-505-MAYA, in Mexico, 983/8-04-27, restaurant, gift shop, group facilities, kayak and windsurf rentals, prices include breakfast and dinner*). *Encontado* means charmed or enchanted in Spanish and this lovely tropical-style hotel – tucked down a hollow along the edge of the Bacalar lagoon – is both. The American owners have spared little expense in making each of their 12 rental units cool and inviting. The bungalows, or *casitas*, have tile floors and a definite colonial hacienda ambiance. Tropical hardwoods and tasteful Mexican decorations are in both the *casitas* and the thatched-roof palapa cabañas, which are near the edge of the lagoon (wear insect repellent here). The capable manager is Luis Téllez, an amateur nature photographer who is well-versed in the area's attractions, especially the Maya ruins. Encontado provides guided educational trips to a variety of archeological sites, including the hard-to-get-to newly opened ones. Birders also love it here. The Hotel Rancho Encontado offers a provisional checklist of birds sighted in and around its property. It lists over 150 different birds. Many more can be found in the region, especially in migration. Birdwatching is best early in the hot tropical day. Excellent restaurant, no red meat served. **$$$**

Puerta Del Cielo (*Hwy 307,* ☎ *983/7-19-93 pool, restaurant and bar*). If it wasn't situated between two more noteworthy competitors, the Puerta would merit more consideration. It looks more like a store front from the road, but in back, 13 basic but brightly painted connected bungalows zig-zag down the hillside toward the lagoon. Each simple room has a view and a tiny patio. The large suite with two beds and kitchenette (#11) has worn, overstuffed furniture and is overpriced for all but two couples. The restaurant and bar are at the water's edge. **$**

Hotel Laguna (*Hwy 307,* ☎ *983/2-35-17, restaurant, swimming pool, bar, 27 rooms with fan or 3 bungalows that sleep 5 to 8*). This hard-to-miss whimsical Mediterranean-style hotel, built 25 years ago and frozen in time, is white with tons of turquoise trim and an orange roof. It's definitely one of a kind and the place grows on you. We think it's very special. All the rooms have white wrought-iron furniture on balconies that face the lake. Thick wooden louvered windows in the tidy rooms allow in the fresh breeze or the light from one of the area's incredible sunrises. Immaculately landscaped walkways and terraces lead from the deep swimming pool down the steep hill to a boat and swimming dock. Sea shells of all shapes and sizes cover the hotel. Truck loads must have been hauled from the Caribbean to create the picturesque decor. Small hand-painted wall tiles with amusing observations and Spanish sayings are also ubiquitous. Good restaurant. The only drawback we found was very slow toilets, which took several flushes to remove waste. **$**

Hotel Laguna.

Cenote Azul Restaurant (*Hwy 307, along the Bacalar lagoon, no phone*). Woven wicker covers the support columns and ceiling of this mostly seafood restaurant perched on the edge of a deep turquoise cenote (one of many with the "Azul" name). The restaurant is also a local swimming hole. The cenote, the largest in the world, looks like an oval lake, some several hundred feet across, with a depth of 300 feet. Fish hang around the edge waiting for food scraps. The seafood or Mexican dishes at the restaurant are tasty (mosquitoes are a problem at dinner), the service friendly and the swimming or snorkeling loads of fun. There's usually an unemployed man or some boys hanging around the parking lot who will wash your car for a tip while you're inside. $-$$

Cenote Azul Trailer Park (*Hwy 307, electric, bathrooms, showers, dump, wash room, no phone*). If you're RV-ing or camping, a very friendly family runs this convenient trailer and camping area right next to Cenote Azul and the Bacalar Lagoon, less than a mile south of the Hotel Laguna. Flat, quiet, shady and convenient to just about anywhere, it's one of the cheapest campgrounds around. Tenters or hammockers need mosquito netting in the evening.

Birding

For good scrub birding within walking distance of Rancho Encontado, walk south about 200 yards until you reach the "Playa Centroamericana" sign on your left. Turn right and follow the dirt track about 100 yards to a large orchard of lime trees. Walk around the edges of the orchard, close to the surrounding forest. Before reaching the orchard you will have crossed under some power lines where a path leads several miles in either direction through good scrub and second-growth habitat.

Three miles north of the hotel there's a sign for a nature reserve five miles up the road. The federal reserve has good forest where biologists are raising great curassows and crested guans for later release into the wild. Ask at Encontado for details. For more forest birding, try one mile farther north at the *Campo Experimental Forestal*. A dirt track toward the lake goes through good forest habitat for about two miles. You may have to ask permission of the watchman to get into the *campo* before office hours.

Chetumal

Time is a river without banks.

– Traditional folk saying

 On May 5, 1898 the Mexican Navy founded a settlement they called Payo Obispo along the mouth of the Hondo River where it flows into the bay. It was part of an effective military strategy to end the Caste War by cutting off the supply of arms purchased by the Maya from English merchants in Belize and smuggled up the Hondo. In 1936, the name changed back to a version of the area's pre-Hispanic name, *Chechemal*. Chetumal became the capital when Quintana Roo became a state and since then the population has grown to nearly 250,000, including suburbs.

When Prince Bernhard of Holland visited, local cooks honored him by creating a delicious new regional dish, a hollowed-out ball of Dutch cheese filled with a mixture of ground pork, capers, olives, raisins, tomato, onion and sweet chile, covered in sauce. He was so delighted, he asked for the recipe, took it back, and it's now a favorite dish in Holland. A popular local bread, *pan bon*, is based on an English recipe.

Chetumal was never a tourist destination in itself, but it does have a unique Caribbean feel due to its proximity to Belize. This is a good base for day trips into southern Quintana Roo. The surrounding countryside offers some pleasing diversions.

Orientation

 GETTING AROUND: To enter the city from the north and west, follow the signs or turn left on Av. Insurgentes to the circle then turn right (south) into town. The city's heart contains an excellent "must-see" museum, the **Museo de la Cultura Maya**, on Av. Heroes. Its permanent exhibition introduces visitors to the complex Maya culture. A leafy forest cuts across several floors centering around a life-size reproduction of a sacred Ceiba tree of life. A working clock effectively explains the Maya calendar. If you see only one thing in Chetumal, this museum should be it. Across from the Monument to the Mestizo Race is the **Altamirano Market**, an art deco-style *mercado*, also on Av. Heroes.

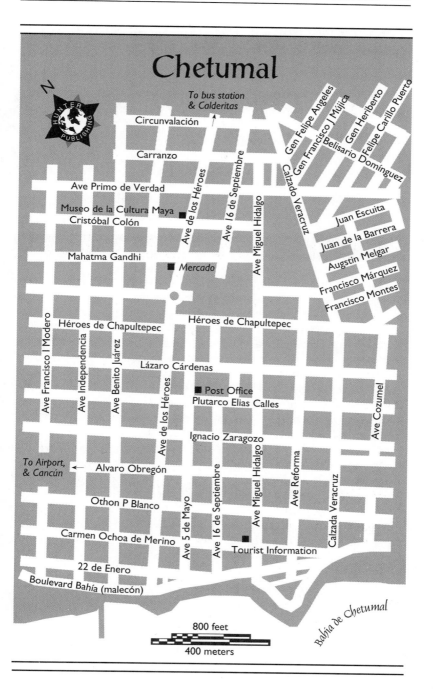

Chetumal

To bus station
& Calderitas

Circunvalación

Carranzo

Gen Felipe Angeles
Gen Francisco J Mújica
Gen Heriberto
Belisario
Felipe Carillo Puerto
Domínguez

Ave Primo de Verdad

Museo de la Cultura Maya
Cristóbal Colón

Ave de los Héroes
Ave 16 de Septiembre
Ave Miguel Hidalgo
Calzado Veracruz

Juan Escuita

Juan de la Barrera

Mahatma Gandhi

Augstin Melgar

Mercado

Francisco Márquez

Francisco Montes

Héroes de Chapultepec

Héroes de Chapultepec

Ave Francisco I Modero
Ave Independencia
Ave Benito Juárez
Ave de los Héroes

Lázaro Cárdenas

Post Office

Plutarco Elias Calles

Ave Cozumel

Ignacio Zaragozo

To Airport,
& Cancún

Alvaro Obregón

Othon P Blanco

Carmen Ochoa de Merino

Ave 5 de Mayo
Ave 16 de Septiembre
Ave Miguel Hidalgo
Ave Reforma
Calzada Veracruz

Tourist Information

22 de Enero

Boulevard Bahía (malecón)

Bahía de Chetumal

800 feet

400 meters

The long Chetumal Bay waterfront is a great walk, bike ride, or drive and a **bandstand** near the hulking Obelisk features Sunday concerts.

A wooden, English colonial-style building to the northwest of the Legislative Palace contains an intriguing scale model of the former **Payo Obispo**, reconstructed from the memories of old residents and built by Luis Reinhard Macliberty. The wooden Caribbean-style town depicted was all but destroyed by Hurricane Janet in 1955. Janet also killed 800 residents.

If you're looking for that special gift for yourself or loved ones, check out the **Artisan** store downtown on Av. Heroes. Some very creative and unique pieces are for sale. We were dying to bring home a 6'5" wooden Carnival skeleton carved by a local artist.

Adventures

 Besides visiting the impressive prehispanic ruins off the highway east toward Xpuhil, day trips to the surrounding area could include **Calderitas**, a small weekend getaway north of the city with good restaurants and a rocky beached bay. **Oxtancah**, a Maya and colonial Spanish ruin three km (1.8 miles) from Calderitas, contains a period painting of three Spanish ships on the wall of the baptistery, perhaps done by a Maya who saw them anchored in the bay, or by a conquistador, wishing for home. **El Palmar** is a tiny village 51 km (32 miles) to the southwest, near Ucum. It has a huge crystalline swimming pool fed by a natural spring. It is a bit out of the way but cool and pleasant. **Tres Garantías** is a remote area in the low jungles southwest of Kohunlich where local villagers are attempting to combine ecology and tourism by offering a jungle stay with hiking trails and birdwatching. Very rustic and natural. Check with the tourism office first, and bring your own water.

Milagros Lagoon (Miracle Lake) is an inviting swimming and camping spot on the edge of *Huay Pix*, 14 km (9 miles) west of Chetumal. Along the banks are some restaurants that reportedly serve tasty regional dishes, including wild boar and *tepescuincle* (*haleb* in Mayan). This large rodent (scientific name, *Agouti paca*) looks a little like a giant chipmunk without a tail. It has short gray to brown fur with four or five rows of buff-colored spots, a buff belly and small ears. It's an intrinsic part of the jungle ecosystem because, like a North American squirrel, the paca buries seeds and fruits that germinate later. Pacas use bony swellings on their cheekbones as resonating chambers to produce sounds and their calls can be quite loud. Due to their good tasting meat, they are in danger of extinction.

In an effort to save them in the wild, breeding farms have been created in Central America and tropical Mexico. Although they are a traditional Maya treat, please decline these when you see them on the menu.

A small village up Rt. 307, the village of **Xul Ha** sits on a circular lagoon that feeds Lake Bacalar through an inlet with a strong current. Swimming these "rapids" takes you past some interestingly carved designs in the bedrock.

Rent a boat at Hal-Ha restaurant along the Chetumal waterfront or from Calderitas and nip over to the uninhabited **Isla Tamalcab** to see the fuzzy wild capybaras, large native rodents of South America that look like furry pigs, run like horses and swim and float like hippopotami. The boat rental provides navigational maps for as far away as Ambergris Caye and San Pedro, Belize.

Chetumal sponsors an **International Automobile Road Race** in early December. Hotels will fill up. The **Fiesta de San Ignacio** is a big fiesta held the last week in July that features reggae, calypso and Mexican music. From Chetumal it's an easy jaunt down to *Belice* (**Belize**) for a day or longer. You're not supposed to take a rental car in, but if you do, you can buy car insurance just over the border. Look for the sign on the right or ask a guard.

Practicalities

 Chetumal averages 95°F in August and 85° in December. It gets copious amounts of summer rainfall. There's no need for a **visa** to enter Belize, but if there's a chance you'll be going into Guatemala, you'll need a tourist card, available at the border or the Guatemala Consulate on Av. Obregon (☎ 983/2-13-65). To extend your Mexican **tourist card** you can try to find the immigration office (☎ 983/2-62-74) off Av. Insurgentes, a few blocks from the sad-to-see zoo. Bring two copies of everything. If you need only 30 days or less, you'll get that as you re-enter Mexico from Belize.

Chetumal **tourism information** is located on Av. Obregon, near the Municipal Palace, with another in the *Palacio del Gobierno*, second floor, on Av. Heroes. That same avenue has several **money change** booths, but the rates are not as favorable as those at the banks. A *largo distancia* **telephone** shop is on Obregon at Heroes. The Bancomer on Obregon has an **ATM**. The **police** are available at ☎ 983/2-15-00 and a **pharmacy**, Farmacia Social Mechaca (☎ 983/2-00-44), is on Av. Indepencia.

A SIDETRIP TO BELIZE: The road to Belize is outside town; it's a short drive to the border. Two **bus lines** serve Belize: **Batty's**, a local service with buses that look like its name, and **Venus**, which also features a 2 p.m. express to Belize City. Buses depart near the *mercado* or the main bus terminal two km (1.25 miles) north of the city center.

Accommodations

Making Chetumal City your base means you also have a fair variety of agreeable and inexpensive hotels to choose from. See page 3 for price chart.

Hotel Marlon (*Av. Juárez No 87,* ☎ *983/2-94-11, fax 983/2-65-55, 50 rooms with 2 junior suites, air, TV, pool, all major credit cards*). The Marlon is a modern business hotel with a reputation as an excellent value. Downstairs is a lobby/bar with a colorful stained-glass window, the Montecarlo restaurant and an inviting pool in the center courtyard. You get more for less staying here. $

Hotel Principe (*Av. Heroes No. 326,* ☎ *983/2-47-99, fax 983/2-51-91, pool, restaurant, private parking*) is also a modern and clean hotel, set back from the busy main street and a real bargain 10 or more blocks from the bay. $

Holiday Inn Caribe (*Av. Niños Heroes No. 171, 983/2-11-00, fax 983/2-16-76, TV, telephone, pool, 86 rooms and suites with air*). Across the main shopping street from the *Museo de Cultura*, the hotel was remodeled in 1995 and now delivers the kind of room quality expected of the Holiday Inn chain – as well as a spacious pool and dependable restaurant. The owner is active in promoting Chetumal tourism and, fortunately, her interest begins with pleasing her guests. $$

Hotel Los Cocos (*Av. Niños Heroes No. 134, restaurant, pool, 70 rooms and 8 suites with air*) is strong competition for the Holiday Inn across the street. An independent "luxury" hotel, Los Cocos has good sized rooms with air-conditioning, an appealing swimming pool and a cool and attractive entryway. $$

Hotel Maria Dolores (*Av. Obregon No. 206, 41 rooms with fan*) is a basic Mexican budget hotel: clean and adequate. Enter up a driveway along the front of the building or through their very good little restaurant, the Sosilmar. $

Hotel Ucum (*Mahatma Gandhi No. 4,* ☎ *983/2-04-10*). Its name only sounds amusing if you pronounce it in English instead of Mayan – and you share our sophomoric sense of humor. Basic accommodations in this friendly but not fancy hotel come with fans in rooms around a massive open courtyard. A clean budget hotel. Supposedly, a daily bus for Xcalak leaves near here. **$**

CREA Youth Hostel (*Obregon and Anaya,* ☎ *983/2-34-65*). Dormitory accommodations in the government-sponsored chain of youth hostels.

Sunrise of the Caribbean Trailer Park (*8 km/5 miles northeast of the city toward Calderitas Bay from Av. Insurgentes*). If camping is your pleasure you may enjoy staying at this breezy bayside trailer park just north of the city. It offers full trailer hookups along a beautiful palm-tree lined portion of the bay. It's a quiet alternative for explorations into Belize and the southern Maya ruins. As the name implies, the sunrises are impressive.

Dining

 As it is in restaurants along most of the long shoreline of the Yucatán Peninsula, fresh seafood is a major menu item here in Chetumal. What distinguishes it from Cancún, however, are the bargain prices. All the restaurants we list here qualify from budget to moderate. Two well-known seafood restaurants are **Emiliano's**, usually packed for lunch, on Av. San Salvador at Calle 9, and **Mandinga**, on Av. Belice No. 124, revered for its octopus and conch seafood soup. See page 4 for price chart.

Hal-Ha (*on the malecón at Punta Maya*). One of Chetumal's newest and most attractive eating places is under a giant palapa among a grove of trees along the edge of the breezy bay. Previously, the Hal-Ha's manager, Alfredo Montalvo Osorio, ran the restaurant at the luxurious El Presidente hotel in Cozumel, so the service, food and decor here are first rate. American soft-rock plays in the background and local families reserve tables for special occasions. The restaurant's Maya name means "close to the water" so, naturally, they have a dock into the Chetumal Bay. They offer rental awning-covered motor-boats to tour the bay ($25 hour, seats up to six) or you can spend $90 for a day and go as far away as San Pedro, Belize (which, like the Gilligan's Island, is a three-hour tour). Photocopied navigational maps provided. **$$**

Puente al Sol (*Blvd. Bahia at the southern end of the malecón*). Dine or drink under this big palapa-roofed eatery on a wooden deck that goes right out over the water. The open southwest end, facing the water, shaped to resemble the bow of a ship, gives it the name "Bridge to the Sun." Live music every evening. **$$**

Sergios (*Av. Obregon at Av. 5th de Mayo*) is a particularly popular place to pick up pieces of pizza pie or grilled steaks. **$**

Restaurant Arcadas (*Av. Heroes and Zaragoza*). This restaurant in the downtown area offers dependable Mexican cooking at reasonable prices. Open 24 hours a day. With a handy mini-supermarket in back, it's a local favorite. Large open windows face the street, making it a great place to watch people in the heart of the shopping district. **$-$$**

Sosilmar Restaurant (*Av. Obregon*). Manager Martin Medina is a Richard Simmons look-alike. He even speaks with the same lilting inflection – but in Spanish. It's easy to gain weight eating in this diner where the servings are generous, delicious and inexpensive. Downstairs from the Hotel Maria de Lourdes, it's open 7 a.m. - 10 p.m. **$**

La Troje de Sergio's (*on the malecón,* ☎ *983/2-72-49*). A popular upscale seafood restaurant with an extensive menu that includes Italian dishes. It has a relaxing atmosphere with a great view across the street to Chetumal Bay. **$$**

Belize

Enough scraps and rocks and countries are conveniently distributed across the face of the earth so that the sun still always shines on something British.

– Pamela Marsh, in a review of Simon Winchester's
The Sun Never Sets

 If you're planning to spend more than a day in Belize, formerly known as British Honduras, pick up a copy of Hunter Publishing's *Explore Belize*, by Harry Pariser. It's got all the details on the **Rio Bravo Conservation Area**, **Cockscomb Jaguar Reserve**, **Bermudian Baboon Sanctuary**, the **Maya Mountains**, **Ambergris Caye** and more. It's a bible to the ins and outs of this eccentric little English-speaking country wedged between Mexico and Guatemala and the worlds of the Maya, Hispanic, Caribbean and British cultures, as well as that of the US (superstation WGN is on satellite TV so everyone is a Cubs fan).

Every March 9, Belizians celebrate **Baron Bliss Day**. The British baron with a Portuguese title – the "Fourth Baron Bliss of the former Kingdom of Portugal" – died of food poisoning while fishing off the coast in 1926. Though he never actually set foot in Belize, he left the bulk of his estate to the colony. Today, that legacy continues to finance public works and an annual regatta in his name.

For a quick and pleasant day trip into Belize, try **Corozal Town**, nine miles south of the border and 96 miles north of Belize City. Originally a private estate on the banks of Corozal Bay, it was settled by refugees from Bacalar during the Caste War. In 1955, Hurricane Janet blew many of the wooden houses akimbo. It's a quaint easygoing and safe Caribbean town.

Orientation

 GETTING AROUND: Entering Belize from Mexico is easy, even on a bus. Stop at the office on the Mexican side, have your passport stamped and hand in your Tourist Card. On the Belize side, stop in the office and fill out a form of intent and a customs declaration. If you're driving, be sure to declare your car because they stamp your passport with an additional receipt. Rental cars are not supposed to be taken in, but if you do, be sure to buy Belizian car insurance just over the border.

Money changers conveniently wait outside the border office. You can spend US dollars if you don't want to bother exchanging, especially if you are only going in for a short trip. The exchange rate was BZ$ 1 = US $2.

Corozal Town

 In the small wooden town hall on Corozal's main square is a lively **wall mural** painted in 1953 by a famous local artist, Manuel Villamore Reyes, depicting the area's history. Older and wiser by 1986, when asked to restore it, he repainted it instead, treating the plight of the Maya in a more sympathetic light. Using deep natural colors and skillfully weaving scenes together, he connected lives through history – the good and bad, happy and sad.

The main square also houses the **post office**, where you can buy some of Belize's very attractive stamps. Next door is the **magistrate's court** and if it's in session you can see judges in English white wigs, presiding over trials. Nearby, only the four corners of the old fort that once stood there are still visible.

Completely ringing Corozal Town are the post-Classic **Santa Rita Maya ruins**, originally explored by British medical practitioner, Thomas Gann, in the late 19th century. The tallest site is a little difficult to find, set among a few homes near the northern edge of town. Wear long pants and insect repellent because no-see-ums are not no-feel-ums.

The **Cerro Maya ruins** are visible as a lump in the trees across the bay from town. The Maya abandoned this important trading center around A.D. 100. A canal 4,000 feet long, 20 feet wide and six feet deep encloses a pyramid plaza complex that features carved masks and two ceremonial ballcourts within a total of 90 acres. Once planned for a tourist attraction, the Cerro ruins are accessible only by hired boat from Corozal.

One of Belize's most impressive Maya ruins is **Lamanai** ("Submerged Crocodile"), set along the New River Lagoon within a 950-acre archeological reserve. It was occupied from B.C. 1500 to the 19th century, one of the longest occupied sites in *Mundo Maya*. The jungle setting and impressive ruins are a worthwhile excursion into the countryside. Although it's not particularly close to Corozal Town, **Henry Menzies** at the Caribbean Village Resort (see below) organizes boat trips up the unspoiled New River to explore the abandoned city. It's an expedition-style adventure and a good day's pleasure, with plenty of wildlife on the overhanging jungle shore. Henry acts a travel agent and facilitator for any itineraries in Belize, including those awkward connecting flights.

ACCOMMODATIONS & DINING

Tea to the English is really a picnic indoors.
– Alice Walker, *The Color Purple*

Caribbean Village Resort (*on the bay, PO Box 210, Corozal Town, Belize, C.A.,* ☎ *501/4-23415 or 22725, fax 501/4-23414, cabins, trailer park & camping*). Despite its pretentious name, the Caribbean Village Resort is a jumbled collection of camping and trailer spots and individual cabins in an ideal location on a palm-covered bulge along the bay south of town. In the center of the horseshoe-shaped complex is an inexpensive family seafood-specialty restaurant run by the Menzies family. Here, locals and friends, as well as guests, enjoy simple but tasty Belizian cooking. The guest cabins are clean and neat and, although not up to resort standards, are very comfortable. The owner, Henry Menzies, is a personable and knowledgeable guy who can arrange bike rentals and boat trips in Belize. $

Tony's Inn & Beach Resort (*south end, PO Box 12, Corozal, Belize, C.A., major credit cards,* ☎ *501/4-22055, fax 501/4-22829*). Tony's Inn is the best place in Corozal Town for quality in accommodations and food. Set on the water's edge, with its own dock and beach, the stylish inn features clean and comfortable deluxe and moderate guestrooms with double or king-size beds, air-conditioning, private bathrooms and cable TV (let's go Cubs!). Their dining area boasts linen tablecloths set in a glassed-in dining room overlooking the bay. If you're looking for a change of pace – a bit of Britain in Belize – stop here. Reasonably priced. **$$**
See page 3 for price chart.

Forest of Kings

*Those who walk through the roots of life
arrive here with the great lady of the land,
who sees and reflects the truth,
to go teach her sons where the only light lies...*

– fragment of an inscription on the Chicanná facade

The southern portion of Quintana Roo and Campeche is rich in spectacular Maya ruins that until recently have been next to impossible to visit. Now, besides the Rio Bec-style ruins at Becán and around Xpuhil, several new sites have been opened to the public. You have a chance to see ruins in all their magnificence without the crowds of Tulum or Chichén Itzá. One can walk in ancient ruined cities and be the only human there, surrounded by the ghosts of the Classic Maya and watched by the living inhabitants of the jungle – wild animals and birds. This little-explored corner of the Yucatán is worth a close look.

Xpiuhil is becoming a mecca for tourists visiting the Maya ruins and many of them are taking advantage of experienced guides to the area (although none is necessary to find the larger sites). There's an extremely knowledgeable guide in Becán, Juan de la Cruz Briceño, who has discovered several sites and worked with INAH and also Moisés Carreón at the Maya Mirador Maya restaurant (see below). He has no phone, so just ask around town. Another guide is tri-lingual Serge Rìou, a transplanted Frenchman who is an acknowledged authority on the surrounding Maya ruins. You may be able to arrange for him at the Mirador and will definitely be contacted at Rancho Encontado in Bacalar. Either Mirador or the Calakmul Hotel

& Restaurant (see below) can also get in touch with William Chan Cox, an archeological specialist. He lives north of Xpuhil in Dzibalchén.

The ride between Chetumal and Escárcega is a long one, six hours or better. Consequently, even if you're not into the ruin route, an overnight in Xpuhil might be a good idea. That's especially true if you're driving straight from Chiapas to Chetumal. There are very few accommodations or sights to recommend in Escárcega, a dusty highway crossroads town in Campeche state (see the listing in Campeche). Xpuhil, on the other hand – located on the border of Campeche and Quintana Roo – is an ideal base to explore the many ruins in the area or the Calakmul Biosphere.

The little town offers a *largo distancia* telephone and several clean hotels and restaurants. Read the scam part in our "Time to Go" section, page 75, for a caution about the town's only Pemex station.

Xpuhil

ACCOMMODATIONS & DINING

Ramada Chicanná Ecovillage (*Highway 186 just across from the turning for Chicanná ruins, no phone, reservations taken at Ramada Campeche:* ☎ 981/6-22-33, fax 981/1-16-18, pool, restaurant). Hacked out of the jungle in the rich archeological area along the Campeche-Quintana Roo border, this property hopes to attract busloads of tourists to the under-visited Maya sites nearby. Rooms are four to a thatch-roofed building made of stucco, stone and tile, with a polished hardwood trim. They are of typical Ramada quality and very Polynesian looking. Terraces and balconies with rustic leather tables and half-round chairs (known as *equipales*) look over manicured lawns and landscaped gardens. It's a little isolated. They're building additional rooms in anticipation of more visitors using this as a base to the Rio Bec and Calakmul areas. As of now there are no Ramada organized tours into the Biosphere or ruins. Putting the "Eco" in "Ecovillage" is the design for the rooms' air circulation, which eliminates the need for air-conditioning and the solar hot water heaters, which don't always work well.

Pluses include a quality restaurant, tasteful furnishings and immaculate cleanliness. On the down side they don't have 24-hour electric (so you hear the annoying generator running at night) nor phone or fax, except for emergencies. $$$ (See page 3 for price chart.)

Mirador Maya Hotel & Restaurant (*Highway 186, ☎ 982/2-91-63*). At the far western end of town, Mirador Maya sits under a giant palapa roof. Although the cabins behind it are spartan, the meals in the restaurant are substantial and tasty. A daily special for around US $3 makes it a long-haul truck "must-stop" for dinner. The manager can help make arrangements for a guide in advance.

Hotel and Restaurant Calakmul (*Km 153 Highway 186, ☎ & fax 983/2-91-62*). Doña Maria Cabara Dominquez offers a big smile to all who come into her pleasant little restaurant and hotel on the edge of dusty little Xpuhil, more or less halfway on the Chetumal-Escárcega highway. The food is excellent: generous, delicious and economical. Menus are written in German, English, Spanish and French.

It's a good place to stop if you're tired of driving as her six modern stucco bungalows with private bath and shower (soon to be 13 bungalows) are clean and neat. She also has eight wooden palapa-topped cabañas that share a communal bath for about $12 a night. Good bi-lingual guides to the Maya ruins can be arranged here. $

The Road To Ruin

 Highway 186, between Chetumal and Escárcega, runs past some magnificent Maya cities from the Classical Age (admission approximately US $1.50). The list of some of those ruins below is presented from Chetumal heading west. With some hard driving you could visit some of the more important ruins and still make Campeche or Chetumal in a very long day. An overnight in Xpuhil is a good idea if just for driving safety, but is a great idea if you're going to spend time at the rarely visited ruins of the southern zone.

Do not drive this road at night and use some common-sense precautions, such as tagging along with another vehicle for safety in numbers. There have been *rare* reports of robberies in the central sparsely populated region. An army post in Xpuhil patrols the area.

DZIBANCHE & KINICHNA: These two Classic-era ruins, within hiking distance of one another, were newly opened to the public in 1996 and are a tremendous find. Dzibanché, "Written on Wood," was the most important Maya city of the region. This complex of impressive pyramids and stone buildings will take your breath away, especially early in the morning or late in the afternoon when there are literally no other living people among the massive structures and tall jungle trees. This site – with its solitude – was perhaps the best of the Maya ruins we visited. And if it wasn't the

The hidden ruins at Dzibanché.

"best," it had the authentic ambiance of a city lost to time and hidden for ages by the verdant forest. Its name comes from the large lintel made of *quebracho* wood that bears a glyph date of A.D. 618. Besides its natural water sources, Dzibanché has several *chultunes*, underground excavations that served as water reservoirs. An important jade pendant dated A.D. 909 was uncovered here as well as a stairway with four carved steps and a carved stone lintel. Nearby **Kinichná** features a tall pyramid with a clear view across miles of virgin jungle. The turnoff for both ruins is 38 km (24 miles) from the beginning of Highway 186 near Bacalar. You can't miss the giant sign. Follow the narrow paved road through the Maya village of Morocoy for a total of 17 km (10.5 miles) until you see a metal barn on the right. That turnoff snakes two km (1.25 miles) to the ruins.

Stone mask at Kohunlich.

KOHUNLICH: Best known for its Pyramid of the Masks, the turn for Kohunlich is less than a mile farther west on the Chetumal-Escárcega Highway 186. It flourished from A.D. 350-900 and contains an esplanade that served as a base where water flowed down to an artificial lagoon. The most important building is the famous Los Mascarones, decorated with various stucco face designs from around A.D. 500, representing the different ages of the sun. The Olmec-looking faces are protected from the elements

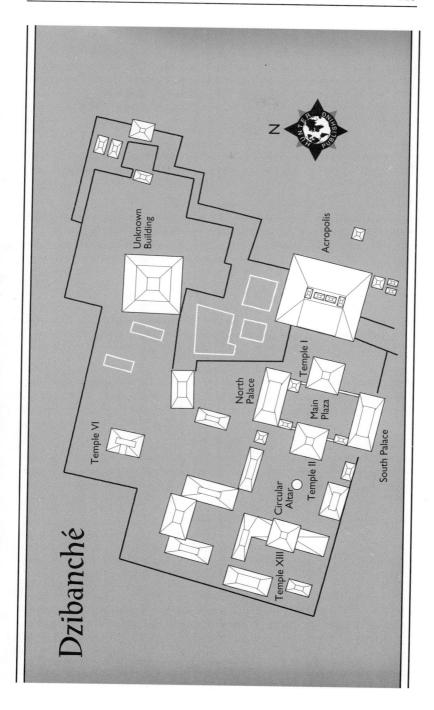

Dzibanché

by thatched roofs and flash photography is prohibited. There are public bathrooms here. INAH, the National Institute of Anthropology and History, is training and employing Guatemalan refugees to work in conserving the archeological zone of Kohunlich. This effort duplicates one at Edzná near Campeche, where the objective is to provide work and social benefits to the displaced Maya who fled political persecution in their own country.

CHAKAMBAKAM: Heading west again from Kohunlich brings you past the village of Caobas, 93 km (58 miles) from Chetumal. Four km (2.5 miles) of unpaved road to the right leads to the ruins, whose name means "Surrounded by Mangroves." The road isn't marked, so you might ask for directions. The Classic-era civic-religious center with a tall pyramid sits on a small peninsula that juts into a lagoon. Stucco and stone sculpture (including Olmec-style masks) have been found here and a *sacbé* leads to the north. Excavations are on-going.

XPUHIL: The tall towers of the Xpuhil ruins, derived from the Mayan for "Place of Cattails," are typical Rio Bec-style architecture. Mask panels flank doorways to lower rooms. Although weather-worn, the small set of ruins is worth a quick look. "Camp services" are offered by Señora Leticia Valenzuela, ☎ 982/2-33-04.

RIO BEC: The ruins known as Rio Bec are actually five separate sites. You wouldn't want to see all five, and they're next to impossible to reach, but a guide can take you to Rio Bec B, Structure I, to see one of the best preserved buildings in the region. Discovered in 1906 – then lost again until 1973 – the interesting site contains an aura of intrigue and romance. If Rio Bec B were easier to reach it would attract many more admirers. The facade features huge face masks and the interior boasts Maya graffiti on its plaster walls. Also of interest if you have the guide and the time is **Hormiguero**, Spanish for "Anthill," a site from the Late Classical period.

BECAN: About seven km (4.4 miles) east of the town of Xpuhil are the impressive ruins of Becán, visible on the right. Surrounded by a long moat-like fortification, its name means "Water Formed Gorge," even though it never was. The seven causeways that cross the earthen fortification are believed to have led to the seven cities under Becán's authority. Built on an outcropping of limestone, its massive towers and enclosed plaza are magnificent. Best time for photos is the late afternoon when the golden-red light of the setting sun causes the east- and west-facing structures to glow.

CHICANNA: Down the road on the left, nearly opposite the entrance to the Chicanná Ecolodge, is the short road to the Chicanná ruins, most notable for the Chenes-style monster mouth doorway. Chicanná, which means "House of the Mouth with Snakes," has a well-preserved building that features a wide doorway into the distinctive slack-jawed monster mouth. Great photo op to show the folks back home.

CALAKMUL: Calakmul, the ancient "City of Adjacent Mounds," was once a victorious rival against Tikal across the border in Guatemala. Its area of influence is now part of a huge nature preserve that borders another in Guatemala. Excavation of this important city has yielded some incredible precious-stone pieces, including the fabulous jade mask now on display in Fort San Miguel at Campeche. Numerous steles are among the 7,000 buildings (most are small and unnoteworthy for tourists) that make up the site. A guide is helpful here, but not absolutely necessary. Too difficult to reach during the rainy season. The turnoff 186 is marked (near Km 97) and there's a guard house with a gate. The ruins are about 62 km (38 miles) down a paved but narrow and twisting road. Ask at the guard house if anyone else has gone in so you can beware of head-on collisions along the sharp curves.

Mexico's largest preserve, the **Calakmul Biosphere**, was created in 1989 in a rainforest that stretches as far as the eye can see both north and south of the roadway. In its vast area spider monkeys, ocelots, tapirs, peccaries and deer are still the prey of *Señor de la Selva*, lord of the jungle – the jaguar. Some guided naturalist and archeological activities can be arranged in Xpuhil or with Rancho Encontado in Bacalar. The Campeche tourist board is working on a five-day "Eco adventure" in Calakmul that sounds quite promising. It includes archeological and naturalist activities in the "zone" as well as cultural interaction with local Maya communities. Try ☎ 981/6-33-00.

BALAMKU: Balamku – rescued from looters in 1990 – is an excellent and undiscovered (at least by tourists) Maya ruin in the jungle of Campeche. Local people, who call the site *Chunhabil*, fortunately reported the looting activity to INAH before too much damage was done. Its most impressive feature is the bas relief stucco facade, well preserved with some visible remains of the yellow, red and black paint that once covered it. A stylized jaguar graces the center of a main panel. Sitting on a zig-zag border, the powerful animal with an apparently skeletal head wears a belt, bracelets, a collar and pectoral. The figure gives the site its archeological name: "Jaguar Temple."

At Km 93.3, turn at the dirt road cutoff, two km (1.25 miles) west of the village of Conhuas (1.6 km/1 mile west of the Km 95 sign).

A people without history is like the wind on the grass.

– Sioux saying

THIS OLD RUIN

Everyone is the son of his own works.

– Cervantes

Three main styles named for the regions in which they are predominant characterize Maya architecture in the peninsula. The styles overlap and share influences with each other. The blocks of stone you see in restored ruins today were originally covered with a plaster often painted either in specific designs or solid colors.

Rio Bec: This Late Classic style, characterized by tall towers and unusable stairways with faux temples on the second level, can be seen in the southern sites of Xpuhil and Rio Bec. Facades feature ostentatious adornments of carved stone.

Chenes: Buildings are typically one story with a central doorway elaborately designed as a monster's mouth. Chenes and Rio Bec styles were contemporaneous and are close enough to be almost indistinguishable.

Puuc: Named for the Puuc Hills of Yucatán, classic Puuc style features structural corners of ornately decorated masks of Chac and the rain gods. Round columns in rows also distinguish this most impressive of classical styles. Uxmal is an excellent example.

Common features of most Maya sites are elevated causeways called *sacbes* ("White Roads"). These pathways linked ceremonial sites within civic centers, but, more interestingly, they also connected Maya urban centers. *Sacbes* are elevated as much as 4.5 meters (15 feet) above the terrain and are as wide as 18 meters (60 feet), but most are of more modest proportions. Builders edged them with cut stone, filled the core with rubble, then paved them over with a hard white stucco, cambered in the center for drainage. Evidence indicates their use was primarily ceremonial, but their commercial and military advantages are obvious.

The longest single *sacbé* stretches 100 km (62 miles) from Cobá to the minor site of Yaxuná, southwest of Chichén Itzá. Unfortunately, very few of these fascinating white walkways are in good enough condition to function as hiking trails. The rough jungle has long ago reclaimed them.

Campeche

Spanish language dictionaries define campechano *as cheerful, good-hearted, genial and generous.*

At A Glance

NAME: The name "Campeche" (cam-PAY-chay) derived from the name of the former Maya trading town of Ah-Kin-Pech. (The town was situated close to where the Maya repulsed the initial attempt to conquer the peninsula. Later it became the first stronghold of the colonists on the Yucatán.)

LOCATION: Campeche is situated on the southeastern corner of the Yucatán Peninsula, bordering Quintana Roo and Yucatán state to the north and east; Guatemala and the Mexican state of Tabasco to the south; and the Gulf of Mexico to the west.

CAPITAL: Campeche city.

MAJOR CITIES: Campeche city, Ciudad del Carmen, Escárcega, Champotón, Calkiní and Hopelchén.

MAJOR INDUSTRIES: Oil and commercial fishing.

POPULATION: 536,000 – indigenous Mayan and Spanish descent.

CLIMATE: Tropical, hot and humid. Coastline cooled by soft winds. Rain in the summer. Average year-round temperature, 27°C.

VEGETATION: Jungle, mangrove swamps and savanna.

GEOGRAPHY: Lowland, hilly in some areas, lagoons, Gulf coast beaches.

SIZE: 20,325 square miles (50,812 square kilometers).

WILDLIFE: Iguana, parrot, monkey, deer, jaguar, tapir, water birds.

ECOLOGICAL RESERVES: Calakmul Biosphere.

MAJOR ARCHEOLOGICAL SITES: Edzná, Calakmul, Xpuhil, Becán, Chicanná, Balamku and Hochob.

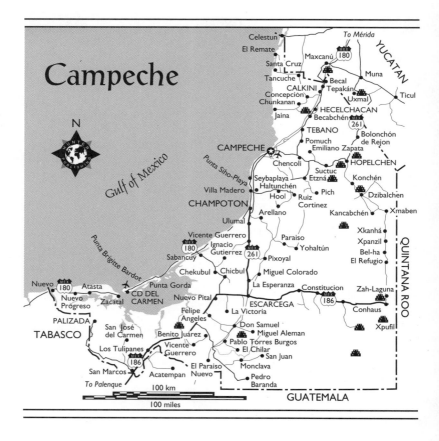

Campeche City

*The history of Campeche, written in stones, fortresses, gates
and walls, tell us of the past; of Maya warriors, Spanish
seafarers and fearsome pirates.*

– Roman Piña Chan, Campeche historian

 The Maya settlement of *Ah-Kin-Pech*, which meant "Priest of the Tick," became the port city of Campeche, one of the peninsula's most colonial cities. Enclosed by a massive medieval wall and guarded by flanking forts, one can feel Campeche frozen in time. The capital city, famous for its hospitality, is quiet and reserved, yet vibrantly alive with a culture that's unique. What makes Campeche doubly attractive to *Adventure Guide* travelers is that it tends to be bypassed by most tourists to the Yucatán. Their loss and our gain. Campeche city and the off-the-beaten-trail attractions of its countryside make for a great uncrowded vacation.

Situated on the warm and shallow Gulf of Mexico, the city was officially founded in October of 1540, though its first attempt at settlement came in 1517. It became the main Spanish port and the city from which roots of colonial influence spread over the Yucatán. Perhaps because of its importance – and certainly because of its location – Campeche fell prey to constant attacks by pirates and plunderers, many of whom based themselves at Ciudad del Carmen. In 1663, pirates massed a savage attack and overran the vulnerable settlement, butchering its men and raping and enslaving its women. In 1685, the pirate Lorencillo occupied the city for 56 torturous days. Finally, after 130 years of continuous harassment, the city had enough of being raped and pillaged by the likes of Francis Drake, John Hawkins, Peg-leg the Pirate, Henry Morgan and Bartolomé the Portuguese. They hired French engineer Louis Bouchard de Bocour to build a huge, hexagonal stone-walled fortress, 2.5 meters thick (eight feet) and guarded by eight towers (*baluartes*) to repulse the buccaneers. On the bluffs either side of the city, forts armed with cannon could put attackers in a withering crossfire. The defenses stopped the bloody pirate attacks, but Campeche's walls were needed again when Maya armies regained the peninsula in the 1840s and drove survivors inside the bulwarks, which saved the lives of thousands of *Campechanos* from slaughter. Lacking Campeche's battlements, the old corsair hang-out of Ciudad del Carmen – where the last of the buccaneers were routed in 1717 – hired ships from the

Republic of Texas, before Texas became a state, to protect it from Maya Caste War attack.

Today, Campeche (population 175,000) extends inland and north and south from the confines of its former defenses. Unfortunately, in the 1960s the city fathers implemented an ill-conceived modernization plan that filled in the waterfront from the old gates and seawall out into the Gulf, to accommodate new buildings. That, combined with the fact that several large portions of the wall were destroyed over the years in the growth of the town, makes us wonder how magnificent the old city must have been when it was completely enclosed. Still, once inside Campeche, the inner city's charming cobblestone streets and ancient colonial buildings enchant and inspire. The neat and clean **Colonial Centro** is a convenient base to explore the sights and a rewarding place to simply stay and enjoy. Lacking the noticeable Maya influence of Mérida, provincial Campeche still appears to revel in its Spanish colonial past.

DISTANCES FROM CAMPECHE

Edzná	65 km/40 miles
Champotón	65 km/40 miles
Seybaplaya	32 km/20 miles
Cd. del Carmen	212 km/132 miles
Escárcega	150 km/93 miles
Calakmul	360 km/224 miles
Chicanná	270 km/168 miles
Becán	250 km/155 miles
Xpuhil	290 km/180 miles
Sabancuy	130 km/81 miles
Palizada	360 km/224 miles
Villahermosa, Tab	450 km/280 miles
Mérida	192 km/119 miles
Chetumal	422 km/262 miles
Palenque	366 km/227 miles

Orientation

 GETTING AROUND: Campeche city was originally divided into three sectors: San Francisco to the north, where the Maya population lived; San Román in the south, where *mestizos* and *mulattos* lived; and the Walled City, where the Spanish elite resided. This separation of races was typical of colonial times and contributed to the Caste War uprising many years later. Those distinctions are no longer a part of Campeche's make-up.

The city rests on the edge of the Gulf of Mexico, its shallow harbor port facilities long since made unusable for large modern ships. The main routes in and out of town run north and south. The southern road splits at Champotón, due south for Escárcega or southwest along the coast for Ciudad del Carmen, the "economic engine" that powers the state economy. The way north to Mérida also splits into long and short cuts. Route 180 takes you 175 km (110 miles) directly to Mérida, while Route 261 loops east then north past the deep underground caverns of Xtacumbilxuna, near Bolonchén, as well as the famous Maya ruins at Uxmal and Kabáh.

Monument to the Maya,
South Entrance to Campeche City.

A road known as the *Circuito Baluartes* rings the walled city's exterior. Odd-number streets run east-west, perpendicular to the sea, and even-number streets run north-south. Although you may have arrived in Campeche by car, vehicles are a liability in the colonial part of town. The streets are exceedingly narrow and parking is at a premium. If your hotel doesn't have private parking and you find a space on any of the criss-cross one-way streets, leave your car there. Old Campeche is a city made for walking.

Practicalities

The banks with **ATM** machines are Bancomer and Atlántico on Av. 16 de Septiembre; Banamex on Calle 53 and 10; and Serfin, on Calle 18 No. 102. The **post office** is in the Federal Palace building on Av. 16 de Septiembre and the **Teléfonos de Mexico** office is 10th and Calle 63. Hertz **car rental** can be found in the Baluartes Hotel Lobby (☎ 981/6-39-11) or at the airport (☎ 981/6-88-48). The ADO **bus station** is on Av.

Gobernadores in the Santa Ana District, 2 km (about 10 long blocks)
northeast of the Sea Gate. The *mercado*, on Circuito Baluartes near
the Baluarte de San Pedro, is the place to catch local buses. Ask a
merchant for help figuring out which goes where.

A good **laundromat**/dry cleaners in the heart of the colonial
section is Tintoria y Lavanderia Campeche, Calle 55 (8-4 p.m., Monday-Saturday). The Panificadora Nueva España is a sweet-smelling
bakery on Calle 10, between 59 and 61. Large selection of delicious
goods, fresh out of the oven. A San Francisco de Asis **supermarket**
is one block north of the Ramada, along with a sports complex.

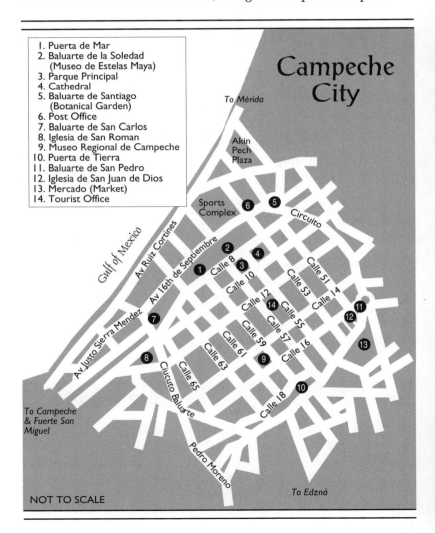

1. Puerta de Mar
2. Baluarte de la Soledad
   (Museo de Estelas Maya)
3. Parque Principal
4. Cathedral
5. Baluarte de Santiago
   (Botanical Garden)
6. Post Office
7. Baluarte de San Carlos
8. Iglesia de San Roman
9. Museo Regional de Campeche
10. Puerta de Tierra
11. Baluarte de San Pedro
12. Iglesia de San Juan de Dios
13. Mercado (Market)
14. Tourist Office

Campeche
City

To Mérida

Akin
Pech
Plaza

Sports
Complex

Circuito

Gulf of Mexico

Av Ruiz Cortines

Av 16th de Septiembre

Av Justo Sierra Mendez

Ciucuito Baluarte

Calle 8

Calle 10

Calle 12

Calle 51

Calle 53

Calle 14

Calle 55

Calle 57

Calle 16

Calle 59

Calle 61

Calle 63

Calle 65

Calle 18

Pedro Moreno

To Campeche
& Fuerte San
Miguel

To Edzná

NOT TO SCALE

Several **craft stores** with some great regional and national crafts are in the colonial downtown. The best of these is the Casa de Artesanías, on Calle 55 No. 25 (☎ 981/6-90-88), between 12th and 14th. This is a beautifully remodeled colonial building made even more comfortable with central air-conditioning and several small tables in an indoor courtyard for refreshments, coffee and soda. Proceeds benefit local family assistance programs. Other worthwhile handicraft places include Veleros Boutique in the Ah Kin Pech Plaza, stand 119, and Típica Naval and Coral, next to each other on Calle 8, near the Baluarte de la Soledad. Another *baluarte*, San Pedro, has a regional handicraft exhibit and sells arts and crafts. The town's lively *mercado* surrounds it.

Nightlife in Campeche revolves around the very popular **Atlantis Disco** in the Hotel Ramada and another dance club across the street in the Hotel Baluartes. **Tourist information** is available on Calle 12 No. 153. The **police** number is ☎ 981/6-36-35 and the **General Hospital** is at ☎ 981/6-42-33. Renew your **tourist card** at the immigration office run by Sr. Jorge Hernández, ☎ 981/6-28-68.

Adventures

Campeche's colorful colonial buildings and confined spaces make a walking tour (or two) a wonderful way to appreciate the city. Though it's a diminutive city, seeing its points can require a long walk. Wear comfy shoes and don't plan on walking around during the hottest part of the day. An afternoon siesta or a long leisurely lunch is called for. Fortunately, dusk and the early evening are magical times downtown. Remember, when it comes to museums: if it's Sunday, it's free; but if it's Monday, it's closed.

ON FOOT

Start at the **Puerta del Mar**, the "Sea Gate," on Calle 8 where it meets Calle 53. This was one of the four main entrances into the walled defenses. Walk inland on 53 to the corner of Calle 10 and turn left, north, along the street to the **Parque Principal**. This is the life center of the old town, the place where couples stroll and families gather on Sundays. The **bandstand** is new and actively used for concerts and fiestas. On your right is the **Los Portales** building with its graceful arches. The massive but plain facade of the **Catedral de la Concepción** (open mornings and evenings) dominates the plaza.

Begun almost as soon as the Spanish had established themselves, it wasn't finished for a century and a half. The cathedral occupies the site of the first mass held on firm land in the New World (an earlier one was held on Cozumel island). One of its spires is known as the "Spanish Tower" because it was finished during colonial rule. Farther down Calle 10 is the **Mansion Carvajal**, a stately building with rich marble floors, undulating Arabic arches and a sweeping staircase. It was the former home of Don Fernando Carvajal Estrada, one of Campeche's richest hacienda owners. The magnificent mansion now houses government offices and handicraft shops, open daily except Sunday. Some of the other good areas for substantial colonial homes are on Calles 55, 57 and 59, in the heart of the Centro.

Turn left on the Circuito Baluartes to reach the **Baluarte de Santiago**, filled with a tiny but exotic *jardín botánico*, a **botanical garden** refuge from the city traffic. Also called *X'Much-Haltun*, the garden nurtures 150-plus species of regional flora. English-language tours are given and admission is by donation. Next, head south on Av. 16 de Septiembre and cut across the park to the Baluarte de la Soledad that contains an attractive museum, *Museo de Estelas Maya*, the **Museum of the Maya Steles** (open 8 a.m.-2 p.m. and 5-8 p.m.). Besides Maya records carved in stone, the museum contains colonial-era artifacts.

Continue south on Calle 8 past the Sea Gate again till you see the garish government buildings that include the "UFO," as Campechanos have nicknamed the clam-shaped silver building that houses the **State Congress**. The **Baluarte de San Carlos**, next door, houses the city museum, with a fascinating collection of old maps and a scale model of the colonial walled town. Head inland on Calle 65 past the polished and proud **University**, *Institutito Campechano*. Return to the Circuito if you want to peak at the **Baluarte de Santa Rosa**, now a library. A few blocks south is the **Church of San Román**, constructed in the 16th century and home of the *Cristo Negro de San Román* – the "Black Christ" – carved from ebony hardwood. One of the miracles attributed to the statue occurred when an attempt to move it to another church resulted in the statue raising its arms high enough to make it impossible to get out the door. There is no record of whether they tried turning it on its side, but it still resides in San Román.

Otherwise, walk back to the Centro, north on Calle 12 or 14 and, if you're starved, head over to Calle 55, between 10 and 12 and stop at **La Parroquía** bar and restaurant for an inexpensive lunch.

The **Regional Museum**, *Museo Regional de Campeche*, on Calle 59 between 14 and 16, is the largest and best of the city's modest museums (open 8-2 and 5-8 p.m.). The building is the former mansion of the *Teniente del Rey*, the "King's Lieutenant," and contains an extensive collection of Maya artifacts and stone carvings, as well as an example of the wooden contraption that deformed baby's skulls by flattening the forehead – a mark of beauty to the ancient Maya. Tattoos were also favored by the Maya, the skin cut and infected so that the resulting scars made the design. Also housed here is the companion jewelry to the jade mask found in Structure VII in Calakmul, on display at Fuerte San Miguel. Backing the Regional Museum on 10th and 63rd is the **Museum of Campeche** in the former Temple of Saint Joseph.

At the west end of 59th sits the **Puerta de Tierra**, the "Land Gate," through which people entered and exited the city overland. The enormous thick door is the original from 1732 made of *jabin* wood. A drawbridge adds further protection to the entrance. From here there's a **city tour** (in Spanish) offered every Saturday at 9 a.m. and 2 p.m. Every Friday at 8 p.m. there's a **Light and Sound Spectacular** at the gate that explains – through the use of spotlights, slides and actors – the history of Campeche. You'll get the gist of it even though it's all in Spanish. As part of the show you're invited to walk the ramparts of the wall from the Puerta to the Baluarte de San Juan, where an authentic-looking pirate "spirit" fights it out with a noble Spanish soldier below. A folk dance is also performed. Diorama rooms within the stone walls portray life in the fortress during those days.

Pirate fight.

The northern end of the walled city across the street is home to Campeche's main *mercado*. The Baluarte de San Pedro on the corner stands sentinel.

A **trolley tour** of town on the *Tranvia* leaves (US $1) leaves at 9:30 a.m., 6 p.m. and 9 p.m. from Parque Principal.

José Maria Sansores Abraham has a fishing lodge and organizes wildlife photo safaris and fishing expeditions. His number at the Hotel Castlemar is ☎ 982/6-23-56, home 982/6-55-38.

FORTS: Campeche has two formidable forts flanking the old city. The **Fuerte San José El Alto** is a few kilometers north of town on a bluff overlooking the city. It offers a great view of the giant statue of Benito Juárez, the Mexican hero. Below it, one of the oldest **lighthouses** in the Americas (1864) sits in front of the **ex-Convent of San José**, built by the Jesuits in 1700. An **art museum** has opened in its beautiful baroque-tiled church.

Corner turret of Fort San Miguel.

Campeche's pride and joy, however, is the **Fuerte San Miguel**, about four km (2.5 miles) south of town atop a steep hill. It's above an industrial waterfront section, just past the huge statue of a Maya with his arm holding a torch entitled "The Resurgence of Campeche." The stone fort is in excellent condition and from its parapets one can sense the power and security this fort must have given those under its protection. At sunset, alone on the rampart with only the black-barrelled cannon, purple sky and blue water, your senses are overwhelmed. Evoke history by crawling around the sentry towers and imagine firing cannon down upon the ruthless pirates. Be a kid again – it's even got a moat!

In the stone floor interior there is a magnificent little museum that boasts some incredible Maya pottery and stonework and the priceless and breathtaking jade mask recovered from Calakmul. An intricately carved ship's prow in the graceful and sleek shape of a greyhound, recovered from the mud of the Champotón River, is also on display. This is a stunning place to visit at sunset (but don't try to walk it; take a cab or drive). No flash photography is allowed in the museum rooms.

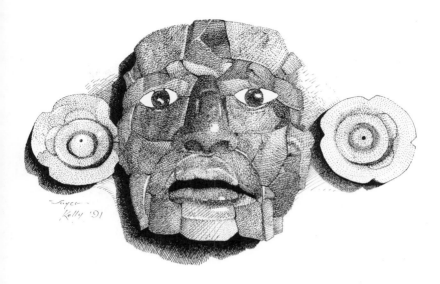

Sketch of the fabulous Jade Mask found at Calakmul.
© Joyce Kelly, *An Archeological Guide to Mexico's Yucatán Peninsula,*
published by the University of Oklahoma Press.

Maya Ruins

Campeche's southern zones of enigmatic Maya cities around Xpuhil and the Calakmul Biosphere are covered at the end of the Quintana Roo chapter.

The north-central part of Campeche features several Maya city sites, the most notable, **Edzná** and **Hochob**, detailed below. Another, the **Isla de Jaina**, off the coast north of Campeche city, is a partly man-made island with little of obvious interest to tourists, but archeologists thrilled at the discovery of an elite Maya burial ground – the largest known necropolis in the Americas. The site has yielded clay figurines (on display in the Camino Real Museum in Hecelchakán and in Mexico City) representing the deceased Maya nobility, a quarter of whom were female.

EDZNÁ

The act of writing requires a constant plunging back into the
shadow of the past where time hovers, ghost-like.
– Ralph Ellison, American author

 The best of Campeche's central and northern abandoned Maya sites is Edzná, which means "House of Grimaces," an easily accessible and magnificent ruin about 50 km (31 miles) southeast of the capital. A long-hidden jewel in the ring of Maya cities, the European and American explorers and archeologists that swarmed over the Yucatán in the late 19th century failed to find the lost city of Edzná. It wasn't until 1927 that the ruins were "discovered," although local people knew of them for years.

Occupied from around B.C. 400 to A.D. 1500, the huge ceremonial center's significant standing architecture is all within easy walking distance. Evidence indicates that a population of 70,000 may have lived there by A.D. 650.

The first building inside the complex is the 20-room residence, the **Platform of the Cuchillos** (Knives), named for the rich find of obsidian knives discovered there. One important aspect hidden from the casual observer in Edzná is the great hydraulic works that provided irrigation and perhaps drinking water through 12 canals and a series of reservoirs. One canal travels eight miles in a southerly direction.

Edzná

Parking
Restaurant
Monolithic Columns
Altar
Tourist Information & Restrooms
Palace of the Knives
Puuc Arch
Gran Acropolis
Gran Tribune
Gran Plaza
Templo Delsor
Ball Court
Pyramid of the 5 Niches
N
Templo de los Mascarones

South of the platform is **Nohoch Na** ("Great House"), which appears to be bleachers for the **Grand Plaza** (525 feet long and 330 feet wide). Its function may well have been for viewing tremendous ceremonies on the Grand Plaza and excavations indicate it covers an earlier building. The south end has the Petén-style **Templo Delsor** and small **ballcourt** with a surviving ring (the goal) in the middle of the west side. On a long flat platform east of the Grand Plaza is another magnificent complex known as the **Great Acropolis**, anchored by the monumental Late-Classic **Temple of Five Stories**, which absolutely overwhelms the impressive buildings that surround it. Twice a year the sun illuminates the holy chamber through the doorway on the top. Check out the vaulted arch beneath the stairway on the first two levels. It is at least 1,300 years old and still standing. Best photos come in the afternoon.

Ruins at Edzná.

Many of the workers on the restoration today are Guatemalan refugees, displaced Maya from across the border. If you're in Campeche, Edzná is a sight not to be missed. Some people even come down for the day from Uxmal and the Puuc ruins to see it.

There are two ways to reach the ancient city from Campeche. The most common way is east on Highway 180 to the cutoff for Edzná on the right (Route 188). Our *Adventure Guide* way is out from the Land Gate on Calle Pedro Moreno through the little town of China (chee-na). Our guide, Erik, calls it "Bump Town" because of the numerous *topes* in town. At the 10 Km mark there's a large field on the left with some modern farm buildings set back. This is **Rancho El Ramonal**, where the owners keep four huge **jaguars** for breeding. The wild cats are incredibly strong and to view them up close, without a cage, is dangerously exciting. They are not normally loose, but held by thick steel chains. Erik tells us that the owners let them loose some evenings to hunt in the forest and local farmers complain of losing chickens to the supple felines. The family that owns them is helpful and doesn't mind visitors, but please remember to tip for the animals' upkeep.

Erik Medicuti Polanco is an excellent guide to Campeche – its attractions and ruins – and he often works with the tourist board. His English is very good and he knows of what he speaks. He has no car, but will accompany you in yours or arrange good taxi fares or even go on a bus with you. You can reach him through the tourist board on Calle 12, ☎ 981/6-55-93 (Alejandro Serrano speaks English there). He also works for a good local travel agency, **Picazh Travel**, ☎ 981/6-44-26. There's a tour to Edzná with a bilingual guide offered by several travel agencies and hotels in town that has an option of stopping here. Departures at 9 a.m. and 2 p.m. (about US $25).

HOCHOB

Harder to get to and well off the beaten trail, Hochob (Mayan for "Maize Storage Place") is a small but spectacular Late Classic Chenes-style site. Several structures are arranged around a plaza, the most interesting of which is the **Principal Palace**, decorated with an intricate monster mouth mask doorway and Chac corner masks. Pottery found at the site indicates it was still occupied when the Spanish landed. On the road from Hopelchén to Dzibalchén you'll have passed **El Tabasqueño** ruins, a Chenes site not yet excavated. A guide to Hochob is the caretaker Hortensio Camál Ku, who lives in Chencoh near the ruins. Ask for him there or at Hochob. Other bilingual guides are José Williams and William Chan Cox, both residents of Dzilbalchén and experienced guides to Campeche's ruins. They are well known; ask anyone in town.

Accommodations

 There are hotels around Campeche and in the suburbs, but we prefer to stay close to the old colonial center. Because so few tourists crowd the narrow streets of Campeche, rooms cost a fraction of what they do near Cancún and are even lower than Mérida. Most people stay only one night in Campeche and that's a shame – it's a good place to relax and enjoy. See page 3 for price chart.

Budget Hotels

CREA Youth Hostel (*Av. Agustín Melgar, 981/6-18-02, pool, cafeteria, sports facilities*). It seems only natural in Mexico to make the "Villa Deportiva Juvenil" hard to find – it's an object lesson in geography for student travelers. Get on a bus marked "Lerma" or "Playa Bonita" heading south along the shore road, get off and turn inland at the Pemex station at Av. Jose Lopez Portillo. The Youth Hostel is in the University Sports Complex. If you're walking, it's a 30-minute hoof from the Centro.

Samula Trailer Park (*Samula, full hook-ups, showers*). Take Av. Jose Lopez Portillo east at the Pemex station, past the University and around some curves past a large shopping center. Go up a small hill and look for a tiny sign on your right. Good luck. The campground and Anita, the woman who runs it, were immortalized (more or less) in *Temple of the Jaguar*, by Donald Schueler, a fascinating book about his cathartic wanderings about the Yucatán.

Hotel Castlemar (*Calle 61 No. 2, ☎ 981/6-51-86, fax 981/6-28-86, 18 rooms with fans*). The airy front rooms facing the narrow street are the better ones in this small hotel in the southern part of the old city. Ornate tile work, balconies, interior courtyard – all say "colonial." Some of the bathrooms are showing age.

Hotel Campeche (*Calle 57 No. 2, ☎ 981/6-51-83, 38 rooms with fans, restaurant*). This hotel, converted from a huge private mansion in 1939, is on a convenient corner of the park square. It's unadorned, with two aged, tiled open-center courtyards. Some rooms (relatively small) have short crooked doorways – built for people under 5'4" – so you know it's authentically colonial. The mattresses are foam rubber and the pillows are tiny, but the rooms are clean and it's definitely a big step up from the dark Reforma. Usually fills up with European tourists. Economical and good, Restaurant del Parque is downstairs on the corner.

Hotel Reforma (*Calle 8 No. 257, ☎ 981/6-44-64, 22 rooms with fans*). This hotel, diagonally across from the Puerta del Mar (Sea Gate) is a real backpacker's special. Primitive accommodations in rooms that are close to depressing, partly because the building is such a great old colonial structure and deserves better, but mostly because it's just grungy.

Hotel Regis (*Calle 12 between 55 and 57, ☎ 981/6-31-75, 7 rooms with fans or air, TV*). The Centro's newest converted hotel (1996) is in a beautifully restored old corner building. The rambling open bedrooms have typically high (18-foot) ceilings with new modern bathrooms, furniture and tiled floors. The combination of colonial charm with modern sensibilities of comfort makes the Regis perhaps the best value in accommodations in the Centro. Each bedroom has tall windows that access a small private balcony overlooking the narrow streets. The exterior and interior walls are one foot or more thick, keeping rooms as quiet as a church. The hulking two-story structure also boasts marble stairs and wide hallways around a center courtyard. A real gem. $

Hotel America Plaza (*Calle 10 No. 252, ☎ 981/6-45-88, 42 rooms with fans or air*). Travelers who enjoy staying in a Spanish-styled hotel in the heart of the oldest part of town often opt for the America, one block south of the main plaza. Big and white with dark wood trim and walkway, its ample rooms surround a tiled open courtyard, complete with hacienda artifacts such as wooden carts and farm tools. Unfortunately, standards of cleanliness in the public areas are lower than the hotel deserves, so we hope the owners wake up to the problem. Room cleanliness is sometimes spotty so don't be afraid to complain squeaky wheels get the most attention. Parking anywhere in the Centro is scarce. $

Colonial Hotel (*Calle 14 No. 122*, ☎ *981/6-26-30, 30 rooms with fans, some with air*). This distinguished hotel in the middle of the Centro has been operating since 1946. A century before that it was the private home of the King of Spain's former colonial Governor – Brigadier Don Miguel de Castro y Araos and his wife. The family-run hotel is friendly and well-kept with a communal sitting area next to its tiled center courtyard and tropical plants. The rooms are small, with typical high ceilings and intricately designed tile floors. It's gracefully old and simple, but with a strong appeal all its own. $

Posada San Angel Inn (*Calle 10 No. 307*, ☎ *981/6-77-18, 14 rooms with air*). The *posada* features neat, modernized rooms in a colonial building across the street from the side of the Cathedral de la Concepción. Its clean, trim square rooms are an excellent value – comfortable and appealing – but they do not retain much of the old-world flavor the edifice evokes. $

Hotel Lopez (*Calle 12 No. 189*, ☎ *981/6-33-44, 39 rooms with air or fans, restaurant*). Colorful but not colonial inside, the Lopez is simple, clean and reasonably priced. $

Moderate Hotels

Baluartes (*Av. Ruíz Cortines*, ☎ *981/6-39-11, fax 981/6-57-65, 104 rooms with air, restaurant, parking, pool*). The boxy Baluartes sits next to the Ramada along Campeche's park-like waterfront. It's less expensive but also less attentive than its brand-name neighbor. Renovated rooms are comfortable but the common areas are a little lacking. Good points include a bright and friendly café/restaurant, La Almena, and a swimming pool that can be used by non-guests for a small fee. Excellent location. $$

Ramada Hotel Campeche (*Av. Ruíz Cortines No. 51*, ☎ *in US: 800-272-6232 or in Mexico: 981/6-22-33, fax 981/1-16-18, 148 rooms and suites with air, pool, jacuzzi, cable TV, secured parking, gym & sauna*). The staff at the Ramada in Campeche is absolutely first rate. The hotel has long been acknowledged as the best in the city for both business travelers and tourists. It's the kind of place where they make you feel at home by remembering your name. All the rooms have private balconies that face the tranquil Gulf of Mexico and, although slightly worn around the edges in some of the public areas, the guest rooms are pleasing and comfortable. The Ramada's popular restaurant, Café Poquito, is frequently full of *Campechanos* as well as hotel guests – and for good reason. The food and service are excellent and reasonably priced and the Sunday buffet brunch here is particularly popular. The glass-enclosed sunny dining area is also one of the largest no-smoking sections we've seen in Mexico. The hotel's Atlantis Disco, Grill Restaurant and Piccolo Bar are also local favorites. Ask for a promotional rate from the 800 number; it saves about 20% off rack rates. $$

Dining

 Seafood is Campeche's specialty and there are several good restaurants along the waterfront south towards Lerma. Shrimp cocktails were invented here so all the signs you see advertising *cocteles* are not mixed drinks but shrimp. Ironically, mixed drinks are said to have been invented in the saloons of colonial Campeche and the combination of two drinks was called *campechana* – cheerful and happy. You can't beat the care and pride *Campechanos* put into their gastronomy, nor will you won't find better prices. "*Key hanal*," is phonetic Mayan for "good tasting food," so compliment the chef!

See page 4 for price chart.

Marganzo Regional Restaurant (*Calle 8 No. 267*). Almost in front of the Puerta del Mar, the Marganzo is an elegant restaurant with starched white table linens and waitresses dressed in colorful Mexican folk dresses. It has always been special to visitors and residents alike, offering the best of Mexican cooking with seafood specialties, such as stuffed pompano and *pan de cazón* (layered tortilla, shark and tomato sauce). This moderately priced restaurant is worth every peso. $$

Los Portales de San Francisco (*Calle 10 No. 86*). Established in one of the oldest neighborhoods of the city, Los Portales lures diners with fine food and an intimate ambiance. Open seven days, 6 p.m. to midnight, this family restaurant is a great place to try local and national *antojitos* (appetizers), such as *panuchos* (a tortilla stuffed with bean, egg and meat) or turkey *tortas* (sandwiches). If you're not stuffed after that, order dinner. You'll waddle home. $

Miramar (*Calle 8 on the corner of 61*). The Miramar has been serving seafood and regional specialties to both *Campechanos* and visitors for over 45 years, so they must be doing something right. It has a colonial atmosphere with high ceilings and long open windows. Ask for a recommendation. The waiters know their menu inside and out; some of them have worked here for more than 25 years. Many believe the area's best seafood is served here, on the corner facing the Government Palace. $-$$

Cactus (*Av. Ruíz Cortines*). If you're tired of seafood choices, you can always get a thick juicy steak here at Cactus, a Mexican chain restaurant. They specialize in fine cuts of beef from the northern state of Sonora. Cozy and agreeable atmosphere for late lunch or dinner. Overlooking the Gulf. $$

RECETAS TIPICAS DE CAMPECHE

*The feminist movement has helped open minds and kitchens
to the notion that men can be at home on the range.*
– René Veaux, chef, Lasserre restaurant, Paris

Pampano en Verde (Pompano in Green Sauce)

Ingredients: *6 large pompano fish fillets; 9 garlic cloves; 2 tomatoes; 1 onion; 2 chiles* xcatic *– not generally available in the US (substitute 2 Italian frying peppers, seeded and cut into thick strips); 1 cup of vinegar; oil; parsley; juice of 3 or 4 lemons; peppercorns; oregano; cumin; salt to taste.*

Blend the parsley, oregano, peppercorns, cumin, 6 crushed garlic cloves, vinegar and salt. Pour lemon juice over the fish fillets and marinate them in the blended sauce. Finely chop the remaining garlic cloves, slice the onion and tomatoes. Cook the fish in a frying pan, adding the chopped garlic cloves, tomatoes and onions, together with the chiles. Allow this to simmer slowly, adding water if necessary, until fish is flaky. Makes six servings.

Aqua de Horchata (Rice Drink)

Ingredients: *1 cup of rice; 1 cinnamon stick; cane sugar or sweetener of choice; powdered cinnamon.*

Rinse the rice and set aside to soak with a cinnamon stick in 2 quarts of water for 24 hours. Blend and strain. Sweeten to taste. When serving, sprinkle powdered cinnamon on each glass. Horchata is an acquired taste, but once acquired it seemed to be the one drink we craved when we were hot and tired. We like to put our horchata into a blender with a little cracked ice and buzz on high for a second or two. *Fantástico!*

La Pigua (*Malecón Miguel Aleman No. 197A*). A *pigua* is a small crustacean similar to the shrimp, so you know this eatery's specialties are from the sea. The chef, Darío Chi Jesús, developed a Campeche-style "caviar" that is now imitated in many other restaurants. La Pigua is often packed for leisurely lunches, its customers encouraged by the sunroom-style glass windows and profusion of tropical plants. $-$$

Restaurant Bar Familiar La Parroquía (*Calle 55 between 10 and 12*). If one restaurant says "Campeche" and everything about it, it's La Parroquía. All at once it's a family restaurant, a pub, a hangout, and a meeting place for old men reliving their glory days or young lovers whose best is yet to come. Open 24 hours a day, this immensely popular spot serves up regional dishes and typical Mexican food in a large fan-cooled open dining area at prices that barely lighten the wallet. This is one of the few places whose atmosphere is created by people rather than pictures on the wall. $

Southern Campeche

 Thirty-three km south of Campeche city (20 miles), along the road that hugs the shoreline, lies **Seybaplaya**, the coast's first good swimming beach. The road offers great scenery and it's fun to drive the hairpin turns, but it's a real bugger if you get behind a smelly truck or bus. There is no passing. A new toll road direct between Campeche and Champotón bypasses the torturous twisting and hilly coast road that used to be the only route south from Campeche.

Seybaplaya's fishing boats are picturesque, with colorful flags, denoting their ownership, flapping in the breeze. A dirt road north from the port around the big hill leads to a pleasant secluded rocky beach, a popular spot for locals. South of Seybaplaya is a hotel that looks like an old fort, Hotel Siho Playa, originally part of a sugar cane hacienda. The Spanish introduction of sugar cane for a short while made the area a major rum and candy source. The sweet tooth stuck and Campeche is still known for its candy confections.

Champotón is a historically significant fishing town with some decent restaurants that face a charming harbor where the river curls around before entering the Gulf. It has almost an English village look to it, though the climate is a wee bit warmer. It was in Champotón where a Maya ambush repulsed the first invading Spanish soldiers, discouraging them from the staying in the Yucatán. North of town there's a series of palapa seafood restaurants on the beach and all looked clean and inviting. Follow the seabirds all along the Gulf seafront to basketball-size cement courts where local fishermen's families dry minnows for *charalitos,* a crunchy snack food for sale in the *mercados.*

Ciudad del Carmen

At the tip of a long sliver of sandbar island between the huge Laguna de Terminos and the Gulf of Mexico, sits Ciudad del Carmen – "Carmen," as everyone calls it. Maya fishermen fished from here and the tradition continues with the city's large but rusting fishing and shrimp fleet. Pirates used the lagoon's protected waters as their lair. From here they attacked merchant vessels bringing cargo back to Spain. It was also from here that they sacked Campeche numerous times. Legend has it that during this time the citizens of Carmen developed a curious defense against pirate abductions: men dressed as women when they went to the *mercado* to shop. In 1717, forces from Campeche routed and killed the remaining corsairs in a surprise attack.

Orange "Frères Martin," French roofing tiles from Marseilles, used as ballast for clipper ships, tile many of Carmen's oldest roofs. In the center of town's old *zócalo,* three concentric paths circle the bandstand. Wealthy men of Spanish lineage used the inner circle for traditional Sunday strolls, women of the same class used the middle, peasants and workers used the outer ring. This vestige of segregation is evident in other town plazas throughout colonial Yucatán.

The state of Campeche is trying to develop tourism in the southern part of the state and it hopes to make Carmen the focal point. Certainly hiring a fishing boat for fishing or touring the lagoon is worthwhile, but the city of Carmen is too spread out, too commercial to be a destination of its own. There is great potential, however, in the surrounding countryside and getting there is an experience that makes the trip worthwhile. The coast road skirts miles and miles of open empty beaches, ideal for **beachcombing** and **exploring**. Unfortunately the idyllic dunes, once shaded by swaying coconut palm trees, are now lined by tall leafless tree trunk skeletons, victims of a combination of yellowing disease and Hurricane Roxanne. But life goes on and the beautiful beaches here are the favorite nesting area for hawksbill turtles. There's also a **turtle research center**, about halfway between Champotón and the fishing village of Sabancuy, where you can stop and see any babies they're holding for release.

Sabancuy isn't on the long sand dune of the coast road; it's about 500 meters inland, across the bridge over the northern end of the Laguna de Terminos. It's a pleasant little town with a colonial church and swimming in the lagoon is refreshing here. There are several inexpensive restaurants in the center and the road inland from here connects with the one to Escárcega. Snorkeling and diving are good in the northern part of the lagoon. Just south of the turn for Sabancuy is a big, shady, thatch-roofed restaurant, **Viaductoplaya**, at Km 77.5. Along with its main dining area, numerous small tables under individual shade palapas line the white Gulf coast beach offering an unbeatable view of the water. Moderate prices, a specialty in seafood and its large size mean that buses often a stop here. Unless your mother warned you about waiting an hour after eating, the swimming along the white sandy beach is excellent. The coral reefs offshore, Los Bajos, are alleged to be good for diving.

Someday, the Laguna de Terminos' rich ecological attractions will be more fully exploited for visitors. **Dolphins** reproduce in numbers there and the surrounding jungles and rivers offer countless opportunities for ecological tourism. Campeche has the largest wild bird reserves in North America. The Palizada River and the small town of **Palizada**, reached by land from the road to Palenque, offer some fascinating fishing and exploration opportunities, including seeing the prehistoric *pejegarto*, a crossbreed between a fish and alligator. The undeveloped southern area near the Tabasco border is particularly wild and beautiful.

Bridges have replaced the ferries that used to bog down travelers in Carmen going to or coming from Tabasco, but watch your speed, the police are vigilant on the bridge. If you do stop in Carmen, expect prices to be a little higher than Campeche because it's a business town.

Accommodations

Hotel Acuario (*Calle 51 No. 60,* ☎ *and fax 948/2-59-95, 34 rooms and 4 suites with air, TV, restaurant*). This hard-to-find new hotel is an appealing place to stay, halfway between the best beach (Playa Norte) and the downtown. Its customers are mostly middle executives in town on business and its owner, former lawyer Pedro Fonz, is a jovial host. The modern two-story hotel offers secure parking on a quiet residential street and has a small pool and jacuzzi. The excellent little restaurant, facing a verdant courtyard with a stone fountain, specializes in fresh seafood and shrimp cocktail. **$**

Hotel Los Alpes (*Calle 22 No. 160,* ☎ *948/2-22-26, 12 rooms with air*). This streetside, downtown hotel is a best buy in the budget category. Only 12 basic rooms line a small garden courtyard with a particularly inviting entrance that includes a tiny restaurant. Two queen-size beds are in each small room. The cute three-table porch café has French clay roofing tiles, brought as sailing ship ballast in the 1800's. The "Frères Martin" (Martin Brothers) name is still clearly visible overhead. Gray stone block and hardwood enhance the mood. **$**

Eurohotel (*Calle 22 No. 208,* ☎ *948/2-30-90, 80 rooms with air and 12 suites, pool, restaurant, bar, disco*). Eurohotel is Carmen's most prestigious overnight address and it deserves to be. Accommodations are modern and comfortable in a tall bright white building surrounding a deep blue pool. Definitely a high class business hotel, it offers twice-a-day free shuttles to Carmen's busy airport. You get much for your money here. Compared to the United States' or Cancún's hotel prices, this is a certifiable bargain. **$$**

Hotel Del Parque (*Calle 33 between 20 and 22,* ☎ *948/2-10-46, 24 rooms with air, TV, restaurant*). This business hotel is centrally located right next to Carmen's main *zócalo* and is in the process of remodeling its already modern rooms, all of which face south, with big windows and large balconies. The rooms are huge, with two queen-size beds in each. **$**

See page 3 for price chart.

Dining

Los Robles (*Calle 26 No. 157*). In what was once their house, the Robles family serves Saturday and Sunday meals. A stylish conversion with good food. Try the lamb Barbacoa. **$-$$**

La Flama (*Calle 35 No. 39*). One of Carmen's newest restaurants, La Flama brags about its filet fajitas, accompanied by vegetables sautéed in butter and their American meat cuts. **$-$$**

San Carlos "El Chelo Baeza" (*Av. Periférico Norte No. 20*). This simple restaurant is well known for its excellent seafood. Pompano, delicate *pan de cazón* and a bouillabaisse with a touch of butter are among the house specialties. Reportedly, even some other restaurant owners recommend the San Carlos. **$-$$**

Piamonte (*Calle 22 No. 208*). Within the stylish Eurohotel, the Piamonte lives up to the hotel's elegance. Chef Emilio Alvardo Castro's favorite is the *Tin-Kin-Ti*, a Maya spiced fish. **$$-$$$**
See page 4 for price chart.

Escarcega

There's little to attract tourists to the crossroads bus-stop town of Escárcega, 150 km (93 miles) south of Campeche and 300 km (186 miles) from Villahermosa, at the junction of Highways 186 and 261. Most people who stay overnight are on the long trip between Palenque and Chetumal. Xpuhil is about two hours east; Campeche one and a half hours; and Palenque is a little over three hours.

The big lagoon about 50 km (32 miles) east of Escárcega is the **Laguna Silvictuc**, at a village of the same name. Rich in flora and fauna, the lagoon had been tagged as a possible site for a resort. The region has a sea bass, white turtle and clam hatchery and reportedly interesting caves called "Montebravo."

Accommodations

If it's getting late you could stay at the **Posada Escárcega** on Calle 25, a half-block north of the Pollos y Huevos fast food shop on the corner. It offers private parking in a center courtyard and costs about US $10 for a double with air. Basic but quiet. The **Hotel Maria Isabel** on Avenida Justo Sierra, a topiary-lined street parallel to 186, is better than its restaurant. Decent rooms and a green courtyard. The best hotel in town is the **Hotel Escárcega** on the main drag, west of the downtown. Sixty-six rooms around a pool and new palapa-roofed bar and pavilion.

These places are never full, so reservations are not necessary.

Dining

The restaurant at the ADO bus terminal is an OK place to pick up a bite to eat and at least there are lots of people to watch. There are many small eateries on 186 near the train tracks and in the surrounding *mercado*, including the **Pollos y Huevos** (Chicken and Eggs). Unfortunately, there is nothing out of the ordinary in town.

Palenque (Chiapas)

They'll like you because you're a foreigner.
They love foreigners: it's just strangers they hate.

– Jonathan Raban, British scholar and author

The ride into Tabasco and Chiapas from Escárcega is a long (216 km/135 miles) but straight foray past what's left of the jungle in the south of Campeche. Cleared for cattle ranching by slash and burn techniques, as you come into Tabasco the vegetation becomes lush and verdant again, but it is still hot and humid. The troubles of Chiapas, namely the Zapatista upheaval, have not affected the area around Palenque and the road from Escárcega is secure. As a ruined city, Palenque (Place of the Sun's Death) has to be seen to be believed. If you're this far south and have the time, it's well worth it. There's a new visitors center and museum where guides to the ruins are available.

The staggering structures, surrounded by the rainforest of the Palenque National Park, feature extraordinary bas-relief sculpture and magnificent well-preserved details. Perhaps the best time to see them is in the ethereal early morning rainforest mist. The **Temple of the Inscriptions** – which makes a great climb, 69 steps, steep and tall – is where the crypt of the King Pacal was uncovered in 1952. Carry a flashlight for the steps down inside. The impressive structure, known as the "Palace," rests on a plot the size of a full city block, highlighted by an architecturally rare (for the Maya) four-story tower. Inside there's a labyrinth of hallways and tunnels ripe for your exploration. Or you can hike paths in the surrounding jungle (wear mosquito repellent).

One of two luxuriant attractions in the nearby countryside is **Misol Ha**, Mayan for "Waterfall," about 20 km (12.5 miles) down on the road toward Ocosingo. Falls plunge steeply into a large sparkling pool, perfect for swimming. Another 45 km (28 miles) on the Ocosingo road leads to a right turn for **Aqua Azul** (*Yax Ha*, or "Blue Water") National Park. Cascading waterfalls of turquoise streams, white foam and fine soft mist make the atmosphere mystically magical. Hiking, camping, swimming, even kayaking, are spellbinding adventures here. This can be a day trip in itself – roundtrip combi buses leave from the Palenque downtown daily. The drawbacks are the persistent Maya vendors and the need to watch your valuables.

Palenque has an airport served from the Yucatán, especially Cancún, and there are air hops from here to the other big Maya sites nearby, Bonhampak and Yaxchilán. A good **travel agency** is the **Viajes Misol-Ha** on Juárez No. 48 (☎ 934/5-09-11).

SPEAKING STONES

Over all the world men move unhomeing and eternally
Concerned: a swarm of bees who have lost their queen.
– Christopher Fry, English writer

One of the most spectacular late discoveries at Palenque was a royal tomb with a well-preserved skeleton inside. The bones are presumed those of a queen, thought to be either the mother or grandmother of the powerful ruler, Pacal. Two companions were also buried with the queen, a common practice in Mesoamerica, and archeologists found a jade mask within. The tomb, unlike other royal burial areas, is a simple stone vault, devoid of any fancy decorations. Pacal, whose tomb was found in the Temple of the Inscriptions in 1952, was buried in a much more ornate manner with a sarcophagus decorated with hieroglyphics and beautiful stone carvings. Seven companions accompanied him to the Otherworld, a sign of his exalted status in the dynasty. His tomb also contained a false chamber, built to foil grave robbers.

During a visit to Pacal's tomb, a French psychic sensed strong "energies" coming from Temple 13, next to the Temple of the Inscriptions. She informed archeologists of a tomb inside and told them they must ask the permission of the queen to enter. Remembering that psychic energy also accounted for a discovery at Chichén Itzá (Augustus Le Plongeon) the skeptical scientists began to dig. Relics from the tomb are scheduled to be exhibited in the on-site museum.

Accommodations

The town of **Palenque** (12 km/7.5 miles from the ruins) has a plethora of small hotels and inns. Due to the large number of tourists, however, hotel prices are relatively high, especially for what you get. For good-valued budget stays try the clean and neat **La Posada** (☎ 934/5-04-37) off

Calle Merle Green (aka Calle Hidalgo) behind the Maya Tulipanes, or the cabañas at the **Hotel La Cañada,** down the same street in a shady spot (☎ 934/5-01-02). You might ask for a recommendation at the **tourism office** in the Casa de Cultura (Calle Jiménez) for more budget digs.

At the higher end, we prefer either the charming and enchanting **Chan-Kah** (☎ 934/5-11-00, fax 934/5-08-20), three km (1.8 miles) south towards the ruins, made of individual cottages with a big palapa restaurant and swimming pool, or **Hotel Nututum Viva** (☎ 934/5-01-00) also on the road toward the ruins, overlooking the Rio Usumacinta. Both boast excellent restaurants but the accommodations at Chan-Kah have a touch more ambiance.

Dining

 For eats, stop in **Cafe y Arte,** a coffee shop kind of place that sells books and magazines on Calle Independencia; bar and restaurant, **La Jaibita II** on Perferico Norte; **La Selva,** offering great atmosphere under a cool palapa roof; or for good regional food try the **Restaurante Maya,** on the plaza where Independencia intersects Av. Hidalgo (since 1958). There's a supermarket, **Supermercado Central,** on Av. Juárez.

Two Routes North

When you come to a fork in the road, take it.

– sage advice from Yogi Berra,
baseball player and manager

 There are two northern routes leading to or from Campeche city and each has its own advantages and attractions. For the reader we are listing most things here as if you were traveling south to north, although it is just as common to find adventurers traveling the circuit the other way: Cancún, Mérida, Campeche, Chetumal, Cancún. If your destination from Campeche is **Uxmal,** both routes can get you there. On the fast route, a right turn for Opichén, just past the railroad tracks in Yucatán, leads to the town of Muna, then south to Uxmal (see also Oxkintok in the Yucatán chapter).

The Fast One

 The direct route between Mérida and Campeche is the *corta*, or shortcut. Opened in 1540, it was the first overland road laid by the Spanish, who called it the *Camino Real* or "Royal Road." As you travel either the slow or fast route, you'll pass through numerous Maya villages where the inhabitants still earn their livelihood in agriculture.

Seventeen km (10 miles) north of Campeche is **Hampolol**, a nature reserve. Near **Tenabo** is a series of roadside shops selling gifts, especially wooden ship models – a signature handicraft of the state – and *nance* (nan-say), a sweet fruit soaked in a sugar liquid and touched with *Xtabentun*, an anise and honey liquor. Arranged in bottles, the delicious small orange and black fruit look like eyes. A traditional Maya treat.

The city of **Hecelchakán** (pop. 12,000) contains an 18th-century church and the **Museo Arqueológico del Camino Real** that displays some of the fantastic clay burial figurines found on Isla de Jaina, as well as representative pieces from all of Campeche's archeological zones. The museum boasts an indoor display as well as an outdoor corridor and garden area. Farther north in **Calkiní** there are plenty of artisans that make distinctive pottery. In town, the Franciscan San Luis Mission features an outstanding baroque principal altar.

Just below the border of Yucatán state is the center of **Panama hat** making: the tiny town of **Becal**. This distinctive headgear is made in over 2,000 subterranean workshops where skillful craftsmen hand weave the delicate leaves of the *jipijapa* palm tree into wonderful hats. The damp caves keep the fibers moist and pliant, essential for the tight weave needed in a top-quality hat. The finer the weave, the more supple and softer the feel – and the more wear-resistant and better looking. You'll be welcomed into many of the workshop caves to watch the hat makers at their craft. It's amazing to see the amount of work that goes into creating a hat that is fancy enough for dress and versatile enough to roll up in your suitcase, then massage back to its original shape when you reach your destination. We have found that gently unfolding our crushed hat, spraying it with water and placing over an inverted bowl helped return the headpiece to its original shape. Then, the brim should be placed on a flat surface, shaped and left to dry. When you're in Becal, select the style and look that looks best on you and buy it. The artisans will thank you and you'll thank them for the many years of use.

If you're hungry, just before (or maybe it's just past) the border with Yucatán is **Los Sombreros**, a roadside restaurant and cheesy gift shop. It's run by a mother and son who serve simple but excellent

Mexican food at prices that make it hard to justify not eating here. A great tasting and generous plate of *poc chuc* (Yucatecan pork) is less than US $3.

The Slow One

The long route on Highway 261 (264 km/165 miles, but more visually interesting than the shorter one) is best known for its northern Maya sites, most across the line in Yucatán. They include **Uxmal**, **Kabáh** and other **Puuc ruins**. However, a series of small colonial towns inhabited by the Puuc Maya dot the southern rural route that bends north in **Hopelchén** ("Five Wells"), a colonial town with a colorful country market. Sixty-three km (40 miles) southeast is **Dzibilchaltún** and the ruins of **Hochob**. Some 31 km (19 miles) north from Hopelchén, near Yucatán and a cement arch marking the border, is the tiny village of **Bolonchén** ("Nine Wells"), where the **Gruta de Xtacumbilxuna** ("Cave of the Hidden Girl") lies. When John Lloyd Stephens visited the seven natural cenotes of water in the cavern between 1841 and 1842, he described it this way: *"Gigantic stalactites and huge blocks of stone assume all manner of fantastic shapes and seemed like monstrous animals or deities of a subterranean world.... The fame of the Cueva of Bolonchén extends throughout the Yucatán."* Who are we to argue? The cavern is huge and impressive but not quite as grand as Loltún.

El oro y amores eran malos de encubrir
(Gold and love affairs are difficult to hide)

– Spanish proverb

Yucatán

I must learn Spanish, one of these days,
Only for that slow sweet name's sake.

– *The Flower's Name*, Robert Browning, 1812-1889

At A Glance

NAME: The name "Yucatán" may have originated from a classic New World misinterpretation. When the Spanish put ashore and asked the native Maya to tell them the name of the land, the Maya replied *"u'y than, u'y than,"* meaning, "We don't understand, what the hell are you talking about?" That was eventually corrupted to "Yucatán" (youk-a-TAN).

LOCATION: Yucatán is a wedge-shaped state covering most of the northern part of the peninsula. It borders the Gulf of Mexico, where the Gulf meets the Caribbean.

CAPITAL: Mérida.

MAJOR CITIES: Mérida, Motúl, Izamal, Valladolid, Tizimin and Progreso.

POPULATION: 1,500,000 – indigenous Maya and Spanish descent.

CLIMATE: Hot and humid inland, but the coastline is cooled by ocean breezes. Dry in the winter.

 VEGETATION: Scrub forest, mangroves and cattle and farm land.

GEOGRAPHY: Lowland, many cenotes, Gulf coast beaches and a range of hills (Puuc region).

SIZE: 16,000 square miles (40,000 square kilometers).

WILDLIFE: Pheasant, deer, jaguarundi, flamingos and armadillos.

ECOLOGICAL RESERVES & PARKS: Parque Natural del Flamenco Méxicano de Celestún, Dzibilchaltún, San Felipe, Rio Lagartos.

MAJOR ARCHEOLOGICAL SITES: Chichén Itzá, Ekbalam, Dzibilchaltún, Uxmal, Kabáh, Sayil and Labná.

Mérida

You are in love with a country where people laugh in the sun and the people are warm as the sunshine and live and move easily, and women with honey colored skins and men with no frowns on their faces sit on white terraces...

– A.S.J. Tessimond, 1902-1962

 It doesn't take long to realize that Mérida is the cultural focal point for the entire peninsula. Despite its size (over 600,000 square km/240,000 square miles) and urban inconveniences, Mérida is one of the Yucatán's most hospitable and nostalgic of cities. Its colonial center thrives and is full of Maya men and women dressed in traditional country garb; round-faced children with sheepish grins and bright laughs; young, fresh-faced college students in the city's several universities; businessmen in *guayaberas* and businesswomen in modern dress; young European tourists bearing backpacks; older North American adventurers in hiking shorts from L.L. Bean; loving Mexican couples strolling the Plaza Mayor; vendors clamoring for business; families on their way to church or a fiesta. Mérida seems to be a living, breathing entity.

Mérida's heart is the **Colonial Centro,** much larger than Campeche's walled city. Central to its existence are the venerable old churches, the *mercado,* a meeting place for two cultures, and the unique and delicious Yucatecan cooking.

The Yucatán's largest city was founded as the peninsular capital by Francisco de Montejo, *El Mozo* (the Younger or the Son), at the ancient Maya city of T'ho (Maya in the countryside still use the traditional name, Place of Five Temples, when referring to Mérida).

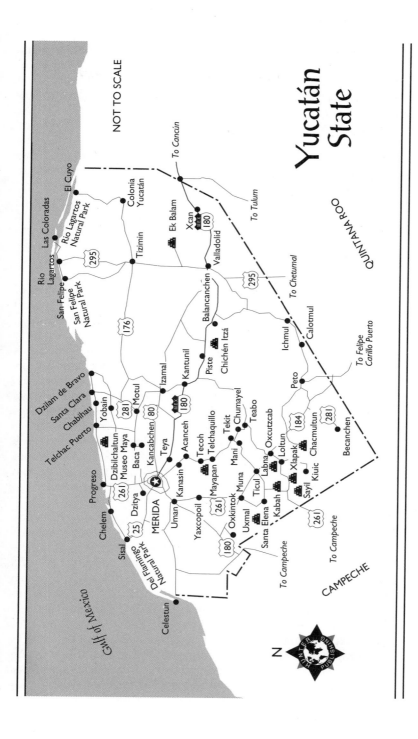

NOT TO SCALE

Yucatán State

Gulf of Mexico

QUINTANA ROO

CAMPECHE

To Cancún
To Tulum
To Chetumal
To Felipe Carrillo Puerto
To Campeche
To Campeche

El Cuyo
Las Coloradas
Río Lagartos
Río Lagartos Natural Park
Colonia Yucatán
San Felipe
San Felipe Natural Park
Tizimin
Ek Balam
Xcan
Valladolid
Dzilam de Bravo
Santa Clara
Chabihau
Telchac Puerto
Progreso
Chelem
Sisal
Celestun
Del Flamingo Natural Park
Yobain
Motul
Izamal
Kantunil
Balancanchen
Chichén Itzá
Piste
Ichmul
Calotmul
Peto
Becanchen
Chacmultun
Oxcutzcab
Teabo
Chumayel
Mani
Tekit
Loltun
Labna
Xlapak
Sayil
Kiuic
Kabah
Santa Elena
Uxmal
Ticul
Oxkintok
Muna
Yaxcopoil
Uman
Kanasin
Mayapan
Telchaquillo
Tecoh
Acanceh
Teya
Kancabchen
Baca
Dzibilchaltun
Museo Maya
Dzitya
MERIDA

295
176
295
281
80
180
261
25
180
261
184
281
261
180

N

HUNTER PUBLISHING

T'ho's impressive buildings reminded Montejo of the Roman ruins in the Spanish city of Mérida, sealing T'ho's fate and its name. He inaugurated the new capital on January 6, 1542 with the words "... *I wish to populate [and] construct a city of 100 neighbors.... May Our Lord keep it in His Holy Service for all time."*

The blueprint called for a rectangular-shaped city graced by wide avenues and a large *zócalo*, or main square. They began building the city from the ruined Maya pyramids found there, which provided enough stone to create all the edifices bordering the downtown Plaza and more. Surrounding the city center, where the Spanish and creoles lived, were *barrios* – lower-class residential neighborhoods – Santiago and Santa Catarina in the west for the local Maya; San Cristóbal to the east for highland Maya; and Santa Lucia in the north for blacks and mulattos. El Mozo began building his own house – Casa Montejo – on the square during the time his wife Andrea gave birth to their daughter, Beatriz, in 1543. The house still stands (now a bank) and its ornate entrance facade features the Montejo coat of arms flanked by gruesome symbols of his power: two Spanish conquistadors each with their feet on the neck of two defeated Maya warriors.

The occupation of T'ho was not easy for the Spanish. Six months after Montejo founded Mérida, thousands of Maya warriors attacked. Somehow, they failed to dislodge the beleaguered conquistadors. In many ways that fateful battle marked an end to the Maya era and the beginning of a colonial system, with huge landholdings by the Spanish, upon which the Maya labored as virtual slaves.

A rustic church served the growing capital until 1561 when work began on the huge cathedral at the west side of the *zócalo* using stones from some of the dismantled T'ho pyramids. The **Catedral de San Ildefonso** was finished in 1598, making it the oldest cathedral on the American continent.

By the late 1800s, henequen was king and *hacendados* (hacienda owners) and wealthy families built opulent homes along the Paseo de Montejo in the north end of town. Usually referred to as the "**White City**," due to the large number of white buildings, Mérida also became known as the "Paris of the West" because of the French baroque influence of its baronial mansions and its thriving culture.

To enjoy Mérida at its finest today calls for time. Time for leisurely lunches under the *portales* across from the Plaza Mayor. Time for Sunday strolls along the paseo's leafy green walkway or listening to choral serenades in a park under the stars. Time to watch courting couples or old friends sit in S-shaped cement park seats known as *confidenciales* – close enough for secrets but far enough apart for propriety. Sit in one and absorb the rhythm of life as it reverberates through the park. Or see the city's sights in a romantic horse-drawn carriage called a *casela*. There's always something interesting going on in Mérida.

Orientation

 GETTING AROUND: If you've been out wandering the countryside, Mérida may come as a surprise. It's a big, cosmopolitan city with big city drawbacks: crowded streets and traffic pollution. The very things that make the Colonial Centro so attractive are responsible for some of its problems – narrow streets built for horse and carriage were never intended to hold jockeying cars or lumbering buses spewing exhaust. Busy season is in the summer, when Europeans and Mexicans on holiday throng the city, while Meridanos flee the high heat and humidity for the cooler countryside and shore, mainly at Progreso. Still, none of these disadvantages should inhibit your enjoyment of a truly unique city.

All roads in the Yucatán lead to Mérida, 320 km (200 miles) west of Cancún and 190 km (119 miles) from Campeche. Like the hub of a wheel or the center of a spider web, roads spoke out from Mérida in several directions: Highway 261 north to Progreso and south to Muna; Highway 180 south to Campeche and east to Valladolid and Cancún; roads west to Celestún and east to Motúl. A bypass road (*periférico*) rings the city but requires paying close attention to the signs if you want to find your desired exit.

Once a walled city like Campeche, Mérida still has three standing Moorish-style gates through which ran *camino reales*, royal roads, overland to Valladolid, Campeche and Champotón. The painted red cobblestone vestige of those roads can be found in the southern and western parts of the old city. Left over from colonial times are the unique and artistic **name plaques** set into the walls of building corners all over the old city. They are remnants of the Spanish attempt to teach the Maya their language and to provide easy reference points for directions for their own illiterate people. For example, a ceramic tile plaque with a picture of a parrot and its name underneath in Spanish, became the name of the corner. Consequently, people could meet on "Flamingo" corner or could reference their address as between "Monkey" and "Drop of Water." The surviving plaques are protected by building codes that prevent their destruction.

DISTANCES FROM MERIDA

Acanceh	30 km/19 miles
Celestún	85 km/53 miles
Chichén Itzá	120 km/75 miles
Chumayel	82 km/51 miles
Dzibilchaltún	15 km/9 miles
Dzilam de Bravo	107 km/67 miles
Dzitnup	167 km/104 miles
Grutas de Balancanche	122 km/76 miles
Grutas de Loltún	138 km/86 miles
Izamal	70 km/44 miles
Kabáh	101 km/63 miles
Labná	119 km/74 miles
Maní	127 km/79 miles
Mayapán	102 km/64 miles
Motúl	44 km/27 miles
Muna	62 km/39 miles
Oxkutzcab	138 km/86 miles
Progreso	33 km/21 miles
Sayil	110 km/68 miles
Teabo	87 km/54 miles
Tecoh	36 km/22 miles
Tekit	66 km/41 miles
Telchac Puerto	69 km/43 miles
Telchaquillo	46 km/29 miles
Teya	10 km/6 miles
Ticul	84 km/52 miles
Umán	17 km/11 miles
Uxmal	80 km/50 miles
Valladolid	162 km/101 miles
Xlapak	116 km/72 miles
Yaxcopoil	33 km/21 miles

The grid-like construction of Mérida's streets makes finding your way easy. Odd-number streets run east and west, with higher number streets to the south of the main plaza. Even-number streets run north and south, with higher number streets to the west. Most of the references we offer in this guide are within walking distance of the *zócalo*, or Plaza Principal, and up the Paseo de Montejo, a Champs-Elysées-like boulevard between Calles 56 and 58. Alternate streets run one-way for vehicular traffic. **Traffic police** control the amazing amount of traffic clogging the narrow streets in the city center. Be aware they will ticket you for driving infractions so pay attention to the traffic flow, traffic lights and their hand signals.

Besides walking, **taxis** are the best way to get around. In-town **bus** routes are difficult to figure out unless you're familiar with the names of the neighborhoods. Nearly all the buses that run on the Paseo Montejo, however, get you downtown near the main plaza. Ask someone on the street or a shopkeeper; Meridanos are friendly and helpful folk. Taxis can be difficult to find because they're not always roaming the streets looking for passengers. Have your hotel, or any hotel, call for one. Alternatively, there are taxi stands at most of the parks and squares, so you'll usually find one waiting there. Negotiate your fare beforehand, as prices are generally higher in Mérida than anywhere else due to a very strong *taxistas* union. Bicycles are probably a "no-no" on the narrow inner-city streets. Mérida has a large airport but international service has all but switched to Cancún. Check with your carrier if you want to fly here. Aeromexico and Mexicana have connections.

Buses into and from Mérida use the new first-class bus depot, **CAME**, on Calle 70 between 69 and 71, about seven blocks southwest of the Plaza Mayor. The second-class terminal, **Autobuses Unión,** is nearby on Calle 69 between 68 and 70. The **train station** is at Calles 48 and 55.

Practicalities

 The **tourism office** is behind thick and tall wooden doors on the corner of the huge Teatro Peón Contreras on Calle 60, two blocks north of the Plaza Mayor. There is a **US Consulate** in Mérida on Paseo Montejo near the Holiday Inn. The phone is ☎ 99/25-63-66. The **U.K.** consul is staked out on Calle 53, ☎ 99/21-67-99. **Canadians** have to call either Mexico City or Cancún. You can reach the **immigration office** for Tourist Card extensions by phoning ☎ 99/28-58-23.

If you're tired of speaking English, live with a local family and study Spanish in immersion classes at the **Centro Idiomas del Sureste**, with three locations (one downtown and two in residential areas) close to the city center. Classes of three hours per day run a minimum of two weeks and there's a grueling but effective option for a full five hours of tongue-numbing lessons daily. All levels, from beginners to advanced. We took classes for four weeks in San José, Costa Rica a few years ago and found the experience invaluable. A half-day of class and the balance practicing your new skills is a quick and painless way to speak like a native. Call Charlene Biddulph,

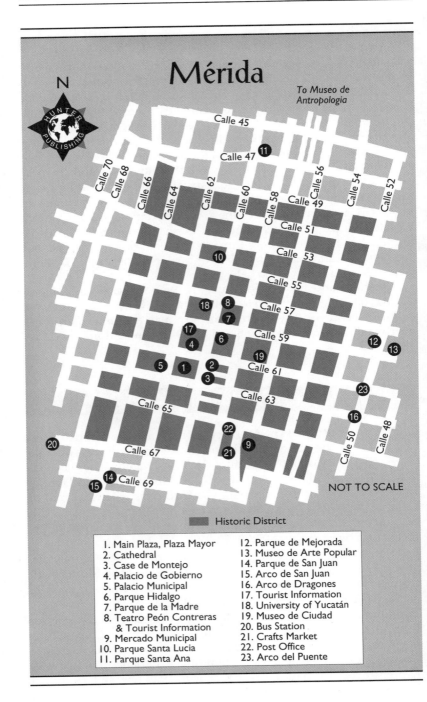

Mérida

To Museo de Antropologia

NOT TO SCALE

■ Historic District

1. Main Plaza, Plaza Mayor
2. Cathedral
3. Case de Montejo
4. Palacio de Gobierno
5. Palacio Municipal
6. Parque Hidalgo
7. Parque de la Madre
8. Teatro Peón Contreras
   & Tourist Information
9. Mercado Municipal
10. Parque Santa Lucia
11. Parque Santa Ana
12. Parque de Mejorada
13. Museo de Arte Popular
14. Parque de San Juan
15. Arco de San Juan
16. Arco de Dragones
17. Tourist Information
18. University of Yucatán
19. Museo de Ciudad
20. Bus Station
21. Crafts Market
22. Post Office
23. Arco del Puente

their US agent, at **Language Studies Abroad**, to register (☎ 800/424-5522). *Entiende?*

In addition to running a good travel agency, **Yucatán Trails Travel,** on Calle 62 between 57 and 59 (☎ 99/28-25-82), Canadian Dennis LaFoy (denis@pibil.finred.com.mx) organizes a monthly get-together of the English-speaking community. He'll make individualized tour and travel arrangements to the ruins and other exciting Yucatecan sights, or you can nip over to Cuba. **Taino Tours**, on Paseo Montejo No. 442 (☎ 99/26-26-92), and **Havanatour,** on the Paseo as well, between 43 and 45 (☎ 99/23-23-96), push the forbidden Cubano trip. Flights stop in Cancún.

There's a small inexpensive hole-in-the-wall **laundromat**, Lavanderias Automatics, on Calle 59 near 74. They do a good, dependable job cheaply. Another worthwhile **laundromat** can be found two blocks due west of the Fiesta Americana hotel, on Av. Cupules and Av. 62.

Instead of gun-toting Army patrols to help tourists, Mérida boasts a **Tourism Police Force**, graduates of the Luis Sotelo Regil Police Academy. They patrol the downtown in distinctive white shirts and light brown uniform with a *Policía Turística* patch on their right sleeve. Although not completely fluent in English, the 41 officers are eager to help and can do so. ☎ 99/25-25-55.

The **Green Angels** (and they are) are at ☎ 99/83-11-84. The **post office** is an elegant building in the middle of the busy *mercado* on Calle 65, near 56. It closes at 1 p.m. on Saturdays. The **Red Cross** is good in an emergency, ☎ 99/24-98-13. The big **hospital** in town is the Hospital O'Horan on Av. Itzáes (☎ 99/24-7-11). **American Express** has an office in the Hotel Aluxes on Calle 60.

Work out your kinks in **Gym Biceps Mixto** on Calle 62 between 57 & 59 (☎ 99/23-28-87). About US $3 per day as a guest gets you access to a full line of modern exercise equipment and free weights. You can put the fat back on at **Capuchino Cheesecake Deluxe** at the corner of 47 and 64 and by its name you know what we mean. There are a couple of **motorcycle and bicycle** shops in town, notably **Bicimaya** (☎ 99/24-80-34) on the corner of 69 and 56.

FESTIVALS AND EVENTS: There is no city in the Yucatán that puts on a happier face than Mérida. Check our list of "Holidays" for special celebrations during the time you'll be in town (pages 64-68). But every night of the week there's a fiesta, a concert, a show – something to see or do. The added bonus is that the events were never meant for "tourists" but for Meridanos themselves, and they're an integral part of local culture.

One fiesta was hardly ended when another began.

– John Lloyd Stephens, writing of Mérida, 1841

Sunday – Mérida en Domingo. All day long on Sundays the downtown area around the main *zócalo* (aka Plaza Mayor or Plaza Principal) closes to vehicular traffic and becomes a giant bazaar and picnic with musical concerts, puppet shows, folk dancing and activities for children. All activities are free. At 11 a.m. there's a concert under the arches of the Palacio de Gobierno, while the police band strikes it up at the Santa Lucia Park. Marimba music makes its mark at the Parque Hidalgo on Calle 60 at 59 at 11:30 a.m. At 1 p.m. a *folklorico ballet* recreation of a mestizo wedding occurs in front of the Palacio Municipal on the Plaza Mayor. There seems to be music, fiestas and flea markets in every park around town. On Sunday, 10 a.m. to 2 p.m., there's a popular browsing **bazaar** market at the Parque Santa Lucia. Good place to buy colorful old stamps. In front of the cathedral you can rent **pedal carts** with canvas roofs for a fun trip around the traffic-free streets.

Monday – Vaquería Yucateca takes place at 9 p.m. (be there early) in front of the Palacio Municipal at the Plaza Mayor. This free concert and show features folk dancers and the police band performing traditional *jarana* dances where the dancers balance trays with bottles and glasses full of beer on their heads as they dance. How do they do it? This celebration is traditional with *vaqueros* (cowboys) who hold a fiesta after the hacienda cattle round-up. Free.

Tuesday – Musical Memories is a free concert of familiar 1940s Big Band, as well as 50s and 60s modern music at 9 p.m. at the Parque Santiago, Calle 59. Very popular. Next to the park there is a charming local *mercado* with flower vendors and lots of little places to eat. It's quieter and less pressured than larger *mercados*. On the bend on Calle 70 is the venerable **Panaderia Flore de Santiago**, where local people gather for breakfast and long lunches. Their fresh coffee is excellent, brewed in an majestic coffee/cappuccino maker that looks old enough to be out of the Ark. Also at 9 p.m. the talented **University de Yucatán Ballet Folklórico** performs "Yucatán and Its Roots" at the Teatro Peón Contreras (worth seeing and the theater is gorgeous inside). Admission about US $4.

Wednesday – At 8 p.m. there's a **music and poetry performance** at the Mayab Culture House on Calle 63 between 64 and 66. The **Retreta**, a concert of music from the 18th century to the present, is performed at 9 p.m. in Ermita Park, the corner of Calles 66 and 77. Both are free.

Thursday – Serenata Yucateca. First begun on January 14, 1965, the free weekly vocal, folk dance, poetry and musical entertainment has become one of the most popular traditional evenings for Meridanos and tourists alike. There are plenty of seats under the stars but if you want to eat dinner at the outdoor tables of the Restaurant Santa Lucia, get there early. Starts at 9 p.m.

Friday – University Serenade. Students from the university perform a collection of songs and dances typical of the Yucatán in the college garden. 9 p.m., free admission. **Catholic Mass in English** is held at the Santa Lucia church facing the park of the same name, 6 p.m.

Saturday – Noche Romántica, or "romantic night," means that trios and musical groups perform in restaurants and bars throughout the town. Try the Holiday Inn's outdoor buffet, which also features musical serenades and candlelight.

Sports

Bullfights are held nearly every Sunday, but big name matadors appear only during the "season," January through March, at the Plaza de Toros, Paseo de Reforma, near Colon. A **baseball team** plays February through July at the Kukulcán Sports Center on Calle 14, next to the Santa Clara Brewery in the south of town. Many hotels have **swimming** pools and Hotel Colon (☎ 99/23-43-55) has a steam room. Otherwise Meridanos go to Progreso to swim in the Gulf. The Holiday Inn has a **tennis** court and there are several courts at Club de Golf La Ceiba, which also has a nine-hole **golf** course (☎ 99/27-00-35). The Club de Golf Yucatán (☎ 99/24-75-25), 16 km (10 miles) north of town on the way to Progreso, offers 18 holes with a par 72.

Shopping

The peninsula's Yucatecan artisans produce some of the finest handicrafts in Mexico. *Hamacas* (hammocks) are a major item, as are *huipiles* and *guayaberas* (traditional clothing) and *huaraches*, leather hand-tooled sandals. Masks, baskets, pottery, Panama hats made from *jipijapa* palm leaves, gold and silver jewelry, leather crafts and belts, wood carvings and colorful party piñatas – all can be found in Mérida's major shopping area, the municipal market, south of the Plaza Mayor and on Sundays in the park bazaars. For handicrafts, try **Casa de Artesanias** on Calle 63, between 64 and 66. They have a wide selection of folk art and regional crafts. Watch your valuables when you're in the crowded *mercado* area. Although not a common occurrance, we once lost a camera to pick-pockets here. **El Arte Maya** is upstairs on Calle 60 between 63 and 65 facing the Plaza. Also try the **Crafts Market** in the green *mercado* building at Calle 67 and 56. When you're in the *mercado* here, or in any country village, pick up some **copal**, a sticky resin incense in colors ranging from pale yellow to deep amber, and used by the Maya for the last three thousand years. Shave thin slivers off the lump and burn or, even better, place a small amount on a lighted charcoal cone. It gives off an evocative, earthy fragrance that is redolent of myrrh, musk and pine. You'll probably find it in a stall that sells religious items.

HOW TO BUY A HAMMOCK

God's blessing on the man who invented sleep.
– Sancho Panza in Cervantes' *Don Quixote de la Mancha*

Long before Columbus, Yucatecans slept on *hamacas* strung from wall hooks or outside between trees. When Spanish conquistadors arrived, they quickly recognized the advantages of hammocks and incorporated them into their night life. Comfortable, durable, portable and easy to clean, they make safe cribs for young babies. The best hammocks made in Mexico are from the Yucatán and in Mérida – the heart of hammock industry – they are sold on almost every street corner. They make great gifts and, once you get used to lying in one, you'll be drilling holes in your bedroom walls for the one you bring home.

Hammocks come in four sizes: *sencilla* (single), *doble* (double), *matrimonial* (queen-size) and *matrimonial especial*, the largest of all. Singles are really for children. Most tourists are amazed at the size of singles and some can be convinced into believing singles are queen-size by an enthusiastic vendor. Genuine *matrimonials* are about 16 feet long, one third of that being the main body. They should weigh an average of four to five pounds.

To check the weave, hold the hammock loosely in your hand and gently spread the strings apart. Spaces between the weaves should be no bigger than two inches or so. Good ones will have double or triple string weaves. It should also have a hundred or more pairs of strings (*brazas*) at each end gathered into the hanging loops and these should be thick and tightly wrapped.

To see if a hammock is long enough for you, grab it at the edge where the body and the end-strings meet and hold your hand level with your forehead. The opposite end of the body should touch the floor. Most of the colorful ones that you see for sale will be nylon (the best choice), although cotton and silk are sometimes available.

Hammocks are in great abundance in Mérida and you will almost certainly be approached by a vendor. Despite their aggressive sales pitches, they're not all out to cheat you. But don't shop only by price. Quality counts, so ask to see the best first. You'll probably find a better selection in the *mercado* at slightly higher prices. There are also some excellent shops that deal almost exclusively in hammocks where you can try out the goods before you buy. **La Poblano**, at Calles 60 & 58, has always been highly recommended. It's worth a visit just to see their extensive inventory. Open Monday-Saturday, 8 a.m. - 7 p.m. Also recommended is the family-run **Hamacas El Aguacate** on Calle 58 at 73. Or you can drive or catch a bus to see them made in **Tixkokob**, a colonial town east of the city, where a large percentage of the hammocks for sale are hand-made in family workshops.

For jewelry look in **La Perla Maya** on Calle 60 No. 485, or **Las Palomas**, also on Calle 60, between 53 and 55. A **Sam's Club** is located in the north of town off the continuation of the Paseo Montejo on the way to Progreso. There's also a big suburban-style shopping mall out that way. A **Sears** department store is on Calle 63, between 56 and 58. Several men's clothing shops are along Calle 59, including the well-known **Jack Guayaberas**, where you can also have comfortable *guayabera* shirts made to order.

Night Spots

Although Meridanos love their fiestas, their city isn't a late-night party town. For some dancing and music try **Pancho's,** on Calle 59 between 60 and 62, or **Carlos 'n' Charlies**, an import from Cancún, on the Prolongación Montejo No. 477. The **Hotel Calinda Panamericana** has a disco on Calle 59 and 52 and so do the **Holiday Inn** and **Hyatt** hotels, side-by-side on Av. Colon off the Paseo. If you want to see a movie, there's **Cine Cantarell** on Calle 60, near the Restaurant Express. We once saw *Schindler's List* subtitled in Spanish here – now that was an experience! Nearby is the **Cine Fantasio**, facing Parque Hidalgo and squeezed between the Gran Hotel and the Hotel Caribe. At the **Cinema 57** on Calle 59 between 68 and 70, Arnold Schwartzeneger once saved the United States while we were away. **Cine Premier** is on Calle 57 and 62. Real nightowls will find Yucatecan **Restaurante Caleca**, at 62 and 61 off the Plaza Mayor, open 24 hours.

An abandoned plantation outside of Mérida.

Adventures

ON FOOT

 Most of Mérida's in-town adventures involve absorbing the soul of the city through the souls of your feet. A morning **walking tour** of Mérida is a wonderful way to see the town. Start at the **Plaza Mayor**, the center of the original walled city. The plaza went through several names, beginning with the Plaza de Armas, where Montejo's original troops paraded. It still can't make up its mind because it's also known as the Plaza Principal and the *zócalo*. A large circular walkway under shade trees centers around a garden and laurel topiaries, a magnificent Mexican obsession. Iron benches and *confidenciales* offer perfect places to people-watch. Friendly Meridanos may approach you to practice their English.

To the west of the park on Calle 60 at 61 is the hulking **Catedral de San Ildefonso**, begun in 1561 with stones from the Maya pyramids at T'ho and finally completed in 1598. It is the oldest cathedral in North America. The plain, fortress-like exterior was part of a functional design. The indigenous people of the Yucatán didn't take too kindly to the Spanish invaders and, time and again, churches served as a last line of defensive fortification. Inside the thick walls the interior decor is equally unadorned but the main altar is impressive and supposedly the second largest in the world. To the side of the altar is the small shrine to the charred crucifix of **Cristo de las Ampollas**. Carved from a tree struck by lightening that burned all night but remained unscathed by the flames, a subsequent church fire left it with the blisters that give it its name: "Christ of the Blisters." When church is in service, there are poor and crippled people asking alms just inside the doorways. We couldn't help but give.

The **Casa de Montejo** is the stately mansion across from the south side of the plaza, built by Francisco Montejo for his family beginning in 1542. Incredibly, his family descendants lived there for 435 years until the late 1970s when Banamex Bank bought and restored the property. The colonial facade is typically high-walled and plain but an intricate bas-relief around the doorway reminds the Maya daily of the Conquest and the power of the Montejos: Two Spanish knights stand upon the heads of defeated Maya warriors, whose mouths cry out in pain. The stone inscription in Spanish reads: *"The Adelante Don Francisco Montejo caused this to be made in the year 1549."* You can walk inside to some public areas whenever the bank is open.

Detailed facade of Casa Montejo.

On the west side of the plaza is the yellow **Palacio Municipal**, site of much of Mérida's Sunday entertainment and reportedly the site of the last Maya building to be dismantled. It's also the locale for Monday night's Vaquería Yucateca exhibition. Under the arches along Calle 61 on the northern border of the plaza is the **Palacio del Gobierno**, open to the public with a fine collection of paintings depicting the Yucatán's tragic history. The vividly colored murals were completed in 1978 by local artist, Fernando Pacheco Castro, upstairs in the Salon de Historia.

The Salon hosts a performance every Sunday at 11 a.m. Outside its high French windows are wrought-iron balconies with wonderful views of the park and cathedral. Under the *portales* that run the length of the building there are several restaurants, including **Pizzeria Bella**, a very tasty pizzeria, and the **Dulcería y Sorbeteria** ice cream parlor, where a dreamy assortment of ice creams and sherbets come in exotic tropical flavors. If it's lunch time try the Yucatecan **Restaurante Caleca,** at 62 and 61 on the corner of the Plaza Mayor, in the next building west. There's also an excellent hairdresser-barber shop next door on Calle 61.

The opposite corner of Calle 61 at Calle 60, along the side of the cathedral, is a good place to pick up a *casela*, a horse-drawn buggy for touring the town. One block east is the **Museo de la Ciudad**, a small museum of the city in a former convent chapel.

Back on Calle 60 heading north are several touristy gift stores and on your left is the **Teatro Daniel Ayala**, a professional theater. On the right is the **Parque Hidalgo** where small outdoor restaurants line the side and hammock vendors lie in wait. Next comes the ancient **Iglesia de Jesus,** built in 1618 by the Jesuits. It's one of Mérida's older buildings. This church, with the quiet little **Parque de la Madre** in front, is a favorite site for weddings and its antique exterior is a great backdrop for photos. The west wall has faint markings of Maya carvings from the stones of the building that stood on this site.

The huge Italianate **Teatro Peón Contreras** is next with the **tourist information center** in the corner office. On the cobblestone sidestreet is the **Café Peón Contreras**, a romantic sidewalk restaurant that features cappuccino and Cuban coffee. Unfortunately, the food doesn't quite live up to the inviting atmosphere, but it definitely has the best outdoor seating in Mérida.

The theater was designed in 1908 by Italian architect Enrico Deserti along the lines of the great European opera houses. The sweeping marble staircase and frescoed dome were restored in the 1980s to their earlier glory. The height of culture in Mérida, it attracts international stars.

The **University of the Yucatán** stands across the street behind black iron gates and big wooden doors. Inside, the courtyard looks up at Moorish-style arches on the hallways surrounding the building that dates from 1711. Site of a Jesuit college, the State University was founded in the 1920s by Felipe Carrillo Puerto.

The **Parque Santa Lucia**, small and rather plain during the day, is a popular place on Thursday evenings when the Yucatecan Serenade occurs. Regulated to a **Poets' Corner** are busts of some of Yucatán's beloved musicians and poets. A small church across from the park, built in the late 1500s for African and Caribbean slaves that lived in the district, offers an English Mass on Saturday evenings at 6 p.m.

Another pleasant way to get a city overview is the **Discover Mérida** two-hour sightseeing tour in an open-sided trolley bus. It leaves beautiful Santa Lucia Park at 10 a.m. and 1, 4 & 7 p.m. daily (about US $4). A bilingual guide (ours was named Misty Chuc – talk about cross-cultures) accompanies the run, which stops at the sculpture park, **Parque de las Americas**, midway, to stretch your legs. Another trip around Mérida, then up to the ruins of **Dzibilchaltún**, leaves at 9 a.m., Tuesday through Sunday (US $10). Horse-drawn carriages also tour the downtown and Paseo Montejo attractions.

ADDITIONAL SIGHTS: The **Paseo de Montejo** is a wide tree-lined boulevard that begins at Calle 47 and runs north through the fine homes and mansions built in the Belle Epoque style by wealthy families and hacienda owners who made fortunes on the near-monopoly the Yucatán had in henequen. Some of the mansions are still private homes, but many are now used as office space. Still others have been replaced by more modern and garish office buildings. The trolley tour from Santa Lucia Park will include other impressive homes in a nearby neighborhood. The Paseo is a popular place to take *calesa*, horse-drawn carriage rides, day and night. Check for them near the Holiday Inn on Av. Colon and the Paseo. At the circle with Av. Colon near the American consulate and Fiesta Americana Hotel is the monumental **Monumento a la Patria**, created by Colombian sculptor Romulo Rozo, depicting the tumultuous history of Mexico and its 32 states.

The **Museo Regional de Antropologia** (Anthropology Museum) is in the **Palacio Cantón** (entrance on Calle 43 and Paseo de Montejo, ☎ 99/23-05-57). Designed by Enrico Deserti, the Italian architect who did the *teatro* downtown, the house was built around 1911 for General Francisco Cantón. The spectacular home became the official residence of the governor of Yucatán before opening as the rich anthropological showpiece of the Yucatán's historical treasures. If you're looking for a good inexpensive meal along the pricey boulevard, we recommend **Leo's**, one of a chain of pizza-and-more, very clean, air-conditioned restaurants. Even more native are the eateries surrounding little Parque Santa Ana on Calle 47, a half-block west of the Paseo's beginning. A string of outdoor restaurants there, jammed into the little street, are super-popular for good, inexpensive food and drink. Open early and late. Taxis and *caselas* are available in the park.

Museo Regional de Artes Populares is on Calle 59, between 48 and 50. This free museum displays artwork, textiles and regional handicrafts. Unique gift shop. One block west is the square where you'll find Los Almendros restaurant.

Only three gates remain of the 13 that once permitted entrance into Mérida's walled city. The **Arco de Dragones** is on Calle 63 at Calle 50. The **Arco del Puente** is one block south on Calle 61 and 50 and its most interesting feature is its pedestrian tunnel cut into the south side of the arch, connecting sidewalks. It requires one-at-a-time passage while you bend over to fit through its approximate four-foot height. The most attractive gate is the **Arco de San Juan** (Calle 64 at 69) in front of a park of the same name. The buildings to either side used the old wall as part of their construction and the red cobblestone road, Calle 64, is the former *Camino Royal* – Royal Road – that connected Mérida to Campeche. The narrow street is lined with close-built colonial homes lit at night by golden yellow streetlights. Something is inexplicably attractive about this little section of town around the old gate. Nearby, under a gigantic shade tree, is the tiny **Ermita de Santa Isabel** church, where travelers customarily prayed before setting out along the Royal Road into the countryside. It's the smallest house of worship in the city.

The **Cementerio General** – permanent home of Mérida's citizenry of yore – is south of the colonial center toward the airport on Calle 66 and also Calle 90 off of Av. Itzáes, which is the road south to Campeche. We're cemetery freaks so it appealed to us. Somewhat hard to find, despite its large size, the cemetery is wall-to-wall mausoleums with more angels than there are in heaven. The grave of Felipe Carrillo Puerto and the stone wall where he and his brothers were executed in 1924 flank the little snack bar where the public road bends. Under the pine tree opposite is the grave of his fiancée, American journalist Alma Reed, who pined for him until her death in 1966. Francisco Pancho is the caretaker, but he couldn't help us find Mundaca's grave (see Isla Mujeres, page 129). If you go that way there's a very good grilled chicken restaurant on the west side of Av. Itzáes called **Pollo Brujo**, a clean and very tasty fast-food eatery and a perfect spot to try *pollo asado* or *pollo carbon*.

Parque Zoologico El Centerario sits at the intersection of Av. Itzáes and the west end of Calle 59. A large zoo and children's amusement park, on Sundays families jam its shady wooded walkways, picnic area and small lake where they rent rowboats. Free admission. If you're traveling with children they'll like this better than those boring old ruins you've been dragging them to.

Three restored haciendas close to Mérida offer tours and costumed recreations of life there. The **Hacienda San Ildefonso Teya**, founded in 1683 and beautifully restored in 1991, is just east of the city on Highway 180 (☎ 99/23-00-24). The Teya features an especially fine

restaurant. **Hacienda Yaxcopoil** has a museum with original furnishings. Located south of Umán, Highway 261 on the way to Uxmal
(☎ 99/27-26-06). Escorted tours of both are available through travel
agencies. **Hacienda San Antonio Cucul** (☎ 99/44-75-71), in the
northeast section of Mérida, features antique furniture, landscaped
gardens, a plant nursery, a chapel and a jail. For a very special treat,
see **Hacienda Tabi**, in the Uxmal and Ruta Puuc section below. Tabi
is an undiscovered gem of a hacienda, hidden away in orange groves
and surrounded by a nature preserve, where you can spend an
inexpensive, blissful night in a hammock.

ON WHEELS

There's a **train excursion** on a special rail car to Izamal, the "Yellow
City," and tickets are available at any travel agency or the *Cultur*
office at the Juárez Ex-Penitentiary in front of Parque de la Paz. It
leaves 8:15 a.m. every Sunday from Central Station at the corner of
48 and 55. The US $18 per-person price includes transportation in
town by Victoria horse-drawn coaches with a lunch and folklore
music and dance show at the Parador Turistica. The train leaves
Izamal at 3:20 and returns to Mérida at 5:10. For a "Discover Izamal"
bus tour every Monday, Wednesday, Friday and Saturday, contact
Transportación Turística Carnaval at ☎ 99/27-61-19 or a travel agent.

FOR ADVENTURE GUIDE READERS ONLY

Exclusively for readers of this book, we've arranged visits to a
working **henequen/sisal factory** in the suburbs of Kanasin, five
km (3 miles) east of town from Calle 69. Call Ileana Zapata or
Gustavo Baas in the Kanasin city hall from 8 a.m. - 1 p.m. at
☎ 99/88-01-31. The small plant where the fiber is made is open
from 5 p.m. - 11 p.m., Monday, Wednesday and Friday. Señor
Arsenio Rocha directs the factory where the valuable local fiber is
worked.

ADS bus lines have a **special tour bus** that departs Mérida at 8 or
8:30 a.m. (Calle 69) for the **Maya ruins at Uxmal,** as well as the other
important Puuc sites. It returns to town about 4 or 4:30 p.m. Check
with the bus line for any schedule changes. There is also **second-class
bus** service that stops along the route, but ask before you board to
make sure.

Accommodations

*"If some people didn't tell you, you'd never know
they'd been away on vacation."*

– Elbert Hubbard, 1856-1915

 Mérida has the luxury of being the commercial and cultural center of the Yucatán, as well as a tourist destination in itself. In fact, the city's busiest season comes when Mexican tourists vacation here in July and August. The city center's buildings are almost exclusively turn-of-the-century and older, relics from the halcyon days when Mérida was know as the "White City" and the "Paris of the West." So it's natural that accommodations here would span the range of "contemporary comfortable," "colonial rustic," and "colonial charming." It's the latter that we find most pleasing, a chance to live in the past with the conveniences of today. See page 3 for price chart.

Budget Hotels

Rainbow Trailer Park (*Highway 261 north of the city*). Big enough for RV's, this trailer park in the   shadow of the huge Tejidos de Hennequin Yucatán factory offers hot water, showers, electric and a swimming pool. Without much of a view, the park is close enough to town on the road to Progreso to make it worthwhile for camping or parking the rig while day-tripping the entire northern Yucatán area. Buses and combi's stop out front for rides into the downtown.

   Casa de Huespedes (*Calle 62 No. 507*). For those who don't mind communal arrangements, you can try hammock sleeping where the Plaza's hammock sellers sleep. It's popular with budget-minded European travelers. One block from the main square, this fine old colonial home now has multiple uses, including a few offices in its large salons. There are beds as well in the guest rooms, but only one small bathroom for everyone. If you're only walking by, check out the magnificent stained glass windows above the second-floor balcony.

   Hotel Paris (*Calle 68 No. 474 between 55 and 57,* ☎ *99/23-82-84, 19 rooms with air or fans, secured parking, TV, restaurant open from 8 a.m. to 4 p.m.*). Generic accommodations in small rooms but very clean. Motel-like building on a safe sidestreet.

   Hotel Latino (*Calle 66 No. 505 between 61 and 63, 26 rooms with fans*). Spartan accommodations here are in a motel-looking setting behind a colonial front. OK, but we liked the Hotel Margarita across the street better.

Hotel Margarita (*Calle 66 between 61 and 63,* ☎ *99/23-72-36, 23 rooms with fans, 3 with air, private parking*). The Margarita is fairly inviting from the outside and looks like it's colonial. But a mish-mash of modernization places this somewhere between 1859 and 1959. Reasonably clean, but check your room first. At this price you could stay longer, so it's not such a bad deal.

Hotel Oviedo (*Calle 62 No. 515 between 65 and 67,* ☎ *99/28-56-18, 33 rooms with fans*). The Oviedo is another colonial mansion converted into a hotel. It's clean but rather spartan. It gives you an idea of what it was like sleeping back in colonial times as the rooms haven't changed much since "Zorro" slept here. Private parking is in the center courtyard and huge old doors open into each room.

Hotel Sevilla (*Calle 62 No. 511 near 65,* ☎ *99/28-83-60, 28 rooms with fans*). The Sevilla hangs a wooden sign outside, announcing its membership in the Mérida hotel association. It's such an official-looking sign we first mistook it for government offices. Inside, this very old colonial hotel is awash in marble and tile – check out the carved marble lion next to the patio – with a very pretty garden in the center. But the clean rooms, which are also traditional colonial, are very basic. The Sevilla is one of those frustratingly charming places that has the potential to be great, but isn't.

Casa Bowen (*Calle 66 No. 521-B at the corner of 65,* ☎ *99/28-61-09, 28 rooms with air or fans, 6 of them with kitchenettes, private parking*). Despite the sometimes surly front desk staff, dollar for dollar the Casa Bowen may be the best value in town in the budget category. Colorful tile work and marble grace the public areas, where there are many sitting nooks tucked into corners. There's a small lounging area with a TV next to the attractive cool garden that grows in the first courtyard. The rooms are plain but clean and use a lot of frosted glass. It's a comfortable colonial hotel in two buildings. The building on the side has parking in its courtyard and the upstairs rooms are the ones with kitchenettes. They contain an old fridge, gas stove and sink and a card table for dining; ask for your pots and tableware. Across the street there's an inexpensive small restaurant, Café Terraza, which is much loved by budget-minded Italians who stay at the Bowen. The hotel owner also rents a house in Progreso with four bedrooms and baths for around $600 US per month. **$**

Hotel Ambassador (*Calle 59 No. 546, corner of 68,* ☎ *99/24-21-00, fax 99/24-27-01, 100 rooms with air, pool, secure free parking, restaurant, TV*). The modern Ambassador has aged better inside than out. Attractive and comfortable rooms with two queen-size beds face a small green courtyard, behind which is an inviting pool and restaurant. Outside, the once intriguing exterior of mosaic tiles that face the street on each floor is stained by water from air-conditioners and is in need of a facelift. Marble-tiled room walls and modern bathrooms are great, but the hot water here is lacking. The small restaurant, La Luz, serves good basic Mexican food and very good coffee. Ask about their excellent value package rate that includes breakfast. $

Posada Toledo (*Calle 58 at 57, No. 487,* ☎ *99/23-16-90, fax 99/23-22-56, 23 rooms with air or fans*). The Toledo is a mark above most former colonial homes converted into hotels. Located close to all the action in the Centro, the Toledo is an oasis of cool green garden in its courtyard and in its high-arched, tiled hallways that grace the western side. It's picture perfect – everything you think of when you think colonial mansion. Along the street side, the rooms are more hotel-like, but #25, the upstairs back suite (which cost about $40 US) is the former master bedroom of the Hernández Guerra family, the hotel's owners. Heavy Spanish wood furniture dominates here, even in the fancy dining room (breakfast) at the rear of the garden. The Toledo is very popular, so reservations are recommended in high season. $

Del Gobernador (*Calle 59 No. 535 at corner of 66, in Mexico toll free:* ☎ *91/800-2-04-33 or 99/23-70-01, fax 99/28-15-90, 61 rooms with air, TV, pool, restaurant, telephones, parking*). This is a hotel that delivers comfort, cleanliness and service at reasonable prices. Not luxurious but certainly deluxe, the rooms are modern and homey. A favorite of Mexican travelers who know a good deal when they see one. $

El Español Hotel (*Calle 69 and 70*). You're hot and tired, it's late and you're just off the bus. Head for the El Español Hotel. It's large and modern and very close to the bus station. A favorite of Mexican businessmen and families traveling by bus. $

Hotel Montejo (*Calle 57 No. 507,* ☎ *28-02-77, 22 rooms with air or fans, 1 suite, restaurant, travel bureau*). Two blocks up the street from the Teatro Peón Contreras, the Montejo may be one of the most unchanged of all the hotels that were once the private homes of wealthy Spanish colonials. The ambiance is old, from the heavy wooden ceiling beams to the polished wooden doors. Unfortunately, some of the clean bed linen is somewhat old and worn. The center courtyard drips with cool greenery. Doubles have only two twins, so if you're sleeping together, choose a single. There's a good air-conditioned restaurant downstairs where you can charge to your room. A 24-hour public parking lot is just down the street. Noted Maya scholars such as Michael Coe sometimes stay here while they're in town. $

Hotel Trinidad (*Calle 62, between 55 and 57,* ☎ *99/23-20-33, fax 99/24-98-06, 19 rooms with fans, 3 share a bathroom*). The Trinidad is one of two bohemian colonial hotels owned by noted Mexican artist and collector Manolo Rivero. Walk into the Trinidad and enter a stunning world of eclectic art, including huge colonial mirrors, painted over as if by Picasso, and a hotel staff out of the 1940s. If they played music in the lobby it might be Edith Piaf or Segovia; either would complement the time-warp feeling. The entryway has two dark, art-filled sitting areas with dusty overstuffed furniture. Rooms are built around two courtyards. Those around the first courtyard are more appealing – colonial-styled with high ceilings. A "super artist's suite" with a king-size bed and "luxury" bathroom is also available. Tall trees grow up over the center patio walls so it's cool and quiet. Upstairs there's a sunny lounge area on the roof. You can pay with a credit card if you pay in advance and can use the pool at the nearby sister hotel. Artsy-funky. $

Hotel Trinidad Galeria (*Calle 60, corner of 51, ☎ 99/23-24-63, fax 99/24-23-19, 31 rooms with fans, pool*). The Galeria has a creative, bohemian "coffee shop" atmosphere. If you couldn't guess from all the art work displayed everywhere, it's the other Mérida hotel of artist Manolo Rivero, who also owns Hotel Trinidad Faces in Playa del Carmen. *ArtNexus*, a bilingual art magazine, considers both Trinidad hotels in Mérida to be "museums." The big, open, atrium-like entrance is a jungle of plants and sculpture. In the labyrinth of hallways under large overhangs are sculpture, paintings, plants and art work situated around comfortable sitting areas. In fact, more area is dedicated to relaxing than there is for accommodations. Guests we talked to absolutely raved over the ambiance. The low-ceilinged rooms have only two small windows but are painted completely white to help lighten them. Comfortable beds and clean bathrooms, too. Unique. $

Hotel Santa Lucia (*Calle 55 No. 508 between 60 and 62, ☎ & fax 99/28-26-72, 51 rooms with air, pool, credit cards, security safe, TV, secured parking nearby, National car rental*). Located just across the road from the happening Plaza Santa Lucia, this hotel is an old colonial home converted into a modern hotel, expertly altered from mansion to two-story hotel in 1990. A glass canopy over the entry door welcomes guests into a pleasant reception area. Solid wooden doors lead to cheery rooms that have two queen-size beds and clean tiled bathrooms. Three corner rooms have balconies overlooking a small pool and patio and there's a wrought-iron spiral staircase from the pool to the second floor. The Santa Lucia is a good choice if you're into colonial-era hotel rooms without the dark woods or slight inconveniences associated with other hotel remodelings. They also own the Hotel San Juan down the street and the Hotel San Clemente in Valladolid. $

Hotel San Juan (*Calle 55 No. 497A between 60 and 58,* ☎ *& fax 99/ 24-17-42, 39 rooms with air, pool*). This new (1996) hotel, a half-block up from the delightful Santa Lucia Park, is an attractive conversion of an old colonial building. Like its sister hotel, the Santa Lucia down the street, a big stained-glass sign over the portal announces its name. But with smaller rooms and a higher price (by about $4 US) this is not the same value. Rooms have all light woods and white tiles and outside there's a narrow courtyard for sun worshippers and an appealing little pool. $

Posada 49 (*Calle 49 No. 514A between 62 and 64,* ☎ *& fax 99/24-54-39, 5 apartment-suites and 5 bed-and-breakfast rooms, tiny pool, outdoor breakfast palapa, garden courtyard*). Albert, a retired teacher from Hawaii, has set up this apartment and bed & breakfast combination in two adjacent old homes on quiet and convenient Calle 49. Three back rooms in the B & B will offer air-conditioning and the two colonial high-ceilinged rooms in front have only fans. The apartments run from suite-size to surprisingly large and can be rented on a daily basis if they're available. They were being remodeled on our visit and looked comfortable and appealing. Parking garage across the street. This is a gay-friendly establishment. $

Hotel Reforma (*Calle 59 No. 508 at the corner of 62,* ☎ *99/24-79-22, fax 99/28-32-78, 45 rooms with air or fans, pool, travel agency*). The entry hall walls of the old Reforma colonial hotel feature mosaic tile around a tiny, square-center courtyard. Upstairs rooms are the nicer, with two queen-size beds in each high-ceilinged, tile-floored room. The clean bathrooms are also a plus. The perennially popular Reforma is located on a busy corner close to all the action, so choose a room that faces the deep blue pool or the patio. Friendly, helpful staff. $

Dolores Alba (*Calle 63 No. 464 between 54 and 52,* ☎ *99/28-56-5, fax 99/28-31-63, 40 rooms with air or fans, pool, private parking*). Doña Sanchez and her family converted their own three-story family mansion into an appealing hotel just up the street from one of the colonial gates to the city, the Arco del Dragones. Despite its location only two blocks from the busy *mercado* shopping area, the Dolores Alba is quiet and comfortable. The rooms, which can be small, surround a large, high-arched courtyard that provides private parking. No credit cards accepted. Their restaurant serves one meal, an American breakfast, at one price: $3 US. Around back is a large and inviting pool and sunny patio lined with green tropical plants. The Sanchez family, experienced hoteliers, also operate another Dolores Alba in Chichén Itzá, about three km (1.8 miles) from the ruins. $

Hotel San Luis (*corner of 68 and 61,* ☎ *99/21-75-80, 18 rooms with air or fans*). In a modern looking hotel/motel-styled building, the rooms here are basic. There is a restaurant and small swimming pool. **$**

Hotel Parque (*Calle 60 across from Hidalgo Park*). Great location, great entryway, doubly disappointing rooms. Very budget basic. The best part is their La Belle Epoca restaurant upstairs in a dining area with two tables out on the wrought-iron balconies. Best seats are on the balconies. Great atmosphere, tasty food. **$**

Hotel Colon (*Calle 62 No. 483 between 57 and 59,* ☎ *99/23-43-55, fax 99/24-49-19, 53 rooms with air, 12 junior suites, telephone, TV, pool, restaurant, steam baths and masseur*). The historic Colon was converted into a landmark hotel from an old colonial mansion way back in 1920. Modernized since then, the rooms are clean, comfortable and very large, with both a shower and a bathtub in each bathroom. It's an old hotel with impressive tile work – some of the ceilings are stamped tin from the Victorian era – but has most modern comforts. Fortunately, when it was modernized, they left the gorgeous tiled entry foyer and private steam baths, which local Meridanos have always used – and you can too. Built long before steam baths acquired an unsavory reputation, the individual hot baths here are from a time gone-by. Pastoral scenes and colorful patterns hand-painted on tiles make this a must see even if you don't partake of the delights of your own private steam bath, complete with double shower and a cool in-room deep swimming pool with, for a touch of scandal, a mirrored ceiling. Attractive and well-lit, you can reserve a bath even if you don't stay here (they are open from 3 p.m. to 9 p.m.; bring a decent towel, the ones for rent are thin). Junior suite rental includes free steam bath use. Massage must be arranged in advance. The hotel also boasts a large pleasing outdoor pool and quiet tropical gardens. Shhhh... this is one of our secret favorites. **$**

Moderate Hotels

María del Carmen - Best Western (*Calle 63 No. 550,* ☎ *in US: 800-528-1234, in Mexico: 99/223-91-33, fax 99/23-92-90, 87 rooms and 3 suites with air, pool, restaurant, TV, private parking, travel agency, baby-sitting available*). Cool pool and all the stuff you're used to in American hotels. This modern building is a good value for those seeking modern comforts. Book suites directly with the hotel. Conveniently located near the center square. **$$**

Casa Mexilio (*Calle 68 No. 495 between 59 and 57,* ☎ *in US, 800-538-6802, or in Mexico, 99/28-25-05, 11 rooms total with air or fans, pool, jacuzzi, rates include breakfast*). There are some homes in colonial Mérida – hidden behind centuries-old walls – that are just marvelous inside. This is one of them. Casa Mexilio, an old, multi-leveled Spanish house converted into a hotel, almost defies description. The rooms are each individually decorated and seem to be woven into a quilt of gardens and patios. We "oohed" and "aahed" with each unique guest room as we wandered across a wooden bridge over a lovely garden and up outside steps to a roof-top patio with a magnificent view of the city at night. Then we dipped down again to a high-walled courtyard garden with a cenote-style swimming pool and jacuzzi. The Casa's American owner has quixotic taste in decor and has filled his intimate hotel with collectibles he has acquired in 20 years of wandering Mexico. A stay here is an experience and a delight. He plans to call the converted smaller house across the street, with its three large rooms, *Estudio*. The owner also arranges a unique tour called "Great Railway Journeys of the Yucatán," which sounds intriguing. Book rooms ahead to be sure. But you may pay a little less at the door if you show up without a reservation. **$$**

Gran Hotel (*Calle 60 No. 496 at Parque Hidalgo,* ☎ *99/23-69-63, fax 99/24-76-22, 30 rooms with air, 2 suites, restaurant, TV*). The historic Gran Hotel received a 1987 facelift and looks much as it did when it opened originally in 1901. The French Neoclassic design is painted a cool mint green and faces the popular Hidalgo Park, only one block from the main *zócalo*. The rooms are modern, in an elegant turn-of-the-century building, complete with high ceilings and arches. This hotel is reminiscent of other "Gran" or "Grand" hotels that grace main squares in many Spanish colonial capitals. In the cool entrance way there is a small restaurant, *El Patio*, where you can dine indoors or al fresco. Takes credit cards. **$$**

Hotel Caribe (*Calle 59 No. 500 at Parque Hidalgo,* ☎ *in US & Canada, 800-826-6842, in Mexico, 91/800-20-00-03, or 99/24-90-22, fax 99/24-87-33, 42 rooms with air or fans, restaurant, pool*). In the beginning (1876) it was the "Convent de Monjas," a nun's Catholic high school. After that auspicious inauguration, it became the founding site of the University of Yucatán before finally opening as an elegant hotel in 1941. There's a rooftop pool and sun patio and the Hotel Caribe's accommodations make it a worthy competitor to the Gran Hotel next door. Its interior courtyard is part of the El Rincón ("Corner") restaurant, which serves elegant meals at reasonable prices. Rooms run from colonial to modern in their furnishings, so take your pick. Helpful, courteous staff. **$$**

Hotel Mérida Misión Park Inn (*Calle 60 No. 491,* ☎ *in US, 800-448-8355, in Mexico, 99/23-95-00, fax 99/23-76-85, 140 rooms and 10 suites with air, pool, restaurant, TV, rates include breakfast*). Ideally located across the corner from the university, a half-block from the Teatro

Peón Contreras and two blocks from the main square, the Misión is a plainly modern hotel joined to a stately old colonial edifice. The foyer and entryway look magnificent, with high ceilings, tiled walls and floors and a bubbling old-world fountain, but the simple guest rooms lack charm. **$$**

Holiday Inn (*Av. Colon,* ☎ *in US, 800-465-4329, in Mexico, 99/25-68-77, fax 99/25-70-02, 213 rooms with air, pool, 2 restaurants, exercise room*). The four-story Holiday Inn, nestled next to the Hyatt Regency and the Fiesta Americana, is a good value if you're into American comfort and style in a foreign country. Known both as a business as well as a tourist hotel, this Holiday Inn is as pleasing as any in the States or Canada. Rates are lower than those of its next-door neighbors. Ask for the promotional rate from the 800-number reservationist. The outdoor restaurant in front is an economical place for a romantic night out. It serves up a delicious all-you-can-eat buffet grill with live Mexican music and soft candlelight. **$$**

Expensive

Fiesta Americana Hotel (*Paseo Montejo at the corner of Av. Colon, in the US, 800-345-5094, or in Mexico, 99/42-11-11, fax 99/42-11-12, 350 air-conditioned rooms on 5 floors, 3 phones in each room, including 1 in the bathroom, security safes, TV, pool, sauna, exercise room, non-smoking rooms, shopping mall*). In the battle of luxury hotels in Mérida, the Fiesta Americana is, for our money, the clear winner. Built in a grand belle epoque style, the hotel offers all the luxury accoutrements one would expect, including a pool, gym, spa with sauna and steam room, tennis court, beauty parlor, jacuzzi and satellite TV. The rooms have wrought-iron balconies outside and inside overlook a huge atrium, crowned by an impressive stained-glass roof. We went up and down several times in their glass elevators just to admire the view. If you've been out in the hinterlands of Yucatán, it's quite a treat to be pampered here. **$$$**

Dining

My tummy is smiling.
– Abigail Trillin, age 4

The combination of Mérida's cosmopolitan aspirations, Spanish colonial mindset and its Maya heritage can best be found in the cuisine mix of the old city. Arabic, Italian,

French, Mexican, Yucatecan – even American – tastes are all here. What's equally appetizing is that you can eat very well for very little. See page 4 for price chart.

Café Alameda (*Calle 58 No. 474 between 55 and 57*). Old men tend to hang out at this café smoking hand-rolled cigarettes, arguing animatedly and drinking thick Arabic coffee. In a small open-air courtyard behind a peachy colored colonial wall, the Alameda must have felt like the last bastion of "home" for the Lebanese that flocked to the Yucatán at the turn of the century. You'll probably feel at home and learn to linger here as well. Coffee strong enough to stand your hair on end and typical Spanish and Middle Eastern cooking. Try the shish kabob. $

Vito Corleone Pizza (*Calle 59 No. 508 between 60 & 62,* ☎ *99/23-68-46*). The bright yellow tiles of the counter and streetside pizza oven are the signature of this immensely popular hole-in-the-wall pizza parlor. An upstairs dining area adds to the university student hang-out atmosphere. The parlor makes clever use of pottery, seemingly imbedded in one wall. And the thin-crust pizzas are surprisingly good. If you're stuck in a hotel, they also deliver. $

El Trapiche (*Calle 62 No. 491 between 59 and 61*). A fresh juice bar just around the sidestreet from the *zócalo* and municipal palace, El Trapiche serves a wide variety of fresh juices squeezed to order. Vegetarian food here is big. $

Cafeteria Pop (*Calle 57 No. 501 between 60 and 62*). Open from 7 a.m. to 12 p.m., the coffee shop that invented coffee shops in Mérida is the "cool" place to be – right across the street from the university. Cool because it has a strong air-conditioner and cool because its decor is vintage modern-art 1960's social protest. Called a "cafeteria," it's actually a sit-down restaurant with generous servings of well-prepared dishes at inexpensive prices. The haunting images of the three faces on the wall were painted in 1971 by a local architect. They are an exact copy of a woodcut by Miguel Bresciano, made for a 1968 album of protest folk songs, *Canciones Para Mi America*, by Uruguayan singer, Daniel Viglietti. Packed with people for lunch and breakfast, it also serves excellent brewed coffee in bottomless cups. The rumor is that it shares some high-quality cooking with the pricier Peregrino next door, as they have the same owner. $

Pizza Bella (*on the zócalo*). Pizza Bella, on the square across from the park, has very good pizza and offers clean inside eating when the car fumes or heat become too strong outside. $

Sigueff's (*Calle 59 No. 553 at the corner of 68*). In 1959, this old family mansion was converted into a restaurant around its Moorish-arched open center courtyard and dark wood salon doors with stained-glass lintels. It's another long lunch spot for local Mérida businessmen as well as the descendants of the turn-of-the-century Lebanese immigrants. It fills up for late breakfast, early dinner and all-day lunch crowds seeking good food at reasonable prices. One salon room is air-conditioned. Open at 8 a.m., it closes at 7 p.m. Try their Arab sampler dinner for less than $6 US. $-$$

Pórtico del Peregrino (*Calle 57 No. 501 between 60 and 62,* ☎ *99/28-61-63*). They named this romantic restaurant after a popular folk song about Alma Reed, the American journalist who was the lover of Mexican revolutionary, Felipe Carrillo (see page 40). It offers an enchanting old-world setting in both its dining areas – either al fresco under a clay tile roof (the tiles were brought as sailing ship ballast from Marseilles, France in the 1800s), or inside in the Spanish colonial dining room. The food at the Peregrino brings diners back again and again and again. Try the chicken breast in green salsa; it's fabulous, as are their other Mexican and international dishes. The Pórtico is also a favorite destination for expatriates on a night out. Food with flair, it's an excellent value. $$

Pancho's Restaurant (*Calle 59 No. 509 between 60 & 62*). A bit of a "Playa Del Carmen" atmosphere in Mérida, Pancho's does it right when it comes to decor. Set well back from busy Calle 59, its entryway is filled with artifacts like a turn-of-the-century horse-drawn carriage and dozens of old photos from the era of Pancho Villa and the Mexican Revolution. Inside there are two bars and three dining areas – two of them outside patios under trees decorated by twinkly lights. The sombrero-wearing, bandoleer-toting *campesinos* running around are waiters. The food is fairly good. Live dance music starts at 11:30 p.m. and rocks your socks until 2:30 a.m. $$

Holiday Inn (*Av. Colon*). Horse-drawn carriages drop customers at this romantically lit outdoor buffet dining area on Avenida Colon, near Paseo Montejo. A chef grills chicken, steaks, or fish to order while you choose from the salad bar and hot table of prepared dishes. Mexican appetizers are also made to order by a Maya woman using a convex hot skillet over a fire. Meanwhile a trio of very talented musicians and singers perform live under a palapa bandstand. We once enjoyed a wonderful Christmas Eve dinner here. Friendly staff. Around US $9 per person. $$

Restaurante Express (*Calle 60, across from Hidalgo Park*). This heavily male-dominated restaurant feels like a place where one of Mexico's many revolutions was orchestrated, accompanied by food and beer and wild hand gestures. Facing the street and shady park, the busy eatery attracts regulars and foreigners for its good food and reasonable prices. Open 7 a.m. to midnight.

Los Almendros (*Calle 50 in Plaza de la Mejorada,* ☎ *99/28-54-59*). Chef-founder Rubén Gonzalez Gonzalez opened the first Los Almendros in 1962 in Ticul, a small Maya town on the Puuc Route, south of Mérida. By 1972, his creative cooking had become so well known that he opened this Mérida location. Cancún's downtown restaurant opened in 1979 and another one opened in Cozumel in 1998. Mérida is home to two more locations: Gran Almendros on Calle 57 No 468 (between 50 and 52) and Almendros Aleman on Calle 21 (between 24 and 26). The secret of Señor Gonzalez's success is not a secret, he treats traditional Yucatecan food as if it were gourmet cuisine. It was in Los Almendros that *poc chuc*, marinated pork slices that are topped with onions and grilled, was invented. It's now one of the countryside's most popular (and delicious) dishes. This restaurant is glass and steel modern inside, brightly lit but with the ambiance of a diner. Photo's of the menu's dishes line the wall, offering a wide selection of Mexican food, including a sampler of Yucatecan specialties. As with other Almendros restaurants, when they're on, they're on, but when they're not, you wonder what all the fuss is about. $$

Restaurant Santa Lucia (*Calle 60 No. 481 at the corner of 55,* ☎ *99/28-59-57, live music*). Carlos Alberto Escalante, along with his sister Martha, actively supervises the family's tiny Santa Lucia Restaurant at the corner of the park of the same name. Crusty French bread with a garlic butter dip is served as an appetizer before their delicious Yucatecan and Mexican offerings. Reasonable prices, extensive menu and generous portions make this an extremely popular choice. Intimate, romantic and funky – all at the same time – the crowded two rooms somehow seat 40 (with a teeny bandstand for live music) and each Thursday evening the restaurant spills tables out into the plaza to become part of the weekly fiesta. Orders are taken by waiters with headset radios and filled by runners to the restaurant across the street. It's the best seat in town to wine and dine and listen to the Thursday night "Yucatecan Serenade" music in the plaza, but the service is a little slow. Carlos says "*hola*" to fellow classmates at Glenwood High School, in tiny Glenwood, Iowa, where he graduated as an exchange student in 1982. $$

Alberto's Continental (*Calle 64 and 57,* ☎ *99/28-53-67*). The hosts since 1962, Alberto Salum, his sister Nery or brother Pepe will greet you personally at this very popular dinner destination. The corner site of Alberto's was originally a Maya mound, dismantled in 1727 to build the foundation of today's colonial building. As you might imagine, the interior is rich with ambiance. The dining room's mosaic tile floor was imported from Cuba long ago to replace the original unadorned stone. The food is excellent. Curved Moorish arches and red tile floor invite diners to an outdoor patio, enveloped by rubber trees, for a wide selection of Italian, Yucatecan and

Lebanese fare. There's a sampler dinner of Lebanese specialties or try their fish "Celestun" – sea bass, stuffed with shrimp. Classically intimate and romantic. $$-$$$

Maya kids.

Mundo Maya

All human beings have an innate need to hear
and tell stories and have a story to live by....
Religion, whatever else it has done, has provided
one of the main ways of meeting this abiding need.

– *The Seduction of the Spirit*, Harvey Cox,
Professor of Divinity, Harvard

 In a modern secular society, people usually define a spiritual reality based upon their religious values, while they define physical reality by agreed-upon scientific principles. A chair is a chair, held down by gravity. But the ancient Maya lived (and some still do) in a world in which these two planes of existence inextricably interlock – defining the material world as a manifestation of spiritual reality and vice-versa. Their humanity and the worlds of nature and spirituality were, in some ways, all one. The gods of the Otherworld influenced fate: they were capable of bringing drought or rain, disease or health, victory or defeat, life or death. Yet the gods depended on the actions of mortals for their welfare as well (the cosmic crocodile monster of the sky would shed its own blood as rain in response to the royal sacrifices from the earth below). Leaving nourishment and sustenance as an offering to departed souls is an ancient custom that continues today.

The Maya conceived their world as having three regions: the bright world of heaven, the stony Middleworld of earth and the dark water of the Underworld. These worlds were sacred, alive and bound up with one another. At sunset, for example, the Underworld rotated above to become the starry night sky.

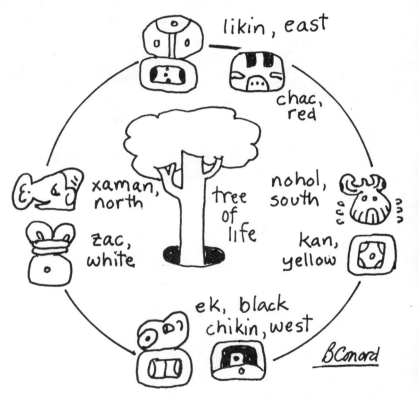

The principal axis of existence was the path of the sun as it blazed across the sky. Each direction of the compass had a god and a color associated with it. East, the most important direction because of the sun's birth, was red, while west, where the sun died, was black. South was yellow and north, from where rain came, was white. In the Maya view of the world east, not north, belongs at the top of maps. These directions were also seen in relation to the center (blue-green, *yax*), where a Ceiba tree, known as the World Tree (*Wacah Chan*), links all three domains – its roots in the Underworld, trunk in the Middleworld and branches holding up the Otherworld sky.

We have divided our adventures in Yucatán state into the four cardinal points of the Mayan world, making red (east) our beginning. Day or overnight trips from Mérida are the best way to get to see the many wonders of the surrounding countryside.

East - Red
(Lakin Chac)

Let others hail the rising sun:
I bow to those whose course has run.

– David Garrick, 1717-1779

East of Mérida there's a countryside rich in history: the magnificent Maya ruins at Chichén Itzá and Ek Balam; the colonial heritage of majestic but tragic Valladolid; beautiful religious Izamal. We suspect most readers will approach the world of the Yucatán heading west, toward Mérida from Cancún. So we arranged the sights in *Lakin Chac* in that order: Valladolid and Chichén Itzá, then points north, finally west to Izamal, only 70 km (43.5 miles) from Mérida. If you're heading east from Mérida, hold the book upside down and read backwards.

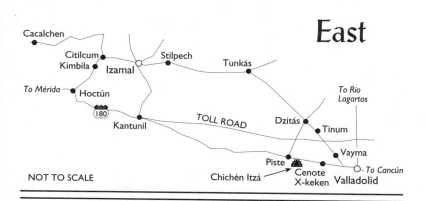

Valladolid

Tradition does not mean that the living are dead,
it means that the dead are living.

– Harold Macmillan, quoted December 18, 1958

 Valladolid rests almost in the center of the Yucatán Peninsula, 160 km (100 miles) from Cancún and 159 km (99 miles) from Mérida. It's a colonial town (pop. 70,000) often overlooked by the rush of tourists heading to nearby Chichén Itzá. This is a great place to spend the night or more if you're exploring the Chichén Itzá and Ek Balam ruins and surrounding countryside.

Tour buses to Chichén are now stopping briefly in Valladolid for a quick shopping trip under the green trees that line the plaza. Maya women sell *huipiles*, hammocks, jewelry and handicrafts there. Harried tourists then re-board the bus, eager to arrive at the Maya ruins before the day gets too hot. Yet pleasant, provincial Valladolid (pronounced "buy-a-doe-leed") is not a city to be hurried. Its rhythm and old-world style need to be savored, absorbed over time. Otherwise you miss little discoveries that make a trip special. We were lucky enough to be sitting in a restaurant during mid-January celebrations, when the next day's bull fight matadors arrived, proudly wearing splendid suits made of lights, to a flurry of excitement. They stopped to pay respect to elderly *hacendados*, dressed in traditional Spanish costume, who were sitting at a nearby table. Soon, the blaring music of a sidewalk fiesta with food and goods lining streets, packed with people, lured us outside. We were two of only a handful of tourists enjoying the festivities. The next day we attended the bull fight – the only *Norteamericanos* – where people welcomed us, encouraged us to take pictures and tried to explain new snack foods. Instead of "hot dogs," stadium vendors sell fresh fruit, dipped in chile powder – POW! The weekend experience felt as if we had gone back in time. And what an appropriate place to regress. The elegant colonial walls of Valladolid have seen much in their long history.

Montejo, the Younger and his cousin, Montejo, El Sobrino, overcame truculent Maya resistance to conquer the ancient city of Zací ("White Hawk") early in 1543. On the site of Zací, on May 28 of that year, the Montejos founded Valladolid, whose colonial coat of arms features a white hawk image and the prophetic slogan, "Heroic City." In the middle of sugar cane and cattle country, but isolated by distance from Mérida, Valladolid matured in relative autonomy and it remained the most "colonial" of the peninsula's larger cities – more conservative and perhaps more proudly aristocratic than Mérida itself.

Its hubris shattered in January 1847 when a Yucatecan secessionist army, using Maya soldiers in its ranks, attacked the garrison of Mexican loyalists. A slaughter of non-Indian civilians resulted. Several months later, an informer named a young Maya, Antonio Ay, in a plot for a revolution to reduce taxes on the Indian population. To set a stern example and to avenge the January atrocities, a firing squad shot young Ay at Santa Ana chapel on July 26, 1847. His death was the catalyst that began the bloody Caste War, with Valladolid in the middle of it. In mid-March, 1848, a more vicious slaughter of *Vallísoletaños* occurred as residents fled the city toward Temax before the ruthless Maya advance.

Orientation

GETTING AROUND: Heading to Valladolid from Cancún you have a choice of two routes, both known on the maps as Highway 180. The first is the **Mérida Cuota**, the only road west made easy to find from Cancún. It's a toll road with very limited exits and two collection booths, one east of Valladolid and one west of Piste. The road is new and allows cars to zip along at a fast clip. If you're going to Valladolid, Chichén Itzá, or Mérida, the Cuota's shortcut through the jungle makes life much easier. For access to the Cuota from Cancún, simply follow the signs for Mérida and Valladolid on Highway 307 South. The Valladolid exit is north of the city. As you drive into town there will be a large, white, castle-like **handicraft market** on your right, worth a stop for the variety of gifts and arts and crafts.

The alternative route is **Mérida Libre,** the two-lane road that goes through the heart of the Maya country. For us it has the great advantage of letting you see the "real" Yucatán and we've had a special adventure of one sort or another every time we've been on it. The road is always interesting, wandering through villages passed by time, but it does require some patience. *Topes* (speed bumps) guard each village and make for a slower journey. However, there's more to life than driving fast, especially in the Yucatán. Private homes along the way sell handicrafts, gifts and bottles of honey.

If you're traveling from Mérida on Route 180, follow the signs at Kantunil for the town of Holca in order to parallel the toll road. Or you can turn north there – or at the town before (Hoctún) – for Izamal and backroads to Valladolid.

Finding your way around town is very straightforward. The city is compact and laid out in the typical colonial grid of mostly one-way streets. Odd-number streets run east and west, even run north and south. Most of the attractions are close to the main plaza. The free highway, Mérida Libre, becomes Calle 39 through town heading west and Calle 41 heading east.

Practicalities

 Local police are at ☎ 985/6-21-00. The **highway patrol**, ☎ 985/6-27-80. The **Red Cross**, for emergency ambulance service, ☎ 985/6-24-13 and the emergency **hospital** is at ☎ 985/6-28-83, behind the San Bernardino church.

Tourism information in this friendly town is next to the city hall on Calle 40 at the corner of 41. A two-hour **bus tour** in an open trolley-style bus, *La Guagua*, departs daily in front of the cathedral at 9 a.m. and 4 p.m. (US $5). Polished and pampered bronze and maroon **taxis** – each city in the Yucatán sports its own individual taxi colors – conveniently hang out along the plaza across from the church. The fare for the half-hour ride to Chichén is around US $15. If you make friends, the Ek-Balam travel agency offers **guided tours** to the Chichén Itzá and Ek Balam ruins that run four and three hours respectively, US $20 & US $25 per person, with a minimum of four people. They also do Rio Lagartos flamingo boat trips, five hours for US $30, including two drinks.

Local bus service is frequent to Chichén Itzá, Cobá, Mérida, Cancún and even Playa del Carmen. The **bus station**, on Calle 54 and 37, is a bit of a hike (seven blocks) to the downtown. The **post office** is on the square, Calle 40, and next to it is a Bancomer Bank, where you should ask for a receipt (*recibo*). There's a **bank** that gives a better rate west on Calle 41 and a money change (*cambio*) booth next to the cathedral. A good, inexpensive **laundromat** is in the Super Maz **shopping center** on Calle 39 near Calle 56, but be sure to specify separation (*separado*) of whites and colors. The shopping center also has a **health food store**.

The best place to rent bicycles is the sporting goods shop of Antonio "Negro" Aguilar, the self-proclaimed "King of Baseball," who once played professional minor league baseball in Tennessee for the old Washington Senators. The former chief of police in Valladolid, he and his family are very friendly and they offer a fair selection of bicycles (all one-speeds) in good condition. He rents them, with a lock, for about US 50¢ per hour; long-term rental is available.

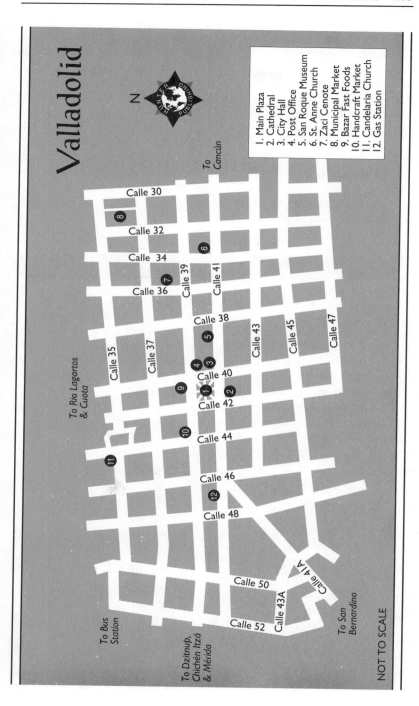

Valladolid

N

To Cancún

1. Main Plaza
2. Cathedral
3. City Hall
4. Post Office
5. San Roque Museum
6. St. Anne Church
7. Zaci Cenote
8. Municipal Market
9. Bazar Fast Foods
10. Handcraft Market
11. Candelaria Church
12. Gas Station

Calle 30

Calle 32

Calle 34

Calle 36

Calle 39

Calle 41

Calle 38

Calle 35

Calle 37

Calle 43

Calle 45

Calle 47

Calle 40

Calle 42

Calle 44

Calle 46

Calle 48

Calle 50

Calle 43A

Calle 41A

Calle 52

To Río Lagartos
& Cuota

To Bus
Station

To Dzitnup,
Chichén Itzá
& Mérida

To San
Bernardino

NOT TO SCALE

The map painted on the exterior wall of his shop, on Calle 44, between 48 and 50 (☎ 985/6-31-15), shows the routes to take to the X-Keken cenote (four km/2.5 miles) and Rio Lagartos, a long 104-km (64-mile) ride. If you want to play some sports in town, see Antonio. He also has four **rooms for rent** in a building above a kindergarten nearby. They feature private parking and a small pool in the budget price range.

Don't miss the new *panaderia*, La Especial, a clean and delicious **bakery** on Calle 41. Jorge Canul owns it, along with one in Tizimín. It has been a family business since 1916. Be sure to try their *pan cubano*, a sweet bread that is as velvet as pound cake and just as delicious. A cousin, Eduardo Canul, owns La Especial bakery in Bakersfield, California. Say *hola* for us.

Sights

Blood and guts are not the only features of Valladolid's history. **The Church of San Bernardino de Siena** and the **Ex-Convent of Sisal**, a religious complex at the corner of Calles 41A and 49 in the Sisal section of Valladolid, are often considered two of the most beautiful buildings of the colonial period and are the oldest Spanish-built structures in the Yucatán. Designed by the architect of Mérida's cathedral, Juan de Mérida, in 1552, the huge stone complex, similar to but not as grand as the one at Izamal, was built over one of the deepest and most extensive cenotes on the peninsula.

Convento de San Bernardino.

Some of the original paintings can still be seen on the walls behind the side altars but former ornate decorations – in all of Valladolid's churches – were stripped in the Caste War and Mexican Revolution, never to be replaced.

The magnificent baroque **San Servacio Cathedral** stands on the square in town. The original one, consecrated on March 24, 1545 (called *San Gervacio*), was torn down in 1706 by the order of Obispo Reyes Rios, who had it rebuilt facing north as a "punishment" to the unknown criminals who stole from the altar of the original church. Their mark of shame means that the entrance door does not face east, as do most other colonial churches in the Yucatán. Valladolid has several other 16th-century churches, including the **Iglesia de Indios del Barrio de Santa Ana**, a chapel built exclusively for Maya Indians, where Antonio Ay was shot, Calles 41 and 34; **Templo de San Juan**, Calles 49 and 40; **Santa Lucia**, Calles 40 and 27; and **La Candelaria**, with a park across the street known as a romantic "lovers' park," at Calles 44 and 35. At the far end of the park you'll find **La Aurora**, a public stage theater. **San Roque Museum**, in a chapel built for the former Name of Jesus Hospital, features a tiny display and a quiet stone memorial park with several benches (Calles 41 at 38) in the rear.

The **central plaza** is especially pleasant in Valladolid. At its heart is a water fountain with a painted statute of a Maya woman pouring water from a clay jug. The circular brick walk that surrounds it, lined with iron bench seats and romantic *confidenciales* for sitting and relaxing. Or getting your shoes shined. The park's trees fill at dusk with hundreds of birds whose combined calls drown out the sounds of traffic. In the evening, wrought-iron lantern lights glow yellow under the shadow of the cathedral that presides over strolling lovers, candy vendors, shoe-shine men and mothers with their children, in awe of the tall *touristas*. Signs in the plaza caution tourists not to tolerate children begging or asking to watch your car, which they pronounce in English as "wash your car." Instead, refuse (it's unnecessary, Valladolid is very safe) and encourage them to go to school.

Stop in the **Palacio Municipal**, where the stone steps to the second floor have been worn into hollows by years of use. A coat of arms and an honor roll of the conquistadors who founded and stayed in the city in 1543 hang on the hall walls. In the upstairs salon, some very impressive historical murals grace the room and portraits of long-dead city fathers and heroes have a place of honor. As in Mérida, window balconies provide a rewarding vista of the cathedral and park.

The **municipal *mercado*** in Valladolid (Calles 37 and 32) is one of our sentimental favorites. It's the town meeting place for *Vallísole-*

Tortilla shop.

taños and plenty of country folk from the surrounding Maya villages. Open daily. Sunday is the big market day, best in the morning. Produce and food dominate the eastern and center stalls (the inside meat market, a staple of village *mercados*, is not the kind of place to take your vegetarian friends) while clothes and sundry crafts fill the rest. This is a good place to buy chile powder, anchiote paste, plastic shopping bags, fruits and vegetables. Visit the *tortillaria* on the corner and see corn tortillas being made.

There's an indoor **Mercado de Artesanías** on Calle 39 near the corner of 44, worth stopping by. **La Antigua gift shop** has a wide array of Mexican handicrafts in ceramic, leather, onyx and wood at fair prices. They're on Calle 37 at the corner of 40, a block back from the plaza. The **El Meson del Marquéz hotel gift shop** boasts an extensive selection of higher quality Mexican collectibles. Under the big trees across the street in the *zócalo*, Maya women line the sidewalks selling hand-made crafts such as *huipiles* – even for Barbie dolls – handkerchiefs, blouses, jewelry and hammocks. If you're not going on to Mérida, this is a good place to buy hand knotted hammocks (see some hints about quality on page 258).

Maya women who wear *huipiles* will also carry a cotton or silk shawl, called a *rebozo*. Many years ago, each village had their own unique pattern and color, but that is no longer true. Around Valladolid, the preference seems to be a clay brown background with flecks of white. Other available hues include black and white, purple and black, black and red, gray and white or generally earth-tone colors. Long and rectangular, *rebozos* are more like stoles than shawls, fringed at both ends. They contain a fancy woven pattern and either a knotted fringe or a macramé-style trim with tassels. *Rebozos*, like hammocks, come in a variety of qualities dependent upon the material and closeness of the weave. They can be gorgeous and eye-catching accessories for an evening or cocktail dress and are a unique gift. You'll find a good selection of *rebozos* at **Casa Miranda** on Calle 39, third floor. While it looks like a five & ten cent store downstairs, upstairs there are some quite fashionable women's clothes and accessories at reasonable prices.

Cenote Zací, the ancient Maya city water source, is on Calle 36 between 39 and 37. If this is your first visit to a cenote, it's worth seeing. The somewhat dramatic large open hole has terraced stone steps coated in a green algae that lead down to the somber water. The owners have built a cool, shady park around the cenote that contains long stone walls, a life-size Chac Mool statue (great for photos), several traditional Maya huts (one of which houses an interesting mini-museum displaying a history of *huipil* embroidery patterns), a rounded stone oven and a modest palapa-covered **café** serving light meals. Unless you're eating, there's a small admission charge. On the high ground above the cenote on Calle 39, the town has erected a small outdoor **artisan market.**

A beautiful and truly unique cenote is **Cenote X-Keken** (ish-kay-ken): two km (1.25 miles) west, on the way to Chichén Itzá, then two km south, toward the village of Dzit-nup. The Valladolid city fathers created a four-km (2.5-mile) bicycle or hiking *sacbé* – parallel to the road – from the edge of town to the cenote, a fairly easy ride or walk, to be rewarded by a cool swim at the end. (See "Practicalities," above, for bike rental details.) X-Keken is best visited early or late in the day (open from 8 a.m. to 5 p.m.), when there are fewer people and no tour

Cenote X-Keken.

buses. Bring a bathing suit (*sin* suntan oil) to this truly magical cenote in an underground cavern. Entrance (US $1) requires stepping down some steep steps carved into the stone – there's a rope to assist you – and going a short distance until the passage opens into a huge underground cavern. Recessed lights highlight the gigantic stalactite that cascades down from the ceiling into the turquoise blue water. A hole in the roof of the cavern allows a thick, brilliant shaft of sunlight to stream into the cave, illuminating the water like an electric spotlight. Some rocky alcoves on a ledge above are useful as changing areas. Snorkeling and swimming are OK, but food, drink, suntan oil and smoking are not allowed. The people of Dzitnup want to keep this enchanting wonder in pristine condition. The interior is quite moist and warm and the rocks can be slippery, so be careful. Handicraft stands surround the parking lot and a public bathroom is available.

The dusty village of **Káua**, about halfway on the free road to Chichén Itzá, has a huge cenote called, in Mayan, **Yaxhek**, or "green glow." This deep open sinkhole offers good swimming in a large, clear lake at the bottom. As you check it out, the local people will check you out – they don't get many *touristas* stopping here. In the other direction, east toward Cancún, is another way to get to the ruins of **Cobá**, either as a side trip or as part of a run to **Tulum** and the Caribbean shore. Turn south in Nuevo X-can, and go 45 km (28 miles) to Cobá.

Twenty-two km (13.6 miles) due south of Valladolid and two km (1.25 miles) south of Tixcacalcupul, on Highway 295, are the remnants of the 100-km-long (62-mile), Cobá to Yaxuná *sacbé* (white road) of the ancient Maya. A sign says "Mirador," meaning a sight, but there really isn't much to see. The sacred raised roadway looks like a clearing in the trees, but if you look closely in the weeds you'll see the outline of the *sacbé*, made of limestone boulders.

Accommodations

Hotels in Valladolid are plentiful and priced right. Most are well below what you may have been paying in Cancún. See page 3 for price chart.

Ek-Balam Restaurant and Cabañas (*Highway 180, 6 km east of town, 6 rooms with fans, restaurant, pool, tennis, camping, disco*). The Ek-Balam ("Black Jaguar" in Mayan) is creating a mini-village with its six pleasant bungalows and pending trailer park and camping area. Tennis courts have been built next to the parking lot. Rooms are very basic but new and clean and the attempt is to provide an attractive place for budget-minded tourists to stay for a few days while they explore the area. A large palapa-covered dining room houses the Ek-Balam restaurant, with some pleasant surprises out back. Descend a stone staircase to a former cock-fighting arena – in a natural hollow beside two caves – currently being converting into a night-time disco with possible *ballet folklorico* shows for daytime groups. A few feet away is a swimming pool, built halfway into a cave where fresh water drips down from above. Diners are welcome to enjoy a dip. Opposite is another cave that can be explored deeper into the earth. Alfonso Madrid, tour guide and manager, donated the animals that were formerly caged here as exhibits to the biospheres at San Felipe and Rio Lagartos, where they were released. He's a personable and knowledgeable contact if you'd like a multilingual guide to local ruins and sights. $

Hotel Zaci (*Calle 44 No 491, between 41 and 39,* ☎ *985/6-21-67, fax 985/6-25-94, 39 rooms with air or fans, TV, restaurant, pool*). The Zaci is magical at night when its two parallel walkways of red tile and white arches are lit. During the day it's pretty as well, painted all white with red roof tiles and terra-cotta floors and decorated with a scattering of green plants in clay pots. The one-story hotel becomes three floors in back, curving around a deep blue pool and a tiny restaurant under a striped awning. Each room is medium-size with modern bathrooms, one queen-size and one twin bed, and big closets. $

Maria de la Luz (*Calle 42 at the corner of 41, opposite the zócalo,* ☎ *& fax 985/6-20-71, 41 rooms with air, pool, restaurant*). Completely remodeled at the end of 1996, the Maria now has eight new rooms and a brand new look in its extremely popular dining room. The medium-size additional rooms have big closets and pleasing tiled bathrooms, with two queen-size beds in each. The older colonial-style rooms have new tile floors and fresh paint, but smaller closets. We still like these, but get one that doesn't face the street. All the rooms wrap around a refreshing kidney-shaped pool. The restaurant serves good meals at reasonable prices, and a daily breakfast buffet for around US $3. Say *hola* to Elio, a waiter here since 1981. The restaurant ambiance is tropical with comfortable bamboo chairs and stained-glass lampshades. $

El Meson del Marquéz (*Calle 39 No. 203, between 40 and 42,* ☎ *985/6-30-42, fax 985/6-22-80, 50 rooms and suites with air, pool, carved wood bar, restaurant, secure parking, gift shop, telephones*). Rightfully considered the best in town, the Meson was originally the ancestral family home of its owner, Mario Escalante Ruiz. In 1966 he converted the large colonial house into a hotel and it has been growing ever since. Quite and cool, it now boasts 18 rooms and 32 suites in three newer buildings behind the original home. Tall bamboo trees wave in the wind three stories above the well-kept grounds and oval pool. Two of the best suites (123 & 127) feature balconies that overlook the blue pool from the shade of a huge tropical tree that grows alongside. Even the mirror in our room was special: it made you look taller and thinner – younger even. This professionally run hotel is a leader in promoting Valladolid tourism and it starts by giving guests the royal treatment. You can get as much – if not more – information from the helpful staff here as you can at the tourism office around the block (clerk Ulises works both places). Besides a well-stocked gift shop, the Meson features a carved wood bar and romantic candlelit patio restaurant with the absolutely finest food in town. **$-$$**

Hotel San Clemente (*Calle 42 No. 206, between 41 and 43,* ☎ *985/6-22-08, 64 rooms with air, TV, restaurant, pool, private parking*). This old colonial hotel across the street from the side of the San Servacio Church at the corner of the *zócalo* has the same owner as the Santa Lucia and San Juan hotels in Mérida. Rooms are large and modern with good-size bathrooms and comfortable beds, although the bed spreads are a bit worn. The owners have put much money into their Mérida properties and will probably redecorate the San Clemente in the future. Not too long ago they improved the center courtyard and small pool, which the three floors wrap around. The fountain in the center is a copy of the one in the middle of the *zócalo*. The second and third floors offer a fantastic view of the church lit up at night. There's also an inexpensive to moderate streetside restaurant, Cupules. **$**

Don Luis (*Calle 39 No. 191, between 38 and 40, 985/6-20-24, 24 rooms with fans, pool, secure parking*). This appealing tropical hotel holds a special place in our heart as it was the first place we ever stayed outside Cancún, many years ago. After a flirtation with higher prices, it is once again a good choice for budget travelers. Tall coconut trees sway in the breeze around a large oval pool in the center. The rooms are basic (thin sheets) but clean and adequate. Some have a working air-conditioner so if it's really hot, ask to see one of those. There's no restaurant, but they do sell water and soda and you're close to the town square, only a few hundred feet east. Two blocks from Cenote Zací, four from the *mercado*.

Hotel Maria Guadalupe (*Calle 4, between 39 and 41, 8 rooms with fans,* ☎ *985/6-20-68*). A tiny hotel with surprisingly large rooms, clean and relatively quiet at night. Within walking distance of everything. Basic accommodations include hot water and firm mattresses.

Posada Osorio (*Calle 40, between 33 and 35, 6 rooms with fans,* ☎ *985/6-26-91*). This no-nonsense little motel has relatively modern rooms with new bathrooms (no toilet seats) and hooks for your hammocks, if you don't like the two queen-size beds. Basic, with good screens on the windows, and clean. It's directly across the street from the incredible private home, designed like a Chinese pagoda, of a very wealthy *Vallísoletaño*.

Dining

 Also check the hotel listings for several notable restaurants. The Casa de Los Arcos, one of the better landmark restaurants in town, closed down in 1996 and will be missed. See page 4 for price chart.

Plaza Maya (*Calle 41, between 48 and 50*). This unobtrusive, green-awning storefront restaurant leads back to a large palapa-covered dining room decorated with Maya frescoes. The kitchen, visible behind a large glass window, is sparkling clean and the cooking staff all wear chef's whites. Professional touches include salsa served in carved stone bowls and if you ask about it, they'll serve you a small courtesy glass of Xtabentun ("ish-ta-ben-tune"), a Maya liqueur made from anise and honey, as an after dinner drink. Try their typical Yucatecan/Valladolid platter (US $6), with eight different local dishes, including *longaniza*, a local sausage that tastes like a juicy Slim Jim, and deer meat (*venado*), which we declined. Deer has been a staple of Maya diet since ancient times, but lately it's overhunted in the Yucatán and we didn't want to contribute to the problem. The Plaza Maya has been a dining treasure since 1988. $-$$

Zazil-Ha (*Calle 42 on the zócalo*, ☎ 985/6-21-71). Inexpensive pizza and a lot more are available from this hard-working restaurant housed in a large colonial-front building on the main square. Featuring good food at low prices, the Zazil has generous servings (big breakfast too) and low-priced drinks. And they deliver pizza! $

Restaurant del Parque (*Calle 42, at corner of 41*). This no-frills restaurant, in another old building at the corner of the zócalo and the San Servacio Church, serves inexpensive Mexican food and great *horchata*. It's a good example of the incredibly high ceilings typical of the colonial era. Good service and specials on beer. $

Restaurant Los Portales (*Calle 41, at corner of 40*). Los Portales has been here perhaps forever. It opens early and is a good place for a light meal or soft drink. Most of the dining is on the tile sidewalk under the portales, so it's a great place to hang out and watch the traffic go by. $

El Bazar (*Calles 38 and 40*). In the open building on a corner across from the main square, the Bazar is a non-bizarre collection of family-owned eateries and a few shops. It's the most fun place to eat in town. There are about a dozen little market-style *loncherias* that open early and close late. Inexpensive, it's our favorite place for breakfast or lunch when we're on the move. You'll have more choices of where to sit and what to eat than you can handle. As the babble of languages overheard attests, everybody eats here – tourist and resident – sooner or later. If you have the stomach for it, this is the place to try *mondongo,* a Yucatecan haggis-like sausage dish made from beef stomach. Those that try it (and it's very popular) say it has a strong taste and smooth texture. Dinner usually features a simple *comida corrida* that will fill you up without cleaning out your purse. $

Don Juanito (*Calle 49, 2 blocks in back of the Convento San Bernardino*). This thatched-roof, stucco-walled restaurant rarely sees a gringo, but if you're in the neighborhood, drop in. It serves authentic Yucatecan food at cheap prices in an atmosphere that looks and feels a little like a cantina bar. $

La Sirenita (*Calle 41, between 30 and 28*). Tired of pork, chicken and beef? Hankering for seafood in the middle of the dry jungle? Let "The Mermaid" lure you with simple but delicious fresh seafood. Follow Calle 41 toward Cancún and it's on your right. $

Chichén Itzá

I would rather live in a world where my life is surrounded by mystery than live in a world so small that my mind could comprehend it.

– *Mystery of Life,* Harry Emerson Fosdick

 The enigmatic ruins of Chichén Itzá ("Mouth of the Well of the Itzás") have intrigued and baffled archeologists and historians since they were first described by Bishop de Landa in the late 16th century. Nineteenth-century books by author and adventurer John Lloyd Stephens and British artist Frederick Catherwood, as well as some by Augustus Le Plongeon and his wife, Alice, fueled imaginations about the mysterious civilization that seemed to have disappeared into the remote jungles of Mexico and Central America.

Today there is no living city. The closest town to the ancient ceremonial center is Piste, two km (1.25 miles) west. If you want to stay overnight to see the light show (in Spanish at 7 p.m. and English at 8), or just to spend more time at these exceptional ruins, the hotel choices include three in the archeological zone itself, one just outside and several in Piste. Every travel agency in the Yucatán hawks one-day tours of the ruins and, while it is possible to see them in one arduous day (open 8 a.m. to 5 p.m.), you may prefer to stay overnight – if only to get there early in the day, before the crowds arrive, or late afternoon, as shadows begin to fall and the sun's glow illuminates the magnificent re-stored structures. The site occupies nearly 10 square km (four square miles), so it takes some time to fully appreciate. Guides are available (try joining or forming a group) at the new visitors center – complete with bathrooms, gift shops (with surprisingly reasonable prices), a bookstore, museum and food court.

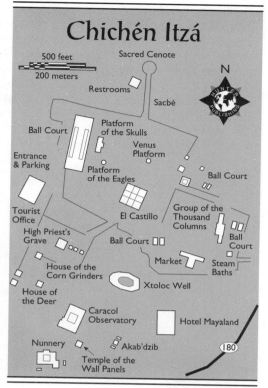

Chichén Itzá

HISTORY: The social catastrophe in the ninth century that caused the demise of the southern Classic cities resulted in Chichén Itzá's gradual rise to rule the northern Yucatán. It was believed to have been settled during the Late Classic period based on the architectural similarities of the "old" part of the city, Chichén Viejo, to the Puuc style. This part of Chichén was abandoned along with the rest of the Classical cities, but was resettled by Chontal Maya, or Itzás, a seafaring tribe who invaded the northern Yucatán in the early Post-Classic period. These people, whom the locals considered barbarians, were in turn culturally absorbed by the Yucatecan Maya along with Toltec warriors who came from Tula in the Mexican state of Hidalgo. Prior to the Toltec presence in the Terminal Classic period, influences from central Mexican culture had already permeated Maya culture. One of those influences was the cult of Quetzalcóatl, the king/god whom the Maya called Kukulcán. The building boom over the 300 years of Chichén's dominance resulted in stunning architectural wonders decorated with images of Chac, the rain god, and Kukulcán, the plumed serpent.

The downfall of Chichén in A.D. 1221 at the hands of rival city-state, Mayapán, purportedly involved the kidnapping of the bride of the king of Izamal. The details are unclear but may be related to the legend of Hunac Ceel, who survived a plunge into the sacred sacrificial cenote at Chichén, which was supposed to take its victims directly to the Underworld. Ceel predicted Chac would bring plenty of rain and shortly thereafter became ruler of Mayapán. He may have engineered the kidnapping dispute that pitched Izamal against Chichén and resulted in the downfall of both, bringing about the rise of victorious Mayapán as the new capital of the northern Maya. Religious Pilgrims continued to visit Chichén even after the Spanish Conquest. Montejo briefly tried to found a city here but, luckily for archeology, found local resistance too fierce to make it worthwhile.

El Castillo.

EL CASTILLO: The 25-meter-tall (82 feet) Temple of Kukulcán, known as El Castillo, "the Castle," dominates the view as it rises majestically in the apparent center of the ruins. Built before A.D. 800, in a Toltec style, but before the Toltec invasion, the pyramid is an eloquent statement of engineering genius and an elegant highlight of a mighty city that stretched at least 25 square km (10 square miles) beyond its wide central plazas. The view from the top is delightful and worth the steep climb.

The impressive structure you see covers a smaller, older one that can still be seen (11 a.m. to 1 p.m. and 4 to 5 p.m.) by entering a narrow stairway at the western edge of the north staircase. Inside, archeologists found a Chac Mool (a reclining statue that holds a bowl over its stomach, thought to be where hearts cut from sacrificial victims were offered to the gods) and a red jaguar altar with inlaid eyes and spots of shimmering jade. It is often hot, crowded and humid inside, not recommended for those who suffer from claustrophobia.

The construction of this temple brought into play the engineering, mathematical and celestial reckoning abilities of the ancient Maya. In some ways it is the Maya calendar embodied in stone. There are 364 steps plus a platform to equal the 365 days of a year, 52 panels on each side representing the 52-year cycle of the calendar round, and nine terraced levels on either side of the stairways that total the 18 months of the Maya solar calendar. El Castillo's axes are so perfectly aligned that the shadows of the rounded terraces fall on the side of the northern staircase where they form the image of an undulating serpent. During the Spring Equinox (approximately March 21), the serpent seems to be slithering down the stairs, while in the Fall (September 21) it reverses and climbs the pyramid. The clever optical illusionists who built it also made it seem taller than it really is. You'll wonder how such diminutive people as the Maya could climb such tall steps. Coming down is harder than going up and, as you use the rope aid, you may notice you have to walk down almost sideways. Some speculate that the reason is so you'll never turn your back on the temple of Kukulcán that crowns the pyramid's top.

BALLCOURT: The largest and best preserved ballcourt in all Mesoamerica is located here, just northwest of Kukulcán's pyramid. It is one of nine ballcourts built in the city, emphasizing the importance of the ceremonial game the Maya called **Pok-Ta-Pok**. It was a religious rite more than a recreational game. Carvings on both sides of the walls show scenes of players dressed in heavy padding (they struck the ball with their hips and body, never their hands or feet). The object was to get the leather ball through one of two carved stone rings placed high on the center of opposite walls. A carved relief also shows a player holding the head of another player kneeling next to him, blood spurting out of the lifeless body. Experts disagree on whether it was the loser or the winner who was sacrificed. If you stand in the **Temple of the Bearded Man** (at the north end) and speak in normal tones the fantastic acoustics of the court's design allow you to be heard clearly over 500 feet away at the southern wall. Above the southeast corner of the court is the **Temple of the Jaguars,** with serpent columns and carved panels. Inside the temple are polychrome bas-reliefs recounting a battle with a Maya village and a sculpture of a jaguar, possibly a throne.

To the right of the ballcourt is the **Temple of the Skulls** (*Tzompantili*, a Toltec name), where rows of skulls are carved into a stone platform. Here, heads of sacrificial victims were put on a pole for display. Eagles tear the hearts from the bodies in another V-for-violence-rated carving. The platform due north of El Castillo is the **Temple of Venus**. Rather than a voluptuous woman in a diaphanous gown, the Maya depicted her as a feathered monster with a man's head in its mouth. Hmmm. This is also named **Chac Mool** because his image was discovered buried inside.

The sacred cenote, **Cenote of Sacrifice**, is a hike (about a fifth of a mile long) up an original *sacbé* to the north. Two hundred feet across and over 115 feet deep, the well was used for ceremonial purposes, not for drinking. To this end, the Maya paid tribute to Chac with gifts of various artifacts and sacrificial victims. Bones of 50 children, men and women have been discovered here. Original dredging was done by American Edward Thompson, who owned the Hacienda Chichén. He sent a huge cache to the Peabody Museum at Harvard University, where much of it is still on display. The National Geographic Society and CEDAM, the Mexican diving association, pulled thousand more pieces from the well in the 1960s.

GROUP OF A THOUSAND COLUMNS: The complex east of the pyramid is named after the many rows of columns, once roofed over, that form a colonnade around the courtyard. Almost Greek or Roman in appearance, the imposing Temple of the Warriors, a huge three-tiered platform with a temple on top, approached by a staircase on the west, dominates its surrounding buildings. There is a large colonnade of stone pillars carved with figures of warriors at its base and a reclining Chac in the temple at the top. Columns wrapped with carvings of serpents served to hold up the roof, now long gone. The temple was built over an earlier one. The inner temple had pillars sculpted in bas-relief (they retain much of their color) and murals painted on the walls. The courtyard to the south contains the **Steam Bath** (No. 2), believed to be a Maya ceremonial sweathouse, undergoing resoration, and a platform at the south end known as the **Market**. Neither of these is in good condition.

SOUTH CHICHEN: The trail south from El Castillo pyramid leads to an area often less crowded with tourists. The first structure you come to is the **Ossuary**, or **Grave of the High Priest**, now being actively restored. A similar design – on a lesser scale – to El Castillo, this pyramidal base covers a natural grotto cave in which bones of a man were found. A small temple further down the trail is the **Red House**, or **Chichán-Chob**, meaning small holes, probably referring to the latticework in the roof comb. With a pleasing view of the other structures, this building is in the Puuc Late Classic style, dated by a glyph at about A.D. 869.

The trail then leads to **El Caracol**, one of the most fascinating structures on site. The name means "Snail" or "Conch" in Spanish, alluding to the spiral staircase found inside (off limits). The round structure, the only one of its kind at Chichén, is the celestial observatory from where the Maya watched the heavens. The slits in the dome and walls aligned with certain stars and Chac masks over its four doors face the cardinal directions. A path to the northeast leads to Chichén's former water supply, the **Cenote Xtoloc**, "Iguana." Due south is the **Temple of Sculptured Panels**, a good spot for photos of El Caracol.

The **Nunnery**, or **Las Monjas**, is next. This impressive structure measures 62 meters (210 feet) long, 31 meters (105 feet) wide and is more than 15 meters (50 feet) high. The construction is Maya rather than Toltec – perhaps the residence of royalty. The resemblance of the myriad rooms to European convents gave it its name. A doorway in the **Annex** next to it forms the open monster mouth associated with the Chenes architectural style. Near the Annex is the tiny **La Iglesia**, whose upper facade and roof comb are a riot of Chac masks and animal gods, *bacabs*. Another building, down a dusty foot trail east of the Nunnery, is the plain **Akab-Dzib**, Mayan for "Obscure Writing," named for some undeciphered hieroglyphics on its lintel.

OLD CHICHEN: A third section of the ruins lies scattered in the brush but connected by trails south of the Hacienda Chichén hotel. Unless you fancy yourself an explorer, it's probably best to have a guide to see these structures. The most noteworthy of these ruins is the **Temple of Three Lintels**, dated A.D. 879, in the classic Puuc style. You might pick up a good local guide, less expensively than at the main ruins, in nearby Piste. Wear slacks and insect repellent; take water and a hat.

The unrecorded past is none other than our old friend, the tree in the primeval forest, that fell without being heard.

– Barbara Tuchman, *The NY Times*, March 8, 1964

A Sidetrip to Grutas De Balankanche

 The caverns of Balankanche, six km (3.7 miles) east of Chichén's ruins, were a center for the worship of the gods Chac, Tlaloc and Kukulcán during the 10th and 11th centuries. Artifacts, sculpture and pottery are found at the crowning attraction of the caves, a thick stalagmite "Ceiba Tree." Open from 9 a.m. to 4 p.m. Guided tours in Spanish or English are the only way to see the caves (relatively large and open). Spanish-language tours are at 9 a.m. and noon; in French at 10 a.m.; and in English at 11 a.m., 1 and 3 p.m. If you're early, hang out in their cool and inviting botanical gardens, with flora identification signs in English and Spanish. Admission is about US $3.

QUEEN MOO & THE EGYPTIAN SPHINX

He and his wife could only report what they actually found, but it was impossible to be in the presence of so many wonders without doing a little wondering themselves.
– Manly Hall, writing of the *Le Plongeons* in *Horizon* magazine, 1948

An investigation into the history of archeology in the Yucatán will eventually come across Augustus and Alice Le Plongeon, referred to as either crackpots or important contributors to the understanding of the lost Maya.

In 1873, Augustus and his young wife landed in the Yucatán to study and document Maya civilization using glass plate photography. He and Alice first stirred up controversy when, in an effort to protect Uxmal from looters, Augustus placed an advertisement in a Mérida newspaper claiming to have set dynamite booby-traps around the ruins. It was to prevent destruction, Alice later explained to the *New York World*, "not at the hand of Indians, who stand in awe of the effigies of the ancient rulers of the country, but the very administrator who is destroying these monuments, by order of the master, to use the stones in the building of his farmhouse."

The ploy blew up in the face of the Le Plongeons when, although it temporarily stopped the plundering of Uxmal's stones, it became a false but oft-repeated story that he had used dynamite to excavate buildings at Uxmal and Chichén Itzá.

But the nail in the coffin of the Le Plongeons' credibility came from their own ill-conceived speculations on Maya history. Augustus and Alice believed the Maya to be descendants of the Atlantis civilization. In their recreation of the story, Queen Móo, leader of the Maya and builder of some of Chichén's marvels, traveled to Egypt where she was welcomed as the god Isis.

Unfortunately for the Le Plongeons, they were attacked in professional circles by jealous archeologists who ridiculed both the conclusions they reached as well as them personally. Lost in the insults from critics who had never studied the Maya nor been to the Yucatán was the Le Plongeons' ground-breaking work and professional methods of excavation – as good if not better than their trained contemporaries – and the important find of Chac Mool at Chichén Itzá.

A very readable and sympathetic book about them is *A Dream of Maya*, by Lawrence Desmond and Phyllis Messenger, published by the University of New Mexico Press.

Accommodations

CHICHEN ITZA ZONA DE HOTELES

 Hacienda Chichén (*Hotel Zone,* ☎ *in US, 800 624-8451, or in Mexico, 99/24-21-50, fax 99/24-50-11, 18 rooms with air, pool, restaurant, safety deposit, babysitting*). A stay here combines three different periods in Mexico's history. Post-Classic Maya from the nearby Chichén Itzá ruins represents the oldest, with some stones were to build the main hacienda house still visible in the interior's west wall. The hacienda was built as a cattle ranch in the 1500s, during the colonial period, and it became a sisal plantation in the mid-1800s. The modern period began in the early 1900s when American Vice-Counsel Edward Thompson bought the hacienda and began archeological work on the nearby ruins. In 1923 the cottages that are now individual guest rooms were built for Carnegie Institute archeologists. Completely remodeled inside, they are still somewhat rustic with wood beam ceilings, but have all the necessaries, including huge bathrooms. The lovely terrace restaurant has seating inside or outside looking out on the lush gardens and swimming pool. The grounds are ripe for exploring the old henequen works, ruined outbuildings and an ancient church. **$$**

  Mayaland (*Hotel Zone,* ☎ *in US, 800-235-4079 or in Mexico, 99/25-21-22, fax 99/25-70-22, 92 rooms, bungalows and suites with air, TV, balconies or terraces, 2 swimming pools, 2 restaurants*). The huge, white, hacienda-style Mayaland is so close to Chichén that many windows overlook several important ruins. Somewhat ugly from the dead-end road, the interior is lavish and luxurious. The 100-acre gardens contain winding paths amid lush tropical flowering plants. Rooms are tastefully furnished with two big beds, a couch and large dresser, giant closets and hand-blown glass lamps. Bathrooms are not so extravagant. Even more attractive are the private bungalows, which are suite-like in size with hand-carved wooden bathroom doors. The two hotel restaurants feature French and international cuisine, with a reputation for excellence. They also offer a buffet lunch and free shuttle to the ruins. $$$-$$$$

Villas Arqueológicas - Chichén Itzá (*Hotel Zone,* ☎ *in US, 800-258-2633, or in Mexico, 985/1-00-34, fax 985/1-00-18, 40 rooms with air, pool, tennis, restaurant*). Some of the rooms here were the original rooms built for the archeologists who worked on the restoration of Chichén Itzá. They're somewhat small with low ceilings and two twin beds snuggled into arched sleeping nooks. It's a warm and cozy use of limited space, like having your own room as a kid. Closets and bathroom are a good size and done in natural woods. The guest-rooms wrap around a pool , which is dwarfed by a huge palapa bar area complete with lazy soft cushions to relax on. There is a formal hacienda-style dining room. For some strange reason we liked it best of three big hotels in the *Zona*. $$

Dolores Alba Chichén (*Km 122 on Highway 180, no phone, 30 rooms with air or fans, pool, restaurant*). This is the original hotel begun by the Sanchez family, which owns the Hotel Dolores Alba in Mérida. The intricately patterned tiles on the floor of the indoor restaurant were hand-painted specifically for the hotel when it was built around 1955. Juan Sanchez now runs it with a smile and a good sense of what's important in modern accommodations. Many guests stay two nights, lured by the nightly laser light show at the ruins. Totally remodeled in 1996, the country house-style hotel consists of attached rose-pink cottages that wander along the extensive gardens. Each medium-size room is cheerful and pleasant with three windows and a modern bathroom. An inviting palapa provides shade for the outdoor restaurant and for several hammocks swinging peacefully near the pool. Free transportation is offered to the ruins. Walk back or negotiate a taxi fare (should be about US $3 or $4; ask first). No phone (except for emergencies), but reservations can be made through the Dolores Alba in Mérida at ☎ 99/28-56-50 or fax at 99/28-31-63. $

PISTE

There are several *posadas* with cheap rooms, such as the clean and basic **Posada Chac Mool**, as well as the upscale **Misíon Hotel**, in the strip mall-like town of Piste. (Neither of these has a phone.) Taxis can run you to the ruins. Inexpensive eateries line the roadway, including **Las Rades**, which also has a mini-supermarket for your camping and RV supplies.

Posada Novelo (*Km 118 Highway 180, 10 rooms with fans,* ☎ *985/1-01-22*). The Novelo has the same owner as the Stardust, so guests can use the next door pool and restaurant. Rooms here are very basic: no toilet seats, worn bed spreads, but clean. **$**

Posada de Paso (*Km 118 Highway 180, 11 rooms with fans, private parking, restaurant*). Upstairs from the plain *posada* hotel is a breezy open-air restaurant under a palapa roof. The rooms and accommodations here are OK for a night, but the restaurant is more noteworthy. Unique, rustic hand-made wooden tables, chairs and sideboards run along a railing looking out on the street. The servings are generous and very inexpensive and it seems not to have been discovered by passing tourists. **$**

Piramide Inn (*Km 118 Highway 180,* ☎ *985/6-26-71, 34 rooms with air or fans, pool, restaurant*). Adequate rooms but a very good restaurant and a large pool mark this grand hotel/motel along the highway in the closest town to the ruins. The original owner started the semi-famous "Explorer's Club" here, but since his death the Club has been lost. Camping is available. **$**

Stardust Inn (*Km 118 Highway 180, 57 rooms with air,* ☎ *& fax 985/1-01-22, pool, TV, restaurant*). No relation to the Las Vegas landmark – although the owner has been to Nevada. The Stardust boasts a very large central pool framed by picturesque coconut palms. The rooms are fairly large, modestly furnished and carpeted upstairs. Ask for a discount. Excellent restaurant. **$$**

See page 3 for price chart.

Dining

The pleasant **Cafetería Ruinas** on the Chichén grounds does a fairly good job offering Mexican and basic meals to weary tourists. In Piste, a few minutes by car, **Restaurant Los Parajos** is popular because of its attractive palapa atmosphere and fair food. **El Carrousel** across the street serves regional meals inexpensively. The **Restaurant Xaybe'h** and **La Fiesta** are both good – air-conditioned, but more expensive – handling a fair number of tour bus diners. **Puebla Maya**, opposite the Pyramid Inn, serves a tasty all-you-can-eat buffet and offers a cool swim in their pool, as does the **Stardust**. Seafood can be caught at **Restaurant Sacbé**. **Restaurant Las Mestizas** is worthwhile, offering home-made regional cooking and a palapa decorated with butterflies and parrots.

If you've gone out for lunch, keep your admission ticket to reenter the ruins the same day, but you may have to pay twice for parking (US $1).

The Road To Rio, Rio Lagartos

Writers and travelers are mesmerized alike by knowing of their destinations.

– Eudora Welty speech at Harvard, 1984

 The road north from Valladolid, Highway 296, passes over the toll road from Cancún to Mérida. It's a broad, flat and straight run to Tizimín, a colonial city in the center of Yucatán's cattle country, then directly up to Rio Lagartos, a working fishing village inside the Rio Lagartos National Park. The 104 km (65 miles) could be a satisfying bike trip if you have the equipment and energy.

In the agricultural countryside, you may be surprised by the number of windmills on metal towers with vanes advertising their manufacturer, "Aermotor Chicago." Galvanized metal windmills were first introduced into the Yucatán by Edward Thompson in 1887, when he imported two from the States and extolled the virtues of the lightweight wind-driven pumps for water. Wells in the Mérida area averaged 30 feet deep and were hand-dug through limestone. By 1903 there were 1,200 American-made windmills whirling above the city. The venerable Aermotor company is still making windmills today in Conway, Arkansas.

The newly opened ruin at **Ek Balam** ("Black Jaguar") is the first stop along the way, 10 km (six miles) north of the Cuota. Follow the sign on the right toward the villages of Santa Rita and Hunukú. Scholars believe that this large site was the center of an agricultural area. At the parking lot follow a *sacbé* 100 meters (330 feet) to the closely clustered ruins enclosed by stone walls. The largest building is an impressive 30 meters high by 150 meters long and 60 meters wide (100' x 495' x 200'). Its rounded corners are climbed by a staircase facing the central courtyard. The views of the surrounding dry jungle are majestic. From here you can see the tallest building at Cobá, nearly 48 km (30 miles) away. Two even taller mounds that look like mountains (but are in reality unexcavated pyramids) flank the structures. A rope aids in climbing the wooded rocky sides and helps adventuresome readers who want to stand where they can see forever – on the top of a structure where no man has stood for a thousand years.

Tizimín

Tizimín, Mayan for "Place of Horses," 50 km (31 miles) north of Valladolid, holds little interest for travelers unless it's fiesta time (and it's a great town for a fair) or as a rest stop or alternative to staying overnight in Rio Lagartos. There's an airstrip in town, built for a visit by the Queen of England but not too active lately. The last time we were there we drove across it on a well-used "shortcut," while several head of cattle grazed along its weed-choked shoulder. A sad zoo also exists on Calle 51, with an appealing restaurant nearby, Las Flamboyanes. The restaurants, bakeries and accommodations in Tizimín (pop. 50,000) are all very inviting and the lack of tourists means they're also low-priced.

A grand colonial **Convento de Los Tres Reyes Magos** (Monastery of the Three Wise Kings) presides over Tizimín's shady main square. If you're just passing through, stop by **La Especial** bakery on the corner of the little pedestrian lane off the plaza and Calle 55. Owner Jorge Canul's family has been baking in Tizimín since 1916 and has recently expanded to Valladolid. A cousin, Eduardo, owns one in Bakersfield, California. Don't miss *pan cubano*, the equivalent of pound cake, sweet and smooth.

Whether we're on Tizimín sidestreets or stretches of lonely roads in the countryside, we can't help but be impressed with the graceful elegance of Maya women sitting side-saddle on bicycles. Just another in our Mexican memories.

Accommodations

 San Carlos (*Calle 54 No. 407 near 51,* ☎ *3-20-94, 28 rooms with air or fans, parking*). On a back street only a block from the main square the V-shaped, two-story San Carlos is easy to mistake for an office building from the front. Run under the auspices of a senior Señora, it's the quietest hotel in town and the one with the best reputation. There's a wild green garden growing in the filled-in swimming pool. The rooms downstairs are a little dark so choose one upstairs. $

Posada Pastora (*Calle 51 No. 413, between 52 and 54, no phone, 19 rooms with fans, TV, private parking*). A half-block off the main square, this new hotel has big rooms but no closets or toilet seats. They use a lot of frosted glass and black wrought-iron doors that give a feeling of even more open space. It's Tizimín's newest hotel and well worth checking out or even checking in. $

San Jorge (*Calle 53 No. 412 on the zócalo, 34 rooms with air or fans,* ☎ *3-20-37, pool, private parking*). Beige and white, this Miami Beach-like hotel has clean, medium-size rooms with tile bath and very big closets. You can't get more conveniently located than this, right on Tizimín's central square. Regular, clean hotel rooms, quite reasonably priced. However, they don't always fill the triangular swimming pool in winter. $

See page 3 for price chart.

Dining

Tres Reyes (*on the zócalo*). A pleasing corner restaurant run by big "Willy Canto," the Three Kings offers good Yucatecan and Mexican cooking (Willy claims it's the best in the world). He offers a varied menu of meats, poultry and fresh fish, all at excellent prices. The town's most popular eatery. $

La Michocana (*on the zócalo*). This is a chain of ice cream parlors and Tizimín's is particularly clean and welcome on a hot day. Try an exotic flavor (of their umpteen choices) and savor it on a shaded bench in the park. $

Los Portales (*under the portales of the Municipal Palace on the zócalo*). Los Portales sits on the main plaza's northeast corner, under the curved arches of the city hall, shaded by bright red Coca-Cola canvas awnings. The few outdoor tables are a popular place to hang out and eat Mexican food and drink beer. There's also an indoor dining area that packs them in for good light food at good prices. $

Armando's (*Highway 295, on the southern outskirts of town*). Armando's is an attractive large thatched-roof restaurant just south of the Tizimín city limits, set back off the road and surrounded by a garden of brilliant red bougainvillea. Open 11 a.m. to 6 p.m., it has been a fixture offering a cool drink and a meal for many years. $

See page 4 for price chart.

Rio Lagartos

The real meaning of travel, like that of a conversation by the fireside, is the discovery of one's self through contact with other people.

– The Meaning of Persons, Paul Tournier, 1957

The road to the fishing port of Rio Lagartos has finally been upgraded to actual pavement rather than rutted *sacbé* and is now fine and fast – 53 km (33 miles) or 30 minutes from Tizimín. Named for the alligator river that no longer contains alligators, the Lagartos is really an inlet to the Caribbean that opens into a huge estuary/lagoon east of town. That lagoon is the home to millions of pink flamingos who come each year in the spring to breed in cone-shaped mud nests. The perfect combination of shallow water and salt in the mud flats accounts for the brilliant pink and salmon color of the gawky but graceful birds. Boat trips out to see them are the big attraction for visitors here.

When they recognized the importance of the flamingo colonies, the Mexican government set aside 118,000 acres in 1979 as a national park to protect the 212 species of native and migratory birdlife. During the summer months, April through August, the colony breeds and tourist access to their breeding area, at the far eastern part of the lagoon, is strictly forbidden. But the areas where they feed are accessible year-round and even during the winter months you'll see huge flocks blanket the shallow mud flats in a coat of pink and white.

Fishermen checking their nets.

Don't be put off when you enter Rio Lagartos. Some dilapidated housing rests in the mangrove swamp south of town, but the community itself is quite quaint and appealing. As you pull toward the riverfront, hawkers may approach and ask if you want to see the flamingos. These young entrepreneurs are legitimate, but check the price quoted with the cooperative kiosk along the *malecón*.

Another attraction of Rio Lagartos is a fabulously photogenic brilliant blue cenote, **Cenote Chiquilá**. It's a cool relaxing swim or snorkel and a great place to camp for free (no facilities) or have a picnic. Located about a half-mile out of town, follow the waterfront to the right (east), past the summer homes that dot the harbor, along the dirt road to a palapa-roofed, open-sided shed. Worth it.

Adventures

ON WATER

Flocks of flamingos dine at several locations along the estuary and lagoon and prices for **boat rides** out to view them depend upon how far you travel. Boats are available on the *malecón* from the fisherman's cooperative. The lagoon begins to widen east of the wooden bridge over the river and it's about 30 minutes to the first feeding spot, Yoluk or Yolv'i (app. US $25). This trip takes about two hours total and can include another smaller colony nearby, Najochin. Adding the Chiquilá colony boosts the price to US $30. The next option takes about 3½ hours total to the larger colony of San Fernando (app. US $40-50). Larger again is the one at Punta Meco, a 4½-hour round trip for about US $75. On all trips, the guide will point out a "white mountain" visible on the barrier peninsula. That's a mountain of salt at Las Coloradas, where it has been mined by the Maya for over 2,000 years!

ON FOOT

Hikers, campers and beachcombers can arrange with local fishermen to be dropped off and picked up later, even the next day, on the virtually deserted peninsula. Ask one of the knowledgeable village youth about the access to the peninsula across the way. While some of it is appealing deserted beaches, other parts are brushy and wild and mangrove swamps to the edge force you to walk in the water. You should be able to plan a day's hike or a camp with some help from the locals. Plenty of solitude, wildlife and nature (including mosquitoes). There's also a good area on the peninsula across from San Felipe, the village to the west, at the mouth of the river.

Accommodations & Dining

La Torreja (*on the malecón near the Rio Lagartos lighthouse*). Look! Under the big palapa! It's a bar! No, it's a restaurant! Either way it's big on fresh fried fish and bottled beer. $

La Isla Contoy (*Calle 19, on the waterfront*). Only fishing boats, tied up along the silty beach, sit between you and the *rio* in this screened-in palapa restaurant. With a great view and a rustic decor, their menu is mostly fresh fish, but they're one of the few seaside places to also offer meat and chicken. Enjoy a fish fillet stuffed with shrimp for about US $4 or the fillet in salsa *à la Veracruzano*. Diego, the manager, offers free tourist information and can arrange trips to see the flamingos or a day of fishing. **$**

Los Negritos (*Calle 10 No. 135*). This large restaurant on the way into town doesn't have the ambiance of the riverside but may still have the best seafood in town. Owner Gilmer Pacheco, whose nickname provided the inspiration for the restaurant's, has a photo menu posted inside and individual wooden fish-shaped menus list the items and prices. His *comida casera* (daily special) is either meat or chicken, but everything else is seafood. Appetizers of *ceviche* come with every drink and the house specialty is a large broiled lobster tail for under US $8. (Mexicans love mayonnaise, so if you're not sure you do, ask for it on the side.) We loved the *mojo de ajo* (fillet broiled in garlic butter). Saturday night from 10:30 p.m. to 2:30 a.m. the tables are pushed back and it becomes the Titanic Discotheque, a hip place to go down with the ship. **$**

Cabañas Los Dos Hermanos (*on the eastern malecón*). Two brothers in the Sanchez Alvarez family built two round stick-walled cabañas and one cement duplex, all palapa covered, in their back yard. They're relatively primitive, but clean and new. You can ask here for Erik Ramos Celis, a good guide and boatman into the lagoon. A bed for the night runs under $10, but this will not suit all tastes.

See page 4 for price chart.

San Felipe & Las Coloradas

Love the sea? I dote upon it – from the beach.
– Douglas Jerrold, 1803-1857

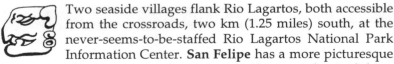 Two seaside villages flank Rio Lagartos, both accessible from the crossroads, two km (1.25 miles) south, at the never-seems-to-be-staffed Rio Lagartos National Park Information Center. **San Felipe** has a more picturesque harbor than Rio Lagartos and if you're into the sea and quiet fishing villages, this is an attractive alternative. Camping is available nearby and the town even offers a modern hotel, something Rio is sorely missing.

Hotel San Felipe de Jesus (*Calle 9 between 14 and 16, 18 rooms with fans,* ☎ *986/3-37-38, extension 127, restaurant*) opened in 1996. It is very attractive and modern with a restaurant that shares a view of the river and Gulf of Mexico. This is a much needed hotel near the increasingly popular flamingo-viewing stop in the Rio Lagartos Reserve. In fact, rates for a boat to go and see the flamingos are less here than they are in Rio Lagartos, even though it's an additional 15 minutes each way in travel time. For swimming and beachcombing, there's a shady palapa across the river where Rio Lagartos opens into the Gulf. The deserted public beach there is fabulous. Local fishing boats will ferry you across for about one dollar (round trip) and will pick you up at any pre-arranged time. For a little over US $10 per hour you can rent a boat to take you on a tour up and down the coast. Ask about fishing. The disadvantage of this hotel is that the best rooms (#1, 2, 3, 8, 9, and 10) share a single large balcony – with a wonderful view – so privacy is technically possible only at night with the light off. $

We can't speak for the name of San Felipe's inviting waterfront restaurant, **El Popular Vaselina** (Favorite Grease Spot?), but it is very popular. No surprise here, fish is the specialty. Its new building is large, clean and palapa-covered and it overlooks an idyllic harbor. What more could you ask?

The brilliant white salt mountain at **Las Coloradas** is fascinating, but there's little to do or see in the village itself. Its fine sandy beach is full of fishing boats flying colorful flags in the strong breeze. Fishing is one of two main occupations at this Maya outpost. The other is salt, which has been gathered here for 2,000 years. The ancient Maya used salt as a trading commodity through all the stages of their civilization. Salt is gathered by filling large ponds with saltwater which is then evaporated, leaving the salt. Mineral deposits make the concentrated ponds gleam purple and red, hence the name of the village. You can try stopping in the modern salt production facilities and ask to look around. At least keep your eye out for wildlife in the low brush that lines the dusty white road. We found a rare jaguarundi's burrow and sat watching him (or her) watch us for five minutes. This area is rich in all kinds of wildlife. The wooden bridge you cross on the way often has fishermen net-fishing from the top, but if you stop to talk or take pictures, be sure to wear either slacks and long sleeves or insect repellent; mosquitoes here love fresh blood.

Izamal

At nine o'clock we entered the suburbs of Izamal....
It was the last day of the fiesta of Santa Cruz....
But amid this gay scene the eye turned involuntarily to
immense mounds rising grandly above the tops of the houses...
proclaiming the power of those who reared them and destined,
apparently, to stand when the feebler structures of their more
civilized conquerors shall have crumbled into dust.

– *Incidents of Travel in Yucatán*, John L. Stephens, 1843

 Known as the "Yellow City," the gold painted strucures in colonial Izamal are built over an Early Classic Maya religious center where pilgrims came to worship the supreme god, Itzamná, and Kinich Kakmó, a manifestation of the sun god, Kinich Ahau. A dozen temples were once in the ceremonial city that lost influence and fell to Mayapán in the Terminal Classic period. Its long occupation and use lasted through the Spanish Conquest. Izamal's holiness among the Maya was based on the legend of a priest-god Zamná (Itzamná), whose body was cut up and buried in the principal temples in town. The religious significance of Izamal to the Maya might explain why the Franciscans chose it as the location for their enormous monastery in the center of town, now one of the two main tourist attractions of this pleasant colonial anachronism. One way to enjoy its flavor is to tour town in a nostalgic Victoria, a horse-drawn carriage that continues to serve as a mode of transportation for visitors and locals alike. Many of the brightly decorated carriages look as though they've been lovingly cared for since the time of Queen Victoria, for whom they're reportedly named.

Orientation

 GETTING AROUND: There are numerous ways to get to Izamal, depending, of course, on where you're coming from and how pressed you are for time. Whether you're coming from Mérida or Valladolid, Izamal can be reached from the town of Kantunil, on Route 180. From Mérida, turn off 180 at either Hóctun (so you can go through Kimbilá) or Kantunil. Or go by way of Motúl, a slower way through many small Maya villages. From Valladolid, take 180 to Kantunil, or the back road that retraces the retreat of the Caste War refugees through Tinúm, Dzitas, Quintana Roo, Tunkas and Stilpech (we loved this route). The road forks (you go right) as you leave town. A train runs daily to Izamal from Mérida with an "Izamal by Train" excursion on Sun. (see page 265). A "Discover Izamal" bus tour leaves Mon., Wed., Fri. and Sat.

Buses serve the city from either direction. If you're in Valladolid, take the daily afternoon second-class train. It might make a story to tell your grandchildren. Be sure to ride in a Victoria horse-drawn hansom in Izamal (found in the shadeless park next to the convent).

Victoria cab in front of Izamal's monastery.

Practicalities

There's a **tourist information** room at the corner of Calles 33 and 30. The **train station** is on Calle 30 and the **bus station** is on Calle 32, No. 302. There are three **gas stations** in town and at least two **pharmacies**, one on Calle 33, opposite the municipal market, and the other inside the **municipal market** across from the convent. **Handicrafts** are special at **Hecho a Mano** ("Made by Hand") at Calles 31 and 34. The **Parador Turístico** on Calle 30, No. 22, has various Maya vendors and puts on cultural shows, including the Sunday show (worth catching even if you aren't with the Mérida train excursion). It starts at about 1 p.m. The cottage-industry village of **Kimbilá** is 12 km (7.5 miles) east of town, where **El Milagro de Dios** and **Creaciones Addy** are noteworthy craft shops.

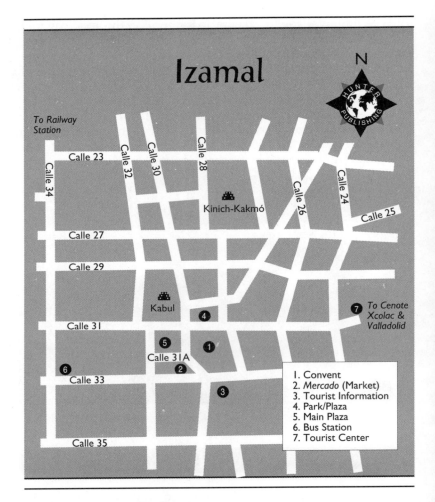

Sights

 The gargantuan golden yellow structure that commands a view of the city and the lives of the people in Izamal (derived from Mayan for "Dew of Heaven") is the **Convento de San Antonio de Padua**. In 1533 the Spanish Franciscan order had the colossal Maya temple Ppal-Hol-Chac demolished down to its base, 180 meters long and 12 meters high (400' x 40'). With the discarded stones, Fray Juan de Mérida began the first monastery in the New World, completed by Fray Francisco de la Torre in 1561. Climbing the long stone steps of the convent leads to the graceful arcade with 75 arches. The strolling covered walkway encloses a grand courtyard, the Atrium. At 8,000 square meters, it is the largest in Mexico and second in size only to the Vatican in the Catholic world. Pope John Paul II spoke in the Atrium of the convent in Izamal on August 11, 1993 and met here with representatives of Latin America's indigenous peoples.

A number of paintings thought to date from the 16th and 17th centuries were recently found on the walls of the church entrance and cloisters when a thick layer of whitewash was removed. One of the most beautiful of the frescoes is dedicated to 4th-century martyr Saint Barbara.

The church interior is relatively stark except for the magnificent gold-leaf *retable* (altar) and the statue of the Virgin carved by Friar Juan de Aguirre and transported from Guatemala in 1558. She resides in a side alcove surrounded by oil paintings of Yucatecan bishops.

At the height of its Early Classic glory, Izamal boasted a plaza surrounded by the pyramids of Kabul ("House of the Miraculous Hand"), Itzamatul ("Dew That Falls From Heaven"), Ppal-Hol-Chac ("Lightening House") and Kinich Kakmó ("Fire Macaw With the Face of the Sun"). The gigantic 35-meter (115-foot) pyramid of **Kinich Kakmó** is visible as you drive into town and from the main plaza, so it should be easy to find, right? Wrong. Once you set out on foot the base disappears in the maze of modern buildings. We felt foolish to have lost it. The base of the monstrous mound is 195 meters by 174 meters (640' x 570') – a big city block. A stairway has been restored so it's an easy, but hot, climb. Since the stairway rises from the street, the full size of the pyramid is not apparent until you reach the first terraced level and discover a second bulky pyramid of another 17 meters (56 feet) rests on top of it. Bishop de Landa described it as *"a building of such height and beauty that it astonishes me."*

We finally found it by hiring a Victoria cab to take us there, but you can get there on foot. Walk north on calle 30 from the front of the convent to Calle 27 and turn right (east) to Calle 28.

About 14 km (nine miles) east of town on the road to Stilpech (follow Calle 31) is the **Cenote X-Kolac**, which makes for a cool and refreshing swim. Some facilities.

Apart from the pagan and religious festivities in honor of the Virgin, held on December 8, the biggest celebration in Izamal is the procession of the **Black Christ of Stilpech**. At dawn on October 18, inhabitants travel to Stilpech to find the statue that they bring back about 7 a.m., heralded by the sounds of hymns, prayers and firecrackers. Then there's an all-day fiesta. Izamal is worth a stop on any Yucatán adventure.

Accommodations

 Green River Hotel (*Avenida Zamná,* ☎ *995/4-03-37, 11 rooms with air, minibar, TV*). According to local folklore there once was a river near the site of this pretty little hotel so it kept the area's traditional name: Rio Verde. Out of the town center by about six blocks, the Green River is a clean, modern one-story building on a wide boulevard of *flamboyante* shade trees. All the rooms are pleasant and adequately sized with closets and new bathrooms, and there are four larger rooms available with three beds. Quiet and very peaceful, it's only a short walk or carriage ride to the convent and ruins. Manager Herbert Sosa is friendly and helpful and speaks fairly good English. If you make reservations, he'll pick you up downtown. Since the Pope's visit in 1993, it's Izamal's favorite overnight stop. $

Hotel Canto (*Calle 31, on the square, 15 rooms with fans*). The Canto is a tremendous disappointment because the entryway in the row of colonial buildings that face the main square is quite inviting. It has beautiful tile work, a green courtyard garden and a locally popular little restaurant. But the dingy small rooms haven't been improved, except perhaps for bathrooms, since John L. Stephens apparently slept here in 1842. This is a place for backpacking hammock-sleepers only. However, the restaurant is cheap and you can go out the back and climb the unexcavated pyramid, "Kabul," that abuts the rear of the building.

Hotel Kabul (*Calle 31, on the square*). The Kabul is the other of two side-by-side colonial-looking hotels on the *zócalo* in front of the plaza next to the convent. Once inside, the hotel looks more like a run-down motel. Its very basic accommodations have no other attraction than the price. $

Macan Ché (*Calle 22 between 31 and 33, fax 995/4-02-87, 10 rooms with fans, rates include breakfast*). Izamal's newest and most attractive accommodations are here at Macan Ché where your host is American, Diane Boyle. On a quiet sidestreet near the El Conejo ruins, it's a short walk to the center of town or the *Parador Turístico*. Crushed stone paths trail back to individual cabañas scattered around her jungle-like tropical garden. Each is tastefully decorated in a different theme: Mexican, African – there's even an English cottage! Rooms are large and comfortable. There's an English-language reading library. The surrounding trees provide cool shade and the noises you hear, day or night, are song birds. Full breakfast is served in the palapa-covered restaurant. There is private parking. Access to swimming is a few blocks away at Diane's ranch with a pool and two other rental rooms. Ms. Boyle, who is active in local community

affairs (organizing dance classes and hosting Piñata parties for children), rents bicycles and offers horseback riding to her guests. $
See page 3 for price chart.

Dining

 Kinich Kakmó (*Calle 27 No. 299, between 28 and 30*). Fifty meters (165 feet) down the street from the new reconstruction on the Kinich Kakmó pyramid, this new intimate and inviting restaurant is Izamal's best. Hidden behind a colonial front, the dining area rests in back under a large palapa roof. It is pleasingly decorated with clay pottery and Maya artifacts. You're invited to wander along a stone path in the garden where two Maya women hand-make your tortillas and grill *poc chuc* or *pollo asado* in their very smoky open kitchen. The attentive staff in the Kinich restaurant offer the most varied menu in town and it's deservedly considered the best. Browse the tiny, reasonably priced gift shop that shares the front of the restaurant. $

Tumben-Lol (*Calle 22 No. 302, between 31 and 33*). Around the corner from the new *Parador Turístico* and the El Conejo ruins is the Tumben-Lol, a large palapa-covered, red-tiled restaurant with a smaller menu than the Kinich Kakmó but slightly lower prices to match. It boasts impressive polished wood entrance doors and a small attractive garden at the edge of the palapa. Clean and cool, the restaurant's name in Mayan means "New Flower," and each of the hand-made chairs has a flower carved in the top. Made-to-order tortillas come from a Maya woman in a separate palapa kitchen. The food is good but service can be spotty, so expect to wait. $

Wayan' Ne' (*Calle 30 No. 303, at corner of 33*). Wayan' Ne' means "Here I am" in Mayan, and on a hot day of visiting the convent across the street you'll be glad they are. The incredibly inexpensive menu is Yucatecan and the food and service are impeccable. Spotlessly clean and pleasant. The restaurant is owned and operated by a Maya woman and her loving touch is evidenced by hand-painted wall plates, cute curtains, noticeably immaculate bathrooms, green plants and an overall welcoming atmosphere. The kind of place you wish you had in your neighborhood at home. $

See page 4 for price chart.

The next compass direction of the Maya world was West, or black, where the sun died. This is the area we will explore next.

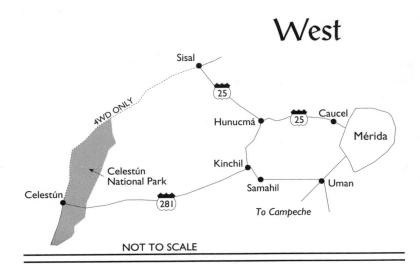

West - Black
(Chikin Ek)

Sisal

In 1810, when Mérida needed another port for transportation and shipping closer than their rival Campeche, they chose **Sisal**, 53 km (33 miles) east, which quickly became a humming little seaport. An escape corridor from Mérida to the port was kept open during the siege of the Caste War. Surrounded by Maya warriors, the Governor of the Yucatán had already decided to evacuate the city and flee to Sisal when, in the middle of the battle, the time came to plant corn. The Maya armies picked up and went back to their fields, snatching defeat from the jaws of victory. But it soon became apparent that Sisal, along the shallow Gulf of Mexico, could no longer fulfill Yucatán's growing need for a deep-water port to handle the increased export of henequen from the haciendas. When the port of

Progreso opened in 1872, in a slightly deeper part of the Gulf, Sisal, which gave its name to henequen fiber, sank back into oblivion. Today, it's a forgotten little sleepy fishing village where you can do nothing because there's nothing to do. Its red-and-white lighthouse is now a private home you can ask to see (don't forget a tip) and a cement pier at the end of the road juts into the Gulf (good for fishing, swimming, taking photos or hanging out with the ever-present kids). A beachside restaurant and bar at the foot of the pier welcomes strangers as friends to this historically rich, backwater village. If it's hot in Mérida and you need beach, this makes a quiet alternative to Progreso. Bus service is available from the downtown station. To drive, take the road (Rt. 281) off the *periférico* (the loop road around Mérida) to Hunucmá (pottery, gasoline and yet another colonial church), 29 km, then follow the signs for Sisal, another 24 km. The road to Hunucmá is also one of two ways to get to Celestún, a fishing village along the beach in the national park of the same name.

Celestún

*Over the long haul of life on this planet it is the
ecologists and not the bookkeepers of business,
who are the ultimate accountants.*

– Stewart L. Udall, former US Secretary of the Interior

There are two ways to reach Celestún and the fabulous flamingo flocks that feed there. Flamingos eat standing in groups of thousands on mud banks in Celestún's shallow estuary. They force the muddy water through the serrated edges of their bill and strain the edible animal and vegetable matter for nourishment. The mineral and salt content of the muddy water is what affects the coloring of the birds – and the Yucatán's salts make for spectacular colors. The birds at Celestún are an electric pink and rose salmon. The first route is the one more clearly marked: Route 281 through Hunucmá, then 64 km to the bridge over Celestún's untroubled water. The second way is faster, more interesting and much narrower. Go south to Umán and follow the signs toward Celestún, through Samahil, then Kinchil, where you connect with Route 281, straight east to Celestún. If you ask directions anywhere in the Yucatán, forget about asking where highway number blah-blah is; Yucatecans don't think of these roads by route numbers.

As you cross the bridge of Celestún estuary, 25-foot launches with outboard motors line the banks and wooden pier on the far side. It is from here that canvas-roofed launches take tourists out into the shallow waters to see the flamingos, native and migratory birdlife (304 species have been identified) and a cenote in the mangrove jungle. In 1979, the Mexican government set aside the surrounding 15,000 acres of beach and mangrove jungle as a bird and nature sanctuary and its popularity as an ecological tourism destination increases each year. If you're planning to spend the night, not a bad idea, go straight to the beach and book a room. The beachfront is where all the town's hotels and restaurants are located.

Tour buses come here daily (leaves Santa Lucia Park at 9 a.m., returns to Mérida at 4:30 and includes a lunch) or you can come by public bus from Mérida (Autobuses de Occidente, Calles 50 and 67). The road to Celestún makes a good but long bike ride if you brought your own. Most guidebooks recommend viewing the birds early in the morning, but we found the late afternoon sun, with its golden-red glow, perfect for photography. Midday is hot.

The boat tours follow two routes. The first leaves from the beachfront on the Gulf, where you ride south in the surf along the pencil-thin peninsula and see an additional flamingo group, then around the point for a stop at a "petrified forest" near the entrance to the estuary. These boats then go on to the first large colony of flamingos north of the bridge, stop at the jungle cenote and return. It takes about three hours. The shorter tour (1½ hours) begins at the bridge and covers two or three massive flocks before stopping at the cenote (sometimes at an "extra" charge) on the way back. The boats, whose prices are more-or-less set by a unionized cooperative, take four to six people for about US $9 per person. Because the water is very shallow and the flamingos are at their best during the dry winter season, boats with four to six people can't always get very close. We rented a launch for two for US $30 and got our money's worth. Launch pilots no longer scare up the flocks for photographs so don't ask. It disturbs their feeding patterns, putting unnecessary stress on the colony.

The Gulf beach at Celestún is good for swimming, shell-collecting, fishing, beachcombing, or watching the frigate birds drift overhead while sitting in one of the many beachfront restaurants that spill out onto the sand.

La Palapa Restaurant is a favorite tour-bus stop, featuring a wooden boat bar and dining tables under an overhang on the beach. Good food at fair prices. The excellent **Restaurant Celestún** gets crowded with local folks chomping on fried fish. Murals of the sea decorate the walls. The cheapest place on the sand is **Restaurant La**

Boya, where locals hang, eating fish and drinking *cerveza*. Just inland across the street is a good inexpensive family restaurant, **Chemas**. At family-run **Restaurant La Playita**, owner Pedro "Pete" Avila Canul runs a tight ship serving delicious seafood to hungry hordes. We became addicted to *mojo de ajo* in the Yucatán, fish grilled with garlic and butter. Superb.

Accommodations

 Hotel María del Carmen (*Calle 12*, ☎ *991/6-20-51, 19 rooms with fans*). The María is the best of the few hotels in downtown Celestún. New in 1992, the beachfront complex added another story in 1997. All the rooms are the same, with small balconies facing the Gulf, tile floors and bathrooms that have hot water (a seaside luxury). A very popular hotel. If you're planning to stay overnight in Celestún and haven't made reservations, stop here first as it fills up fast. There is a well-liked restaurant in front of the hotel, the Villa del Mar, where you can ask owner Señora Carmen Gutiérrez for a room while savoring her good cooking. $$

Eco Paraíso Xixim (*Km 9 on the dirt road north from Celestún*, ☎ *991/6-21-00, fax 991/6-21-11, 15 cabañas with fans, beachfront, safety boxes, pool, tours, restaurant, bike rentals, rates include breakfast and dinner*). This seems to be a serious effort to balance the ecological impact of a hotel with its natural surroundings and still turn a profit. A sister hotel to the Eco Paraíso Caribe in Playa del Carmen, Xixim, which means "sea shell" in Mayan, markets itself as "state-of-the-art" ecological. The conch shell, Mexico's most famous seashell, was the Maya glyph symbol for zero (the Maya developed a numerical concept long before mathematicians in the Old World).

The cool, screen-windowed palapa guest cottages are all new (the hotel opened in December of 1996) with two double beds, seafront porches and gorgeous turquoise-tiled bathrooms. To save on water and waste, guests have the option of not having their sheets and towels changed daily – a painless and effective way to conserve. Electricity, which comes from a distant generator, is restricted to certain hours. Organic vegetables are grown on the 280-acre grounds using composted waste as fertilizer. Even the waste water here undergoes treatment and is recycled.

Most of the guests at Xixim (pronounced "Ish-shim") are Europeans who have bought six-day packages that include scheduled tours of the Celestún Biosphere, Uxmal and other Maya ruins, as well as some haciendas and cenotes. If they're not full you can buy a package or just take a bungalow for a night or two. Reservations strongly suggested. You'll need to slather on eco-friendly mosquito repellent, which they conveniently sell at reception. **$$**

Hotel Gutierrez (*Calle 12, ☎ 991/6-20-41, 15 rooms with fans*). This is a basic, spartan beachfront hotel, with a typical "what-you-see-is-what-you-get" attitude. The sea-view upstairs rooms are basic and acceptable, but they lack toilet seats. The bathroom walls have stains, but are clean. Its ideal location in the center of things on the beach – and the reasonable price – make it more attractive. There's a new construction between the Gutierrez and the María that looked as if it might be a new hotel, so let us know. The Gutierrez also has the local public phone. **$**

See page 3 for price chart.

Moving on around the Maya compass, we now head to the north, from where rain came.

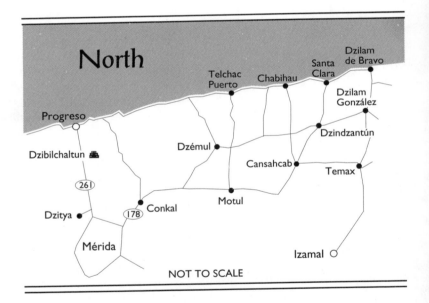

North - White
(Xaman Zac)

The big loop (Mérida to Progreso, along the coast to Dzilam de Bravo, then back through henequen plantations to Motúl and home to Mérida) may be a bit much to appreciate in one day. You might consider doing the ruins and Progreso one day and the coastal route and inland colonial cities on another. If you do go for it, leave early. If you're still shopping for that artisan's special gift, try stopping a few miles north of Mérida in **Dzitya**, to visit in the shops where craftspeople work. Ask to hear the stones that ring at the church.

Dzibilchaltún

The Paseo de Montejo becomes a major highway from Mérida north to the timeworn port of Progreso. The road is a wide, four-lane highway past the giant henequen factory and the flatlands of the north. Despite clearing the land for successive boom-and-bust plantings of sugar cane and henequen, the large Maya ruined city of Dzibilchaltún (tsee-beel-chahl-TOON), where some 20,000 people once lived, was not "discovered" until 1941. Although the interest to casual visitors isn't intense, it is an important archeological site, continually occupied from B.C. 800 until after the Spanish Conquest.

The Mexican Government spent a large amount of money on the new museum at Dzibilchaltún ("Where There is Writing on Flat Stones"). In addition to collected stelae and some of the figures found at the site, the museum features a reproduction of a Maya village where attendants demonstrate traditional folk arts and crafts. It's worth a visit while you're here.

The most interesting area of the spread-out ruins (8,400 rubble structures in 19 square km/7.6 square miles) includes the famous **Temple of the Seven Dolls** as well as a small Terminal Classic building (**Structure 38**) and a **stone chapel** built by the Spanish, circa 1590. Seven clay figurines, each with some deformity, were placed under the temple floor, thereby giving it its name. Possibly these "dolls" were used in ceremonies to cure illness, but no one really knows. The long *sacbé* that leads through the open fields to the temple is a very crunchy white road not to be walked in the heat of the day. Several nature trails have been cut into the scrub forest around the site and they make a great alternative to the *sacbé* that leads to the temple or a worthy shady hike on their own. Pick up the booklet, available in the museum, about birds and plants along the trail. It ends at a pleasant cenote not far from the entrance. The 40-meter-deep (132 feet) **Cenote Xlacah** goes down at a slant and is now a public swimming hole and pleasing picnic area. A *National Geographic* expedition once recovered nearly 30,000 Maya ceremonial artifacts from its cool waters. "Wear a swimsuit," advises a sign.

Tours and taxis will get you there. It's 15 km(9.3 miles) north of Mérida and four km east. The bus to the village of Chanculob (one km/.62 miles from the ruins) leaves from the terminal downtown at Calle 62 between 65 and 67.

Progreso

 If it weren't for the hordes of *Meridaños* escaping the summer heat in town, Progreso might have descended into another sleepy Gulf coast village. Founded in the late 1800s to replace the port of Sisal, which proved inadequate for the booming Yucatecan henequen trade, the port prospered until the decline of the fiber at the end of the First World War. Like Sisal and Campeche before it, the long limestone shelf under its harbor inhibits its ability to function as a deep-sea port. Today, the shallow harbor can't accommodate the deeper draft of many modern ships, although Progreso is able to export sisal, honey, cement, fish and salt in smaller freighters. To continue its role as a shipping port and to attract cruise ships, the government has built a long pier (*muelle*) seven km (4.3 miles) out into the Gulf. One of the longest wharves in the world, on a hazy day it's hard to see the end from the shoreline. It makes a great walk or bike ride but big trucks occasionally rumble by. There isn't a stitch of shade so don't go out during the sunny midday. Even with the pier, the Gulf waters are still too shallow for the gigantic cruise ships that float into Cozumel. Consequently, it hasn't been able to attract that kind of tourism. City fathers are hoping the ships will dock farther out and send passengers in on launches, but so far few cruise lines have expressed interest.

The long pier at Progreso.

*Why can't the captain of a vessel keep a memorandum
of the weight of his anchor, instead of weighing it
every time he leaves port?*

– George Prentice, 1802-1870

The shallow waters that restrict shipping make for great swimming in warm, protected waters. You can walk out into the gentle surf for a great distance before the water even reaches your waist. The wide beach is a favorite spot for Progreso's many fiestas. The *malecón*, which runs east from the *muelle*, is a broad boulevard, home to several good restaurants and a seawall with sidewalks for walking and people-watching.

Besides sea and surf, Progreso is not a particularly worthwhile spot for an extended vacation. It's not all that clean and the folks don't go out of their way to make you feel welcome. Even the **tourist information** is in an awkward spot: Calle 30 and on the way out of town! The best view of the city is from the old white **faro** (lighthouse), built around 1890. Open to the public. Tip the keeper or whoever lets you up. Across the street is an interesting and busy *mercado*, where we often eat in a corner stand, **Loncheria El Angelito**, family-owned for 14 years on the corner of 80 and 27. Another favorite is **Riko's Restaurant and Pizza**, nearby on 80. The absolute cleanest place in town is **Riko's Loncheria** (must be many Rikos here), Calle 68 and 29, four blocks off the beach and three blocks east of the big Telemex microwave towers. Along the *malecón* there are several good seafood restaurants, better looking than the places in town. The one with the best ambiance is **Le Saint Bonnet**, which offers a good menu, but hardly French food.

Hotel pickings in the city are skimpy. Try the **Hotel San Miguel**, Calle 78, a decent place for around US $15, or the basic and clean **Hotel Progreso**, Calle 29 No. 142. Several other **hotels** along the *malecón* are worth looking at. There's also a **supermarket**, San Francisco de Asis, in town. Many well-to-do beachgoers go to **Yukalpetén**, the next town west, where summer homes abound. It is accessible by a paved turnoff before you reach Progreso from Mérida. The **Hotel Sian Ka'an** is on a sand road along the beach.

The Coast Road

As refuge from the harsh cold of Canada and the US in the winter, many *Norteamericanos* own homes or condominiums outside Progreso on the warm waters of the Gulf. They're known as "snowbirds." A 74-km (46-mile) paved road scoots along the northern coast of the Yucatán from Progreso east to Dzilam de Bravo, then turns inland.

It's a fun day trip from Mérida in a car that goes through some places most tourists never see. For the first part of the coastline you have to do as we did: criticize the architecture, from garish to superb, of the many expensive homes that line the shore.

Chicxucub Puerto is the first town you come to, seven km (4.5 miles) east of Progreso. One of the few hotel offerings in condominium-heavy town is the **Chu-Huc-Maria Hotel** (*Calle 25, no phone, 28 rooms with fans, room service, pool*). Up a side road, three blocks from the beach, this is a standard Mexican hotel, with beds and bathrooms (cold water only) and overhead fans. It was new in 1990, so its rooms are in good shape, reasonably clean and in a pleasant setting. About US $15 gets you a decent modern room. Heading east you'll pass through several small fishing villages as the expensive homes peter out and wildlife and sea birds take their place. The next fair-size village is **Telhac Puerto**. You'll come to a little harbor first where a commercial fishing fleet is based. They pack the boats like sardines, tightly woven together, when they're in dock (good photo op). When they're out to sea, it's 15 days at a time. The inland lagoon to which the harbor connects is **Laguna Rosada**, a flamingo nesting area.

The **Pauula Beach Camping**, just after Telchac and before the village of Chabihau, has clean and appealing beachfront primitive spots and you can always ask for a room in the house. The deserted beaches are great for beachcombing and swimming. If you started in Mérida, about now you're hungry again. **Santa Clara** is a charming little fishing village with an appealing inexpensive beachfront hotel, **Hotel Playa Azul** (look for a little sign) and a good seafood restaurant, **Restaurante La Morena**. Latin rock and roll accompanies some great-tasting ceviche as a free *antojito* (appetizer) if you're having beer, or you can order it as meal (enough for two). The other menu item is whole fried fish accompanied by tortillas and a tasty cabbage salad. A local hang-out for fisherman and locals, this makes a welcome break. The beaches are fine for swimming here.

The coast road ends in the fishing village called **Dzilam de Bravo**, where the infamous pirate Jean Lafitte is allegedly buried, along with his brother, Pierre, in the local cemetery. According to legend, Jean was buried under a wooden grave marker found with his name inscribed, although there is no record of his return after he left the Yucatán in 1826. His brother Pierre, however, is buried there. Both pirates were popular with local fishermen because of their kindness. There's a lighthouse at the end of town. If you're out for more than a day-trip, launches hired from Dzilam will take passengers along the coast into the **Parque Natural San Felipe** to see *ojos de aqua*, as well as awesome flocks of pink flamingos and waterbirds galore. There is an inexpensive hotel, **Hotel Dzilam**.

YUCATECAN RECIPES

Ceviche (say-beach-ay)

Ingredients: *2 cups of assorted seafood, 1 tomato, 1 white onion, 2 seeded jalapeño peppers (fresh), 2 cloves of garlic, sea salt to taste.*

Mexican fishermen often prepare this snack at the water's edge from their fresh catch. Eaten with crackers, together with some tequila or beer, it is a pleasurable snack. A variety of seafood can be used to make ceviche, so each batch is unique. Start with a small amount at first, adapting the proportions of ingredients.

Cut skinned and boned raw fish, any kind will do, plus shrimp, oysters, clams or whatever you have available into tiny bite-size pieces until you have about two cup's worth. Place in a ceramic bowl and cover with the juice of two limes. Stir and set aside.

Chop very finely all other ingredients. You'll need sea salt to taste. Add this to the seafood. Optionals: a dash of bottled hot sauce, pepper, cilantro (dried or fresh), even oregano or parsley flakes can add a nice flavor. Marinate at least 10 minutes before serving, longer, if you have the patience. Ceviche is customarily eaten with toothpicks.

Pollo Pibil (Chicken Pibil)

Ingredients: *1 large chicken cut into serving-size pieces (leg, breast, etc.), 3 banana leaves (if not available, we used a "brown and serve" bag with great success; aluminum foil can also be substituted), 1 cup of vinegar, 1 cup of bitter orange juice, 1 white onion (medium-size, roasted), 4 garlic cloves, 8 black peppercorns, 10 grams achiote (hard to find in powdered form in many parts of the US; substitute "Sazon" seasoning with achiote packaged by Goya Foods, available in most supermarkets), ¼ cup oil, salt to taste.*

Blend roasted onion, crushed garlic cloves, peppercorns and orange juice. Pour mixure into bowl together with the oil and achiote, previously dissolved in vinegar. Marinate the chicken pieces in the mixture for 10 minutes. Wrap them in a bed of banana leaves (or substitute). Bake in a medium oven (375°) for 30 minutes or until steam escapes when bundles are pierced. Usually served topped with pickled red onion rings. Makes about six servings.

The narrow paved road inland leads through huge henequen plantations and cattle ranches. This area is chock full of ancient haciendas, some ruined, others still working. We spent some time on this trip chasing chimneys to find old abandoned haciendas.

The crescent of the limestone shelf here in the north is one of the Yucatán's larger *Zona de Cenotes*. A preliminary survey of the state counted over 600 cenotes as possible tourist attractions. In the crossroads town of **Dzilam González** (with a tasty bakery, La Rosita Panaderia), you can turn right to the colonial town of **Dzindzantún**, with a detailed 16th-century church and ex-convent, or go straight south to the larger town of **Temax**, a center for hand-embroidered *huipiles*. Either way, the road back to Mérida is then through **Cansahcab**, another colonial town with a rich folk history. An even richer history and a fascinating city on its own (worth revisiting if you're not too tired by now), is **Motúl**. This colonial city, populated with Maya, 51 km (32 miles) northeast of Mérida, is the birthplace of Felipe Carrillo Puerto, the Socialist reform governor of the Yucatán, assassinated at the behest of reactionary *hacendados* before his planned wedding to American journalist Alma Reed.

Motúl retains some of the tragic romanticism of that story. The town is very clean and well maintained and the airy main plaza features a freshly painted white and green **Palacio Municipal** (a museum dedicated to Carrillo located in his former home), several good restaurants and beautifully decorated horse-drawn carriages that serve as the town's taxis.

The **Hotel Motúl**, on the square above the Banco del Atlantico, seemed suitable for a night's stay. We found two strong reasons for a stop in Motúl. **Restaurant Zac Motúl** serves up air-conditioned comfort and good Yucatecan food in the middle of Motúl's pretty square. It's like eating at a good diner with big windows to watch the world go by. A large circular palapa restaurant, **Cenote Sambula** (Calle 43, about 8 blocks south of the *zócalo*), opened in December of 1996 but the cenote below it – where you can swim free – has been around for eons. The cenote is in a cave, with broad colonial-style cement steps down to a solid cement floor. Legend holds that it once hid Felipe Carrillo and his supporters when the *federales* were searching for him during the Mexican Revolution. Changing cubicles are provided. The clear green waters disappear farther into the cave and brave swimmers can swim inside where there is light from another opening. Did we mention that the food at the restaurant is Yucatecan and delicious and cheap? There are plenty of signs around town advertising this newly popular eatery. Motúl's annual celebration for their patron saint, Juan Bautista, is held on July 16.

If you spend the night in Motúl or plan a separate visit you could include the Maya ruins at **Aké**, south of Motúl through Tixkokob and Ekmul. This sleeper of a ruin, the last one to be visited by Stephens and Catherwood in their second trip of 1842, is hardly ever visited by tourists. It's an Early Classic city in an open field, best known for Structure 1, a pyramidal base supporting a platform with 36 standing stone pillars. Some of the massive stone blocks on the 150-foot-wide stairway from the ancient plaza are over 6.6 feet long and as many wide. How were these enormous heavy blocks quarried, moved and put in place? Mysteries of the Maya. There's a henequen factory nearby.

South - Yellow
(Kan Nohol)

 There are three basic routes into the Yucatán's *kan nohol* with its natural wonders, colonial architecture and Maya sites: Route 180 south toward Campeche, which cuts over to Muna and Uxmal and the Ruta Puuc; directly south on Route 261 through Muna to Uxmal; or meandering down the Convent Route through colonial towns to Oxkutzcab and the Ruta Puuc. Best choice? Do them all.

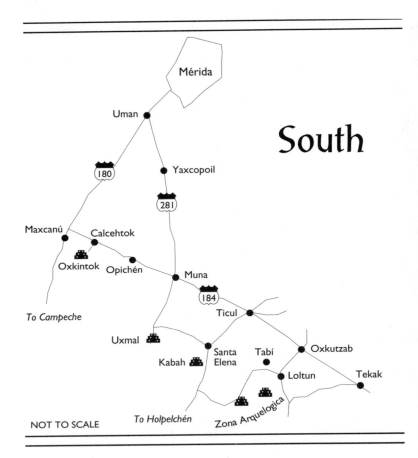

South

NOT TO SCALE

Umán & Oxkintok

 Seventeen km (10.6 miles) southwest of Mérida, at the end of a wide road through an industrial area, lies the colonial city of **Umán**, on Route 180 to Campeche. Here you'll find the massive domed 16th-century church of **San Francisco de Asis** and on the outskirts is the **Hacienda de la Palma**, where there is an antique car collection. From Umán there are two choices south: to Muna and Uxmal direct, covered below, or south for 48 km (30 miles) to **Maxcanú** and the ruins of **Oxkintoc**, retracing the route John Lloyd Stephens followed to Uxmal in 1841. If you're coming up from Campeche, this side road is an interesting detour on the way to Mérida or Uxmal. Follow the sign for Calcehtok and Opichén, near where the railroad tracks cross the highway, on a narrow road along the base of the Puuc hills. In **Calcehtok**, a very typical Maya village, there are signs to turn south for the ruins and caves (*grutas*).

Oxkintoc, which means "Three Day Flint," was a large and important Maya city occupied for 1,400 years between B.C. 300 and A.D. 1100. The 11 large temple mounds spread over many acres are just being excavated by INAH, so you may see workers under the supervision of Mexican archeologists. One of the largest, from the Early and Late Classic periods, is called the "Labyrinth." When John Lloyd Stephens (who seemed to be everywhere first) went to visit a "cave" near Maxcanú, he was actually led to this Oxkintoc mound whose subterranean construction had a "marvelous and mystical reputation." Stephens went on to explain that, *"The universal belief was that it contained passages without number and without end."* He became the first man to discover that these passages and chambers were man-made, not natural. Entrance is on the west side. Bring a flashlight, water and a sun hat. Some of the material found at the site is now displayed in the Mérida Museum.

A good guide to the Labyrinth at Oxkintoc is **Roger Cuy**, a long-time caretaker of the ruins. He lives close-by and can be contacted by the **Al Parador Restaurant and Cabañas** back down the road in Calcehtok. This appealing little new restaurant (no phone), with primitive overnight cabañas and a cool swimming pool, is hoping to lure visitors stopping at the ruins. There are no facilities at Oxkintoc, so the friendly Parador is a very welcome way station. The beer here is ice cold and the Yucatecan food is delicious.

Roger is also the man to have as a guide to the caves that Stephens missed: the **Grutas Calcehtok** (the Mayan name, *Xpokil*). At the end of the paved road, only one or two km (1.25 miles) past the turn into the ruins, is a parking area and turn-around where a marked path leads to the big hole in the ground. A metal ladder descends into a secret oasis of green vegetation – banana trees and jungle plants – all hidden 20 feet or so below the rocky limestone ground. At one end of the depression is a large, rock-strewn cavern that slants down to another, deeper oasis, where shafts of light from openings above are like spotlights on the dark floor. At the foot of this cave, natural tunnels lead off into as much as eight km (five miles) of underground blackness. A boulder at the entrance to the cave advises contacting Roger if you really want to explore, but we were happy simply to climb down the ladder and peek inside.

Continue on through Opichén to Muna, then south to Uxmal or north back to Mérida, or perhaps straight to Ticul.

Uxmal & The Ruta Puuc

... I had seen seven different places of ruins, memorials of cities which had been and had passed away and such memorials as no cities built by Spaniards in that country could present.

– John Lloyd Stephens, on his way to revisit Uxmal, 1841

 The direct route to Uxmal, perhaps the most striking and beautiful ruined Maya city in the Yucatán, runs south on Route 261 from Umán through Muna, then straight ahead to Uxmal. About one-third of the way along 261 is the restored hacienda, Yaxcopoil. After Uxmal and nearby Kabáh, there is a series of ruined Maya cities along a route often referred to as the "Ruta Puuc," named after its proximity to the Puuc hills. In combination, these spectacular ruins represent some of the most provocative examples of Classic Maya architecture in the rococo Puuc style. A quick nip farther south on 261 will bring you to the **Gruta de Xtacumbilxunán,** past Bolonchén (see "Two Routes North," page 244). Remember that video cameras at all archeological and museum sites require an extra fee, while tripods are banned and, in most cases, so is a flash.

AUTHORS' NOTE: If you're planning to spend the night at Uxmal or Santa Elena to see Uxmal's light and sound show, you may prefer to do this route in reverse, starting at the Loltún caves for their first tour (9 or 9:30 a.m.), then following the ruins route backwards. To reach Loltún first, drive Hwy 261 to Muna. Turn left on 184. It's about 65 km (40 miles) to Oxkutzcab. Or combine this with the Convent Route (follow the signs south from Oxkutzcab to Loltún).

The beautiful **hacienda Yaxcopoil** is a restored 17th-century sisal hacienda converted into a museum recreating life as it was for the wealthy *hacendados*. The family that owned it for generations left in the 1950s and the interior has been kept as it was, complete with copper pots in the white-tiled kitchen. The vast estate grew henequen and the museum shows how it was worked into fiber. Original furniture and kitchen utensils on the inside, the exterior of the mansion has a decidedly French influence and it's not surprising that, with its tall, distinctive, Moorish-style double entry arch, it has been used as a film set. About 15 km (9.3 miles) south of Umán, it's a worthwhile diversion, as is the Hacienda San Ildefonso Teya, just east of Mérida.

TIE ME UP, TIE ME DOWN

Such hath it been – shall be – beneath the sun
The many still must labor for the one.
– Lord Byron, 1788 -1824

Henequen is one of the versatile plants in the huge agave family whose plant leaf fibers are used to make cord and rope. Agaves are also used to produce the alcoholic drink, *pulque,* and tequila is fermented from yet another variety. The pulp of other kinds are used as food and to produce soap. You'll see rolling fields of the spiny plants behind rock walls all over northern Yucatán. The other name for them is *sisal* (see-sal) after the Yucatán port.

The plants have leaves up to six feet long and a flower stalk up to 40 feet in height, blooming only once and then dying. They take five to 10 years to mature (lives can be prolonged by cutting some leaves each year). The sword-like leaves are from 30 to 60 inches long and four to five inches wide, ending in sharp points. They are cut by hand, trimmed of their top spine and side needles. One person and helper can cut from 3,000 to 5,000 leaves in a day.

Narrow gauge railways were once employed to transport the bundled leaves to a plantation mill. Now trucks and tractors handle most of that task. At the mill, machines beat and scrape the pulp from the fiber, which is then dried in the sun or in drying machines, and sorted into grades according to length and quality. Originally used in agriculture balers, more recently the natural fiber has found a home in furniture manufacturing.

During the period the Yucatán was the sole source of henequen, extensive plantations allowed hacienda owners to amass enormous fortunes, leading to an economic boom that transformed the countryside.

To provide labor, much of the Indian population was forced into debt peonage – the equivalent of slavery. Today, Tanzania, Brazil and Kenya are the main sources of better quality sisal, though the Yucatán still produces a large amount of commercial henequen.

A place to eat in Muna, **Restaurant Chun Yaax-Che**, brags that it serves the "best food in the Yucatán." Up a sidestreet before the central plaza, it does offer good cooking served on linen tablecloths. Mainly for tour bus lunches, the restaurant (with gift shop) specializes in *pollo pibil*, chicken wrapped in banana leaves and baked in a pit grill. If there's a bus parked near there, you might like to stop and eat. *Pibil* is made only in advance.

Uxmal

> *From its front doorway I counted sixteen elevations with broken walls, mounds of stones and vast, magnificent edifices, which at that distance seemed untouched by time and defying ruin. I stood in the doorway when the sun went down, throwing from the buildings a prodigious breadth of shadow, darkening the terraces presenting a scene strange enough for a work of enchantment.*

– John L. Stephens describing the vista from the top of the Pyramid of the Magicians, 1840

Uxmal (oosh-MAL) means "Three Times Built" – although there is evidence that there were five building periods – and it is one of the peninsula's most beautiful ruined Maya cities. Not quite as grandiose as Chichén Itzá, Uxmal is more magnificent in an ornate Puuc style. Puuc architecture is characterized by finely shaped limestone veneers applied to lime-based concrete over block. The lower facades of Puuc buildings are typically plain, but intricate mosaics decorate the elaborate upper facades. Among the most common motifs are criss-cross lattices, geometric designs, monster serpents and masks.

The city reached its peak of grandeur during the Late and Terminal Classic periods as a contemporary of the great southern city-states of Palenque and Tikal. Unlike many of the Maya ruins, the existence of Uxmal never faded from collective memory. Its existence was first recorded by Europeans when a Spanish priest, Diego López de Cogullado, wrote about it only 15 years after the Conquest. The imposing ceremonial city had been abandoned by the Maya in the late 10th century, with a brief resurgence in the Terminal Classic period by either Toltecs or Itzá Maya or their combination. One persistent theory about Uxmal holds that its location – in a very dry area – was eventually responsible for its downfall. Uxmal is one of the few Classic Maya cities not built near a cenote, but the people overcame that severe disadvantage by building *chultunes*, cistern-style reservoirs that held rainwater. Chac, the rain god, was understandably important to the residents of these arid hills and his image appears frequently.

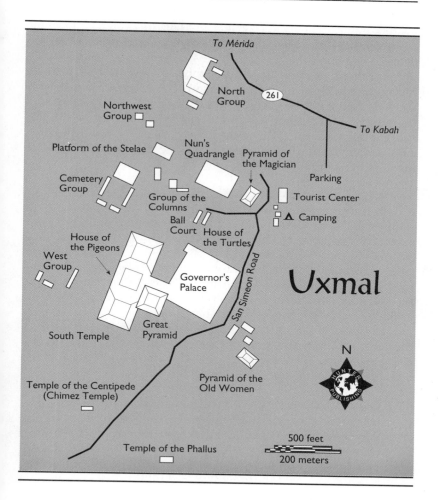

Uxmal's showpiece ruins have added a 45-minute sound and light show during the winter months, one in Spanish at 7 p.m. and one at 9 p.m. in English. We found the experience worthwhile. Colored lights highlight intricate facade features in the Nunnery Quadrangle and color spotlights illuminate the hill-top Governor's Palace and Great Pyramid. The background music adds a regal ambiance. However, in recreating the myths of the Maya and Uxmal, the storyline becomes somewhat disjointed, and we found it possible to see the show in Spanish and still enjoy it.

THE PYRAMID OF THE MAGICIAN: El Adivino is the first majestic structure you'll come across after entering through a new visitors' center. The dwarf-sorcerer in Maya folklore who built the pyramid that bears his name was a mythical figure who hatched from an egg and grew to maturity in one year. The pyramid has a unique shape with a base that appears oval but is actually rectangular, with severely rounded corners and steep sides up to its 100-foot height. What you see now is the fifth construction, each building period adding to and covering the previous. With a stupendous view, the climb to the top is difficult. If you venture up, climb down the other side. Interesting Chac masks flank the fourth level stairway on the west side.

THE NUNNERY QUADRANGLE: This building got its name from a 16th-century priest who thought its 70-odd cell-like rooms reminiscent of an austere convent. Four rectangular buildings flank a compact courtyard. The smaller structure on the east bears a painted capstone with a date of A.D. 907 and the name of Lord Chac, believed responsible for building the Nun's Quadrangle, the Ball Court and possibly the Governor's Palace. The detail on the second-story structure is incredible and is where you see the 1,000-year-old depiction of traditional *na* houses.

A complex of buildings on a rise south of the Quadrangle includes the compact **Turtle House**, a little temple with decorations of turtles along its facade. Turtles were associated with the god Chac because both man and turtles need rain to survive.

THE GOVERNOR'S PALACE: Overlooking the Turtle House, this is a masterpiece of Maya architecture. The exquisite structure, originally three connected buildings, is built upon a natural platform high above the surrounding city. From here a *sacbé* runs to Kabáh, one of the nearby cities thought to be under Uxmal's influence. That *sacbé* was first thought to be the reason the building is at a slight angle to the others but it has been found that the large central doorway, with its elaborate carvings on the lintel, is in perfect alignment with the planet Venus. The upper facade of this well-preserved building is woven with corner Chac masks, lattice work designs and human figures in detailed headdresses that make its decor truly magnificent. When Stephens saw it he wrote: *"... as the stranger ascends the steps and casts a bewildered eye along its open and desolate doors, it is hard to believe that he sees before him the work of a race in whose epitaph –* as written by historians – they are called ignorant of art. If it stood... in Hyde Park or the Garden of Tuileries, it would form a new *order... not unworthy to stand side by side with the remains of Egyptian, Grecian and Roman art."*

THE GREAT PYRAMID has been partially restored and it gleams white against the green jungle. Although not as impressive as other structures at Uxmal, it's a great spot for photography. View the well-preserved step mask in the interior temple and the corner Chac masks in its profusion of decorations, including depictions of the sun god. Below it is the **House of the Doves** and a plaza layout similar to the Nun's Quadrangle, but not as well preserved.

ACCOMMODATIONS & DINING

Misión Uxmal (*Km 78 Mérida-Campeche,* ☎ *in US, 800-448-8355,* ☎ *& fax in Mexico, 99/24-73-08, 70 rooms with fans, restaurant, pool*). The three-story hacienda-style Misión has rooms with large balconies or patios that face the Uxmal ruins about a half-mile away. The top floors offer views of the ruined structures popping up above the jungle. A word of caution: the balcony railings are too low and feel unsteady. And it's a long drop to the ground. Very dangerous.

The huge teardrop-shaped pool is magnificent, perhaps the best we found in the Yucatán, but otherwise there's little to do in the evening except sleep – if only the mattresses weren't so torturously hard. El Mestizo restaurant downstairs serves delicious food and has attentive waiters. Local woodworker, Carlos Cancino Baaz, sells his carving and native art wares daily near the pool. If you're seeking out-of-the-way places nearby, ask him about serving as your guide. He knows his way around but speaks only Spanish or Mayan. **$$**

Villas Arqueológicas - Uxmal (*next to the ruins at Uxmal, 40 rooms with air,* ☎ *& fax 99/28-06-44, pool, restaurant, tennis courts*). A mirror image, approximately, of its sister hotels in Cobá and Chichén. All the Villas are Club Med properties, but none is all-inclusive. Only a few steps from the ruins. See our review of Chichén Itzá's Villas hotel, page 300. **$$**

Hotel Hacienda Uxmal (*next to the ruins at Uxmal,* ☎ *in US and Canada, 800-235-4079, in Mexico, 99/25-06-21, fax 99/25-00-87, 80 rooms with air or fans, 2 pools, 3 restaurants.*) The oldest hotel in Uxmal, Mayaland's Hotel Hacienda housed the archeologists who worked at uncovering the impressive Maya ruins across the street. Big bright bedrooms are highlighted by tile floors, large bathrooms, Spanish furniture and two comfortable queen-size beds, much like those in the Mayaland property in Chichén Itzá. The round palapa restaurant on the corner facing the ruin's entrance is very appealing. **$$$**

Rancho Uxmal (*Km 70 Highway 261, no phone, for reservations,* ☎ *997/2-02-77, 20 rooms with air or fans, pool, restaurant*). If you're not into the bigger bucks of Uxmal's big three hotels, stay here. It's about three km (1.9 miles) up the road and half the price. Pleasant plain

rooms in this simple hacienda-style hotel are perfectly acceptable for a night, or you can camp in back where there are electrical hookups. $
See page 3 for price chart.

Camping Sacbé Bungalows (*Santa Elena, 16 km/10 miles south of Uxmal, 7 km/4.3 miles north of Kabáh, no phone, 3 bungalows, hammock, tent and trailer sites, restaurant*). An excellent alternative to staying at Uxmal is the next town south, Santa Elena (once known by its Mayan name, *Nohcacab*). Santa Elena has a fine old colonial church sitting high on a hill and the burned out ruins of an even older chapel, as well as a road back to Ticul, if you're not going to the other Ruta Puuc ruins. Shortly south of the turnoff into town is Camping Sacbé, with several attractive guest cabins. In 1990, Edgardo Portillo and his French wife, Annette, cleared the land for their dream business, a family campground. They created the most pleasant and tidy campground we found in the Yucatán. Flowering cactus and plants accent level lawns and the three private bungalow *casitas* are immaculately clean. Delicious Mexican meals with a fine French flair are served in a lovely screened palapa next to a huge flowering cactus bush. In the heart of the Ruta Puuc, between important ruins, Sacbé makes an ideal base for explorations. Edgardo is full of information and can direct you to cenotes and ruins that tourists never see. A best buy. Buses stop out front. To visit the Maya ruins of **Sacbé** (*Mascarón*) or to see the overgrown Uxmal-Kabáh *sacbé* that runs behind the campground, ask for guide Emilio Santos Camal in Santa Elena.

Colonial Church,
Santa Elena.

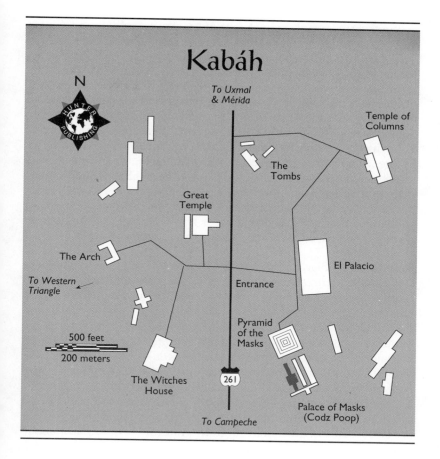

Kabáh

N

To Uxmal
& Mérida

Temple of
Columns

The
Tombs

Great
Temple

The Arch

El Palacio

To Western
Triangle

Entrance

500 feet

200 meters

Pyramid
of the
Masks

The Witches
House

261

Palace of Masks
(Codz Poop)

To Campeche

Ruta Puuc

Man himself is a visitor who does not remain.

– anonymous statement in proposed
environmental legislation in the USA

KABAH: Straddling both sides of the highway south of
Santa Elena are the ruins of Kabáh, which means "He of
the Strong Hand." All the ruins are close to the road,
with the majority of buildings on the east side (the left
if you're traveling south). The best of this interesting site, connected

by the *sacbé* to Uxmal, is the **Palace of Masks** or **Codz Poop** ("Coiled Mat"), a Mayan name referring to the resemblance between the curled snouts of the Chac masks (that also serve as steps to the inner rooms) and a rolled-up sleeping mat. The 148-foot-long building rests on a high terrace platform and absolutely bursts with 300 Chac masks, all with hooked noses. So many identical masks would seem to show a baroque ostentation, as if Kabáh's architects wanted to one-up larger Uxmal. Other buildings on the east side near the Codz Poop are the **Temple of Columns**, famous for rows of semi-columns on the upper part of the facade, and **El Palacio**, the Palace. Across the street on the west side you'll pass the rubble mound of the **Principal Teocalis**, or Great Temple. Climbing is not recommended because of loose stones. Farther up the dirt path is a restored vaulted stone arch that it marks the end, or the beginning, of the *sacbé* to Uxmal. The arch at Labná is grander and in better shape.

SAYIL: The "Place of the Ants," Sayil, offers a fair number of standing structures stretching back on well-cleared paths as much as three-quarters of a mile from the road (although the best pieces are close). The left turn for the Puuc Highway is south of Kabáh and Sayil is about four km (2.5 miles) on the right. The most impressive building by far is a three-tiered palace mounted on a pyramidal base, **El Palacio**, considered another masterpiece of Maya architecture. The Classical-Greek-looking structure rises three stories and contains 94 rooms and a wide central staircase that divides the 280-foot length into two wings. You'll need a wide-angle lens to get a complete picture of this breathtaking building. The wide doorways are supported by thick, free-standing columns, with a frieze above showing images of the descending god (the Bee God) which Stephens described as a *"figure of a man supporting himself on his hands, with his legs expanded in a curious, rather delicate attitude."* At the northwest corner is a *chultun* that held as much as 7,000 gallons.

From the palace, an elevated *sacbé* filled with large stones stretches through the open field to **El Mirador**, currently under excavation and restoration by archeologists. Next to it is the elaborate but ruined **Temple of the Lintel**, with carved glyphs that decorate its facade. Sayil reached its peak (9,000 residents) in the Terminal Classic period. Check out the phallic stone idols lined up along the small structure near the palace or on the **stelae** beyond El Mirador. If you read Stephens' colorful book he mentions the **Well of Chac**, near Sayil, and tells of his harrowing descent to the water level of this deep cavern, depended upon as a community water source as late as the 1950s. The ropes and ladders to the vertical shaft part are rotted away, but extremely curious people will find it 500 feet southeast of the Km 30 marker on the road, up a foot trail. To go beyond the opening to the vertical shaft would be foolhardy. Two good **guides** to the area are Miguel Uc Medina, at Sayil, and Emilio Santos Camal in Santa Elena. (Ask local residents.)

XLAPAK: This is a small site, about six km (3.75 miles) past Sayil, with only one building worth seeing – **Structure I**, also called the "Palace." There are sets of three Chac masks on the corners of the upper facade, with their noses curled up, while each Chac mask above the doorways has proboscis that curls down. The name in Mayan means "Old Walls."

LABNA: Labná is best known for its magnificent arched portal, once connected to a structure that separated two quadrangle courtyards, each of which was surrounded by buildings (now rubble). The corbeled **Arch** (10' x 19') rests on a small platform flanked by two doorways into small side rooms. The west face features decorative moldings of undulating zig-zags and above these are depictions of thatched-roof Maya huts (*nas*) with lattice work accents. In the niche doorways, seated figures are thought to have existed.

The **Palace** is the first building you come to when you enter, built during the Late Classic period around A.D. 850. Not in as good a condition as the Palace at Sayil, this one has a built-in second-story *chultun* and a sculpture of a serpent gripping a human head in its gaping jaw at the eastern corner. Based on the 60 chultunes in and around Labná – "Old House of Women" – archeologists believe that 3,000 Maya once lived here.

There are several other interesting sites in the area, including **Chuncatzim I, Huntichmul** and **Sabacché**, but these are for die-hard amateur archeologists. See "Sayil," above for the name of two local guides if you want to retrace Stephens' visits.

TABI: As the Puuc Highway snakes away from the cluster of ruins toward Cooperativa, orange groves flank the roadway. Approximately four km (2.5 miles) after Labná is a small sign for Tabi, an astonishing hacienda hidden way back on a nature preserve behind the orange groves and anchiote trees. You may have to ask for directions from agricultural workers because it is not well marked. Just before you give up, the entrance appears on a bumpy road into a tall forest. After creeping along the driveway with slits of light slicing between the trees, you come to an amazing sight – an absolutely huge golden yellow hacienda across several acres of lawn in the middle of nowhere. There's not a sound except for the forest birds and hot breeze in the leaves. Tabi is being restored by the

Foundation Cultural Yucatán, a non-profit organization that is hoping to create a cultural center on the 3,900-acre site (10% of its original size).

The 17th-century hacienda is in excellent shape, with a big red-flowering bougainvillea plant gracing the front. Its history began with growing corn, cotton and tobacco in the good soil of the area. Spared by the violence of the Caste War, around 1850 it began sugar-cane production that developed into an excellent business. By 1900, Tabi had been transformed into the spectacular home we see today. As many as 2,500 workers lived on the hacienda property during that time and many of the nearly 500 household and ground servants were Chinese. Eulogio Duarte, the strong-willed *hacendado* who ran the hacienda at its zenith in a style reminiscent of times gone by, died in 1905. His family was unable to cope with the fall in sugar prices combined with the stresses of the Mexican Revolution and by 1907 abandoned it as a working plantation.

It changed owners several times until the Foundation picked up the property in 1992. The kitchen looks as if the last owner had just left and the Maya caretaker is particularly proud of the library. Modern bathrooms have been installed in the upstairs bedrooms where the floors are beautifully tiled in intricate and colorful floral designs and the ceilings are a lofty 16.5 feet. For a small fee you can join the ghosts of the past and sleep overnight in a hammock – a real adventure! Nobody visits here and that's both a blessing and a shame. It's a fabulous place to explore, one that still breathes history. If you visit, the caretaker will show you the property with its ruined chapel (a massive brown beehive hangs in the wooden eaves), a tall furnace chimney you can walk inside, and old sugar cane machinery. Please remember to tip. If the water is high maybe you can swim in one of the hacienda's old built-in swimming pools. Tabi is a total experience not to be missed. Once back on the roadway, turn left for Loltún and Oxkutzcab.

GRUTAS DE LOLTUN: So far, scientists know the history of the people of the Yucatán began here at Loltún Cave, where stone tools and animal remains were radiocarbon dated to B.C. 2200. It also contains some of the earliest ceramics on the peninsula, dating from around B.C. 700. Besides the fascinating natural underworld formations (Loltún means "Rock of Flowers"), there are cave paintings and stone carvings, including a crude imitation Olmec-style head. There are several glyph-carved door jambs and an erect stone phallus on display outside, but it's the splendid natural stalactites and stalagmites inside that capture the imagination. There's a restaurant and bathrooms. Tour guides sell snacks and water in the reception area. Tours (about US $6), the only way to see the caves, run at 9:30 a.m., 11:00, 12:30 p.m., 2 and 3, but double-check with the office. Closed Mondays.

Where you made a left to the caves of Loltún, a right would take you through Cooperativa, then a left to Kancab and a right to **Chacmultún**, a sleeper of a Maya ruin near Tekax that might prove attractive to can't-get-enough ruin enthusiasts. Its name means "Mounds Made of Red Stone," and its low, compact buildings, though not as impressive as Labná or Sayil, are fairly interesting. About 27 km (17 miles) from Loltún.

OXKUTZCAB: This bustling and clean Maya town is in the heart of Yucatán's agricultural district and the fertile soil in the area grows a large percentage of the peninsula's oranges. During the last week of October and first week of November the town erupts in **Orange Festival** festivities, when every day is a fiesta in the town square. The 16th-century church on the plaza is yet another beautiful colonial relic. If you're finishing up the Ruta Puuc or the Convent Route and you're hungry, **Su Cabaña Suiza** restaurant on Calle 54 is open until 6:30 p.m. This family-owned eatery specializes in Mexican and Yucatecan food prepared over charcoal fires. The smell of delicious grilled meats should get your juices flowing before you even enter the palapa-covered dining room. Tables and chairs outside also beckon. Very inexpensive.

The only hotel we know of in Oxkutzcab is **Los Tucanes Hotel** on Calle 64. Reportedly, archeologists working the ruins sometime stay here. See "Ticul," page 347, for the scoop on the three-wheeled bicycles, *triciclos*, that ply the narrow streets.

The Ruta Puuc and the next itinerary, the Convent Route, are arranged so that each can be completed in a day (albeit a long one). You may prefer to stay somewhere along the line and combine the two into a giant loop. A night in Uxmal, Santa Elena, Ticul, or even Tabi, takes the pressure off seeing and doing everything and still getting back to Mérida for the night.

The Convent Route

Hunting God is a great adventure.

– Marie De Floris OSB, to novice nuns making their vows

The third way from Mérida into the south of Yucatán is the meandering local road marked as **Route 18** on maps. Following this off-the-beaten-path itinerary takes you past ancient churches, convents, courtyards and cenotes. If you leave early, before 8 a.m., this makes a pleasant day trip by car. Or you can stay overnight somewhere along the Ruta Puuc for a great combination of Maya and colonial past.

From downtown, take Calle 67 east and rejoin 69 where it's two-way, then go over the bypass highway (*periférico*) and follow the signs for **Kanasin** (not Route 18) to Acanceh. The scrub forest you pass is the Cuxtal Ecological Preservation Zone. The first time we tried to take this route we got on the wrong road to begin with (by

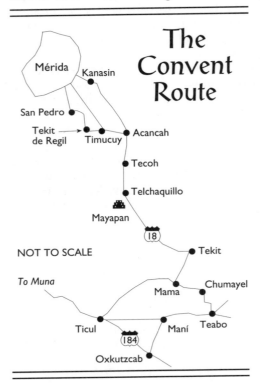

following Calle 42 south) and went through tiny towns, such as Tahdzibilichén and Tekit de Regil. Along the way we found some fascinating diversions, played soccer with local youth on the grounds of one of the several abandoned old haciendas and didn't even realize we were lost until we rejoined the "route" in Tecoh. To us, this simply proves there is much to discover on the little roads around Mérida, even if you don't have an entire day (and these side roads make great bike trips). The first village, 10 km/6.25 miles after Kanasin, is **San**

Antonio Tehuit, a working henequen plantation town. A few miles later is another sisal hacienda town, **Tepich**. Then it's off to Acanceh.

ACANCEH: The central plaza in the busy small village of Acanceh ("Moan of the Deer") hosts both colonial and modern churches, as well as a Maya ruin called the **Grand Pyramid**. About four blocks away are more ruins, including the **Temple of the Stuccoes**, with visible glyphs. Ask someone for directions; if they take you, tip five pesos or so. Acanceh is a total of 22 km (13.75 miles) from Kanasin.

TECOH: This town has a very ornate church and convent complex dedicated to the Virgin of the Assumption, built on the base of a large Maya pyramid. The carved stones, altar, carved statues and paintings are impressive. Tecoh has a *mercado* and a gas station. Eight km (5 miles) from Acanceh.

TELCHAQUILLO: Drive slowly or you'll miss this tiny village. The central plaza has an austere, but photogenic, Catholic church, with carved blocks from the ruined city of Mayapán used to build its walls. Designs on the block are still visible where the stucco has worn off the exterior. The little square across the street has a cenote with carved steps down into it. On Stephens' visit he commented that: *"Women, with their water jars, were constantly ascending and descending; swallows were darting through the cave in every direction and the whole formed a wild, picturesque and romantic scene."*

MAYAPAN: Only a few miles more and you'll come to the historical Maya city of Mayapán. The walled city, the size of Chichén Itzá, with 4,000 mounds, once ruled the northern Yucatán with an iron fist. Legend says that it was founded by the great Kukulcán from Chichén Itzá around A.D. 1000. The dynasty that resulted was the Cocom family, who joined in a federation with Chichén until a war between the two city-states resulted in Mayapán conquering the Itzás in 1221. Buoyed by their victory, the Cocom extracted tribute from other Maya cities and for two centuries consolidated their power. One method was to force members of the rival royal families to live as captives in Mayapán. This included the Xiú family from Uxmal, who finally led a general revolt and successfully sacked the city in the mid-1400s. It was immediately abandoned and never occupied again. The Xiú family founded a new capital at Maní but continually battled the surviving Cocoms for the next 100 years. Their mistrust of one another prevented them from driving out the European invaders. When Montejo successfully defended T'ho (Mérida) in 1542, the Xiú ruler made a fateful alliance with the

Spanish to once-and-for-all wipe out their ancient rivals, the Cocoms. Only too late did it become apparent to the Xiú that the price the Spanish would extract was subjugation of all Maya 100 years later.

Restoration is intense here because the ruins really are ruined. A visit here is a chance to see an ongoing archeological dig. With few visitors, Mayapán is a lonely site, as if the ruins themselves harbor a heavy heart over their role in the demise of the Maya.

Religious procession at Tekit.

TEKIT: Tekit, 30 km/19 miles on after a series of camel-backs past Mayapán, is a larger and more prosperous village. The Moorish-styled 16th-century parish church contains wall niches that house ornate statues of saints and there's an impressive wood *retablo* (altar).

MAMA: Next on the route, seven km (4.3 miles) down the road, is Mama, a small village even your mother would appreciate. Its famous bell-gabled church, thought to be the oldest on the route, features a large garden, a well with a closed atrium, frescos and a baroque altar. As you pass through the village, notice the number of little houses that have Corinthian columns holding up front porches. A mark of status. From Mama you can turn right through **Chapab** straight to Ticul and the fast road back to Muna and Mérida. If you go that way there's an abandoned hacienda about 12 km (7.5 miles) down the road. Turn left to complete the Convent Route.

CHUMAYEL: This is the village where the important Maya document *Chilam Balam* was written. One of the highlights of these books chronicles the rise of Chichén Itzá. **Teabo** is four km (2.5 miles) past Chumayel, and is well known for its hand-embroidered *huipiles* and stately 17th-century temple. Next comes **Tipikal**, a "tipikal" Maya village. Maní is another 12 km (7.5 miles).

Monastery at Maní. It was here that Diego de Landa destroyed the Maya books.

MANI: We've saved the best stop on the Convent Route for last – the tragic town of Maní. Here, in a devil's bargain, the Maya Xiú family dynasty surrendered to Montejo and joined the Spanish in fighting the Cocom clan. Almost immediately Montejo's Franciscan missionaries began building a massive church and monastery using 6,000 Maya slaves. Under Fray Juan de Mérida's direction, workers completed the huge complex in only seven months. The thick stone monastery contains a working church (San Miguel). On our last visit, a choir, composed of young Maya girls, some in *huipiles*, filled the temple with song. In a juxtaposition of the past and present, their sweet voices were accompanied by a modern electric piano and synthesizer that recorded them on multiple tracks. This played back as they sang, making them seem like a huge choir. The haunting sound followed us as we wandered through a labyrinth of cloistered rooms and delightful pocket gardens. The remnants of paintings and faded graffiti from hundreds of years past can be seen on the plaster walls. Inscribed on the wall in a cubbyhole that leads to the bell gable are names of people long forgotten – perhaps a wayward conquistador looking for immortality, an earlier tourist far from home, or a courting couple searching for privacy. Who knows? The walls remain silent.

It was in Maní in July of 1562 that the zealous Bishop Diego de Landa destroyed important Maya documents and statues during the Franciscan movement of converting the indigenous people to Christianity. He gathered and destroyed some 5,000 idols, 13 altars, 27

Rooftop bells on Maní's monastery.

scrolls on deer skin and 197 vases with hieroglyphs that, in combination, represented the history of the Maya. These were the first "books" of the New World, older than any of Europe. He later regretted some of his destructiveness and wrote all he could remember in a book, *Relation of Things in the Yucatán,* the most important contemporary single source of Maya culture and history we have today. Only four works survived the Friar's furious onslaught, but legend maintains that a Maya king buried historical documents in Uxmal, rather than see them destroyed. If they exist, they've never been found. From Maní you can drive to **Oxkutzcab** or **Ticul** for a good meal or a night's sleep.

FAHRENHEIT 451

For thou desirest no sacrifice, else would I give it thee;
but thou delightest not in burnt offerings.

– Christian Prayerbook, ca. 1662

Few Maya writings survived the religious zeal of Fray Diego de Landa. In an effort to convert the Maya into Christians, the good friar destroyed virtually all of their "pagan" texts. A few surviving documents give a glimpse of how the ancient Maya saw themselves.

Popul Vuh is considered to be the most important primary source on Maya mythology. It was preserved through oral tradition until written, anonymously, around 1544 in the Quiché Maya language and Latin. The first four chapters deal with the creation of the world and the creation of man and woman from corn. The middle relates the adventures of young demigods; moral lessons about the consequences of doing evil; and the hubris of Vucub-Caquix, who wanted to be both the sun and the moon. The final part, less literary than historical, lists the kings and conquests of the Quiché Maya up to shortly before the Spanish Conquest.

The *Rabinál Archí* is an historical drama and the only surviving example of pre-Hispanic theater in North America. The plot involves the capture of the Prince of Quiché by warriors from rival tribes. The prince refuses to humiliate himself to avoid death. The audience knows what's coming and, in the end, he is sacrificed. *Anales de los Cakchiqueles* is a work translated from Cakchiquel Mayan language. It's a 96-page legal document that some Cakchiquel nobles used to recover privileges lost during the colonial period. It contains the genealogy of the Xahil family and the history of the Cakchiquel tribe. Another very important work, *Libros de Chilam Balam*, written after the Conquest, is composed of religious texts (Maya and Christian), historical texts, medical writings, astrology and rituals. Several fragments of Maya song lyrics also survive in the *Songs of Dzitbalché*, including one to accompany a "sacrifice by arrows" rite.

Poignantly, a recently discovered Maya ceramic vessel from between A.D. 600 and 900 (covered with glyphs and text) proves that written "books" existed in North America more than 600 years before Columbus arrived.

TICUL: Ticul is the home to a thriving pottery industry and many of its small workshops (*fábricas*) fill its neighborhoods. Artisans are also famous here for their embroidered cotton *huipiles* and these and other craft wares can be found in the *centro mercado* downtown, just off the plaza. Ticul presents you with another ubiquitous old church, this time a grand fortress-like 18th-century cathedral with an older colonial monastery attached. The busy part of this busy town is around the market, whose narrow surrounding streets are awash in *triciclos*, the three-wheeled bicycles that serve (quite well) as people-powered taxis – you'll see a small family crammed onto the seat over the two front wheels – or as carriers, hauling everything from manufactured goods to fire wood, vegetables, or reeds cut as fodder for farm animals. If you stay in Ticul, or just pass through and want to see the sights, park your car away from the *mercado* and hire an inexpensive *triciclo*. Be the Sydney Greenstreet of Mexico.

Ticul is also noted for its cottage-industry shoe manufacturing (buy 'em here). With so much commerce, it has a life of its own besides tourism. Perhaps that accounts for the lack of good tourist amenities. Although Ticul is ideally situated as a base to visit Maya ruins, cenotes and old haciendas, the town doesn't offer a wide selection of places to stay. **Hotel Bougambillias** (Calle 23, ☎ 997/2-07-61) is a two-story modern motel-like inn that provides plebeian rooms with good fans and sky blue walls. Although the rooms are small, they aren't claustrophobic, and the price is right. It's almost across the street from **Hotel Cerro Inn** (☎ 997/2-02-60), which is more like a long motel (larger rooms than the Bougambillias, but more wear-worn). The Cerro does boast a fairly good restaurant under a cool palapa roof, but tall people need to watch their head walking into the entrance as a metal guy wire secures two sides of the thatched roof at about two meters (six feet).

Los Almendros restaurant is in a big colonial house. It got its start in the early 1960s. The venerated restaurant, on Calle 23 No. 27, has grown into a chain of successful Yucatecan (and usually delicious) eateries. Try the *poc chuc*, where it all began, the *picante pollo ticuleño* or *papadzules*, egg-filled tortillas covered in a spicy sauce. Eating in at least one of Los Almendros' locations is a requirement for any visit to the Yucatán, but many other restaurants throughout the peninsula are also "cooking good." Another place to try in Ticul is **Los Delphines**, an appealing little garden restaurant with better-than-usual food. It rests under a palapa behind big metal gates at Calle 27 near 28.

Besides the central market, a good place to shop is the **Centro Artesano**, in front of the cathedral. In addition to other arts and local crafts, Ticuleños also weave Panama hats in some of the numerous caves of the area; some workrooms are even hand-dug. But it is pottery that attracts the most attention in Ticul. **Arte Maya**, on Calle 23 No. 301, is a high-quality shop and gallery that makes Maya reproductions and original stone, ceramic and clay pieces. They are classically beautiful and considered to be of museum quality. Another museum-quality *fábrica* is the **Hacienda Yo'k'at** on the westside of town on the highway to Muna. Though it may look garish, with statues and masks lining the exterior, the workshop of the late artist Wilbert González still produces some notably fine Maya art.

Authors' Farewell

No matter where you go, or what you do, we hope
you enjoy Mexico as much as we have. We've tried to
organize and evaluate the attractions of this fabulous
land in a way that you'll find useful. And we hope to
provide both seasoned and fresh adventurers with
new activities in a destination we're sure you'll want
to visit again and again. See you on the road!

"For memory has painted this perfect day
With colors that never fade,
And we find at the end of a perfect day
The soul of a friend we've made."

– Carries Jacobs Bond, 1862-1946

Smile!

Lazy Day Reading

There is no Frigate like a book
To take us lands away.

– Emily Dickinson, 1830-1886

Mexican Culture & People (fiction)

Aztec, Gary Jennings
The Underdogs, Mariano Azuela
Idols Behind Altars, Anita Brenner
Like Water for Chocolate, Laura Esquivel
Rain of Gold, Victor Villaseñor
Where the Air is Clear, Carlos Fuentes
The Plumed Serpent, D.H. Lawrence
Pedro Páramo, Juan Rulfo
Mornings in Mexico, D.H. Lawrence
The Old Gringo, Carlos Fuentes
Stones for Ibarra, Harriet Doerr
The Treasure of the Sierra Madre, B. Traven
Under the Volcano, Malcolm Lowry

Mexican Culture & History (non-fiction)

Labyrinth of Solitude, Octavio Paz
The Children of Sanchez, Oscar Lewis
Tepoztlán, Robert Redfield
Distant Neighbors, Alan Riding
Mexico, Michael D. Coe
The Modern Maya, Macduff Everton
A Dream of Maya, Lawrence Desmond & Phyllis Messenger
The Ancient Past of Mexico, Alma Reed
The Caste Wars of the Yucatán, Nelson Reed
Archaeological Guide to Mexico's Yucatán Peninsula, Joyce Kelly
The Temple of the Jaguar, Donald Schueler
Incidents of Travel in the Yucatán, John Loyd Stephens

Phonetic Mayan Glossary

We don't pretend to have the spelling correct in the following glossary of Mayan phrases, but we wrote them down phonetically. The Maya are tickled when you greet them in their own language. Try it out on your taxi driver! Everyone we spoke to was pleased at our attempts and they all wanted to help us learn more. Remember an "x" in Mayan is pronounced "ish."

Bash kawa leek?	Hello, what's happening?
Mish baa	Nothing much
Maa'lo	OK or good
Maa'lo ben	I am well
Me nan	None
Sama kin wheel kech	See you tomorrow
Sama	Tomorrow (or short for the above)
Too la Kin	See you another day
Tush ka bean?	Where are you going?
Ine ka bean a Ho	I am going to Mérida
Ine kash tich in bay...	I'm looking for the road to...
Bish aka ba?	What's your name?
Tush ka tah?	Where are you from?
Dios bo teak	Thank you (or God will thank you)
Tech schan	To you also
Wayan nay nay	Here I am
Bash le baa'la?	What is this?
Ba hooush toe hoe lay baa'la?	How much does this cost in money?
Key hannah	Good food
Tzó no hote	Cenote
Otoch or Naa	House
Pack jha'al or Cheena	An orange
Palapa	"Palapa" refers to the thatched palm roofs, which are found on everything from beachside umbrellas to huge halls.

Good luck and let us know how you do!

Spanish Vocabulary

Days of the Week

domingo	Sunday
lunes	Monday
martes	Tuesday
miercoles	Wednesday
jueves	Thursday
viernes	Friday
sabado	Saturday

Months of the Year

enero	January
febrero	February
marzo	March
abril	April
mayo	May
junio	June
julio	July
agosto	August
septiembre	September
octubre	October
noviembre	November
diciembre	December

Numbers

uno	one
dos	two
tres	three
cuatro	four
cinco	five
seis	six
siete	seven
ocho	eight
nueve	nine
diez	ten
once	eleven
doce	twelve
trece	thirteen
catorce	fourteen
quince	fifteen
dieciséis	sixteen
diecisiete	seventeen
dieciocho	eighteen
diecinueve	nineteen

veinte	twenty
veintiuno	twenty-one
veintidos	twenty-two
treinta	thirty
cuarenta	forty
cincuenta	fifty
sesenta	sixty
setenta	seventy
ochenta	eighty
noventa	ninety
cien	one hundred
ciento uno	one hundred one
doscientos	two hundred
quinientos	five hundred
mil	one thousand
mil uno	one thousand one
dos mil	two thousand
un millón	one million
mil millones	one billion
primero	first
segundo	second
tercero	third
cuarto	fourth
quinto	fifth
sexto	sixth
séptimo	seventh
octavo	eighth
noveno	ninth
décimo	tenth
undécimo	eleventh
duodécimo	twelfth
último	last

Conversation

¿Como esta usted?	How are you?
Bien, gracias, y usted?	Well, thanks, and you?
Buenas dias.	Good morning.
Buenas tardes.	Good afternoon.
Buenas noches.	Good evening/night.
Hasta la vista.	See you again.
Hasta luego.	So long.
¡Buena suerte!	Good luck!
Adios.	Goodbye.
Mucho gusto de conocerle.	Glad to meet you.
Felicidades.	Congratulations.
Muchas felicidades.	Happy birthday.
Feliz Navidad.	Merry Christmas.
Feliz Año Nuevo.	Happy New Year.

Gracias.	Thank you.
Por favor.	Please.
De nada/con mucho gusto.	You're welcome.
Perdoneme.	Pardon me.
¿Como se llama esto?	What do you call this?
Lo siento.	I'm sorry.
Permitame.	Permit me.
Quisiera...	I would like...
Adelante.	Come in.
Permitame presentarle...	May I introduce...
¿Como se llamo usted?	What is your name?
Me llamo...	My name is...
No se.	I don't know.
Tengo sed.	I am thirsty.
Tengo hambre.	I am hungry.
Soy norteamericano/a	I am an American.
¿Donde puedo encontrar...?	Where can I find...?
¿Que es esto?	What is this?
¿Habla usted ingles?	Do you speak English?
Hablo/entiendo un poco Español	I speak/understand a little Spanish.
¿Hay alguien aqui que hable ingles?	Is there anyone here who speaks English?
Le entiendo.	I understand you.
No entiendo.	I don't understand.
Hable mas despacio por favor.	Please speak more slowly.
Repita por favor.	Please repeat.

Telling Time

¿Que hora es?	What time is it?
Son las...	It's...
... cinco.	... five o'clock.
... ocho y diez.	... ten past eight.
... seis y cuarto.	... quarter past six.
... cinco y media.	... half past five.
... siete y menos cinco.	... five of seven.
antes de ayer.	the day before yesterday.
anoche.	yesterday evening.
esta mañana.	this morning.
a mediodia.	at noon.
en la noche.	in the evening.
de noche.	at night.
a medianoche.	at midnight.
mañana en la mañana.	tomorrow morning.
mañana en la noche.	tomorrow evening.
pasado mañana.	the day after tomorrow.

Directions

¿En que direccion queda...?	In which direction is...?
Lleveme a... por favor.	Take me to... please.
Llevame alla ... por favor.	Take me there please.
¿Que lugar es este?	What place is this?
¿Donde queda el pueblo?	Where is the town?
¿Cual es el mejor camino para...?	Which is the best road to...?
De vuelta a la derecha.	Turn to the right.
De vuelta a la isquierda.	Turn to the left.
Siga derecho.	Go this way.
Malecón	Road by the sea.
En esta direccion.	In this direction.
¿A que distancia estamos de...?	How far is it to...?
¿Es este el camino a...?	Is this the road to...?
¿Es...	Is it...
... cerca?	... near?
... lejos?	... far?
... norte?	... north?
... sur?	... south?
... este/oests?	... east/west?
Indiqueme por favor.	Please point.
Hagame favor de decirme donde esta...	Please direct me to...
... el telephono.	... the telephone.
... el excusado.	... the bathroom.
... el correo.	... the post office.
... el banco.	... the bank.
... la comisaria.	... the police station.

Accommodations

Estoy buscando un hotel....	I am looking for a hotel that's...
... bueno.	... good.
... barato.	... cheap.
... cercano.	... nearby.
... limpio.	... clean.
¿Dónde hay hotel, pensión, ospedaje?	Where is a hotel, pensión, hospedaje?
Hay habitaciones libres?	Do you have available rooms?
¿Dónde están los baños/servicios?	Where are the bathrooms?
Quisiera un...	I would like a...
... cuarto sencillo.	... single room.
... cuarto con baño.	... room with a bath.
... cuarto doble.	... double room.
Puedo verlo?	May I see it?
Cuanto cuesta?	What's the cost?
Es demasiado caro!	It's too expensive!

Index